Second Edition

Assistive Technology in the Classroom

ENHANCING THE SCHOOL EXPERIENCES OF STUDENTS WITH DISABILITIES

Amy G. Dell

The College of New Jersey

Deborah A. Newton

Southern Connecticut State University

Jerry G. Petroff

The College of New Jersey

PEARSON

Boston Columbus Indianapolis New York San Francisco Upper Saddle River
Amsterdam Cape Town Dubai London Madrid Milan Munich Paris Montréal Toronto
Delhi Mexico City São Paulo Sydney Hong Kong Seoul Singapore Taipei Tokyo

KH

Vice President and Editorial Director: Jeffery W. Johnston
Executive Editor and Publisher: Stephen D. Dragin
Editorial Assistant: Jamie Bushell
Vice President, Director of Marketing: Margaret Waples
Marketing Manager: Weslie Sellinger
Senior Managing Editor: Pamela D. Bennett
Production Manager: Susan Hannahs
Senior Art Director: Jayne Conte
Cover Designer: Suzanne Duda

Cover Photo: Julie Luyber
Full-service Project Manager: Sneha Pant, Element/Thomson North America
Composition: Element/Thomson North America
Cover and Text Printer/Bindery: RR Donnelley/Harrisonburg
Text Font: 10/12 Times

Credits and acknowledgments for material borrowed from other sources and reproduced, with permission, in this textbook appear on the appropriate page within the text.

Every effort has been made to provide accurate and current Internet information in this book. However, the Internet and information posted on it are constantly changing, so it is inevitable that some of the Internet addresses listed in this textbook will change.

Library of Congress Cataloging-in-Publication Data

Dell, Amy G.
  Assistive technology in the classroom : Enhancing the school experiences of students with disabilities / Amy G. Dell, Deborah A. Newton, Jerry G. Petroff.—2nd ed.
     p. cm.
  Includes bibliographical references and index.
  ISBN-13: 978-0-13-139040-9
  ISBN-10: 0-13-139040-6
1. Educational technology—United States.   2. Students with disabilities—United States.   I. Newton, Deborah A.   II. Petroff, Jerry G.   III. Title.
  LB1028.3.D43 2012
  371.33—dc23

2011019865

10 9 8 7 6 5 4 3 2 1

PEARSON

ISBN 10: 0-13-139040-6
ISBN 13: 978-0-13-139040-9

2/28/12

To my son, Matthew, who
"spreads sunshine all over the place."
Amy G. Dell

To my husband, John, for encouraging and supporting the pursuit of all my dreams, and to my
son, Sean, for teaching me how to use a computer so many years ago.

Deborah A. Newton

To my partner, David, and our sons, Parker and Borey,
for their unconditional love and support.

Jerry G. Petroff

ABOUT THE AUTHORS

Amy G. Dell is professor and chairperson of the Department of Special Education, Language and Literacy at The College of New Jersey. She has been involved in assistive technology training for 20 to 25 years, developing and teaching master's-level courses in assistive technology, leading initiatives to infuse assistive technology into undergraduate and graduate coursework, and establishing an Alliance for Technology Access (ATA) center in northern New Jersey. She directs two centers at The College of New Jersey—the Adaptive Technology Center for New Jersey Colleges, and the Center for Assistive Technology and Inclusive Education Studies (CATIES) both of which connect people who have disabilities with technology tools that will increase their independence and participation in school, work, home and community activities.

Deborah A. Newton is currently an associate professor in the Department of Special Education and Reading at Southern Connecticut State University in New Haven, Connecticut, where she teaches graduate courses in adaptive technology. She taught for many years at the elementary level, then served as assistive technology specialist at the Center for Enabling Technology in Whippany, New Jersey. She holds a doctorate in curriculum and instruction from the University of Cincinnati, a master's degree from The College of New Jersey, and a bachelor's degree from the State University of New York at New Paltz. Dr. Newton regularly presents at assistive technology conferences and remains active as an assistive technology consultant.

Jerry G. Petroff is an associate professor in the Department of Special Education, Language and Literacy at The College of New Jersey. He is project director of the New Jersey Consortium for Deafblindness, co-director of the Career and Community Studies Program for young adults who have intellectual disabilities, and director of the Work Skills Prep Program, a residential summer camp program to improve work skills of 20 students who are blind/visually impaired and have multiple disabilities. Dr. Petroff has over 35 years of experience working on behalf of children, youth, and adults with disabilities. Holding a doctorate in psychological studies in special education and a master's degree in speech pathology and audiology, he teaches courses and consults with local school districts on inclusive education, teaching students with severe disabilities, and the transition of students with disabilities from school to adult life.

PREFACE

Assistive Technology in the Classroom, Second Edition, continues the first edition's emphasis on the *integration of assistive technology into the curriculum*—how assistive technology can be used in schools to enhance the teaching and learning of students with disabilities. It addresses the challenge of how *teachers* can use assistive technology in all kinds of classrooms to teach new skills to students with all kinds of disabilities and to provide *students* with access to the general education curriculum. The context for the text's discussions of technology use is always the classroom, the school, and other environments in which students learn. This approach reflects the philosophy of the leading professional organization in educational technology, the International Society for Technology in Education (ISTE), which states that "learning with technology should not be about the technology itself but about the learning that can be facilitated though it" (Knezek, Bell & Bull, 2006).

NEW TO THIS EDITION

The rapid pace of change in the computer industry has the unfortunate side effect of rendering many technology tools—hardware, software programs, assistive devices, Web sites—obsolete within three years, sometimes even sooner. The upside to this speed is that exciting new products and trends become available in the same three-year period. These two trends created a strong need to update the technical information and resources provided in the first edition of this text. Keeping readers abreast of relevant new developments in computer technology and assistive technology that hold tremendous promise for students with disabilities is the primary intent of the revision of this text.

The major changes to the second edition are as follows:

- A new Chapter 4 has been added on Technology to Support Universal Design for Learning (UDL) and Differentiated Instruction. This addition is in response to user feedback and reflects increased interest in UDL in education. In this chapter, students learn about best practices for using technology to include students with disabilities in general education classes.
- The previous Chapter 5 has been replaced by two chapters: the new Chapter 4 and a new Chapter 5—Computers and the Internet to Teach Math. With this changed focus, readers learn about best practices for using technology to teach math skills to students who struggle with mastering math concepts, and how to use technology to provide access to math activities for students who are blind or have physical disabilities.
- New trends in the use of mobile technology such as smartphones, iPods, and iPads are included in this second edition. A number of apps are discussed in the context of how they can support students with disabilities. This is a brand new area of technology for schools and one that is ballooning, so readers need to be aware of its implications and possibilities.
- Information on all technology tools—applications, Web sites, assistive devices, and operating systems—has been updated to reflect the most current products, including the latest operating systems from Microsoft and Apple, Windows 7 and Macintosh OS 10.6, respectively. Readers have access to the most current information and resources related to the integration of assistive technology into teaching and learning.

- A new section has been added to Chapter 3 on providing accessible instructional materials (AIM) to students with print disabilities. Students will learn about the types of alternate formats available, the kinds of playback devices that accommodate each format, and the 2004 Individuals with Disabilities Education Act's new requirement to provide all special education students with accessible instructional materials in a timely fashion.
- Chapter 14 on Implementation of Assistive Technology in Transition Planning has been significantly expanded to reflect the latest development in technology and self-advocacy. In the section on Assistive Technology for Transition from High School to Home, Workplace, and Community, students will learn about applications to teach functional skills; new tools for creating social stories; and new technology to provide visual supports, including apps for iPods, smartphones, and iPads.
- All Internet addresses (URLs) in the Web Resources sections and Reference sections have been updated so that readers will have access to all online resources recommended by the authors.

The text's focus on teachers and their role in assistive technology implementation stems from the authors' recognition that one of the major problems contributing to the gap between the *possibilities* of assistive technology and the *successful implementation* of it in our schools is that teachers lack the necessary knowledge and skills. Even in school districts in which assistive technology teams conduct assistive technology evaluations on students with disabilities and make recommendations for appropriate technology tools, many students do not benefit from the recommendations because the professionals with whom they interact on a daily basis—that is, their teachers—are not aware of what assistive technology can do, do not know how to use it within the context of their classrooms, and do not know how to support their students' use of it.

The technology solutions included in this text are appropriate for students with a wide range of disabilities. Technology tools that benefit students with low-incidence disabilities such as autism and multiple disabilities are presented, as well as technology solutions for students with high-incidence disabilities such as learning disabilities and attention deficit disorders. Although some states have teacher certification requirements that are categorical in nature, other states have generic special education certifications, and as such, teacher candidates need to be prepared to implement assistive technology with *all* students.

A WORD ON TERMINOLOGY

ASSISTIVE TECHNOLOGY.   Other terms are sometimes used to refer to technology that helps students with disabilities. *Rehabilitation technology*, *special education technology*, *educational technology*, *instructional technology*, and *information technology* often overlap and may mean different things to different people (Golden, 1998). Golden points out that this "definitional ambiguity has fostered an atmosphere of confusion in the development and implementation of assistive technology policies in many settings, especially education" (p. 6). This text uses *assistive technology* to refer to any kind of technology (low tech to high tech) that helps students with disabilities succeed in school.

By maintaining a focus on what teachers need to know about assistive technology, this text is not a survey of the entire field of assistive technology. Discussions of assistive technology for positioning and mobility, sports and recreation, architecture, and transportation are not included. Although these are important to quality-of-life issues, they do not directly relate to the instructional process and students' success in schools and therefore are not covered in this text.

Furthermore, selection of and training to use technology devices in these fields typically fall under the domain of rehabilitation professionals such as physical therapists and do not rely on the involvement of classroom teachers for their successful implementation.

What teachers *do* become involved in is teaching and learning: teaching reading and writing, listening and speaking, math, functional skills, and content areas. Because this book's focus is on teaching and learning in the classroom, our use of the term *assistive technology* refers primarily to technology that meets the *learning and communication needs* of children and youth with disabilities in school.

EDUCATIONAL AND INSTRUCTIONAL TECHNOLOGY.   The terms *educational technology* and *instructional technology* have come to be used interchangeably, but as Roblyer (2003) points out, "no single acceptable definition of these terms dominates the field" (p. 5). To ease this confusion, Roblyer has developed the following definitions:

> Educational technology is a combination of the processes and tools involved in addressing educational needs and problems, with an emphasis on applying the most current tools: computers and their related technologies. (p. 6)

> "Integrating educational technology" refers to the process of determining which *electronic tools* and which methods for implementing them are appropriate for given classroom situations and problems. (p. 8)

A close reading of these definitions reveals that *assistive technology* could be considered a subset of Roblyer's definition of *educational technology*. Insert the phrase "students with disabilities" and this becomes a good working definition of assistive technology:

> [Assistive] technology is a combination of the processes and tools involved in addressing educational needs and problems [of students with disabilities], with an emphasis on applying the most current tools: computers and their related technologies. (p. 6)

Insert the phrase "integrating assistive technology" into the second definition and it accurately describes that process as well:

> "Integrating [assistive] technology" refers to the process of determining which *electronic tools* and which methods for implementing them are appropriate for given classroom situations and problems. (p. 8)

Although some writers have used *special education technology* to refer to these processes (e.g., Edyburn, 2003), we have chosen to use the more neutral *assistive technology* because it does not imply that the technology is limited to students who are educated in special education settings.

ORGANIZATION OF THE BOOK

The link between technology and teaching and learning drives this text's organization as well as its content. Part 1 is organized by *school-related tasks* that students must perform on a daily basis to be successful—writing, reading, accessing the general education curriculum, practicing academic skills, demonstrating what they have learned, communicating with teachers and peers, and understanding what their teachers and peers express. Each chapter in Part 1 begins with a description of the problems students with disabilities face with the specific school-related task, and then it goes on to describe how assistive technology can help overcome the problems related to this activity. This structure helps teacher candidates understand how assistive technology fits into their classrooms and curricula. It shifts the focus from training on specific devices and the latest gizmos to training on how to use the technology to learn.

After Part 1 has established the benefits of assistive technology for students with disabilities, Part 2 addresses the question: How can we make computers and the Internet *accessible* to students who cannot type on a keyboard, use a mouse, hear an alert sound, or see a monitor? Chapters in this part discuss ways to adjust operating systems and conventional applications to provide access, specialized access solutions, and the decision-making process for determining the most effective access method for a student.

Part 3 focuses on augmentative communication—the use of computer technology to provide a voice for students who cannot speak. Chapters 10 and 11 provide essential background information on augmentative communication so that Chapter 12 can highlight the *teacher's role* in integrating augmentative communication in the classroom. The background information in Chapters 10 and 11 is provided because most teachers and teacher candidates have had little, if any, previous training in augmentative communication. Chapter 12 presents strategies for teachers to use in their classrooms to encourage students to develop and refine their augmentative communication skills. This chapter describes how to integrate communication objectives into classroom activities and daily routines and how to provide multiple opportunities for students to use their augmentative communication systems during the school day.

Part 4 is titled "Making It Happen." The first three parts of the text established the value of assistive technology and presented a variety of assistive technology solutions. In this last part, the book moves from possibilities to the nitty-gritty: How do we make these exciting possibilities happen for students with disabilities? What do we need to know, and what do we need to *do* to actually get assistive technology to the students who stand to benefit from it? The answers to these questions are complex and involve a wide range of issues, including the laws related to assistive technology, the integration of assistive technology into IEPs, the "digital divide," implementation plans, administrative issues, and funding sources. Chapter 13 summarizes the typical obstacles to assistive technology implementation in the P-12 realm and presents recommendations for getting around these barriers. Chapter 14 addresses implementation issues specifically related to transitioning from high school, with an emphasis on the need to teach students to self-advocate for their assistive technology needs.

Although disability categories are mentioned within the context of technology-based solutions, this text is *not* organized around disability categories. There is a common misconception in special education that Disability X = Technology Tool Y, but this is overly simplistic and misguided. There are multiple factors involved in selecting appropriate technology tools for students with disabilities, and it is a mistake to base selection decisions simply on a child's diagnosis. Therefore, this text discusses disability categories within the context of school-related tasks and technology-based solutions.

PEDAGOGICAL ELEMENTS

The book was designed following the principles of "considerate text": each chapter begins with a set of focus questions, is divided into sections that are labeled with headings, and concludes with a summary of key points. Sidebars highlight specialized information. An important pedagogical element is that the technology presented is continually *linked to real people* though the use of *user profiles*, which are concise summaries of how assistive technology tools have transformed students' school experiences. We recommend that as you proceed through the text, you consciously try to make connections between the information presented and the students whom you teach. Applying the lessons of the text to students with disabilities whom you know will help you understand the subtleties of the assistive technology decision-making process.

Because of the ever-changing nature of technology, the text purposefully presents only a sampling of assistive technology hardware, applications, and related Web sites. A deliberate effort was made to minimize the use of specific product names, and they have been used only for purposes of illustration. For additional information on specific products and to view photographs or screenshots of them, go to the Web sites that are listed at the end of each chapter in the section called Web Resources. This section contains the URLs of manufacturers and publishers of hardware, applications, apps, and assistive devices, as well as links to informative resources. Every effort has been made to provide accurate URLs for all Web sites. However, if you are unable to access the site, we recommend that you go to the site's home page and try to navigate to the specific page using the links included on the home page.

A list of suggested activities is included at the end of each chapter. These are in-class or out-of-class activities that involve students more deeply in the chapter's subject matter. All of the suggested activities have proven successful over the past 17 years in assistive technology courses with students who are studying to be special education teachers or technology coordinators. Instructors are encouraged to assign one or more of these for each chapter or to assign similar activities of their own design. Many of the activities are hands-on and require a computer and specific applications to complete. Others involve interviews of people in the field. All of the activities are designed to *engage students in active exploration* of assistive technology tools or environments in which assistive technology is or could be used to help students make the connection between assistive technology and the learning process.

REFERENCES

Edyburn, D. L. (2003). Technology in special education. In M. D. Roblyer (Ed.), *Integrating educational technology into teaching* (3rd ed., pp. 315–333). Upper Saddle River, NJ: Merrill/Pearson Education.

Golden, D. (1998). *Assistive technology in special education: Policy and practice*. Reston, VA: Council for Exceptional Children's Council of Administrators in Special Education and Technology and Media Division.

Knezek, G., Christensen, R., Bell, L. and Bull, G. (2006). Identifying key research issues, *Learning and Leading with Technology, 33*(8), 18–20.

Roblyer, M. D. (2003). *Integrating educational technology into teaching* (3rd ed.), Upper Saddle River, NJ: Merrill/Pearson Education.

ACKNOWLEDGMENTS

We are very grateful to and deeply appreciative of the many people who generously contributed their expertise to the preparation of this second edition. Many thanks are due to our colleagues at The College of New Jersey who shared their knowledge with us: Noreen Moore on technology for writing; Shrivdevi Rao on transition from school to community life; and Tammy Cordwell on alternate formats, accessible instructional materials, Windows 7, and myriad apps for mobile devices. Eva Scott kindly provided an example of a social story for Chapter 14. Kevin Cohen, Anne Disdier, Michelle Ragunan, Tammy Cordwell, Ellen Farr, and Fran Chase good-naturedly assisted us with taking photographs, and we thank Julie Luyber for providing us with the cover photo. Dianne Gibson and Mary Ann Peterson, office staff in TCNJ's Department of Special Education, Language and Literacy, Kris Anne Kinney of Information Technology, and Michelle Ragunan rescued us numerous times. Once again Ellen Farr took on the onerous tasks of formatting the entire manuscript and organizing all the figures and photos. In addition, she prepared the instructor's manual. Without her superb organizational skills and unflappable nature, this second edition would never have come to fruition.

We would also like to thank current and former students at The College of New Jersey for their contributions. Lisa Pacifico's research on math Web sites was incorporated into Chapter 5, and Dan DeLuca and Lorrie Jo Dirienzo's research on blogs in education was included in Chapter 2. Many of the user profiles that appear in the text were adapted from articles that were originally written for our newsletter *TECH-NJ* by TCNJ graduate students Patricia Mervine, Danielle Niemann, Meenakshi Pasupathy, Gerald Quinn, Christina Schindler, Wolf Shipon, Kimberly Ahrens, Tina Spadafora, and Kavita Taneja. Many students in our courses over the years have provided us with valuable feedback on our teaching that influenced the organization and writing of this text. Students in Amy Dell's Spring 2011 Assistive Technology class brought a young person's perspective to the second edition when they unanimously rejected the word *software* as "old fashioned" and voted for us to use the term *applications* instead.

We are indebted to many people outside our college campuses. Gayle Bowser, Penny Reed, and Joy Zabala, three national leaders in assistive technology, permitted us to quote liberally from their seminal works. Kerry Randle, Provincial Coordinator for SET-BC, not only gave us permission to use the SET-BC materials, but also put us in touch with parents to get permission to use their children's learner profiles. Vicki Spence and students of the John C. Leach School in New Castle, Delaware, provided us with wonderful photographs of assistive technology in action. Once again we want to thank Vincent Varrassi who coined the phrase "There are no IEPs in college" and cheerfully gave it to us to use in Chapter 14, and Bill Ziegler of the Bucks County, Pennsylvania, Intermediate Unit who was Amy Dell's first assistive technology teacher. His beliefs in the incredible possibilities of assistive technology continue to exert a powerful influence on her work.

Over the years we have been inspired by many assistive technology users—students with disabilities, their parents, and adults who have disabilities—who show us by their persistence and accomplishments the power of assistive technology. Thank you to Anthony Arnold, Anthony Bonelli, Dylan Brown, Serena Cucco, Jon Gabry, Michael Lawson, Cory Samaha, and Michael Williams for continuing to show the world what is possible.

We would also like to thank our editors at Pearson and the following reviewers for their helpful comments and suggestions: Barbara Delohery, University of North Dakota; Diana Lawrence-Brown, St. Bonaventure University; Rita Mulholland, Stockton College; Thanh T. Nguyen, Bridgewater State College; and Joe Wheaton, The Ohio State University.

BRIEF CONTENTS

CONTENTS

PART 3: Augmentative Communication 229

PART 1

BENEFITS OF COMPUTER USE IN SPECIAL EDUCATION

1

INTRODUCTION TO ASSISTIVE TECHNOLOGY

Focus Questions

1. How is assistive technology defined in IDEA 2004?
2. What is the assistive technology continuum?
3. What laws mandate the provision of assistive technology to students with disabilities?
4. What is the promise of assistive technology?
5. What principles underlie the philosophy of this text?
6. What are universal design and universal design for learning?

INTRODUCTION

In 1972, when I was a sophomore in college, I met an unusual middle-aged man who made a deep impression on me. Bernie had severe cerebral palsy, a neuromuscular condition that significantly affected his movement and posture. He could not walk and had no control over his arms or hands; in fact, he had one of his arms tied across his chest to prevent it from jerking involuntarily and hitting someone. His head control was poor. Most people looking at him sitting in his wheelchair with his head hanging down assumed he could do nothing; they assumed he was as cognitively disabled as he was physically disabled, and they made no attempt to discover the person inside.

Bernie, however, did not accept other people's low expectations of him. He was determined to find a way around his physical limitations so he could be an active participant in the world around him. Bernie knew that he had a little control over one of his legs, and he wondered if he might be able to do something with that little voluntary movement. A handy friend attached a metal dowel to the bottom of one of his shoes and placed a rubber tip on the end. With this simple contraption, Bernie was able to type on a typewriter. The only assistance he needed was someone to put the shoe with the dowel on his foot and place the typewriter on the floor next to his foot. His typing speed was slow, but he was now able to write letters to his friends (this was before e-mail), type letters to legislators, and write articles expressing his points of view. Although the term did not exist at this time, this kind of creative problem solving is an early example of assistive technology.

I never forgot Bernie. Today, 38 years later, I still remember what I learned from him: (1) Regardless of how disabled a person may appear, inside is a person who wants to be part of life. (2) Taking a problem-solving attitude, instead of a too-bad-there's-nothing-that-can-be-done attitude, can lead to creative solutions that eliminate or bypass obstacles such as physical disabilities. (3) Simple technology can change a person's life. These lessons are what led me to personal computers when they became available many years later. I had seen with my own eyes that "having a disability no longer has to mean that things cannot be done; it means that we can find new ways to get them done" (Alliance for Technology Access [ATA], 2004, p. 3). And I wanted to be one of those problem solvers—"people who ask not *whether* something can be done, but rather *how* it can be accomplished" (ATA, 2004, p. 3, italics added). Marc Gold (1980), an early leader in the field of severe disabilities, expressed this philosophy succinctly: "Try another way."

WHAT IS ASSISTIVE TECHNOLOGY?

The term *assistive technology* is defined in the federal law that provides the foundation for all special education services—the Individuals with Disabilities Education Improvement Act (IDEA 2004). This law's definition of assistive technology consists of two parts: assistive technology *devices* and assistive technology *services*. Both are important and will be discussed in this section.

IDEA 2004 defines an assistive technology *device* as "any item, piece of equipment, or product system, whether acquired commercially off the shelf, modified, or customized, that is used to increase, maintain, or improve functional capabilities of a child with a disability" (IDEA 2004, Sec. 1401(1)(A)). (See Figure 1.1 for the complete definition.) Let's examine this definition in reverse. An assistive technology device must have an impact on the *functioning* of a child with a disability. For example, a portable magnifier enables a child who has a visual impairment to read a worksheet, thereby improving his or her ability to complete schoolwork. A motorized wheelchair increases the ability of a child who has a physical disability to move around the classroom to participate in activities. A talking augmentative communication system that enables a child who has autism to express preferences increases the child's ability to communicate. These three examples show how an assistive technology device can "increase, maintain, or improve functional capabilities of a child with a disability."

If we look at the first part of the definition—an assistive technology device can be bought in a store ("acquired commercially off the shelf"), it can be a purchased item that has been modified, or it can be something that has been customized for an individual's particular needs. A large computer monitor is an example of an assistive technology device that can be bought in a store (for students with visual impairments who need to enlarge the visual display). Another example of off-the-shelf assistive technology is a talking calculator, which provides auditory feedback to a student with learning disabilities who has a problem typing numerals correctly.

Examples of modifications to off-the-shelf products include adding wooden blocks to the pedals of a tricycle so a child who has short legs can reach the pedals, building up the handle of a pencil or eating utensil with foam so a child with poor motor skills can grip and manipulate it better, and adding special software to a standard computer so a child with autism can learn new academic skills.

Customized assistive technology devices include a wide variety of items. Communication boards created with pictures and talking computerized devices that serve as augmentative communication systems are usually customized for each individual student. Teacher-made,

FIGURE 1.1   IDEA 2004 definition of assistive technology.

Individuals with Disabilities Education Act (IDEA) of 2004, 20 U.S.C. § 1401

1) ASSISTIVE TECHNOLOGY DEVICE—
   (A) IN GENERAL—The term 'assistive technology device' means any item, piece of equipment, or product system, whether acquired commercially off the shelf, modified, or customized, that is used to increase, maintain, or improve functional capabilities of a child with a disability
   (B) EXCEPTION—The term does not include a medical device that is surgically implanted, or the replacement of such device.

2) ASSISTIVE TECHNOLOGY SERVICE—
The term 'assistive technology service' means any service that directly assists a child with a disability in the selection, acquisition, or use of an assistive technology device. Such term includes—
   (A) the evaluation of the needs of such child, including a functional evaluation of the child in the child's customary environment;
   (B) purchasing, leasing, or otherwise providing for the acquisition of assistive technology devices by such child;
   (C) selecting, designing, fitting, customizing, adapting, applying, maintaining, repairing, or replacing assistive technology devices;
   (D) coordinating and using other therapies, interventions, or services with assistive technology devices, such as those associated with existing education and rehabilitation plans and programs;
   (E) training or technical assistance for such child, or, where appropriate, the family of such child; and
   (F) training or technical assistance for professionals (including individuals providing education and rehabilitation services), employers, or other individuals who provide services to, employ, or are otherwise substantially involved in the major life functions of such child.

Source: http://uscode.house.gov/download/pls/20C33.txt

computer-based activities to teach specific skills are another example of customized assistive technology devices.

As you can see from these examples, the definition of assistive technology devices is quite broad. A helpful way of organizing all of these possibilities is to place them on an assistive technology continuum—that is, a continuum from low tech to high tech (see Figure 1.2). Low-tech devices use no electronic components and are relatively inexpensive. They are what are often called "gadgets," "gizmos," "doodads," or "thingamajigs," that is, "simple tools that make life's daily activities easier or even possible" (Collins, n.d.).

The kitchen is a good place to find examples of low-tech devices. Can openers and jar openers with thick handles make opening cans and jars easier for people with limited strength. Color-coded measuring spoons with big numbers help people with low vision. Cookbook holders hold open the pages of a cookbook to the correct recipe so the cook can refer to it easily. In the classroom, typical low-tech devices include pencil grips that improve a student's handwriting by building up the shaft of a pencil (see Figure 1.3), clipboards to hold papers steady, masking cards to help struggling readers keep their eyes on the correct line of text, and simple communication boards made out of pictures.

High-tech devices are items that often are based on computer technology. In general, high-tech devices are more complicated to operate and require more training than low-tech devices, and they are considerably more expensive. However, high-tech devices offer unique benefits that often make their expense and training demands worthwhile. They are powerful and flexible devices and can be used for many tasks. For example, desktop computers and laptop computers connected to the Internet and equipped with specialized applications can be used for writing,

Assistive Technology Continuum

Low-Tech Tools

- Pencil grips
- Pens, pencils, crayons markers with extra wide shafts
- Raised line paper, grid paper
- Reading guide
- Slant board
- Paper holder
- Non-slip surfaces
- Magnetic letters, tactile letters
- Bar magnifier
- Rubber stamps
- Sticky notes
- Keyguard
- Moisture guard
- Head pointer/mouth pointer
- Dowel (held in fist)

Mid-Tech Tools

- Digital recorder
- Calculator
- Electronic dictionary/thesaurus
- Portable notetaker
- Audio book
- Talking book
- MP3 player
- Mini-book light
- Switch-operated toys and small appliances
- Step-by-step communicators
- Inexpensive augmentative communication devices

High-Tech Tools

- Desktop computer
- Laptop/netbook
- iPad
- iPod
- Software
- Apps
- Alternate inputs & outputs
- Internet
- Augmentative communication devices

FIGURE 1.2   Assistive Technology Continuum.

reading, information gathering, corresponding via e-mail, and learning new skills. Sophisticated augmentative communication systems can be used for these same tasks, with the important addition of providing a voice for students who cannot speak.

In between sophisticated high-tech and nonelectronic low-tech devices are items classified as mid-tech devices. Mid-tech devices are electronic in nature but are much less expensive and require less training than high-tech devices. Digital recorders for recording teachers' lectures and handheld electronic dictionaries and spell-checkers are examples of mid-tech devices. Oversized calculators and calculators that talk are other examples. Decisions about selecting appropriate assistive technology for students should always consider the low-tech to high-tech continuum.

Before leaving our discussion of IDEA's definition of assistive technology devices, it is important to note that the law includes an exception: "The term [assistive technology device]

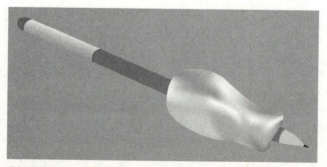

FIGURE 1.3   A pencil grip is an example of a low-tech writing tool.
Source: Courtesy of Onion Mountain Technology.

does not include a medical device that is surgically implanted, or the replacement of such device" (IDEA 2004, Sec. 1401(1)(B)). Implanted devices include feeding tubes for students who cannot eat and cochlear implants for students who are deaf (see Chapter 6).

The second part of IDEA's definition of assistive technology identifies assistive technology *services. Assistive technology service* refers to "any service that directly assists a child with a disability in the selection, acquisition, or use of an assistive technology device" (IDEA 2004, Sec. 1401(2)). Assistive technology services include evaluating a child for assistive technology; purchasing or leasing an assistive technology device for a child; customizing a device to meet a child's specific needs; repairing or replacing a broken device; teaching the child to use the device; and providing training for professionals, family members, and other individuals who are "substantially involved in the major life functions" of the child (IDEA 2004, Sec. 1401(2)(F); see also Figure 1.1). The inclusion of assistive technology services in the law is extremely important as it recognizes that simply *providing* a device is not enough. Making a device available without providing essential supports does not lead to successful implementation of assistive technology. This concept will be discussed in detail in Chapter 13.

Related Terms

Other terms are sometimes used to refer to technology that has been designed for individuals with disabilities. The meanings of *rehabilitation technology, special education technology, educational technology, instructional technology,* and *information technology* often overlap and may represent different things to different people (Golden, 1998). Because this book's focus is on teaching and learning in the classroom, our use of *assistive technology* refers primarily to technology that meets the *learning and communication needs* of children and youth with disabilities in school. We use *assistive technology* to refer to any kind of technology (low tech to high tech) that helps students with disabilities succeed in school. (A more thorough discussion of this "definitional ambiguity" [Golden, 1998, p. 6] is found in this text's preface.)

THE LEGAL BASIS FOR ASSISTIVE TECHNOLOGY

As noted in the previous section, the definition of *assistive technology* is specified in federal special education law. IDEA 2004 includes this definition because the law mandates that assistive technology devices and services be provided to students with disabilities if the technology is essential for accessing education and education-related resources.

Individuals with Disabilities Education Act

Although IDEA 2004 is the most recent reauthorization of the federal law that governs the education of students with disabilities in P–12 settings, it was the 1997 reauthorization that changed the role of assistive technology. Reauthorizations of IDEA prior to 1997 mentioned assistive technology only in provisions related to supplementary aids and services. As a result, consideration of assistive technology was typically limited to students with severe disabilities. The reauthorization of IDEA in 1997 dramatically changed this situation by clearly defining assistive technology and requiring consideration of the assistive technology needs of *every* student receiving special education services. IDEA 1997 adopted the definition of assistive technology established by the Technology-Related Assistance for Individuals with Disabilities Act of 1988 (Tech Act). (See Figure 1.4 for a brief timeline.) By inserting assistive technology consideration into every individualized education program (IEP) development process, IDEA 1997 significantly

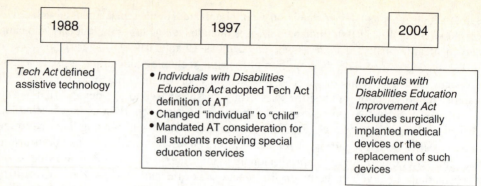

FIGURE 1.4 Brief timeline of assistive technology law.

increased the number of students, as well as the range of disabilities, for which assistive technology solutions are now considered.

IDEA 2004 alters only slightly the 1997 definition of assistive technology by specifically excluding surgically implanted medical devices or replacement of such devices. Assistive technology consideration remains one of the "special factors" that must be considered during the development of the IEP. IDEA 2004 reiterates the importance of assistive technology in the education of students with disabilities by giving priority status to funding "projects that promote the development and use of technologies with universal design, assistive technology devices, and assistive technology services to maximize children with disabilities' access to and participation in the general education curriculum" (Sec. 1481(d)(4)(6)).

In addition to IDEA 2004, two other federal laws have had an impact on the provision of assistive technology to students with disabilities. Section 504 of the Rehabilitation Act of 1973 (and subsequent reauthorizations) and the Americans with Disabilities Act (ADA) of 1990 ensure that students with disabilities have equal access to education and that they are protected from discrimination based on having a disability. Each of these laws has relevance to our discussion of assistive technology.

Section 504 of the Rehabilitation Act of 1973

Section 504, which has been reauthorized several times since its original passage, states the following:

> No otherwise qualified individual with a disability in the United States … shall, solely by reason of her or his handicap, be excluded from participation in, be denied the benefits of, or be subjected to discrimination under any program or activity receiving Federal financial assistance. (Sec. 794(a))

As recipients of federal funds, school districts must comply with Section 504. Because it is a civil rights provision, Section 504 applies to a broader range of students than those who fall within the 13 categories of disabilities specified by IDEA 2004. Section 504 applies to *all* students with disabilities, even those who are not eligible for special education. Students with medical conditions such as heart malfunctions, blood disorders, chronic fatigue syndrome, respiratory conditions, epilepsy, and cancer would be considered to have a disability and are entitled to accommodations under Section 504 if the condition impacts their education (Utah State Office of

Education, 2007). They are entitled to educational accommodations so they will not be denied an education equal to that provided for their typical peers. Therefore, students who are considered to have a disability under Section 504 may be entitled to assistive technology to avail themselves of educational opportunities.

Americans with Disabilities Act

The Americans with Disabilities Act (ADA) is civil rights legislation aimed at preventing discrimination against individuals that is based on disability. The ADA extends civil rights protection to public places, including educational institutions, places of employment, transportation, and communication services whether or not the institution or business receives federal funds. With respect to education, the ADA is especially important for students pursuing postsecondary education because these students are no longer covered by IDEA. Assistive technology is not specifically mentioned in the ADA, but it is generally considered to fit under the phrase "auxiliary aids and services" that must be provided to make programs accessible. Many colleges and universities provide assistive technology as a reasonable accommodation to make their programs accessible to students with disabilities. Chapter 14 provides more detailed information on college students' rights under the ADA. Figure 1.5 shows a visual representation of the relationship among IDEA, Section 504, special education, general education, and the ADA.

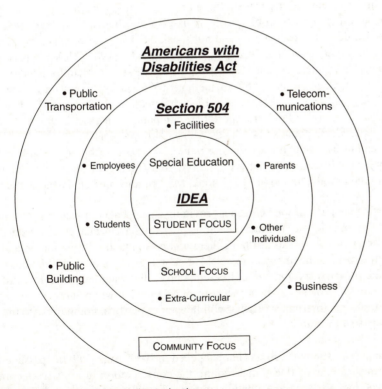

FIGURE 1.5 Laws affecting assistive technology.

Source: Reprinted with permission from *A Parent and Educator Guide to Section 504: Another Service Option for Children with Disabilities,* by J. Copenhaver, 2010.

BRIEF HISTORY OF ASSISTIVE TECHNOLOGY

Before the passage of the laws discussed previously, there were no legal mandates to provide assistive technology to students with disabilities. However, a few people recognized the value of what we now call low-tech devices. The manual typewriter was one of the first pieces of technology adopted by people who could not write due to a disability. The first typewriter was developed in 1808 by a man named Pellegrino Turri, who built it for his friend Countess Carolina Fantoni da Fivizzono, who was blind, to help her write legibly (Jacobs, 1999). In more recent times, Bob Williams, a disability rights advocate who has physical disabilities and cannot speak, identifies a typewriter as his first piece of technology. He was 7 years old when his parents provided him with an IBM electric typewriter. He learned years later that his teacher had not believed he would ever learn to read. His reflection on this first piece of technology provides important insights:

> I am convinced that had I not had the typewriter, my teacher's perception would have likely become very much of a self-fulfilling prophecy. I would have become, like an estimated 50% of my contemporaries with cerebral palsy who, despite their typical intelligence, now face significant difficulties with reading, writing, and comprehending much of the printed word. (Williams, 2000, p. 247)

Fast-forward to the early 1980s when the first affordable personal computers became available. The ability to delete and insert text without having to retype entire pages was quickly recognized as a powerful feature by problem solvers like Bob Williams. Peripherals that turned PCs into talking machines for people who could not speak quickly followed. The first book on this topic, *Personal Computers and the Disabled*, was published in 1984 (McWilliams) with illustrations of the latest computers such as Hewlett-Packard's HP-150, which, for a mere $3,995, came with a 9-inch green screen and 256K of memory (256 *kilo*bytes, not megabytes). The Radio Shack TRS-80 was $1,999 and featured a 12-inch screen but had only 64K of memory. Texas Instruments marketed one of the first "portable" computers —it cost $2,695, had 128K of memory, and weighed *only* 37 pounds (44 pounds with a color monitor)!

Technology enthusiasts thought they saw the future: If only the technology could be faster, have more memory, weigh less, and cost less, the problems facing students with disabilities would be solved. In the introduction to his 1984 book, McWilliams predicted exactly that:

> I hope that people will soon consider providing a personal computer for certain disabilities as automatic and as fundamental as providing a wheelchair or a leader [guide] dog or a pair of crutches.... I hope there will be so much information on and action in getting personal computers to disabled people that this book will be but a minor footnote in a major campaign.... Let's just hope that what happened to word processing from 1982 to 1984 [when it went from being unknown to being a ubiquitous writing tool] is a forerunner of what will happen to personal computers for the disabled from 1984 to 1986. (p. 16)

Did McWilliams say 1986? It still has not happened in 2011. Even with the passage of the ADA and the reauthorizations of IDEA that require the consideration of assistive technology for every student who receives special education services, it still has not happened. Through the 1990s and the first decade of the 21st century, the technology did improve—steadily, rapidly, impressively—yet McWilliams's prediction has not come to pass. The problems of getting technology to students with disabilities and getting the technology used effectively have not been solved. At the time of this writing, numerous assistive technology products are available, many easy to use and at affordable prices, but problems with identifying appropriate tools and implementing plans in schools remain major obstacles that keep students with disabilities from benefiting from assistive technology.

Bob Williams (2000), the disability advocate, identifies additional barriers to assistive technology implementation—society's negative stereotypes and low expectations of people with disabilities:

> Why are so many people consigned to lead lives of needless dependence and silence? Not because we lack the funds or because we lack the federal policy mandates needed to gain access to those funds. Rather, many people lead lives of silence because many others still find it difficult to believe that people with speech disabilities like my own have anything to say or contributions to make. (p. 250)

Assistive technology has the potential to empower people with disabilities with opportunities to participate in their communities and achieve more than ever before (ATA, 2004). Technology has been called "the great equalizer" for people with disabilities because it offers "better opportunities to communicate, learn, participate, and achieve greater overall levels of independence. Perhaps most importantly, new technologies enable people with disabilities to perform competitively in the workplace" (National Organization on Disability, 2006).

Also called "electronic curb cuts," computers provide access to activities and opportunities that people without disabilities take for granted. In education, they can provide access to the general education curriculum and key educational experiences such as typical reading, writing, and assessment activities that take place daily in every classroom. Providing access to the curriculum is an essential component of the successful inclusion of students with disabilities in their neighborhood schools (Nolet & McLaughlin, 2000; Salend, 2004; Villa & Thousand, 2000). Computers can enable students with disabilities to demonstrate their understanding of academic subjects even if they cannot write legibly or speak intelligibly (Male, 2003). They can make textbooks understandable to students who are poor readers (Meyer & Rose, 1998). They can decrease students' reliance on teachers and other adults by increasing students' independence in completing academic tasks (Bryant, Bryant & Rieth, 2002, National Center on Accessible Instructional Materials at CAST, 2010). Computer technology can provide a voice for students who cannot speak (Williams, 2006). The list of benefits goes on.

However, after 25 years of exploring new assistive technology products and teaching teachers, parents, and students how to use them, we have reached one clear conclusion: Technology alone is not enough. Assistive technology is exciting and fun, no question about it, but a computer alone will not increase a student's success in school. A school's simply purchasing an expensive site license for an application will not lead to student gains. Providing students who have disabilities with the latest, most dazzling devices in the world will not make a difference in their lives—unless the initiative integrates the technology into the curriculum and addresses the details of implementation.

Therefore, this text's emphasis is on the *integration of assistive technology into the curriculum*: how assistive technology can be used in all kinds of classrooms to enhance the teaching and learning of students with a wide range of disabilities. It is easy to be seduced by the razzle-dazzle of the latest electronic gimmick, but we have tried to resist that temptation and instead have focused on the *link* between technology and the teaching-learning process. The context for our discussions of technology use is always the classroom, the school, and other environments in which students learn. This approach reflects the philosophy of the leading professional organization in educational technology, the International Society for Technology in Education (ISTE), which articulates that "learning with technology should not be about the technology itself but about the learning that can be facilitated through it" (Knezek, Christensen, Bell, & Bull, 2006, p. 19).

In addition to this curriculum integration philosophy, we share the core principles of the Alliance for Technology Access (ATA), a national network of technology resource centers, organizations, and businesses that seek to connect people with disabilities to technology that will empower them to participate fully in their communities (ATA, 2004).

These principles explain how technology relates to people with disabilities obtaining their basic rights:

- People with disabilities have the right to maximum independence and participation in all environments, without barriers.
- Technology can be harnessed to diminish or eliminate environmental barriers for people with disabilities.
- People with disabilities have the right to control and direct their own choices, and the right to access the information they need in order to make informed decisions according to their goals and interests.
- People with disabilities have the right to employ assistive technologies, strategies for implementation, and necessary training support to maximize their independence and productivity. (ATA, n.d.)

Independence, self-sufficiency, personal choice, participation, inclusion, dignity—these principles are a direct outgrowth of the disability rights movement. In the late 1960s, motivated and educated by the protest strategies and successful outcomes of the civil rights movement, a handful of college students with disabilities began their own self-determination movement in Berkeley, California (Shapiro, 1993). Calling themselves the Rolling Quads and led by Ed Roberts, a young man with severe physical disabilities as a result of polio, these students rebelled against the patronizing, controlling, and limiting bureaucracy and set out to break down "the common barriers they faced—from classrooms they could not get into to their lack of transportation around town" (p. 48). Their goals expanded to "total self-sufficiency," and eventually they founded the first independent living center in the country. The Rolling Quads wanted to be their own case managers, "so they would never again have to kowtow to a bureaucrat who controlled their funding" (p. 48), and they decided that they needed to change the way they thought of themselves—no longer would they be clients of the state; from now on they were "consumers of state services."

With this dramatic change in attitude, the traditional medical model of diagnosis and treatment prescribed by professionals was called into question. Shapiro (1993) explains this change:

> The medical model of disability measured independence by how far one could walk after an illness or how far one could bend his legs after an accident. But [Ed] Roberts redefined independence as the control a disabled person has over his life. Independence was measured not by the tasks one could perform without assistance but by the quality of one's life with help.... Disabled people themselves,

the newly christened "independent living movement" assumed, knew better than doctors and professionals what they needed for daily living. And what disabled people wanted most of all was to be fully integrated in their communities, from school to work. (p. 51)

The continuing efforts of these and other disability activists eventually led to the passage in 1990 of the ADA. This civil rights law for people with disabilities provides the legal basis for the inclusion of people with disabilities in all walks of life, from the workplace to public places such as educational institutions. Assistive technology is a means to these ends. Therefore, we believe that students with disabilities must be provided with access to the assistive technology tools that will increase their independence and participation in school. We also believe that teachers and other school personnel have a responsibility to help students with disabilities find and learn how to use these tools.

In keeping with the philosophy of the disability rights movement, this text does not advocate the medical model of diagnosis and treatment that is accepted practice in rehabilitation fields. Instead the text advocates a decision-making process that places the student at the center (ATA, 2004). Rather than relying on "experts" to "diagnose" a problem and then "prescribe" a "treatment," the student-centered decision-making model actively engages the student with a disability and family members in a collaborative process of finding technology tools that meet the student's needs and preferences.

How does this consumer-directed approach fit in an educational setting? We believe that students and their parents need to be active participants in the decision-making process. They have important roles to play in figuring out which technology tools will best help them with their schoolwork and with which technology tools they are most comfortable. The selection of these technology tools must tie in to the goals and dreams students (and their parents) have. Teachers and assistive technology specialists need to ask students for their input and honor their preferences during the assistive technology selection process (Grady, Kovach, Lange, & Shannon, 1993; Moore, Duff, & Keefe, 2006). This process is discussed in detail in Chapter 9.

ASSISTIVE TECHNOLOGY DECISION-MAKING PROCESS

Chapters 2 to 8 and 10 and 11 of this text introduce numerous technology tools that, when used appropriately, can significantly enhance the school experiences of students with disabilities. With all these choices available, how does one determine which specific piece of assistive technology (AT) will help an individual student? Addressing this issue is key to successful implementation of AT. The previous paragraph begins to answer the question by highlighting the importance of including students and their parents in the decision-making process. Who else needs to be included? What components need to be considered?

A helpful guide for AT decision making is the SETT Framework developed by Zabala (2000 & 2005). This framework reminds us that we must always begin the AT selection process by focusing first on the *Student*. What is the age and grade level of the student? What are the student's strengths? What are the student's interests? In which skills areas is the student weak? After we have gathered this kind of information, we need to consider the nature of the *Environments* in which the student spends time. What is the physical arrangement? Are there special concerns? What equipment and materials are currently available in the environment?

What is the instructional schedule? What supports are available to the student? What resources are available to the people supporting the student?

After we have addressed the "S" and "E" of the SETT Framework, we then need to ask which *T*asks the student must perform to be successful in those environments. What activities take place in the environment that support the student's curriculum, and what are the critical elements of these activities? For example, in a typical fourth-grade classroom, students need to read their textbooks and assigned work; they need to complete worksheets and write short compositions; they need to participate in hands-on science activities; and they need to communicate with other students when working on group projects.

Only after the *S*tudent, the *E*nvironments, and the *T*asks have been addressed, can we begin to consider specific technology *T*ools. How might technology support the student's active participation in those activities? What strategies might be used to improve the student's performance? What no-tech, low-tech, and/or high-tech options should be considered for *this* student in *these* environments? This decision-making process will be discussed in more detail in Chapter 9, but it is introduced here to provide the reader with a practical frame of reference.

UNIVERSAL DESIGN

Another concept that is woven throughout this book is *universal design*, which supports increased independence, participation, and inclusion of individuals with disabilities in all aspects of life and at the same time maintains the dignity of the individual. Universal design is defined as "the design of products and environments to be usable by all people, to the greatest extent possible, without the need for adaptation or specialized design" (Center for Universal Design, 1997, para. 3). Before a product or environment is developed and marketed, universal design recommends considering "the needs of the greatest number of possible users, [thereby] eliminating the need for costly, inconvenient, and unattractive adaptations later on" (Center on Applied Special Technology, 2006). This concept began in the discipline of architecture, then broadened to the fields of hardware and software development, and is now a key principle in instructional design.

Three popular conveniences clearly illustrate the concept of universal design: automatic doors, curb cuts, and captioning of television programs. Automatic doors make stores, airports, and other public spaces accessible to individuals with disabilities, but they also make those places accessible to a broader range of people: shoppers pushing shopping carts, travelers wheeling suitcases, parents pushing children in strollers, elderly people, and others who lack the strength to open heavy doors. In sum, automatic doors benefit a wide range of people and all of them, including individuals with disabilities, can access the facilities in a dignified manner—independently, through the same entrance.

Curb cuts are another good example of universal design. Originally designed to make navigating city streets more accessible to wheelchair users, curb cuts turned out to benefit many more people than just wheelchair users (Jacobs, 1999). Curb cuts are now used by workers making deliveries with hand trucks, elderly people using walkers, roller bladers and skateboarders, as well as people pulling city shopping baskets and pushing baby strollers. (See photo.)

Moving from the field of architecture to that of media, our third example of universal design is the captioning of television programs. Closed captioning was originally developed to enable people who are deaf to access and enjoy television shows. When its use was limited to the deaf, the technology was expensive and cumbersome to find. Today, however,

A curb cut benefits many people, not only those who use wheelchairs.

Photo by Amy G. Dell

captioning is built into television production because it benefits many people. As Jacobs (1999) explains:

> Television (TV) manufacturers in the U.S. will tell you that their caption de-coders for the deaf wound up benefiting tens-of-millions more consumers than origi-nally intended. As the electronic curb cut effect has shown in the past, televisions with decoders are simply better than those without. For example, captioning can enable TV viewers to: …listen to programs in silence while someone is sleeping; and listen to programs in noisy environments like sports bars.

Captioning for television and film has also become a widely used instructional tool for people who are learning English as a second language (National Council on Disability, 2005).

The computer industry has widely adopted the concept of universal design, particularly the principle of "flexibility in use." Wanting to sell as many computers as possible, the industry recognizes the commercial value of designing operating systems that are usable by as many people as possible. This means people who are new to computers, as well as expert users; people who use computers for enjoyment at home, and those who use them in the workplace; young people who have good eyesight, and people over 40 who need reading glasses. Incorporating this concept of flexibility in use in operating systems offers several positive applications for students with disabilities.

For example, having the option to use keyboard commands instead of a mouse enables peo-ple who cannot control a mouse an alternative for computer access. This includes students with fine motor difficulties, limited range of motion, or visual impairments that interfere with seeing or tracking the mouse pointer on the computer screen. Designers take into account variations among the precision, accuracy, and speed of computer users. Both the Macintosh and Windows operating

Other Examples of Technology Innovations Benefiting Large Numbers of People

The list of technology innovations that were originally developed to meet the needs of people with disabilities but ended up benefiting everyone is long (Jacobs, 1999). It includes the following:

- Alexander Graham Bell's invention of the telephone, which he developed while trying to help his deaf students
- Bell Labs' scientists' invention of the transistor, which they developed while trying to develop more reliable, powerful, smaller, and cheaper hearing aids (Jacobs, 1999)
- Ray Kurzweil and his team's invention of the flatbed scanner, which was an unexpected result of their work on a "reading machine" for the blind.

systems provide the means to enlarge the size of icons and slow down the speed of the mouse (Figure 1.6). Larger icons provide a larger target area to accommodate some students' lack of precision and accuracy in directing the mouse pointer. Combined with a slower mouse speed, larger icons make it possible for some students with disabilities to use a computer without the need for additional specialized devices. For students who have hand-eye coordination problems, visual impairments, hand tremors, or cognitive disabilities, these two options are especially helpful.

Being able to make adjustments to the keyboard repeat rate is another helpful adjustment. Users can adjust the delay before a key will start repeating and how fast it repeats once it starts. Increasing the delay before a key begins to repeat makes the computer more accessible for students who have fine motor control or other issues, making it difficult to release a key after it has been selected. Slower repeat rates also benefit students who need to look at the keyboard as they type and have difficulty raising their heads to verify typing accuracy.

UNIVERSAL DESIGN FOR LEARNING

Universal design for learning (UDL) draws on the concept of universal design in architecture and products and combines it with current brain research about how students learn, resulting in an approach that increases flexibility in teaching and decreases the barriers that prevent students from accessing materials and classroom activities (Rose & Meyer, 2002). Just as the original concept of universal design intended to make structures and products usable by the broadest range of individuals, UDL seeks to make curricular content available to the broadest range of students. For example, software programs that provide spoken directions with a simple click of the mouse enable students who cannot read, students who forget directions, and students with attention problems to complete activities without teacher intervention. Digital media, especially electronic text, offer many opportunities to engage students in learning and to enable them to demonstrate what they have learned even if they struggle with traditional reading and writing tasks. Upcoming chapters, Chapter 4 in particular, provide additional information about UDL. Readers should note that UDL makes the curriculum accessible to a broad range of students, including general education students who are auditory learners, visual learners, or difficult to engage or motivate, as well as students with disabilities. When the principles of UDL are applied in classrooms, the need for additional assistive technology solutions for individual students may be reduced or eliminated.

Even in classrooms where UDL is practiced, however, some students will continue to need specialized technology solutions. For example, because the number of students who are blind is comparatively low, the potential market for Braille keyboards is small. As a result, Braille

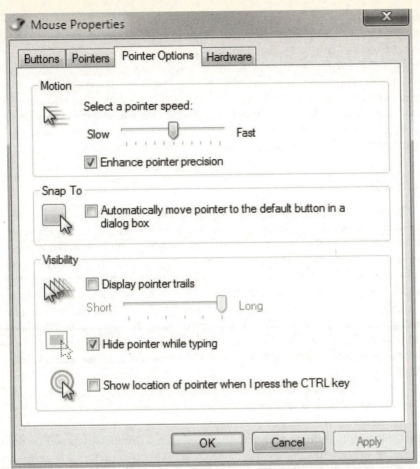

FIGURE 1.6 Mouse Control Panel in Windows 7 showing Pointer Options.

Source: Microsoft Product. Screen shot reprinted with permission from Microsoft Corporation.

keyboards are not likely to become a standard option on conventional computers. Therefore, whereas universal design is an outstanding development for people with disabilities and it remains an essential part of the assistive technology decision-making process, it does not completely eliminate the need for specialized products. Throughout the text, we will provide information on both universally designed features and specialized technology devices, with the emphasis always placed on identifying the appropriate match between students' needs and possible technology solutions.

A NOTE ON TERMINOLOGY

In the years since this text was originally published, two of the most significant changes in computer technology have been the emergence of Web 2.0 and "cloud computing." Web 2.0 refers to applications on the World Wide Web that facilitate interaction, collaboration, and access, such as social networking sites, hosted services, and Web applications. This expansion of the Web has changed the way both software developers and computer users use the Web. Instead of selling CDs of their software and requiring schools to install them on hard drives or local area networks, many developers now store their programs on the Web; teachers and students gain access to the programs by navigating to a Web site through their Internet browser and logging in. (Readers who have used Google Docs or Skype will be familiar with this arrangement.) Since these programs are Web-based ("in the cloud"), they can be accessed from any computer that has an Internet connection, including home computers. Student work is saved online so it too can be accessed from home computers as well as school computers. This text will use the term "applications" to refer to any educational software program, whether it is provided on a tangible media device such as a CD, DVD, or thumb drive, or it is stored "in the cloud." The text will use the colloquialism *app* to refer to educational applications that run on mobile devices such as smart phones and iPads.

CONCLUSION

Do you remember Bernie, the person profiled at the beginning of this chapter who typed on a typewriter with his foot? The dowel that was bolted to the bottom of his shoe was a good example of a low-tech device, and it served him well. However, think of how much more Bernie could have written, how much more he could have interacted with the world, had he lived today and could use his low-tech dowel to access a high-tech computer with a high-speed Internet connection. As you read the following chapters, think of what Bernie could have accomplished with the technology tools that are highlighted. Think of other people you know who have difficulties writing or reading or learning or communicating. Try to make connections between their particular needs and the opportunities offered by assistive technology. You will find powerful solutions to the problems they face, and we hope you will be as excited as we are by the promise of assistive technology.

Summary

- Lessons from people with disabilities: (1) Regardless of how disabled a person may appear, inside is a person who wants to be part of life. (2) Taking a problem-solving attitude can lead to creative solutions that eliminate obstacles caused by disabilities. (3) Simple technology can change a person's life.
- Assistive technology is defined in the Individuals with Disabilities Education Improvement Act of 2004 (IDEA 2004). The definition consists of two parts: assistive technology devices and assistive technology services.
- The assistive technology continuum spans low-tech to high-tech devices. Low-tech devices, such as pencil grips and clipboards, use no electronic components and are relatively inexpensive. High-tech devices, such as laptop computers and augmentative communication devices, are usually based on computer technology, require training to use, and are expensive. However, their power and flexibility usually make the expense and training worthwhile.
- The term *assistive technology* is related to several other terms—*rehabilitation technology, special education technology, educational technology, instructional technology,* and *information technology.* However, this text uses it to refer primarily to technology that meets the learning and communication needs of students with disabilities.
- The 1997 reauthorization of IDEA was the first law to require that assistive technology be considered for every student receiving special education services.
- Two other two federal laws have had an impact on the provision of assistive technology to students with disabilities:

Section 504 of the Rehabilitation Act and the Americans with Disabilities Act (ADA).

- Despite these laws, serious problems remain in getting appropriate assistive technology to students with disabilities who stand to benefit from it.
- This text's philosophy: People with disabilities have the right to independence, self-sufficiency, personal choice, participation, inclusion, and dignity, and technology can be harnessed to achieve these goals.
- The text's emphasis is on the integration of assistive technology into the curriculum—the link between assistive technology and the teaching and learning of students with disabilities.
- The SETT Framework provides a helpful guide for deciding which technology tools will help an individual student.

This framework reminds us that we must always begin the AT selection process by focusing first on the *Student*.

- Universal design is defined as "the design of products and environments to be usable by all people, to the greatest extent possible, without the need for adaptation or specialized design" (Center for Universal Design, 1997, para. 3).
- Examples of the universal design principle of flexibility in use include features in computer operating systems that allow users to use keyboard commands in place of the mouse, enlarging icons, slowing down the speed of the mouse, and turning off the key repeat function.
- Universal design for learning (UDL) seeks to make curricular content available to the broadest range of students.

Web Resources

For additional information on the topics listed, visit the following Web sites:

Low-Tech Tools
Arizona Technology Access Program (AzTAP)—Assistive Technology for the Home: Resources for Older Adults and Individuals with Disabilities
http://www4.nau.edu/ihd/AzTAP/Library/AzTAP_ResourcesforOlderAdults.asp
Onion Mountain Technology, Inc.
http://www.onionmountaintech.com

Other Kinds of Assistive Technology
Family Center on Technology & Disability
http://www.fctd.info/resources

Laws Governing Assistive Technology
Wrightslaw
http://www.wrightslaw.com

History of Assistive Technology
Disability Museum: Search "assistive technology" in Library
http://www.disabilitymuseum.org
American Foundation for the Blind's Assistive Technology Timeline
http://www.afb.org/Section.asp?SectionID=4&DocumentID=4368
Legends and Pioneers of Blindness Assistive Technology, Part 2 by A. R. Candela American Foundation for the Blind's AccessWorld, September 2006
http://www.afb.org/afbpress/pub.asp?SectionID=1

Philosophy of This Text
International Society for Technology in Education (ISTE)
http://www.iste.org

Norman Kunc
http://www.normemma.com→Schools

Disability Rights Movement
Smithsonian's Disability Rights Movement Virtual Museum
http://www.americanhistory.si.edu/disabilityrights/welcome.html

Oral Histories of the Disability Rights and Independent Living Movement
http://bancroft.berkeley.edu/collections/drilm.html

Universal Design
Center for Universal Design at North Carolina State University
http://www.design.ncsu.edu/cud/about_ud/udprinciples.htm

Center on Applied Special Technology (CAST)
http://www.cast.org/research/udl

Universal Design in Computer Operating Systems
Keyboard shortcuts in Windows operating systems
http://www.microsoft.com/enable/products/keyboard.aspx

Suggested Activities

1. *Recognize the power of assistive technology.* Observe or interview a person with a disability who uses assistive technology in daily life. The technology could be a computer, an augmentative communication system, or any low-tech or mid-tech device.

   a. *Introduce the user:* Write a paragraph introducing the person. Make him or her come alive as an individual first and foremost. Mention school or work and the person's interests. Then include some information about his or her disability.

   b. *Discuss the benefits and purpose of assistive technology use:* What does assistive technology enable this person to do? Discuss specific activities.

2. *Demonstrate low-tech assistive technology.* Visit a dollar store and find an item that could be used as low-tech assistive technology. Bring the item to class to share your idea and demonstrate its use (e.g., a clipboard to hold papers securely or rubberized shelf liner to keep books from slipping).

3. *Research universal design.* Visit the Web site of the Center for Applied Special Technology (CAST) at http://www.cast.org. Read up on the latest research and developments in universal design for learning. Write a summary of one of them and post it to your class's discussion board.

4. *Start an assistive technology portfolio.* Begin gathering resources on assistive technology. The portfolio can be compiled and presented electronically using PowerPoint® or a Web site, or it can be compiled in hard copy, using a binder or accordion file. The key is to organize the materials and clearly label them. The following categories are suggestions: product flyers and catalog excerpts, standards or guidelines from your professional organization regarding assistive technology skills, or informative Web sites or print materials that would be useful resources for colleagues and parents. Add relevant materials to the portfolio after reading each subsequent chapter in the text.

References

Alliance for Technology Access. (n.d.). *Principles.* Retrieved May 26, 2010, from http://www.ataccess.org/

Alliance for Technology Access. (2004). *Computer resources for people with disabilities* (4th ed.). Alameda, CA: Hunter House.

Bryant, B. R., Bryant, D. P., & Rieth, H. J. (2002). The use of assistive technology in postsecondary education. In L. Brinckerhoff, J. McGuire, & S. Shaw (Eds.), *Postsecondary education and transition for students with learning disabilities* (pp. 389–429). Austin, TX: Pro-Ed.

Center for Universal Design. (1997). *About universal design.* Retrieved May 26, 2010, from http://www.design.ncsu.edu/cud/about_ud/about_ud.htm

Center on Applied Special Technology. (2006). *Research and development in universal design for learning.* Retrieved May 26, 2010, from http://www.cast.org/research/index.html

Collins, R. (n.d.). *Independence can be cheap and easy with low tech assistive technology.* Retrieved May 26, 2010, from the Arizona Technology Access Program (AzTAP) Web site: http://www4.nau.edu/ihd/AzTAP/Initiative_on_Aging/AzTAP_AssistiveTechnologyandAginginPlace_Article2.asp

Copenhaver, J. (2010). *A parent and educator guide to Section 504: Another service option for children with disabilities.* Logan, UT: Mountain Plains Regional Resource Center.

Gold, M. (1980). *Try another way: Training manual.* Austin, TX: Marc Gold & Associates. ERIC# ED172507

Golden, D. (1998). *Assistive technology in special education: Policy and practice.* Reston, VA: Council for Exceptional Children's Council of Administrators in Special Education and Technology and Media Division.

Grady, A. P., Kovach, T., Lange, M., & Shannon, L. (1993, February). "Consumer knows best": Promoting choice in assistive technology. *PT: Magazine of Physical Therapy, 1*(2), 50–56.

Individuals with Disabilities Education Act of 2004, 34 C.F.R. § 300.5 & § 300.6. Retrieved July 18, 2010, from http://www.nectac.org/idea/300regs.asp

Jacobs, S. I. (1999). *Section 255 of the Telecommunications Act of 1996: Fueling the creation of new electronic curbcuts.* Retrieved May 26, 2010, from the Center for an Accessible Society Web site: http://www.accessiblesociety.org/topics/technology/eleccurbcut.htm

Knezek, G., Christensen, R., Bell, L., & Bull, G. (2006). Identifying key research issues. *Learning and Leading with Technology, 33*(8), 18–20.

Male, M. (2003). *Technology for inclusion: Meeting the needs of all students.* Boston, MA: Allyn & Bacon.

McWilliams, P. A. (1984). *Personal computers and the disabled.* Garden City, NY: Quantum Press/Doubleday.

Meyer, A., & Rose, D. H. (1998). *Learning to read in the computer age.* Newton, MA: Brookline Books.

Moore, V. M., Duff, F. R., & Keefe, E. B. (2006, October/November). The importance of student preferences, human rights, and dignity. *Closing the Gap, 25*(4), 1, 12.

National Center on Accessible Instructional Materials at CAST (2010). *Text-to-Speech (TtS) and Accessible Instructional Materials (AIM): An Implementation Guide for Use of TtS and AIM in Secondary Classrooms, April 30, 2010 Update.* Retrieved May 2, 2011 from http://aim.cast.org/experience/training/aim_implementation_guide

National Council on Disability. (2005). *Information technology and Americans with disabilities: An overview of innovation, laws, progress and challenges.* Retrieved May 26, 2010, from http://www.ncd.gov/newsroom/publications/2005/innovation.htm

National Organization on Disability. (2006). *Economic participation: Technology.* Retrieved May 26, 2010, from http://www.nod.org/index.cfm?fuseaction=Page.viewPage&pageId=16

Nolet, V., & McLaughlin, M. J. (2000). *Accessing the general curriculum: Including students with disabilities in standards-based reform.* Thousand Oaks, CA: Corwin Press.

Rehabilitation Act of 1973, Section 504, Pub. L. No. 93–112, 29 U.S.C. § 794 (1977).

Rose, D., & Meyer, A. (2002). *Teaching every student in the digital age: Universal design for learning.* Alexandria, VA: Association for Supervision and Curriculum Development.

Salend, S. J. (2004). *Creating inclusive classrooms: Effective and reflective practices* (5th ed.). Upper Saddle River, NJ: Merrill/Pearson Education.

Shapiro, J. P. (1993). *No pity: People with disabilities forging a new civil rights movement.* New York: Times Books.

Utah State Office of Education (2007). A Parent Guide to Section 504 of The Rehabilitation Act Of 1973 and the Americans With Disabilities Act (ADA). Salt Lake City, UT: Author. Retrieved June 14, 2011 from http://www.utahparentcenter.org/

Villa, R. A., & Thousand, J. S. (Eds). (2000). *Restructuring for caring and effective education: Piecing the puzzle together* (2nd ed.). Baltimore, MD: Brookes.

Williams, B. (2000). More than an exception to the rule. In M. Fried-Oken & H. Bersani (Eds.), *Speaking up and spelling it out* (pp. 245–254). Baltimore, MD: Brookes.

Williams, M. B. (2006). *How far we've come, how far we've got to go: Tales from the trenches* [DVD]. Monterey, CA: Augmentative Communication, Inc.

Zabala, J. S. (2000). *Setting the stage for success: Building success through effective selection and use of assistive technology systems.* Retrieved May 26, 2010, from LDonline: http://www.ldonline.org/article/Setting_the_Stage_for_Success%3A__Building_Success_Through_Effective__Selection_and_Use_of__Assistive_Technology_Systems

Zabala, J. S. (2005). Ready, SETT, go! Getting started with the SETT Framework. *Closing the Gap, 23*(6), 1–3.

2 | ASSISTIVE TECHNOLOGY TO SUPPORT WRITING

Focus Questions

1. What are the major components of the writing process?
2. What kinds of problems do students with disabilities have with writing?
3. Which technology tools can address problems with prewriting activities, and how?
4. Which technology tools can address problems with drafting, reviewing, and editing, and how?
5. Which technology tools can assist with publishing or sharing of students' work?
6. Which technology tools can address problems with note taking and how?
7. What else, in addition to appropriate technology selection, is essential to improve the writing of students with disabilities?

INTRODUCTION

Whether the assignment is writing book reports, writing answers to test questions, writing a persuasive essay, or writing a science lab report, students need to be able to write to be successful in school. Through their writing, students are assessed on their factual knowledge, their ability to synthesize and evaluate information, and their facility with language skills. Students also can express their creativity through their writing.

Before we can discuss how assistive technology can support writing, we need to define the term *writing* and consider the problems students with disabilities experience with writing. What *is* writing? Is it simply holding a pen and moving your hand from left to right to leave meaningful marks on a page? The process of physically producing text—that is, handwriting—is one aspect of writing. Forming letters correctly, forming them quickly, and aligning them properly on paper can be difficult for many students with disabilities. What *else* is involved in the process of getting one's thoughts down on paper?

A huge body of literature addresses this question, including the specification of content standards for language arts developed by the National Council of Teachers of English and the International Reading Association (1996). Although it is beyond the scope of this text to present this literature in detail, a brief summary will provide a helpful context to our discussion.

Writing is a complex problem-solving activity that involves thinking, planning, and decision making, in addition to the mechanics of transcription. Flower and Hayes (1981) present a cognitive process model in which emphasis is placed on the underlying *thinking skills* involved in writing. They characterize the act of writing as consisting of three major elements: the task environment, the writer's long-term memory, and the writing process itself:

> The task environment includes all of those things outside the writer's skin, starting with the rhetorical problem or assignment…. The second element is the writer's long-term memory in which the writer has stored knowledge, not only of the topic, but of the audience and of various writing plans. The third element… contains writing processes themselves, specifically the basic processes of Planning, Translating, and Reviewing. (p. 369)

The process Flower and Hayes (1981) call "planning" has come to be known as **prewriting**. This process takes place before any sentence is put on paper. Prewriting involves planning for writing; generating ideas, which may include brainstorming activities and/or collecting relevant information; organizing the ideas into some kind of meaningful structure and sequence that may take the form of a concept map or outline; and setting goals for the composing activity. Tompkins (2000) suggests that 70% of writing time should be spent on these prewriting activities.

The second process, translating, is usually referred to as **drafting**. In this process, students develop their ideas and thoughts into meaningful words, sentences, and paragraphs (Scott & Vitale, 2003). Drafting requires both thinking and mechanical processes such as handwriting or keyboarding.

In the third process, **reviewing**, students *reread* and *evaluate* what they have written. In the fourth process, **editing**, they *edit* and *revise* their drafts. These self-evaluations, edits, and revisions focus on all aspects of writing—spelling, grammar, organizational structure, word choice, and content.

Although at first glance these concepts may look like an ordered sequence, it is important to emphasize that in good writing, these processes do not proceed in a linear fashion. Good writers continually generate new ideas; reorganize their thoughts; and set new goals as they compose, edit, and revise (Flower & Hayes, 1981). The writing process, then, is more like a series of interconnected loops than a straight line. This recursive nature of the writing process has important implications for the teaching of writing (Lipson, Mosenthal, Daniels, & Woodside-Jiron, 2000) and for the use of technology to enhance writing.

Once the writing process is completely finished (usually after multiple drafts and revisions), a fifth and culminating activity is **sharing** the final product with others, or **publishing** it. Publishing can be done in a variety of ways, such as through bulletin board displays; class books or newsletters; school newspapers; or postings online on class Web sites, blogs, or wikis. The purpose of publishing is to provide a specific audience for the writing and "to instill pride of authorship" in student writers (Scott & Vitale, 2003).

PROBLEMS THAT STUDENTS WITH DISABILITIES HAVE WITH WRITING

Students with disabilities often have difficulty with *all* of the processes previously described (MacArthur, 2009), and it is not uncommon for them to try to avoid any kind of writing assignment. "I don't like to write. It's hard and it hurts my brain to think so hard," wrote a student in a journal that was part of a research study on struggling writers (Tompkins, 2002, p. 179). Another student in Tompkins's study said, "When I have to write, I'm thinking about being done because I really don't like to write" (p. 179). Students with learning disabilities and attention deficits, in particular, find the writing process overwhelming. In their research on the perceptions of students with language and learning disabilities (LLD) about instruction in the writing process, McAlister, Nelson, and Bahr (1999) found that "students with LLD may not plan because they do not know how to plan" (p. 170). The students in their study could not articulate what it means to plan or why they should plan. One interviewee said, "I just do [planning] in my head, and sometimes I just type words out, and it becomes a story." These researchers summarize writing samples of students with LLD as being "shorter, less coherent, and less refined" than those of normally achieving students (p. 160). Other experts have characterized their writing as "lifeless" (Baker, Gersten, & Scanlon, 2002).

Spelling is particularly troublesome for students with learning disabilities. Their writing is often filled with misspelled words that are not corrected because students with learning disabilities have difficulty detecting the spelling errors in their writings (Darch, Kim, Johnson, & James, 2000; Jones, 2001). MacArthur, Ferretti, Okolo, and Cavalier (2001) summarize the writing problems displayed by students with learning disabilities:

> Their revisions are limited primarily to correction of mechanical errors.... They experience difficulties with transcription processes, both spelling and handwriting, and these struggles affect the overall quality of their writing because cognitive resources devoted to transcription are not available for higher-order processes.... Students with writing difficulties are also less knowledgeable about criteria for good writing and about writing strategies.... Their written products, in comparison to those of their normally developing peers, are typically shorter; contain more errors in spelling, punctuation, and capitalization; lack organization; are less cohesive; omit important genre components; and are lower in overall quality. (p. 288)

Students with other kinds of disabilities may also face obstacles when writing. Students who are deaf and communicate primarily through sign language have literacy levels well below grade level because English represents a second language for them (sign language is their first language). Students with cerebral palsy, muscular dystrophy, and other physical disabilities struggle with the mechanics of writing. They cannot hold a pencil or do not have the fine motor skills needed to manipulate a pencil.

Other students, including many with learning disabilities, may be able to hold a writing implement but they struggle with forming letters correctly, forming them quickly, and aligning them properly on paper. These students may have lots of ideas and may be strong editors, but they cannot get their thoughts on paper. Some students with autism, Down syndrome, or visual-motor learning disabilities may have poor fine motor coordination that results in dysgraphia, which, in the context of writing, means their handwriting is illegible. Not only are they unable to share their final products with others, but their handwriting is illegible to themselves as well, making the rereading and revising process impossible. In addition, for many students on the autism spectrum, struggling with the mechanics of handwriting can be frustrating and stressful and can lead to behavior problems (Broun, 2009).

One final problem related to writing faced by many students with disabilities is note taking. Taking notes, which is an essential activity in many educational situations, is a specialized form of writing. Although it does not require prewriting and revising per se, it requires the ability to listen and write at the same time, the ability to organize the ideas that are presented, and the ability to distinguish what is important from what is not, all carried out simultaneously and speedily. This is a serious obstacle to learning for all students with disabilities.

TECHNOLOGY TOOLS THAT SUPPORT THE WRITING PROCESS

Low-Tech Adaptations for Writing

Low-tech solutions may be all that a student needs, or they may be just one part of the solution for handwriting difficulties. For students who have barely legible handwriting, several low-tech items can improve their ability to manipulate a pencil and write legibly. For example, building up the shaft of a pencil with modeling clay, foam, or a commercially available pencil grip can help a student control the pencil better (Georgia Assistive Technology Project Tools for Life, n.d.). Sometimes placing the paper on a board that is slanted (at a 15- to 30-degree angle) provides better control. Students who have use of only one hand can sometimes benefit from anchoring the paper on a clipboard. Paper that has raised lines or bold lines helps students stay on the lines when writing. This can help students with learning disabilities, as well as students with visual impairments. Students who are blind need to be taught to use signature guides, which are small plastic cards that have a cutout the size of a typical signature. A sighted person places the signature guide on the appropriate spot on the paper, and the person with vision loss signs his or her name in the cutout space.

Other low-tech solutions are available for students who cannot manipulate a pen or pencil at all. Some students who have a whole-hand grasp can use rubber stamps for certain writing activities. For example, number and operation sign stamps can be used for simple arithmetic worksheets. Having a stamp made with a student's name can enable a student with physical disabilities to sign his or her name. Rubber stamps with a wide variety of pictures are available in craft stores and could be used to answer questions on worksheets or quizzes. These are all examples of easy-to-use, inexpensive items that can support the activity of writing.

Prewriting: Graphic Organizers

Most writers, both professional and amateur, are apprehensive when faced with a blank piece of paper or a blank computer screen (optimistically called a "new document"). How can students get past this hurdle?

Remember that the writing process does not begin with drafting. It begins with prewriting activities such as brainstorming and getting organized. Even before computers, teachers discovered that using diagrams called *graphic organizers* could help students in the planning process. Sometimes called *think sheets* (Englert, Raphael, Anderson, Anthony, & Stevens, 1991), these prewriting activities encouraged students to think about what they wanted to write and helped them organize their ideas into a logical order. Now with computers, graphic organizer software programs offer students a seamless connection between a diagram that shows the relationship among ideas (*concept map*) and a text outline. Students no longer have to copy their ideas from the concept map to their paper or word processing document. They can spend their time thinking about their ideas and manipulating their graphical representation on a computer screen, and then—with one click of the mouse—they can turn their concept map into a text outline.

Graphic organizer software is particularly well suited for brainstorming activities. Inspiration software (by Inspiration Software, Inc.) has a feature called "rapid fire" that enables users to record ideas quickly; then the ideas can be manipulated on the screen until they are arranged into a meaningful structure and sequence, and the connections and subconnections among them are clearly represented (see Figure 2.1). This kind of activity can help students organize information and their ideas for a writing assignment.

FIGURE 2.1 Sample graphic organizer: Concept map to help a student get organized for an essay on "My Summer Vacation." Clicking on the Outline icon on the toolbar converts the diagram to a text outline for further development.

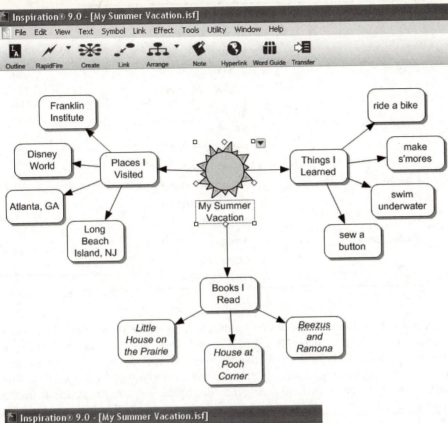

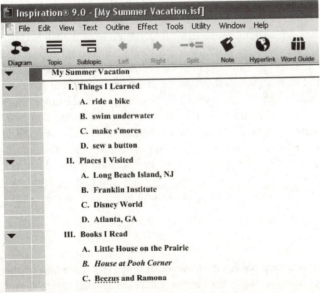

Source: Diagrams created in Inspiration® by Inspiration Software, Inc.

TABLE 2.1 Sample Templates Provided in Inspiration®	
Subject Matter	**Template Title**
Language arts	Literary Web
	Literary Analysis
	Persuasive Essay
Science	Lab Report
	Scientific Method
	Simple Cycles
Social studies	Cause and Effect
	Historical Period
	Pro and Con
Planning	Assignment Plan
	Research Strategy
	Goal Setting
Thinking skills	Analogy
	Comparison
	Venn Diagram

Many students with learning disabilities or attention deficits do not yet have the skills needed to turn a brainstorming activity into an organized concept map. For these students, teachers have found that **templates** are a helpful scaffolding technique. Templates provide a predesigned format that matches the specific organizing task. The student's responsibility is simplified to filling in the content only. With the organization being provided by the template, the student is free to concentrate on the subject matter. Table 2.1 lists various templates provided in Inspiration.

For example, in science classes students usually have to write lab reports. Students with learning disabilities or attention deficits often fail to demonstrate their understanding of the lab because their lab reports are disorganized and poorly written. With the science lab template that is provided in Inspiration, these students are able to enter the information in the correct place, click the Outline button, and create an organized text outline from which they can finish the lab (see Figure 2.2).

The benefits of using visual concept maps are supported by both cognitive learning theory and the research. Graphic organizers have been shown to improve students' outlining and writing skills, and to help students with learning disabilities organize information (Inspiration, 2003; James, Abbott, & Greenwood, 2001). Computer-based concept maps offer additional advantages (MacArthur, 2009). They are easily revised and expanded; they can include prompts from a teacher that can be hidden when not needed; and most importantly, they can be converted to a text outline with a single mouse click. The transition from prewriting to the next stage—drafting—is, therefore, seamless.

Drafting

Technology has been helping people get their ideas down on paper since the invention of the typewriter in the 1800s. (The first commercial typewriter appeared on the market in 1874, and electric typewriters became available in the 1950s.) You could say that the typewriter was the

FIGURE 2.2 Part of Inspiration's science lab template and outline.

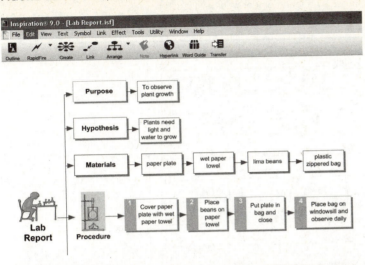

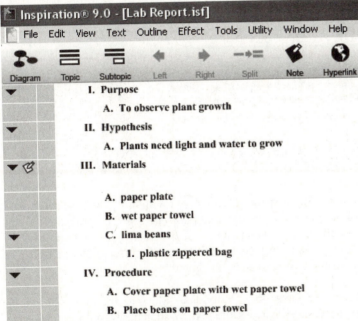

Source: Diagrams created in Inspiration® by Inspiration Software, Inc.

first high-tech writing tool used by individuals with disabilities. Michael Williams, a writer and disability advocate who has cerebral palsy, identifies his grandfather's standard manual typewriter as his first piece of assistive technology. He used typewriters to communicate all through grade school, high school, and college (Williams, 2006).

Bob Williams (no relation to Michael Williams), who held administrative positions in the U.S. Department of Health and Human Services during the Clinton administration, also

FIGURE 2.3 Word processing allows students to write clear, legible text. A portion of a handwritten draft prepared by a fourth grader who has learning disabilities for the writing assignment "Should Peanuts Be Banned in School?"

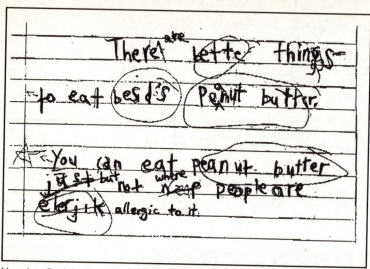

Here is a final draft prepared by the same student using word processing.

Should Peanuts Be Banned?

". . . I think peanuts should be banned from schools. I see more lives have been lost because, when people that even touch it, they can die. That's how bad peanut butter is. There are better things to eat besides peanut butter. You can eat peanut butter but not where people are allergic to it."

Source: From "AlphaSmart a Success in Inclusive Classroom," by K. Taneja, 2000, *TECH-NJ, 11*(1), p. 4.

identifies the typewriter as his first piece of writing technology (Williams, 2000), as mentioned in Chapter 1. Unable to control his fingers due to cerebral palsy, he typed by grasping a small dowel in his fist. And Dick Boydell, an Englishman with cerebral palsy who could not use his hands at all, taught himself to type using his big toe. (See Chapter 8 for discussion of alternative access methods for students who cannot use a standard keyboard.)

WORD PROCESSING APPLICATIONS. These three individuals illustrate the first solution offered by technology: the ability to create clear, legible text by students who do not have the motor skills to grasp a pencil or the fine motor coordination to master the mechanics of penmanship. This, of course, is accomplished through the use of **word processing applications** such as Microsoft Word and Google Docs. Even the simplest document created in these applications is neat in appearance and legible. There are no smudges or tears in the paper where the writer had tried to erase a phrase. There are no messy cross-outs or arrows going in every direction to indicate changes in the order of sentences or paragraphs (see Figure 2.3). Richard Wanderman (2000), a leading educational technology consultant who has learning disabilities himself, explains why he embraces word processing for composing: "Being able to make perfectly formed letters by hitting a key is a lot easier than struggling to write by hand."

Seven Ways Word Processing Helps Developing Writers

1. Legibility of text
2. Potential for publishing in a variety of formats
3. Ease of revision
4. Fluent production of text (while composing, note taking, etc.)
5. Likelihood of supporting applications (for spelling, grammar, concept mapping)
6. Portable, easy-to-replicate electronic text (easy to share, hard to lose)
7. Potential links to electronic source material

Source: From "The Power of Word Processing for the Student Writer," by S. Graham, 2008, Renaissance Learning, Retrieved May 26, 2010, from http://research.renlearn.com/research/321.asp

When viewed in the context of the writing process, you can see that word processing programs support the generative nature of writing. The tasks of inserting new text, deleting unwanted text, and replacing text through cut-and-paste commands become effortless, allowing writers to change their minds about sentence constructions and idea development without penalty. There is no drudgery involved in recopying. Quoting Wanderman (2000) again:

> Just being able to change things without a rewrite frees us from worry about making mistakes. With the ability to change things comes:
>
> - no emphasis on spelling during composition
> - less emphasis on getting the ideas in the right order the first time
> - more emphasis on content....
>
> Being able to concentrate on what you are trying to say rather than struggling to get the spelling right, or worse, choosing only words you know how to spell, is what electronic editing allows.

These anecdotal comments about the benefits of word processing are supported by the research. A landmark report from the Carnegie Corporation, *Writing Next* (Graham & Perin, 2007), includes the use of word processing as one of 11 elements of writing instruction that have been found to be effective in helping adolescent students—especially low-achieving students—learn to write well.

Writing Tools at the Emergent Literacy Level

Students with disabilities who have not yet developed literacy skills, such as young children and children with cognitive or multiple disabilities, can experience success in early writing when provided with appropriate technology tools. Clicker 5 (Crick Software), for example, includes several features that make it particularly effective for this population: a simple interface with a child-friendly font; text-to-speech to create "talking books"; a picture library to help students find and read the right words; and teacher-created word grids that provide point-and-click access to whole words, phrases, and pictures (see Figure 2.4). The topic of emergent literacy is discussed in more depth in Chapter 11.

(continued)

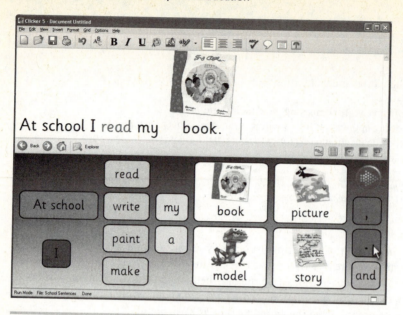

FIGURE 2.4 Clicker 5 (Crick Software) offers word grids, text-to-speech, and a simple interface to support the writing of young children and children with severe disablities.

Source: Reproduced with permission of Crick Software, www.cricksoft.com

WORD PREDICTION APPLICATIONS. The drafting (composing) process can also be supported through the judicious use of **word prediction applications**. Word prediction programs, such as Co:Writer (Don Johnston), Word Q (goQ Software), WriteOnline (Crick Software), and Google Scribe make an educated guess about the next word a student wants to type and presents a list of choices (see Figure 2.5).

The student glances over the list of choices and, if his or her word appears in the list, selects it simply by clicking on it or typing the corresponding number. The word then appears in

FIGURE 2.5 WordQ word prediction software used in conjunction with Microsoft Word.

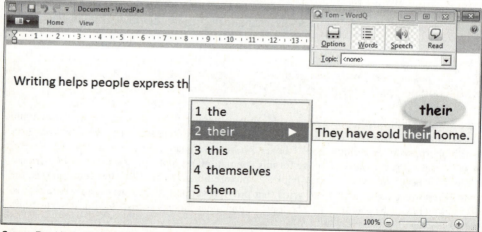

Source: Reprinted with permission of Quillsoft.

the sentence followed by an appropriate space. Some word prediction applications must be used in conjunction with a second application, such as a word processing or e-mail programs; others, such as Google Scribe, are a feature of an application. (In some text messaging applications on cell phones word prediction is called auto-complete or word completion.) In this way, word prediction can support users in all writing environments.

The use of word prediction technology can reduce the number of keystrokes needed to express a thought and therefore has been widely used by individuals with physical disabilities. It is especially helpful for students who type with a single finger (or dowel like Bob Williams) or those who use an alternate access method (see Chapter 8) and whose typing speed is extremely slow. It has also become a helpful writing tool for students with learning disabilities who have severe spelling problems.

Word prediction programs usually predict based on the initial letter that is typed by the user. Sophisticated programs can also predict based on the rules of grammar. For example, if a student types "Yesterday we ..." a grammatically sensitive word prediction program will guess that the next word is going to be a verb and will present mostly verbs in its initial list of guesses. These programs can also be set to "favor" previously used words: The program "remembers" the words a user typed earlier and presents these words first in the lists of guesses. For example, if the user's name is Jujuan, anytime he types a Shift-J and the program infers a noun may be needed, "Jujuan" will appear as one of the choices in the list.

One of the most powerful features of word prediction programs is the ability to set up **custom dictionaries**. Custom dictionaries include vocabulary that is specific to a particular writing activity or subject. Often they include technical terms that are not included in a program's standard dictionary. For example, if a student is writing a paper on dinosaurs, a custom dictionary can be set up that includes words such as *Triassac, Jurassic, Early Cretaceous, Late Cretaceous, Allosaurus, Plateosaurus, Coelophysis, Erythrosuchus, Scutellosaurus, Heterodontosaurus, Megalosaurus,* and other technical terms that are not found in a typical spell-check dictionary. When a student types the letter *A*, for example, *Allosaurus* is likely to be one of the choices. See Figure 2.6.

Custom dictionaries can be extremely helpful for students with learning disabilities who have severe spelling problems. These are the students whose spelling is so out of the ordinary that standard spell-checks are not effective because they cannot guess the intended word. For these students, word prediction programs that use **phonetic dictionaries** are more effective. Phonetic dictionaries are programmed to identify misspelled words by the way they sound, not just by the way they look. So if a student tries to sound out the word *physical* and begins typing "fzic" in Co:Writer (Don Johnston, Inc.;), the list of predicted words will include the following:

1. physics
2. physical
3. fickle
4. FICA
5. fiction

Or if a student tries to sound out the word *photosynthesis* by typing "fotosi," the program will provide the following choices:

1. fantasy
2. photosensitive
3. photostatic
4. photostatting
5. photosynthesis

FIGURE 2.6 Sample screen in Co:Writer, a word prediction program, with the topic dictionary "dinosaurs" selected.

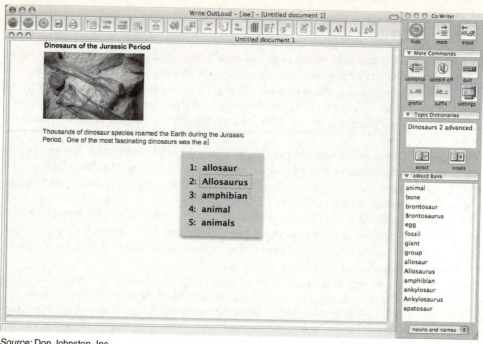

Source: Don Johnston, Inc.

An additional feature that helps poor spellers is that when the mouse is moved over a choice in the predicted words list, the program speaks aloud the word. Students who cannot visually recognize the correct spelling of a word can often make their selection based on the way the word sounds.

Web-Based Integrated Writing Application

WriteOnline (Crick Software) is a talking word processing and word prediction program that is Web based. This means it does not require installation and it is accessible from *any* computer that is connected to the Internet—computers in school and computers at home. Its text-to-speech feature enables students who have weak reading skills to review what they have written and find and correct their writing errors. Its word prediction feature provides spelling and grammar support. It also offers a "Wordbar," which is an on-screen word bank that offers point-and-click access to words and phrases for specific curriculum-related writing tasks. The advantage of accessing the program via the Internet is that students (and teachers) have access to the program's specialized features—text-to-speech, word prediction, and the word banks—from their home computers as well as from any computer in their school. Since many writing assignments are completed as homework, this enables students to have the technology supports they need in all environments. Considering technology trends at the time of this writing, it is expected that other writing applications will soon be available as Web-based applications.

Research on the use of word prediction by students with learning disabilities provides helpful direction regarding its use. The size of the vocabulary available in the dictionary or custom dictionary, as well as the content, must be tailored to the specific writing task (MacArthur et al., 2001). Early writers perform better when the dictionary selected is a small one and includes a focused set of words. Students writing a research paper on a particular topic will perform better if a larger dictionary is selected and relevant proper names and technical vocabulary are added to the dictionary. When the match between a writing task and predicted words is a good one, students can easily find the words they are attempting to spell. Conversely, if the match is a poor one, students can quickly become overwhelmed by lists of irrelevant choices and will not find word prediction to be a helpful tool.

AUTOCORRECT. For students who enter text very slowly because they have physical disabilities, a common feature of standard word processing programs called AutoCorrect can speed up the drafting process. AutoCorrect, usually found under the Tools menu, allows users to create typing shortcuts. Using abbreviations or function keys set by the user, AutoCorrect enters an entire phrase after the abbreviation is typed. For example, in typing this chapter we recorded a macro ("AT") for the phrase "assistive technology." Every time "AT" was typed, the entire phrase "assistive technology" was automatically entered. This feature is especially useful for students' names and specialized vocabulary words that are needed for a writing assignment.

USER PROFILE

Josh

Josh is an eighth-grade student who enjoys many of the pastimes that other 14-year-olds do. He listens to music and talks to girls on the phone. He likes to play baseball, soccer, and roller hockey and attends sleep-away camp in the summer. At a young age, Josh was found to have severe learning disabilities that resulted in significant academic deficits, specifically in written language. Josh's learning disabilities are evident in any subject that requires organization, handwriting, spelling, or composition.

In the short amount of time that I spent with Josh and his parents, I was able to catch a glimpse of the intense frustrations that they have all experienced as a result of these deficits. Josh's parents handed me a stack of letters that Josh had written the previous summer from sleep-away camp. I glanced through the crumpled pages trying to make out a word here or there. In most of the letters, I was able to decipher only the date, the greeting "Mom & Dad," and the closing "Love, Josh." The illegible words were not even written on any lines. They zigzagged up and down the page, looking as if they were not organized in any logical fashion. His parents described to me how they would sit together and try to read the letters. Usually, they could not decipher more than a sentence or two. They explained the frustration of not knowing what their son was trying to tell them.

Josh's parents pointed out that even if you can get used to his handwriting, the next obstacles are spelling and composition. Josh has difficulty understanding the connection between sounds and letters. This, in turn, creates big problems with spelling. His phonemic unawareness was evident as I tried to read through the camp letters.

When Josh was in seventh grade, his parents were referred to an Alliance for Technology Access (ATA) center in their state. The assistive technology specialist at the center tried several different software programs to help Josh with his writing. When she introduced him to word prediction, Josh typed a complete sentence and then turned to his mother and asked, "Can I write some more?" Josh's mother was overcome—this was the first time she had ever seen her son show any competence or interest in writing.

(continued)

Josh uses word prediction to complete his writing assignments in school and homework assignments. For example, he now does his weekly vocabulary assignments on the computer. For these assignments, he has to write original sentences using his vocabulary words. In the past, Josh would either write out the sentences, which usually meant that they were illegible, or he would dictate the sentences to his mother and she would type them on a word processor. Now, Josh is able to do these types of assignments on his own. This is important progress for an adolescent in middle school. His parents are very pleased with the way his writing has progressed. ■

Source: From "Word Prediction Makes the Difference: Learning Disabilities in Middle School," by D. Niemann, 1996, *TECH-NJ, 8* (1), p. 4.

SPEECH RECOGNITION APPLICATIONS. One final technology tool that must be mentioned in a discussion of drafting or composing is **speech recognition.** Speech recognition applications such as Dragon NaturallySpeaking (Nuance), SpeakQ (goQ Software), or MacSpeech Dictate (Nuance) enable a user to dictate his or her words into a computer that is equipped with a microphone (see Figure 2.7). This technology bypasses the keyboard completely and holds promise for people who struggle with handwriting and keyboards. However, although the accuracy of

FIGURE 2.7 Dragon NaturallySpeaking dictation box as it appears in Microsoft Word.

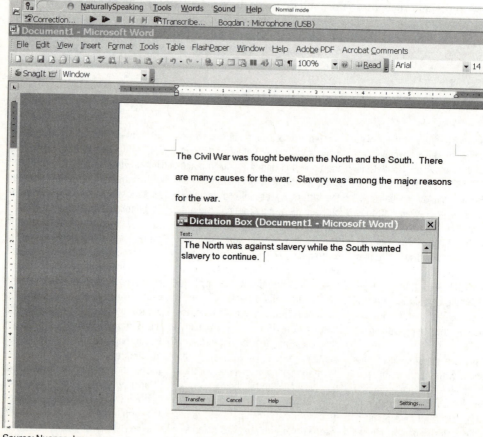

Source: Nuance, Inc.

speech recognition improves with every upgrade, it continues to have a number of limitations that make it a useful writing tool for only a small number of students with disabilities.

Although the accuracy rates of programs such as Dragon NaturallySpeaking are said to be 95% when used by trained users, the accuracy rate is likely to be lower for children with disabilities (MacArthur, 2009), and any percentage of inaccuracies poses problems for the writing process for students with disabilities. Consider that speech recognition requires students to do the following tasks, sometimes simultaneously:

- Think about what they are going to say
- Speak the thought aloud
- Speak any punctuation and capitalization
- Read on the monitor what the program understood them to say
- Decide if that was actually what was said (recognize mistakes)
- Correct the program if it misunderstood
- Go back to picking up the train of thought

Therefore, instead of making writing simpler, speech recognition adds a substantial burden to the writing process. It is not likely to help the composition process for students who are weak in reading or have difficulty multitasking. MacArthur (2009) points out other limitations of speech recognition in schools:

> Despite its potential, speech recognition raises many practical issues. It is difficult to use speech recognition in a school environment because the software requires a reasonably quiet environment for accurate recognition. Also, it makes composing a more public effort, which may be embarrassing, especially for struggling writers. . . . In addition, students must make a commitment to learning to use the software effectively. (p. 252)

However, for a small number of older students with disabilities who meet the following criteria, speech recognition has been shown to be an effective writing tool: (1) The students are computer savvy and enjoy solving technical problems, rather than getting discouraged by them; (2) they have strong oral language skills and understand the differences between spoken and written language; (3) they and their teachers and parents receive extensive training on how to use speech recognition; and (4) they are highly motivated to make it work and are willing to persevere (Speaking to Write, 1999). In addition, even for these highly motivated students, speech recognition will be effective as a writing tool only if school personnel devote several hours of time to a student training program and follow-up (Cavanagh, 2009).

Reviewing

The reviewing part of the writing process, which is so difficult for students who have poor reading skills, is made easier by the use of **text-to-speech.** Text-to-speech reads aloud whatever a student writes. It can read aloud word by word, sentence by sentence, or entire paragraphs or documents. The "reading chunk" feature is easily set by the user from a menu or submenu. The speed of the reading and the quality of the voice are also easily adjustable. "Just being able to hear your writing read aloud is enough … to allow some writers to hear problems in their syntax or even spelling where they might not be able to see them" (Wanderman, 2000). Figure 2.8 shows the toolbar for Write:OutLoud. Note the "read aloud" icons. A study of college students

USER PROFILE

Megan M.

Megan M., a 23-year-old college graduate, uses *Dragon NaturallySpeaking Professional* (Nuance), a voice recognition program, to write on her computer. By dictating into a microphone, she is able to control both the mouse and the keyboard solely with her voice. Megan needed to explore different access methods because she has very limited use of her arms due to a form of muscular dystrophy called Werdnig-Hoffmann's Disease Type II.

Before learning *Dragon,* Megan's computer access was very limited, and she was dependent on other people to write for her. Typing "just became too troublesome and time-consuming, so I would end up dictating in the end. Dictation was my method of 'typing' for years." Megan typically relied on "my student aides or brother or sister, or whoever was around, to do the physical typing while I dictated. It was extremely time-consuming, not only for me, but for the people helping me as well."

At age 18, Megan worked with an assistive technology specialist to find a better solution for her computer access. "The technician evaluating me thought I would be a great candidate for using *Dragon* because I had fine speech and the cognitive ability to handle the training." Megan began using the program at college where she received technical support from the director of the disability support office. She started with a tutorial, but it was through use over time, and much trial-and-error, that Megan fully grasped the program's capabilities.

"As time went on and I began mastering *Dragon,* I began doing my own work completely independently. I started out with small papers and assignments, then I started surfing the Internet for research and whatnot, and before I knew it, I was doing a 22-page senior seminar paper, research and all."

Megan emphasizes that this efficiency did not occur overnight. It took her 3 to 5 months to feel comfortable with the program, and it was not until a year of use that she felt she had truly mastered the software:

Learning this program is very much like learning another language. At first I was very slow, saying only short sentences and making sure the process was actually working. It's a very strange feeling talking to a computer and seeing visual results in front of you immediately. As time went on and I had a better understanding of how the program worked and how I could work with the program, my speed and accuracy became faster and greater. The language of *Dragon* has become second nature to me. Now I can talk for sentences without worrying about how the program is responding. If a problem arises, I know I can fix it. ■

Source: Adapted from Schindler (2005).

---

with learning disabilities using text-to-speech supports the idea that the feature can help students find errors in their writing on their own (Raskind & Higgins, 1995).

The more sophisticated text-to-speech programs also offer a **highlighting** feature that helps students read and evaluate what they have written. Users can choose to have their writing highlighted word by word, phrase by phrase, sentence by sentence, or paragraph by paragraph. A common choice is to have the chunk of text being read aloud (such as a sentence) highlighted

FIGURE 2.8 Write:OutLoud toolbar showing "read aloud" icons.

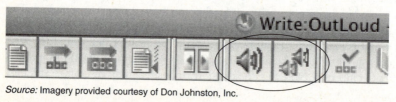

Source: Imagery provided courtesy of Don Johnston, Inc.

in one color, while having a second color highlight what is being spoken word by word. This arrangement supports students with reading difficulties by helping keep their eyes on the chunk of text they are trying to evaluate and revise.

Editing

We have already mentioned that the ability to manipulate text afforded by word processing applications "makes revision possible without tedious recopying" (MacArthur et al., 2001, p. 288). Research supports the idea that allowing students who have learning disabilities to write with word processing applications, in combination with instruction on revising strategies, improves the overall quality of their writing (MacArthur, 2009). In addition to this editing power of word processing, the revising process can be significantly enhanced through the use of several other technology tools, some that we have already described. In the following text, we will discuss spell-checks, thesauruses, grammar checkers, homonym finders, text correction software, and Track Changes and Insert Comments features.

SPELL-CHECKS. Built in to all word processing programs and many Internet browsers, spell-checks quickly find words that have been misspelled. If the writer chooses, spell-checks also guess which word the writer intended by presenting a list of possibilities and spelling each guess correctly. This is an extremely helpful tool for skilled readers and writers because it picks up typographical errors as well as true spelling errors, and these users can quickly correct their mistakes by choosing the right word from the word list. However, for many students with learning disabilities, standard spell-checks present a new set of problems: (1) For students who are poor readers, the list of suggested words can add to the confusion. For example, a student who types "redy" for "ready" is presented with the following choices:

> reedy
>
> red
>
> rely
>
> redeem
>
> ready
>
> redo
>
> reds
>
> redeye

Many of the words look similar, and the poor reader or speller cannot distinguish the correct word from the list of choices. (2) For students who have severe spelling problems, conventional spell-checks often do not guess correctly; as a result, the list of choices presented does not include the student's intended word. For example, if a writer spells the word *reference* as "refrins," the spell-check in Microsoft Word presents the following choices:

> refrains
>
> refries
>
> refines

This list of choices will not help the writer who needed to spell *reference*.

Spell-checks that use phonetic dictionaries are a better choice for poor spellers. As mentioned, phonetic dictionaries are programmed to identify misspelled words by the way they

FIGURE 2.9 Talking spell-check in Write:OutLoud.

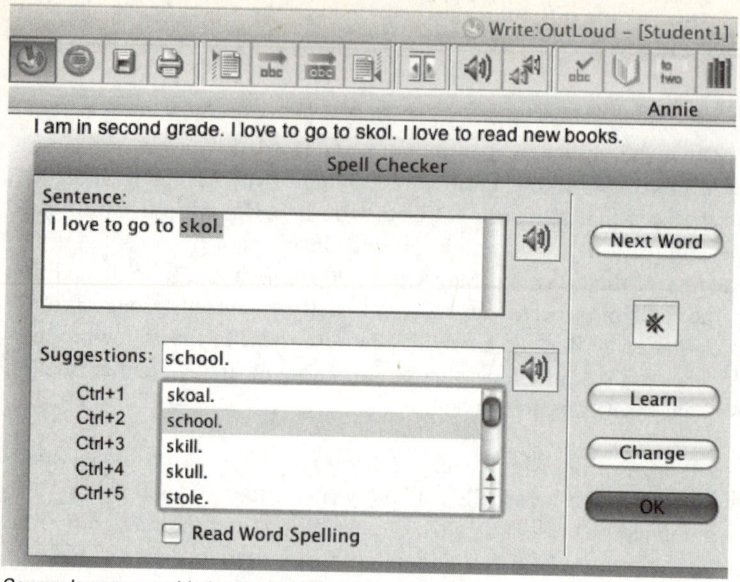

Source: Imagery provided courtesy of Don Johnston, Inc.

sound, not just by the way they look (see the earlier example). Spell-checks based on phonetic dictionaries are available in Franklin's handheld dictionaries and in most text-to-speech and word prediction applications designed for people with learning disabilities.

Poor spellers are also helped by spell-checks that talk. **Talking spell-checks** read aloud the misspelled word and every suggestion in the list of correctly spelled words. Students who are poor readers can listen to the words and choose the correct word based on how it sounds. If the student is still uncertain of the correct word, talking spell-checks read aloud the words' definitions, and the student can make a choice based on the correct definition. (See Figure 2.9)

THESAURUSES. Many skilled writers use a **thesaurus** to help them with their word choices. This is another electronic tool that can help improve the writing of students with learning disabilities. Sometimes called a "synonym finder," these tools present a list of words with similar meanings to the selected word. If users find the choices in Microsoft Word's thesaurus too limiting, there are several Web sites that offer more comprehensive lists of choices. (See Sidebar: Online Synonym Finders.)

Using a talking spell-check is one way to deal with the problem of homonyms. Homonyms are words that sound the same but have different meanings (e.g., *there* and *their*; *to*, *two*, and *too*). A conventional spell-check presents homonyms as choices in its word lists, but this does not help

Online Synonym Finders

http://www.thesaurus.com
http://www.visualthesaurus.com
http://www.dictionary.com

FIGURE 2.10 Confusing Words Web site.

Confusing Words

Confusing word: [   ] [Find]

----

affect   to influence, to pretend (verbs); feeling (noun)

effect   a result; being in operation (nouns); to make happen (verb)

Examples   Self-concept affects learning.[1]

            She affected intellectualism by wearing glasses and using long words

            Her affect is always sour in the morning.

            One effect of lunar gravity is tides.

            The new state income tax was in effect last fall.

            The president effected a new policy on international trade.

Notes   1 Most often affect is used as a verb and effect is used as a noun.
            Something that affects you will have an effect on you.

© 2004 Confusing Words   **About Confusing Words**

Source: Reprinted with permission of R. Wanderman.

the writer who does not know which spelling goes with which meaning. The Franklin handheld dictionaries include a "confusable checker," and some word processing programs include a feature called **homonym finder** that identifies words that are homonyms and presents definitions of them to assist the writer in selecting the correct word. A Web site called Confusing Words offers an extensive inventory of homonyms and helpful definitions, taking into account regional differences in pronunciation (Wanderman, Wanderman, Clark, & Koethnig, 2004; see Figure 2.10).

GRAMMAR CHECKERS. Professional writers and teachers are divided on the value of grammar checkers. Grammar checkers are tools that are available within word processing applications such as Microsoft Word. When activated, they underline grammatical errors such as incomplete sentences, capitalization errors, punctuation errors, subject-verb disagreement, and a whole host of other errors in syntax.

The problem is Word's grammar checker also looks for and underlines phrases and sentences that do not match its particular writing style. Unless you specifically tell it not to, it will underline passive sentences, sentences that are longer than 60 words, clichés and colloquialisms, successive nouns (more than three), first-person uses, gender-specific words, and "wordiness." Professional writers strongly object to what they consider Word's "dubious advice on grammar" and Microsoft's attempt to "reengineer the language" (Teresi, 2000). To check the accuracy of Word's grammar checker, Teresi ran the Preamble to the Constitution through it and was told, "Consider revising. Very long sentences can be difficult to understand." The Gettysburg Address was also criticized. When Word's grammar checker encountered the phrase "dedicated to the proposition that all men are created equal," it said, "men is a gender-specific expression. Consider replacing with person, human being or individual" (Teresi, 2000)

The most recent versions of Word do allow users (including teachers) to specify which aspects of the grammar checker they want activated. This is easily done through Word 2007 and

Text Correction Application

Ginger™ is a Web-based application that combines spell checking and grammar checking in a single mouse click. By running sentences through its online database, Ginger corrects errors of spelling and grammar based on the context of each sentence. For example, when a student types the following sentence: "He leaves on the outskirt of cambrige and everidai he go artside to sea the butifl bards," Ginger will suggest the following corrections: "He lives on the outskirts of Cambridge and everyday he goes outside to see the beautiful birds." The difference between Ginger and other text correction programs is that Ginger reviews entire sentences and suggests corrections for spelling mistakes, typos, grammar errors, and homonym errors. Since these corrections are based on context, Ginger can often tell when a correctly spelled word is misused and can replace it with the right word (such as "see" for "sea"). When Ginger is unable to determine the proper term, it suggests other possible corrections. Each option is presented with a sample expression, allowing users to consider the usage when choosing the correct word.

Word 2010s Proofing feature (which is accessed via Word's Options button or through Word 2008's Preferences on Macintosh computers). It is possible, therefore, to turn off any stylistic evaluations and limit the grammar checker to identifying only a few selected grammatical errors. A creative teacher could integrate this focused use of the grammar checker into students' writing assignments.

TRACK CHANGES AND INSERT COMMENTS FEATURES. Technology also offers a convenient way for teachers to communicate with students about the editing process. An important component of writing instruction is that student writers receive feedback on their drafts—from either their teacher or peer editors—in a timely manner (Zeitz, 2003). Using two tools in Microsoft Word, Track Changes and Insert Comments, and the speed and convenience of e-mail, teachers or peer editors can provide feedback quickly without erasing the student's original writing. When Track Changes is activated, an editor's deletions are marked in ~~strikethrough~~ font and insertions are indicated by <u>underlined text</u>. The writer can see both the editor's suggestions and the original text, and the decision to accept or reject the editorial changes is left to the writer.

The Insert Comments tool is helpful for notes and questions that the editor wants to share with the writer. "The real learning process occurs when the reviewer discusses the content and poses thought-provoking questions about how the material is presented.... [Insert Comments] allows the reviewer to make annotations in a separate window on the screen without changing the actual text of the document" (Zeitz, 2003, p. 16). The student can then consider the editor's questions and comments and decide how he or she wants to proceed. The Track Changes and Insert Comments features are powerful editing tools used by experienced writers; students with disabilities can certainly benefit from their use in writing instruction.

Sharing or Publishing

Sharing what students have written with others is the culminating experience of most writing activities. Technology has much to contribute to this stage. Simply using computers (with word processing applications) connected to printers for the drafting, editing, and revising processes ensures that the final product will be legible and attractive. When the teacher assembles a library of stories published by his or her students or posts students' writings on the bulletin board, students with disabilities—even those with illegible handwriting and poor spelling—can be proud of their printed stories.

Sharing what students have written can also be accomplished through the creation of class (or school) newsletters and newspapers. This is easily done using advanced features of word processing programs such as formatting a document in columns, changing text direction, inserting graphics and digital photos, and automatically wrapping text around pictures. Publishing newsletters that can be distributed around the school or community often motivates students who have come to dread any writing assignment. It gives them a clear purpose and a real audience for their writing—not just the teacher, but their families and peers as well.

Combining graphics, video, and sound with text can be an enjoyable method of getting students interested in writing. Story-writing programs combine features of word processing applications with features of graphics applications and seamlessly integrate the two. Just as primary grade students may be asked to draw a picture in preparation for a writing assignment, story-writing programs allow students to begin their writing activity by creating elaborate images on the computer. Not only is the final printed product enhanced by the creative illustrations, but anecdotal evidence suggests that the added dimension of images enhances the prewriting process, motivates students to write, and leads to more intricate writing (Daiute, 1992). One concern expressed by researchers is that students may become distracted by the bells and whistles of graphics, video, and sound, and they will end up paying less, not more, attention to the writing of text (MacArthur et al., 2001).

Multimedia presentation applications such as PowerPoint® offer another method for publication that combines graphics, video, and sound. The strength of a PowerPoint presentation is that it neatly presents a summary of complicated information or a longer document through the skillful use of bulleted phrases. As such, creating a PowerPoint presentation does not lend itself to improving students' composing skills. What it can do is (1) provide an engaging environment for prewriting—in particular, for determining an appropriate organization for a writing assignment and (2) offer an alternative to writing a paper in a content area for students who have weak writing skills but need to demonstrate knowledge of a topic.

Students Sharing Writing on the Internet

A good example of using the Internet to share students' writings is described by Strassman and D'Amore (2002). Seeking to provide opportunities for her high school students who are deaf and hard of hearing to think and write about controversial issues, the teacher arranged online *synchronous chats* (a technical term for a form of "instant messaging") and Electronic Read Arounds. Students were asked to discuss their opinions about school uniforms on an online chat, which served as a prewriting activity. A printout of the completed dialogue was given to students to help them organize their thoughts. From there, students expanded their ideas and edited them into a document.

The Electronic Read Arounds combined the sharing process with the editing process. Students' written drafts were shared with other students who added questions and comments about the effectiveness of the writing. This helped the writer see the strengths of his or her writing and the sections that were unclear; getting feedback from fellow students, rather than just the teacher, provided students "practice in real-world styles of writing while simultaneously helping them to improve the process by which they write" (Strassman & D'Amore, 2002, p. 31).

Digital storytelling is another option for motivating students to write and for sharing their writing with a wider audience. It has been described as "a new twist on the ancient art of the oral narrative" (Salpeter, 2005, p. 18). Students are encouraged to tell their own personal story through a process sometimes called "PowerPoint on steroids." The process begins with the writing of a story or script. After editing and rewriting the story, students add photographs, other images, sound, and/or video to further personalize the story. Students' emotional attachment to the people or events in the story is considered a key to the success of this use of technology.

The Internet offers multiple opportunities for publication (MacArthur, 2009), and research shows that publishing student writing on the Internet motivates students to write well (Karchmer-Klein, 2007). Discussion boards are useful for sharing short pieces of writing. Teachers can begin a discussion thread by posting questions or topics on a class discussion board. These questions or topics establish a clear purpose for this writing activity. Students can be required to post replies to each thread and to read what their peers have written. On class discussion boards, the audience for students' writing is clear, and knowing that their peers, not just their teacher, will be reading their words often motivates students to put forth an effort.

Blogs are another online method for sharing students' writing. The origin of the word *blog*—a blending of *Web* and *log*—explains its basic characteristic: It is an online journal. But for educators, the characteristic that makes it a valuable writing tool is that it is interactive: Students can easily respond to the writer with their own comments (Britt, 2006). Teachers can set up a blog on a particular unit of study, assign students to research different topics and post their write-ups on the blog, and require students to provide feedback to their fellow students. This can be used to teach editing and revising skills, as well as to encourage ongoing written dialogues about the topic of study.

Intercultural communication projects, which can involve discussion boards, blogs, or e-mail, have been shown to enhance students' motivation to write and to write clearly (MacArthur, 2009). For these Internet-based projects, classes from one part of the country or world collaborate on a curriculum project with a class from another part of the country or world. Students in a different place and culture read the students' writing, which adds to the need to communicate clearly.

Wikis are another online avenue for publishing students' writing. Wikis are "collaboratively authored, searchable documents.... For classroom purposes, wikis are designed to be created by more than one student" (Morgan & Smith, 2008, p. 80). Whereas with blogs, students can only add comments, with wikis students can change content. Therefore, wikis are ideal for writing workshop activities in which students confer with one another and edit one another's work (Teachers First, 2003). Since wikis offer a Track Changes feature, students can see the editing process in action. In addition, the wiki environment provides "immediate, contextualized feedback, thus strengthening the relations among audience, purpose, and structure of the writing" (Morgan & Smith, 2008, p. 81).

Table 2.2 summarizes technology tools that can enhance the writing process.

TECHNOLOGY TOOLS THAT SUPPORT NOTE TAKING

As mentioned at the beginning of this chapter, taking notes during lectures is a specialized form of writing. It requires students to listen and write at the same time, and it must be done quickly. Students need to be able to see the instructor and the blackboard or whiteboard. In most middle schools, high schools, and colleges, methods of note taking must also be

TABLE 2.2 Linking Technology Tools to the Writing Process

Writing Process	Technology Tool	Sample Products
Prewriting	Graphic organizer	Inspiration Kidspiration MindView
	Outlining application	DraftBuilder
Drafting	Word processing	Microsoft Word Google Docs
	Word prediction	WordQ
		Co:Writer Google Scribe
	Macros	Microsoft Word
	Speech recognition	DragonNaturally - Speaking SpeakQ
Evaluating what was written	Text-to-speech	WordQ Write:OutLoud Read & Write Ginger
Editing and revising	Text-to-speech	WordQ
	Talking spell-checks	Write:OutLoud
	Homonym finder	Read & Write
	Word prediction	Confusingwords.com
		WordQ
		Co:Writer Google Scribe
	Grammar checker	Microsoft Word
	Text correction	Ginger
Sharing and publishing	Track Changes and Insert Comment features	Microsoft Word
	Multimedia application (combining text with graphics, sound, and video)	PowerPoint
	Internet	Discussion boards Blogs Wikis
Note taking	Portable note takers	Neo CalcuScribe
	Smartpen	LiveScribe Pulse Pen LiveScribe Echo Pen
	Braille note takers	Braille Lite M40
	Application with captionist and second display	C-Print CART
	Capturing devices	mimio SMART Board Promethean ActivBoard

portable because students typically attend classes in different rooms. These requirements preclude the use of desktop computers for most note taking. Laptops are one alternative but present another set of shortcomings: (1) Battery life on laptop computers is limited, meaning students either need to sit near a power source (not always possible in typical classrooms), or they need to carry an extra battery with them and remember to change it before the laptop loses its charge. (2) Laptops take a few minutes to boot up. While they are starting up, students may miss the first part of lectures. (3) Laptops are vulnerable to damage. They will not withstand being thrown on the ground in students' backpacks or being accidentally knocked off a desk. (4) Students who have attention issues may be easily distracted by the many non–note taking options available on laptops such as Internet browsing, video games, and social networking sites.

Portable Word Processors

For students who can take their own notes by typing on a keyboard, portable devices are available that meet the following criteria: (1) They have a longer battery life than a laptop, (2) they have a simple on/off switch and require no time to start, (3) they are durable and are less likely to break than a laptop, and (4) they are relatively inexpensive. These devices are called portable word processors or portable note takers. The Neo 2 (Renaissance Learning) is an example of this kind of technology tool. It has a full-sized keyboard; is lightweight; and features basic editing commands, a thesaurus, a spell-checker, and a Spanish-English word lookup. It connects easily to a printer for printing or to a computer for downloading files for later editing (wireless versions are available). The Neo 2 also has a pre-installed keyboarding tutor to help students build their keyboarding skills. Add-ons are available to provide text-to-speech and word prediction capabilities. CalcuScribe (SmartPad, Inc., d.b.a. CalcuScribe) is another portable, battery-operated word processing device. This lightweight device also includes a calculator keypad for completing math activities. Both the Neo's and the CalcuScribe's visual displays are relatively small, so they are not appropriate for in-depth editing, but they work well for note taking.

The Neo 2 is a portable word processor and note taker.

Photo courtesy of Renaissance Learning, Inc.

Smartpen

A different kind of tool for note taking is a device called a smartpen (Pulse Pen and Echo Pen, both from Livescribe). This is a pen-sized computer that captures both handwriting and audio recordings, that is, the student's handwriting and the instructor's lecture, and syncs them together. The pens record the audio while digitizing the handwritten notes that a student takes on Livescribe's special "Dot Paper." This paper is printed with microdots that facilitate a dot positioning system (DPS). The smartpen has an infrared camera at its tip that takes 72 snapshots per second, giving it the ability to capture and recreate handwriting based on the dot patterns at the pen's location. What this means for students is that when they open their notebooks to review their notes, they simply tap the pen any place within their notes, and the smartpen will replay the audio from the moment the note was written. This enables students to check the accuracy of their notes and to add information to their notes. Both the notes and the audio recording can be uploaded to the Internet so they can be saved, replayed and shared with other students. Although the Pulse and Echo Smartpens are amazing and reliable technology tools, it is important to note that they will be effective only for those students who are committed to reviewing their notes regularly.

Using the Pulse Smartpen by LiveScribe to record a teacher's lecture and take notes on LiveScribe's special "dot paper".

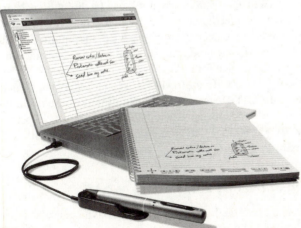

Transferring notes and the audio recording taken with a Pulse Smartpen to a computer for editing and saving.

Photos courtesy of LiveScribe, Inc.

Other Options for Note Taking with Audio Recording

The ability to sync audio recordings of lectures or lessons with handwritten or typed notes is available in Microsoft Word 2008 for the Mac and in several apps for the Apple iPad. In Word 2008, open a new document and choose Notebook Layout from the View menu. The Audio Notes toolbar will appear. Clicking the red circular button will begin audio recording while you type your notes; clicking the black circular button will end audio recording. To hear a specific part of your notes, just click the speaker icon that appears to the left of the first line of each paragraph.

The Apple iPad can serve as a note taker through a handwriting recognition app, the use of an external keyboard, and/or the use of an app that offers notes with sound recording. AudioNote (Luminant Software) and SoundPaper (David Estes) both use the iPad's built-in microphone to capture a teacher's voice. The app then syncs the recording with the user's notes and allows the user to tap the screen to hear what was said when the note was taken. If the current enthusiasm for the iPad continues, we can expect to see many new apps become available that will have applications in the classroom.

Portable Braille Note Takers

For students who are blind, a line of portable note takers, such as the BrailleNote by HumanWare, is available that provides a choice of adaptive inputs and outputs. Some students prefer a portable note taker that has a standard Braille keyboard, whereas others prefer a regular QWERTY keyboard (see the User Profile of Serena in Chapter 14). Both kinds of devices can be connected to a computer, a printer, or a Braille printer for downloading files and printing. The use of Braille as a computer access method will be discussed in more detail in Chapter 8.

Capturing Devices

Some students with disabilities are not able to take their own notes in class. In the past, they have had to rely on photocopies of notes taken by fellow students, or they were provided with a personal note taker who may or may not have been familiar with the subject matter. This was particularly problematic for students in math and science classes. Today technology tools called *capturing devices* offer note-taking alternatives.

By attaching a portable capturing device to any whiteboard, notes can be digitally recorded in real time and color format. These notes can then be disseminated through print, e-mail, a class Web site, or any other type of electronic media. One such capturing device, the mimio (Virtual Ink), can be attached directly to any whiteboard, and notes can be displayed in real time on a student's computer, or they can be stored in the device for upload later.

Another type of capturing device, the SMART Board (SMART Technologies Inc.), functions as an interactive whiteboard. Using SMART Board applications, all notes written on the device can be digitally recorded in real time so students can rewind and fast-forward to specific sections of lectures for review. Additionally, the SMART Recorder feature of the application allows audio to be added to notes for an extra level of support.

Note-Taking Services for Deaf/Hard of Hearing Students

For students who are deaf or hard of hearing, two methods of note taking have been developed that rely on professional note takers. Communication Access Realtime Translation, or CART,

SMART Board.

Photo courtesy of SMART Technologies Inc.

is a system that is used in the courts because it results in a verbatim record of proceedings. CART captionists are specially trained to transcribe every word that is spoken, much like a court stenographer. The verbatim transcription is displayed on a large light-emitting diode (LED) display or a laptop computer so that individuals with hearing loss can read it. This kind of verbatim record is required in legal proceedings. Some colleges provide CART for students who are deaf as a complete record of class meetings. For students who need only lecture notes, however, CART is usually considered excessive.

For these students, a more affordable accommodation is C-Print. C-Print was designed by the National Technical Institute for the Deaf specifically as a note-taking system. Using a special application and trained captionists, C-Print produces paraphrased records of class lectures. The captionists have received intensive training in text-condensing strategies and in typing using an abbreviation system so they can keep up with the instructor's lecture. For students who want to see the notes as the instructor lectures, the captionist's laptop can be connected to the students' laptops for simultaneous display or to a projected display. Some students prefer that the captionist e-mail them the notes after they have been edited.

TECHNOLOGY ALONE WILL NOT IMPROVE STUDENTS' WRITING

Although technology offers powerful tools that can improve the writing of students with disabilities, the research on computers and writing conveys a consistent message: Assistive technology will succeed in helping students improve their writing skills *only if* it is paired with good teaching strategies (MacArthur, 2009). Simply providing graphic organizers, word processing applications, word prediction applications, speech recognition, text-to-speech, talking spell-checks, homonym finders, or portable note-taking devices will not lead to improvements in the writing skills of students with disabilities. Students need to receive three-pronged training: (1) instruction on the *writing* process, (2) training on specific *technology tools*, and (3) training on how to use these technology tools to enhance the writing process.

Instruction on the Writing Process

The literature on how to teach the writing process is extensive. Tompkins (2002) recommends instructional scaffolding, such as having the teacher model the writing process—that is, directly demonstrate in a step-by-step fashion how to plan, create a draft, evaluate what was written, and then revise and edit. She also recommends teaching mini-lessons on specific writing-related skills, collaborative writing assignments, and guided writing assignments, in addition to independent writing activities. Baker et al. (2002, p. 70) suggest that teachers model the "inner dialogue expert writers engage in during the writing process." James and colleagues (2001) describe a model for teaching writing to students with learning disabilities that combines process writing with an assessment process for monitoring student progress. They recommend providing explicit instruction on the skills that are included in their Six-Trait Writing Assessment Rubric, such as organization, voice, word choice, and writing conventions (e.g., punctuation and grammar).

Scott and Vitale (2003) developed a scaffolding technique called the Writing Wheel that serves as a visual guide to the writing process for students who need help focusing and sequencing (see Figure 2.11). The Writing Wheel is divided into five *unequal* sections, each devoted to a major subprocess of the writing process and each containing a list of the activities students need to do. By allocating half of the circle to prewriting, the Writing Wheel conveys at a glance the relative amount of time students should spend on each stage. An overlay with a cutout can be placed on the wheel to help students focus on one task at a time. The Writing Wheel can help students with learning disabilities be more aware of the processes involved in writing, provide monitoring information for teachers and students, and help students focus on the individual components of the writing process.

Loeffler (2005) provides a helpful strategy to teach students with learning disabilities how to monitor their misspelling of words. She points out that traditional spelling tests have a narrow focus on memorization and do not teach students spelling strategies. As an alternative, she recommends modeling a "spelling self-check routine" and using a spelling rubric that teaches students a variety of strategies. The first task on the rubric is to identify misspelled words. One of the acceptable strategies is to use a spell-check. Loeffler's rubric is a good example of combining instruction in writing tasks with instruction on appropriate technology tools.

Instruction on Technology Tools for Writing

When the technology tools described in this chapter are first introduced to students, the tools "create new burdens at the same time that they remove other burdens" (MacArthur et al., 2001, p. 298). For example, although word prediction can help poor spellers, to use it successfully students need to continually read over the list of suggested words, decide if one of them is appropriate, and select the desired word, all the while holding their intended sentence in their memory (MacArthur, 1999).

For technology to be helpful to students with disabilities, students need to be *comfortable* using the technology tools. This means they must learn how to use it *skillfully* so that their minds can focus on the writing process and not be distracted by the technology. How do they get to this point? They need to be taught explicitly how to use each application and each relevant feature, and they need plenty of time and opportunity to *practice* using the tool. "Do a lot of something and it gets easier," notes Wanderman (2004), adding "Once enough practice takes place the tool starts to fall into the background and what the user wants to

FIGURE 2.11 The Writing Wheel.

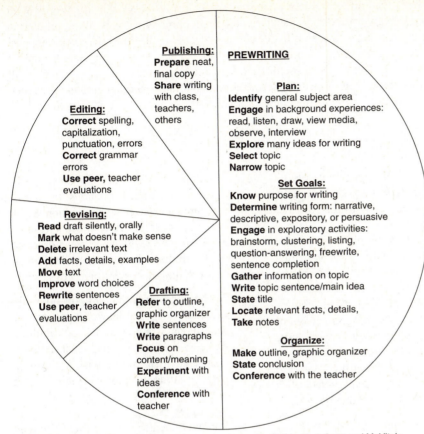

Source: From "Teaching the Writing Process to Students with LD," by B. J. Scott and M. Vitale, 2003, *Intervention in School and Clinic, 38*(4), p. 222. Reprinted with permission.

do with the tool starts to come into the foreground. In the end, the tool ought to be almost taken for granted and the focus completely on the application." Wanderman reminds us that the practice itself must have meaning. Without a meaningful task to accomplish, such as composing an e-mail message to a friend, practicing using a piece of writing software will be meaningless.

In addition to learning specific applications, students need to acquire basic keyboarding skills (MacArthur, 1996). Typing is very different from handwriting and requires a different set of skills. Students need to become familiar with the location of the letters on the keyboard so they can quickly locate the keys they desire. It is not necessary for them to become skilled touch-typists, but they need to reach a level of proficiency at keyboarding. Several good applications exist that teach keyboarding in an entertaining way. (See Web Resources.)

Putting It All Together

Just as teachers need to model the writing process, they also need to model the use of technology to support writing. They need to teach skills such as using a graphic organizer to brainstorm and/or organize a writing assignment, using a talking spell-check to find the correct spelling of a word for students who are extremely poor spellers, or using the Confusing Words Web site (http://www.confusingwords.com) to identify and correct homonym errors. Word prediction requires that students learn how to scan a list of choices, decide if the word they want appears on the list, and hit another key if the desired word does not appear. These steps must be taught to students in the context of writing and spelling strategies (MacArthur et al., 2001). In fact, all of the technology tools described in this chapter need to be demonstrated, taught, and practiced within the context of writing activities if students with disabilities are to benefit from their use.

Summary

- Writing is a complex problem-solving activity that involves thinking, planning, and decision making, as well as the mechanics of transcription.
- Writing is an iterative process that can be broken into various steps: prewriting, drafting, reviewing, editing, and sharing or publishing. Students with disabilities often have difficulty with all of the processes involved in writing, so it is not uncommon for them to try to avoid writing assignments.
- A variety of helpful writing tools are available to assist individuals with disabilities in each part of the writing process:

  - *Prewriting:* graphic organizers (e.g., Inspiration)
  - *Drafting:* word processing, word prediction with custom dictionaries, speech recognition
  - *Reviewing:* text-to-speech
  - *Editing:* text-to-speech, phonetic spell-checks, talking dictionaries, thesaurus, grammar checker, text correction, Track Changes and Insert Comments features
  - *Sharing or publishing:* word processing, multimedia presentation applications, digital storytelling, blogs, wikis

- Technology tools that support note taking include portable word processors, SmartPens, Braille note takers, capturing devices, and CART and C-Print services.
- Assistive technology will succeed in helping students improve their writing skills only if it is paired with good teaching strategies.
- Students need to receive three-pronged training: (1) instruction on the writing process, (2) training on specific technology tools, and (3) training on how to use these technology tools to enhance the writing process.

Web Resources

For additional information on the topics listed, visit the following Web sites:

Writing Process

ReadWriteThink, a Project of the International Reading Association, National Council of Teachers of English & the Verizon Foundation
http://www.readwritethink.org

Graphic Organizers

Inspiration Software, Inc.
http://www.inspiration.com/examples/search

Mindview 3
http://www.matchware.com/en/products/mindview/education/examples.htm

Word Processing for Drafting
LD Resources
http://www.ldresources.org/?p=171

Write:OutLoud
http://www.donjohnston.com/products/write_outloud/index.html

Word Prediction
Co:Writer 6
http://www.donjohnston.com/products/cowriter/index.html

WordQ
http://www.goqsoftware.com

Write Online
http://www.cricksoft.com/uk/writeonline

Read & Write
www.texthelp.com → US → Education

Google Scribe
http://scribe.googlelabs.com/

Speech Recognition
Dragon Naturally Speaking
http://www.nuance.com/naturallyspeaking

SpeakQ
http://www.goqsoftware.com

MacSpeech Dictate/Dragon Dictate
http://www.macspeech.com

Text-To-Speech
ReadPlease
http://www.readplease.com

TextAloud
http://www.nextup.com

WordQ
http://www.goqsoftware.com

Write Online
http://www.cricksoft.com/uk/writeonline

Read & Write
http://www.texthelp.com → US → Education

Ginger Software
http://www.gingersoftware.com

Clicker 5
http://www.cricksoft.com/uk/products/clicker/

Phonetic Dictionary
Write:OutLoud
http://www.donjohnston.com/products/write_outloud/index.html

Digital Storytelling
Center for Digital Storytelling
http://www.storycenter.org/index1.html

Microsoft Education
http://www.microsoft.com/education/atschool.mspx

Blogs in Education
Kidblog
http://kidblog.org

Free site designed by a teacher
http://www.classchatter.com

Note Takers
Neo 2
http://www.renlearn.com/neo

CalcuScribe
http://www.calcuscribe.com

BrailleNote
http://www.humanware.com/en-usa/products

Pulse and Echo Smartpens by Livescribe
http://www.livescribe.com

Capturing Devices
mimio
http://www.mimio.com

SmartBoard
http://www.smarttech.com

Teacher resources from SmartBoard
http://www.education.smarttech.com/ste/en-US/Ed+Resource/

StarBoard Educator Resource Center
*http://resourcecenter.hitachi-software.de/us/http://www.prometheanworld.com/
server.php?show=nav.16053*

Captioning for People Who Are Deaf/Hard of Hearing
CART
http://www.netac.rit.edu/downloads/tpsht_cart.pdf

C-print
http://www.ntid.rit.edu/cprint/

Keyboarding
Type to Learn 4 free demo
http://commerce.sunburst.com/freeTools.aspx?id=0

Mavis Beacon Teaches Typing® Platinum 20
http://www.broderbund.com

SpeedSkin
http://www.speedskin.com

Talking Typer (designed for blind users)
http://www.aph.org/tech/tt_info.htm

Low-Tech Tools for Writing
Georgia Assistive Technology Project Tools for life
http://www.gatfl.org/LearningDisabilitiesGuide/WritingDifficulties.aspx

Onion Mountain Technology
http://onionmountaintech.com

Suggested Activities

1. *Explore word prediction.* Type a short paragraph (3–4 sentences) and count the total number of keystrokes you needed to make (every letter, number, punctuation mark, space, and Shift key hit). Now type that same paragraph using a word prediction program that is set to "remember recent words." Keep track of the number of keystrokes you use. What is the difference in the number of keystrokes between the two times you typed the paragraph? Now type the paragraph a third time. Again, keep track of the number of keystrokes you use. What is the difference in the number of keystrokes between the first time you typed the paragraph (without word prediction) and the third time, when the word prediction program had had a chance to learn your vocabulary? What are the implications of this finding for students with disabilities?

2. *Make the writing components of a unit accessible to students with disabilities.*

   a. Select a unit of study for a grade level. It can be a unit you that you currently teach, have taught in the past, would like to teach in the future, or one that you have been asked to support by another teacher. Or you can select lesson plans from a Web site such as www.teachnology.com.

   b. Identify the writing components in the unit (e.g., completing worksheets, taking a quiz, writing a story, writing a letter). Then explain how you would make the writing components accessible to a student who has learning disabilities and a student who has physical disabilities. Be specific. Make sure your recommended solution or solutions match the task and the students' needs.

3. *Create topic dictionaries in word prediction.* Using vocabulary from your unit, create a topic dictionary in Co:Writer or another word prediction program. Include at least 10 words in it. Type a writing sample using the topic dictionary, and take a screenshot of the topic dictionary in use. Print the screenshot. Then write a brief narrative explaining the formatting options you would select to meet your students' needs (e.g., number of choices, flexible spelling, background color).

4. *Find low-tech solutions for writing.* Put together a kit of simple low-tech writing aids. Go to a local crafts store and an office supply store and gather items such as clipboards, pencil grips, appropriate rubber stamps, items that can be used as a slant board, pens and markers with wide diameters, different kinds of paper, and so on. Organize them in a plastic bin.

References

Baker, S., Gersten, R., & Scanlon, D. (2002). Procedural facilitators and cognitive strategies: Tools for unraveling the mysteries of comprehension and the writing process and for providing meaningful access to the general curriculum. *Learning Disabilities Research & Practice, 17*(1), 65–77.

Britt, J. (2006). Go blogging with social studies field trips. *Learning and Leading with Technology, 33*(6), 29.

Broun, L. (2009). Take the pencil out of the process. *Teaching Exceptional Children, 42*(1), 14–21.

Cavanagh, C. (2009). Speech recognition trial protocol. *Closing the Gap*, December 2008/January 2009, pp. 8–11.

Daiute, C. (1992). Multimedia composing: Extending the resources of kindergarten to writers across the grades. *Language Arts, 69,* 250–260.

Darch, C., Kim, S., Johnson, S., & James, H. (2000). The strategic spelling skills of students with learning disabilities: The results of two studies [Electronic version]. *Journal of Instructional Psychology, 27*(1), 15–27.

Englert, C. S., Raphael, T. E., Anderson, L. M., Anthony, H. M., & Stevens, D. D. (1991). Making writing strategies and self-talk visible: Cognitive strategy instruction in regular and special education classrooms. *American Educational Research Journal, 28,* 337–372.

Flower, L., & Hayes, J. R. (1981). A cognitive process theory of writing. *College Composition and Communication, 32*(4), 365–387.

Georgia Assistive Technology Project Tools for Life. (n.d.). *Learning disabilities and assistive technologies: Reading.* Retrieved June 29, 2006, from http://www.gatfl.org/ldguide/read.htm

Graham, S. (2008). The power of word processing for the student writer, Renaissance Learning, Retrieved May 26, 2010 from http://research.renlearn.com/research/321.asp

Graham, S., & Perin, D. (2007). *Writing next: Effective strategies to improve writing of adolescents in middle and high school—A report to the Carnegie Corporation of New York.* Washington, DC: Alliance for Excellent Education. Retrieved May 26, 2010 from http://www.all4ed.org

Inspiration Software®, Inc., & Institute for the Advancement of Research in Education (IARE) at AEL. (2003). Graphic organizers: A review of scientifically based research. Retrieved April 2, 2007, from http://www.inspiration.com/vlearning/research/index.cfm

James, L. A., Abbott, M., & Greenwood, C. R. (2001). How Adam became a writer: Winning writing strategies for low-achieving students. *Teaching Exceptional Children, 33*(3), 30–37.

Jones, C. J. (2001). Teacher-friendly curriculum-based assessment in spelling. *Teaching Exceptional Children, 34*(2), 32–38.

Karchmer-Klein, R. (2007). Best practices in using the Internet to support writing. In S. Graham, J. Fitzgerald, & C. MacArthur (Eds.), *Best practices in writing instruction* (pp. 222–241). New York: Guilford.

Lipson, M. Y., Mosenthal, J., Daniels, P., & Woodside-Jiron, H. (2000). Process writing in the classrooms of eleven fifth-grade teachers with different orientations to teaching and learning. *The Elementary School Journal, 101*(2), 209–231.

Loeffler, K. A. (2005). No more Friday spelling tests? An alternative spelling assessment for students with learning disabilities. *Teaching Exceptional Children, 37*(4), 24–27.

MacArthur, C. A. (1996). Using technology to enhance the writing processes of students with learning disabilities. *Journal of Learning Disabilities, 29*(4).

MacArthur, C. A. (1999). Word prediction for students with severe spelling problems. *Learning Disabilities Quarterly, 22*(3), 158–172.

MacArthur, C. A. (2000). New tools for writing: Assistive technology for students with writing difficulties. *Topics in Language Disorders, 20*(4), 85–100.

MacArthur, C. A. (2009). Using technology to teach composing to struggling writers. In G. Troia (Ed.), *Instruction and assessment for struggling writers* (pp. 243–265). New York: Guilford.

MacArthur, C. A., Ferretti, R. P., Okolo, C. M., & Cavalier, A. R. (2001). Technology applications for students with literacy problems: A critical review. *The Elementary School Journal, 101*(3), 273–301.

McAlister, K. M., Nelson, N. W., & Bahr, C. M. (1999). Perceptions of students with language and learning disabilities about writing process instruction. *Learning Disabilities Research & Practice, 14*(3), 159–172.

Morgan, B., & Smith, R. D. (2008). A wiki for classroom writing. *The Reading Teacher, 62*(1), 80–82.

National Council of Teachers of English and the International Reading Association. (1996). *Standards for the English language arts.* Urbana, IL: Authors. Retrieved from http://www.ncte.org/standards

Niemann, D. (1996). Word prediction makes the difference: Learning disabilities in middle school. *TECH-NJ, 8*(1), 4, 8. Retrieved from http://www.tcnj.edu~technj/fall96/writeaway.html

Raskind, M. H., & Higgins, E. (1995). Effects of speech synthesis on the proofreading efficiency of postsecondary students with learning disabilities. *Learning Disability Quarterly, 18*, 141–158.

Salpeter, J. (2005). *Telling tales with technology. Technology & Learning,* February, 18-24.

Schindler, C. (2005). Voice recognition provides independence for Ramapo College student. *TECH-NJ*, Vol. 16, No. 1, Retrieved April 2, 2007, from http://www.tcnj.edu/~technj/2005/ ramapo.htm

Scott, B. J., & Vitale, M. R. (2003). Teaching the writing process to students with LD. *Intervention in School and Clinic, 38*(4), 220–224.

Speaking to Write. (1999). *Spotlight on speech recognition.* Retrieved June 2, 2010, from http://www2.edc.org/NCIP/vr/VR_HTMLdoc.html

Strassman, B. K., & D'Amore, M. (2002). The write technology. *Teaching Exceptional Children, 34*(6), 28–31.

Taneja, K. (2000). AlphaSmart a success in inclusive classroom. *TECH-NJ, 11*(1), 4.

Teachers First. (2003). *Writer's Workshop: Making writing a lifelong habit for elementary students.* Retrieved on March 23, 2010, from http://www.teachersfirst.com/lessons/writers/writer-4.html.

Teresi, D. (2000). Call me Fishmeal. *Forbes, 166*(13), 39.

Tompkins, G. E. (2000). *Teaching writing: Balancing process and product* (3rd ed.). Upper Saddle River, NJ: Merrill/Pearson Education.

Tompkins, G. E. (2002). Struggling readers are struggling writers, too. *Reading & Writing Quarterly, 18*, 175–193.

Wanderman, R. (2000). *How computers change the writing process for people with learning disabilities* (First Person feature). Retrieved June 2, 2010, from the LD OnLine Web site http://www.ldonline.org/firstperson/How_Computers_Change_the_Writing_Process_for_People_with_Learning_Disabilities?theme=print

Wanderman, R. (2004). *Tools and dyslexia: Issues and ideas* (LD Resources). Retrieved June 2, 2010, from the LD Resources Web site http://www.ldresources.org/2004/07/08/tools-and-dyslexia-issues-and-ideas/

Wanderman, R., Wanderman, A., Clark, D., & Koethnig, M. (2004). *Confusing words.* Retrieved June 2, 2010 from the Confusing Words Web site http://www.confusingwords.com

Williams, B. (2000). More than an exception to the rule. In M. Fried-Oken & H. Bersani (Eds.), *Speaking up and spelling it out* (pp. 245–254). Baltimore, MD: Brookes.

Williams, M. (2006, April). How far we've come, how far we've got to go: Tales from the AAC trenches. Presented as part of *Building and Maintaining Social Networks by Strengthening Communicative Interactions* by S. Blackstone, D. Wilkins, & M. Williams, at the California Speech-Language-Hearing Association's Annual State Convention in San Francisco on April 1, 2006. Retrieved from the AAC-RERC Web site on July 18, 2010, http://aac-rerc.psu.edu/index_Williams.html

Zeitz, L. E. (2003). Electronic editing. *Learning & Leading with Technology, 30*(7), 14–17, 27.

3 | ASSISTIVE TECHNOLOGY TO SUPPORT READING

Focus Questions

1. What is the difference between learning to read and reading to learn?
2. What are the five areas of reading instruction that were identified by the National Reading Panel as being essential for children to learn to read?
3. How can computers be used as a reading remediation tool (to teach reading skills)?
4. How can computers be used as a reading compensation tool (to help students compensate for their reading difficulties)?
5. What does the research say about the impact of text readers and scan/read programs on students with learning disabilities?

INTRODUCTION

Reading is both a subject area that students must master *and* a means by which students learn other subject areas. In the early grades (K–3), the primary focus of schools is on reading *instruction*, on children **"learning to read,"** whereas it is said that in grades 4 and up, the focus shifts to children **"reading to learn."** The skills involved in reading to learn are called *content literacy skills*, which are defined as "the ability to use reading and writing to acquire new content" (Zorfass, Fideler, Clay, & Brann, 2007, p. 1). Computer technology has a powerful role to play in both learning to read and reading to learn.

This chapter is divided into four parts. The first part provides a *context* for using computer technology as a tool to teach reading. It presents what we know about teaching children to read (evidence-based strategies). The second part summarizes the typical problems faced by children who have trouble reading. Children with reading difficulties are given many labels: struggling readers, learning disabled, dyslexic, print disabled. The strategies discussed in this chapter apply to all of these children, regardless of their label. The focus in the third part shifts to how computer technology can be used to teach children to read (i.e., as an instructional tool). The fourth part addresses how computer technology can help older students whose reading remains inadequate even after intensive instruction (i.e., how computer technology can be used as a compensatory tool to provide access to grade-level texts).

TABLE 3.1	Topic Areas Identified by the National Reading Panel
Phonemic awareness:	Understanding the *sounds* of a language
Phonics:	Recognizing the correspondence between sounds and letters
Fluency:	Reading orally with speed, accuracy, and proper expression
Comprehension:	Understanding the meaning of the text
Vocabulary:	Understanding the meaning of words both orally and in print

WHAT WE KNOW ABOUT TEACHING CHILDREN TO READ: EVIDENCED-BASED STRATEGIES

In 2000, the **National Reading Panel (NRP)**, a group that was convened at the request of the U.S. Congress, published a seminal report titled *Teaching Children to Read*. The report reviewed the published research on reading, pinpointed the types of skills children need to learn to become independent readers, and summarized the evidence relating to how those skills are best taught to beginning readers (NRP, 2000). The panel recommended specific instructional approaches and strategies ("evidence-based practices") that its members believed "hold substantial promise for application in the classroom at this time." These findings and recommendations have had far-reaching effects on reading instruction in the early twenty-first century and, therefore, are summarized in the next section.

Findings of the NRP: Topic Areas

To become proficient readers, children need to be taught skills in five topic areas. These areas are described in the following sections and listed in Table 3.1.

PHONEMIC AWARENESS.   Phonemes are the smallest units of sound in the spoken language, and *phonemic awareness* refers to the ability to "focus on and manipulate phonemes in spoken words" (NRP Subgroup on Alphabetics, 2000, p. 3). The term relates to children's understanding of the *sounds* of their language. English, for example, consists of 41 different phonemes. The word *book*, for example, consists of three sounds or phonemes /b/, /u/, and /k/. Explicitly teaching children to recognize and manipulate phonemes is the first recommendation of the NRP's report.

PHONICS.   Phonics instruction teaches the correspondence between sounds and letters: "The primary focus of phonics instruction is to help beginning readers understand how letters are linked to sounds (phonemes) to form letter-sound correspondences and spelling patterns and to help them learn how to apply this knowledge in their reading" (NRP, 2000, p. 3). The NRP's report found that "systematic phonics instruction produces significant benefits for students in kindergarten through 6th grade and for children having difficulty learning to read" (p. 4). Instruction in phonics also "improved the ability of good readers to spell" (p. 4). The NRP concluded that "explicit, systematic phonics instruction is a valuable and essential part of a successful classroom reading program" (p. 5).

FLUENCY.   "Fluent readers are able to read orally with speed, accuracy, and proper expression" (NRP, 2000, p. 6). Fluency is necessary for reading comprehension; disfluent readers have difficulty gaining meaning from what they read. One major approach to teaching fluency is guided oral reading. The NRP report found that "guided oral reading procedures that included guidance from teachers, peers, or parents had a significant and positive impact on word recognition, fluency, and comprehension" (p. 7).

COMPREHENSION.   Reading comprehension is the ability to understand what is read (Spear-Swerling, 2005). It is enhanced when students "actively relate the ideas represented in print to their own knowledge and experiences and construct mental representations in memory" (NRP, 2000, p. 10). This is usually accomplished through the use of various cognitive strategies such as making predictions, questioning, summarizing, clarifying, visualizing using graphic organizers, and self-monitoring (Rose & Dalton, 2002). Palincsar and Klenk (1991) point out that children learn to use these strategies when their teachers explicitly model them. For example, a good reading teacher will pause while reading aloud and say, "I'm predicting that he is going to get in trouble." Or the teacher might say, "I don't know what this word means so I'm going to try to figure it out by reading the rest of the sentence."

VOCABULARY.   The larger the child's vocabulary—both oral and print vocabulary—the easier it is to understand text. A child with a weak vocabulary will have difficulty comprehending what he or she is trying to read. The findings of the NRP show that direct and indirect instruction in vocabulary leads to improvements in reading comprehension. The report recommends both repetition and multiple exposures to vocabulary as approaches to teaching vocabulary.

READING PROBLEMS IN STUDENTS WITH DISABILITIES

Which of the five topic areas discussed present problems for children with disabilities? You probably know children who have difficulties in *all* of the areas. Some reading experts believe that decoding or "phonological processing is the core deficit in dyslexia" (Ross-Kidder, 2004). For these children, explicit instruction on phonemic awareness and phonics is critical to improving their reading skills. Reading programs such as the Wilson Reading Program (www.wilsonlanguage.com) and Orton-Gillingham (www.orton-gillingham.com) stress these phonological skills. Other reading experts emphasize the need for children with reading disabilities to be taught specific reading comprehension strategies *and* how to use these strategies. For example, struggling readers need to be taught to monitor their comprehension *and* to take some kind of productive action when they do not understand what they are reading (Lipson & Wixson, 1997).

One group of students who often have problems with reading comprehension are those who have attention disorders (Schulte, Conners, & Osborne, 1999). These students have difficulty focusing on the text; they may "lose their place, have trouble keeping what they read in short-term memory, and have to read the same paragraph repeatedly to get any meaning out of it. As a result, reading becomes mentally fatiguing" (Robin, 1998). For students with these kinds of reading problems, access to content is severely diminished. This results in problems with *learning* because their weak comprehension skills interfere with their ability to read to learn (Ming & Dukes, 2010). Many students with learning disabilities "find that books and other texts that constitute the general curriculum function as *barriers* rather than gateways to learning. Decoding difficulties block students from access to important content, and comprehension problems block students from responding to and learning from text in meaningful ways" (Rose & Dalton, 2002, p. 9, italics added).

HOW TECHNOLOGY CAN ADDRESS THESE PROBLEMS

Learning to Read: The Computer as a Remediation Tool

The computer can be a powerful teaching tool. Its ability to present systematic, repetitive, engaging, and individualized instruction makes it particularly well suited for providing students who have disabilities with the practice they need to master specific skills (Wehmeyer, Smith, Palmer, & Davies, 2004). This section will examine how computers can be used specifically to teach the five skill areas identified in the NRP's report.

PHONEMIC AWARENESS AND PHONICS.   Well-designed educational applications are particularly good at teaching phonemic awareness and sound-letter correspondence. This is due to the computer's ability to present both visual displays (color and animation) and sounds to highlight patterns and to engage students. Whereas the workbooks and worksheets typically used in elementary school classrooms can represent sound only with letters, computers can speak phonemes aloud and provide practice with the actual sounds that students need to learn (Meyer & Rose, 1998). Both the short /a/ sound in *apple* and the long /a/ sound in *gate*, for example, can be presented and practiced when the computer says the actual sounds.

There are many applications on the market — both for computers and for mobile devices like the iPad — that claim to teach phonological processes. The key is to select programs that (1) are designed around the principles of good reading instruction and (2) meet the criteria for effective instructional software (Meyer & Rose, 1998) (see Chapter 5). Good reading applications do the following:

- They highlight patterns among sounds, letters, and letter-sound correspondence.
- They provide multiple opportunities for meaningful practice.
- They engage students through interactive activities and interesting displays (colors, animation, sounds) that motivate students to practice and learn.
- They allow for customization for individual differences. (Meyer & Rose, 1998)

Starfall (http://starfall.com), a Web-based application that focuses on phonemic awareness and phonics, provides many activities that meet these criteria.

One special application of computers for teaching phonological processes to students with learning disabilities involves slowing down, exaggerating, and altering sounds to make sound patterns easier to recognize. Intensive technology-based interventions such as Fast ForWord (Scientific Learning Corp.) or Earobics (Cognitive Concepts Inc.) are designed

> to train the brain to speed its auditory information processing. As the child becomes more proficient at recognizing the sounds, the Fast ForWord Language program adjusts to the child's improving level of competence by continually shortening the duration of the sound, requiring the brain to process at faster rates of speech. (Ross-Kidder, 2004)

This specialized intervention seems to be most effective with children whose reading difficulties are due to problems in phonological processing. The developers of Fast ForWord have published several studies whose results show noteworthy improvements in oral language and skills on several measures in children with dyslexia who used the program for 8 weeks (Temple et al., 2003). These kinds of results are achieved only when students follow a rigorous schedule of completing the Fast ForWord activities for at least an hour each day for a minimum of 8 weeks.

FLUENCY.   The *National Reading Panel Report* recommends several strategies for teaching fluency that can be directly provided by computer technology. The strategies include modeling fluent reading and then having students read the same text aloud; providing students with opportunities for repeated oral reading with support (e.g., help with unknown words) and feedback; using audio recordings, peer readers, or other means of providing both modeling of fluent reading and feedback; and providing students with opportunities to practice reading with a high degree of success (Northeast and the Islands Regional Technology in Education Consortium [NEIRTEC], 2004).

The multimedia capabilities of computers make them an ideal technology for providing these kinds of fluency-building activities. Human speech can be electronically recorded (i.e., digitized) to provide models of good reading. Without the need for adult intervention, students can see text and graphics displayed on the computer monitor while they listen to it being read with appropriate speed, accuracy, and expression.

Computer technology interventions provide a variety of ways in which students can practice their reading to improve their fluency. After viewing and listening to stories, students may participate in a series of timed reading sessions with the computer recording their reading rates and representing their improvement in graph form. Students can read along as the computer highlights and speaks the text, features that help them practice their pacing and expression. Hearing the text also helps students identify unfamiliar words. Students can record themselves reading aloud for subsequent review by themselves or their teachers. Students can also read aloud and have the computer provide immediate assistance if needed. Table 3.2 lists a sampling of applications that offer these kinds of fluency-building strategies.

VOCABULARY.   The findings presented in the NRP report (2000) suggest that the most effective vocabulary instruction includes direct instruction on vocabulary items related to a specific

TABLE 3.2	Applications that Support Fluency	
Software Name	**URL for Additional Information**	**Description**
Read Naturally Software Edition	http://www.readnaturally.com	At each level, students complete a 1-minute "cold timing" in which they read a story independently to establish a baseline reading speed, expressed in words per minute (wpm). Next, they listen to the story being read aloud and are encouraged to read along. They then complete several 1-minute practices with the same text, each time trying to increase their wpm. Comprehension activities follow, and as a final step, students read the text aloud to their teacher who determines whether they have passed the level.
Reading Assistant Expanded Edition	http://www.scilearning.com/products/reading-assistant/	Records students while they read aloud, and using voice recognition capabilities, provides students with immediate support and feedback when they misread or struggle to pronounce words.
Raz-Kids	http://www.raz-kids.com	Provides an Online Leveled Reading Library of more than 190 books at K–6 reading levels. Students listen to self-selected or assigned books while each word is highlighted as it is spoken aloud. After listening to stories, students record themselves reading the text. They can listen to their recorded reading, share the recording with their teacher and others, or record again if they wish to improve their reading.

Software Name	URL for Additional Information	Description
Start-to-Finish Library	http://www.donjohnston.com	Provides high-interest/low-level titles. After listening to excellent models of fluent reading, students can record themselves reading a passage aloud as many times as they would like until they are satisfied with their reading. A bar graph displays feedback on the accuracy of their reading. The first and last recordings are saved and can be reviewed later by the teacher.

text students will be reading, not isolated vocabulary drills. The panel's work shows that students need multiple exposures to the vocabulary words in rich contexts, including reading and writing. Importantly, the NRP report (2002) finds that "computer vocabulary instruction shows positive learning gains over traditional methods" (p. 4-4).

It is difficult to find applications dedicated only to vocabulary development that conform to the findings of the NRP. There are commercial and freeware applications that teach pre-defined vocabulary lists; however, they do this in isolation rather than in relation to authentic reading tasks as recommended by the NRP. Additionally, these programs often do not offer the supports that students with reading disabilities may require, such as auditory access to text-based practice exercises, adjustable response time, and adjustable visual display.

Although not specifically created for vocabulary building, applications with authoring capabilities are useful tools for supporting vocabulary development. **Authoring applications** are programs that allow teachers to create customized activities by adding their own content to pre-existing templates. For vocabulary development, authoring programs provide teachers with an opportunity to create activities that align with NRP recommendations, that is, using word lists and content directly related to the material that students will be reading. Digitized (recorded) speech or synthesized (computer-generated) speech can be used to provide clear instruction so students know what they are expected to do. The speech output features also provide auditory access to unfamiliar words, definitions, or other text; thus, students with reading disabilities can concentrate on the learning task rather than on decoding. Activities can be customized to optimize the visual presentation for individual students, including preferred background color; font color, size, and style; and the amount of material presented at one time.

Authoring applications designed for use by educators are easy to use, even for novices. Examples of authoring programs that can be used to create curriculum-related activities are provided in Table 3.3.

READING COMPREHENSION. Technology tools for developing reading comprehension revolve around specific strategies recommended by the *National Reading Panel Report*. The shift in instructional applications from the older, primarily "drill and practice" formats to the more constructivist approach of computer-supported strategy instruction has been particularly valuable in the area of reading comprehension (Rose & Dalton, 2002). The ability of the computer to manipulate text, read text aloud, provide a range of supports, and maintain records of performance is now being put to use in applications that model and explicitly teach strategies for reading comprehension. See Table 3.4 for a sampling of these programs. Thinking Reader (Tom Snyder Productions) is highlighted in the next section because it is a good example of a series that teaches explicit comprehension strategies to struggling readers (see Figures 3.1–3.3).

TABLE 3.3 Applications to Support Vocabulary Development

Software Name	URL for Additional Information	Description
ClozePro v.2	http://www.cricksoft.com	Cloze activities provide sentences or passages with selected words missing. Students use the context of the sentences or passages to select the missing words. With ClozePro, teachers create customized cloze activities by typing or pasting text into the program and then choosing the words to be removed. A text-to-speech feature speaks the text as well as the word choices provided.
Clicker 5	http://www.cricksoft.com	Talking grids can be created for students to match words with their definitions; video clips that build students' background knowledge and/or illustrate concepts can be embedded in grids; text passages can be read aloud; student-created sentences or stories can be written and recorded. A broad array of premade templates is provided.

FIGURE 3.1 Screenshot of Thinking Reader showing all the tools that are available to teach reading comprehension strategies.

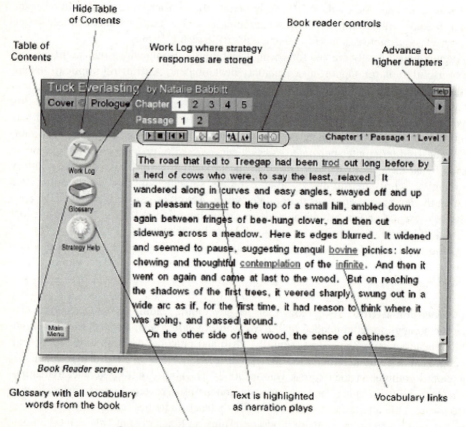

Source: Reprinted with permission from Tom Snyder Productions.

	URL for Additional	
Software Name	Information	Description
Thinking Reader	http://www.tomsnyder.com	Teaches comprehension strategies using the unabridged text of middle school–level literature. Students can listen to the story being read aloud while the text is displayed on the screen. Seven comprehension strategies are modeled by on-screen characters to help students practice using the strategies (see Table 3.5)
Destination Reading	http://www.hmlt.hmco.com/DR.php	On-screen characters create a dialogue with the student to invite active engagement. Topics for reading passages were voted on by 3,000 students who also contributed ideas to the design of the program. Instruction and themes reference popular culture, allowing students to practice skills in contexts they find relevant.
UDL Editions from CAST	http://udleditions.cast.org	Provides a series of reading selections along with support tools such as text-to-speech, Spanish translations, and definitions of unknown words.

TABLE 3.4 Sample Applications for Developing Reading Comprehension

Thinking Reader presents the unabridged text of high-quality, middle school–level literature on a computer so that students can (1) listen to the story being read, (2) read along with a visual display that has been adjusted to meet their individual preferences, (3) observe on-screen characters model reading comprehension strategies, (4) quickly access definitions of unfamiliar vocabulary, and (5) practice using the reading comprehension strategies. The books in the series include *The Giver* (Lois Lowry), *Tuck Everlasting* (Natalie Babbitt), *Roll of Thunder, Hear My Cry* (Mildred Taylor), and *Bud, Not Buddy* (Christopher Paul Curtis). Because the story can be read aloud by the computer, students who are poor decoders (i.e., those who have not mastered phonemic awareness and phonics) can still enjoy the books and can still work on improving their comprehension by learning the reading comprehension strategies. The seven strategies that are embedded in the program are summarizing, questioning, clarifying, predicting, visualizing, feeling, and reflecting (Tom Snyder Productions, 2004; see Table 3.5). Students are reminded of the strategies at appropriate times while they are reading and listening to the text via an elaborate system of prompts, hints, models, and feedback (see Figures 3.2 and 3.3). For teachers, the series includes an extensive system for gathering assessment data on every student and for providing feedback to each student.

Web-based subscription services offer other options to improve the higher level reading skills of fluency, comprehension, and vocabulary. KidBiz3000 and TeenBiz3000 (Achieve3000) are good examples. Every day, KidBiz3000 sends students in specified grades a news-based reading assignment that is customized for their reading level. TeenBiz3000 focuses on grades 6–12. The reading passage could be about national or world events, science, technology, trends, or sports. All children read about the same topic and complete a set of related writing activities, but the levels of the passages differ depending on how the students performed on a reading pretest. A customized dictionary and reference materials are also provided. So although each student works at his or her own level, all students read about the same topics and can participate in class discussions (Achieve3000, n.d.).

TABLE 3.5 Seven Reading Comprehension Strategies Taught in Thinking Reader

Strategy	Description
Summarizing	Students are asked to summarize what they have read.
Questioning	Students pose a question about book content that is important to know and remember.
Clarifying	Students have the opportunity to ask about something they do not understand in the text. Their question may be about a word or phrase, historic/background information, or anything else requiring additional explanation.
Predicting	Students use what they know to make a prediction about what will happen next.
Visualizing	Students visualize the setting or an important event.
Feeling	Students are asked to make a personal connection to the text or to put themselves in a character's place.
Reflecting	Students reflect on their progress as a reader.

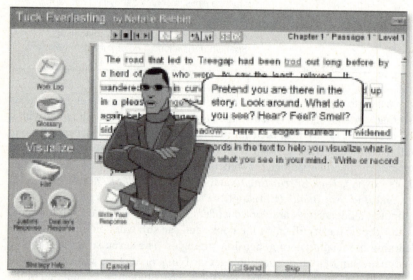

FIGURE 3.2 After clicking on the Hint icon on the left, students are presented with a hint for the comprehension strategy of "feeling."

Strategy Hint

Source: Reprinted with permission from Tom Snyder Productions.

INTERESTING READING MATERIALS ON THE INTERNET.   In addition to the strategies and technology tools already discussed, children who struggle with reading can benefit from careful selection of their reading material. Meyer and Rose (1998) point out that "engagement is essential to successful reading" (p. 56), and that "deep engagement depends on *interesting material*. For individuals with skill deficits, interest can lead to remarkable engagement and success. It can motivate them to make extraordinary efforts to overcome difficulties that would stop them cold if they did not care so much about the subject" (p. 61, italics added). Letting students *choose* their own reading material is one way to enhance their engagement with the text (Rothman, 2004).

With an Internet connection finding reading material that matches students' interests is as simple as a few mouse clicks. Teachers can find all kinds of reading material online—books, articles, newspaper stories, Web sites, wikis, and blogs. Teachers (or students) can

FIGURE 3.3 Thinking Reader Strategy Help screen.

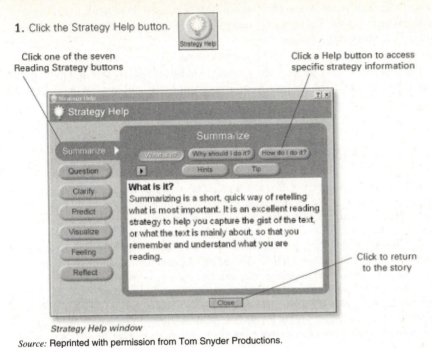

Source: Reprinted with permission from Tom Snyder Productions.

download these materials, save them as text documents in a word processing application, manipulate the text for a comfortable visual display (e.g., increase the font size, double-space the text, increase the margins so the line of text is shorter), and then print them for reading or save them to be read aloud by a computer using applications that we discuss in the next section (Meyer & Rose, 1998).

Subscribing to a leveled reading Web site is another option for locating reading materials that match students' interests. Reading A-Z, Scholastic Book Wizard, and Raz-Kids, for example, offer thousands of online books (e-books) that can be searched by subject and reading level. Books that are designated "multilevel" provide three reading levels for the same title. These kinds of Web-based applications make it easy for teachers to locate books that will pique their students' interest.

Reading to Learn: The Computer as a Compensation Tool

In the upper elementary grades, just as direct reading instruction begins to taper off, the nature of the material students must read begins to change. Whereas in K–3, children read mostly narrative fiction and nonfiction stories, in fourth grade they begin to read textbooks in the content areas, called expository texts (Rothman, 2004). Being able to read and understand these textbooks is critical for academic success, especially as the student moves on to middle school, high school, and college. Middle, high school and college students are required to complete extensive amounts of reading on a daily basis—textbooks, works of literature, journal articles, reference materials—most of which have readability levels well beyond the skills of most students with disabilities (Boyle et al., 2002). Slow readers and students with reading comprehension problems struggle to complete their reading assignments and fall behind in their work because they cannot keep up with all the reading. This not only causes anxiety and frustration, but also interferes with their learning of the subject matter.

Some students get through high school by having their parents or instructional aides read their textbooks to them. (Some simply do not complete the reading and get by through paying attention to class lectures.) These may be short-term solutions, but in the end they are a disservice

Low-Tech Adaptations That Support Reading

Special education teachers and reading specialists use a range of strategies to improve the literacy of students with reading problems. Students are taught to use highlighter pens and sticky notes, for example, to call attention to certain text passages or pages, especially when reading long selections. Highlighting makes important information stand out and helps students locate it later (Assistive Technology Training Online Training Project [ATTO], 2005). This is especially helpful for students who cannot skim text when studying. Using different-colored highlighters for different types of information can help cue students to where in the passage they can find the information they need (Georgia Assistive Technology Project Tools for Life, n.d.). For example, students can be taught to use a yellow highlighter for topic sentences, a blue highlighter for unfamiliar vocabulary, and a green highlighter for important names. Sticky notes can be used to jot down reminders and questions about the reading passage. For library books or other books that cannot be marked, removable highlighter tape is a good alternative.

For students who have physical disabilities, a book holder can be an essential low-tech device. A good one holds a book of nearly any size at a comfortable reading angle and provides adjustable pegs that prevent pages from flipping inadvertently (ATTO, 2005). Some students can use a pencil eraser or rubber-tipped head stick or chin stick to turn pages when the book is positioned in a book holder. To make it easier for students to read worksheets and other single sheets of paper, teachers can place them in an inexpensive holder called a Page Up (MTM Corp). These simple adaptations enable many students who have physical disabilities to read independently, freeing them from the need to ask another person to hold the paper or turn the page for them.

to students; when teenagers attempt to attend college or hold a job, they find they are unable to complete their reading assignments on their own. Therefore, students with reading difficulties stand to benefit significantly from technology that can increase their comprehension of text and their independence in reading.

Several different kinds of technology can provide access to the printed word. Portable devices are available, as well as desktop computer solutions. Collectively the term for this kind of technology is providing books (or text) in **alternate formats**. Two complementary components make up alternate formats: the file (or format) type and the device used to access the file. The section that follows will discuss the different file types and the hardware (or playback device) that is needed to access each kind.

The 2004 reauthorization of IDEA (Section CFR 300.172) added the requirement that states and local education agencies must ensure that "**accessible instructional materials**" are provided to students with print disabilities in a timely manner. The term *print disabilities* is defined by two federal statutes (see Sidebar). *Timely manner* is generally understood to mean at the same time that a student's nondisabled peers receive their instructional materials (Iowa Department of Education, 2009). *Instructional materials* refers to core curriculum materials and textbooks.

Students With Print Disabilities Eligible Under the Copyright Act as Amended (Chafee Amendment)

A student with a print disability is one who is unable to gain information from **printed materials** and needs a specialized format (i.e., Braille, large print, audio, digital text) to access that information (accessible instructional materials). Eligible students* are

1. Students with visual impairments that keep them from reading standard print (blind, legally blind, or with other functional vision limitations).
2. Students with physical disabilities that prevent them from reading print or using a print book or without the ability to hold or manipulate information in printed form or not able to focus or move their eyes. Such a limitation could be a result of a spinal cord injury, cerebral palsy, traumatic brain injury, a neurological condition, etc.
3. Students with a reading disability based on an organic dysfunction that keeps them from being able to effectively read standard print. The reading disability must be of sufficient severity to prevent reading regular or standard printed materials in a normal manner. The cause of the reading disability must be physically based, that is, it must be an organic dysfunction and the person certifying the reading disability must be medically** able to judge whether the disability has a physical or organic basis.

Who does not qualify as having a print disability?

- Students who do not speak the language they want to read.
- Students with disabilities that do not impact the ability to read (for example, most hearing and behavioral disabilities).
- The following groups of students are not automatically eligible or automatically ineligible: those who have learning disabilities, dyslexia, attention deficit disorder, attention deficit-hyperactivity disorder, chronic-fatigue syndrome, autism, functional illiteracy, or mental retardation, unless there is a specific accompanying visual or physical disability.

Source: Iowa Department of Education (2009). True AIM: http://trueaim.iowa.gov

*[As defined by] The Library of Congress regulations (36 CFR 701.6(b)(1)) related to the Act to Provide Books for the Adult Blind (approved March 3, 1931, 2 U.S.C. 135a) ...

**Competent authority is defined in 36 CFR 701.6(b)(2) ...

ALTERNATE FORMATS.   There are six major types of alternate formats that can provide access to instructional materials. They are available from a number of sources and they must be used in conjunction with a playback device or an application. Table 3.6 provides an overview of the different kinds of file formats and their corresponding playback devices.

TABLE 3.6   Alternate Format File Types and Playback Devices

Alternate Format	File Types	Options for Reading on Computer	Portable Playback Devices
Electronic text (e-text)	.doc or .docx (MS Word) .txt (plain text) html	• Text-to-speech (text readers) such as Text Aloud, Read Out:Loud, ReadPlease, ClaroRead, Blio • Scan/read programs such as WYNN, Kurzweil, Read & Write	• ClassMate Reader • Intel Reader • KNFB Mobile • kReader Mobile • Victor Reader Stream
DAISY (navigable)	DAISY files Bookshare.org files RFB&D (audio only)	• DAISY reader such as ClaroRead, Dolphin Easy Reader, Victor ReaderSoft, Read Out:Loud Bookshare Edition	• Victor Reader Wave • Victor Reader Stream • Read2Go on mobile devices • ClassMate Reader • Intel Reader • BrailleNote series
PDF files	PDF	• Adobe Acrobat Reader with built-in text-to-speech (v.6 & higher) • Scan/read such as WYNN, Kurzweil, Read & Write (after completing "virtual scan")	• BrailleNote series • (Most portable devices will read only those PDF files that have been converted by an application)
MP3 (not navigable)	Audio only	• Windows Media Player • iTunes	• iPod • iPad • MP3 players
Large print	.doc or .docx	Microsoft Word	
Braille format	.brf	refreshable Braille display	• Braille note taker with refreshable Braille display such as BrailleNote or PacMate Omni

e-Text: Electronic text is a computer file such as a Microsoft Word document (.doc or .docx), a file in Rich Text Format (rtf), plain text (.txt), or html (a Web site). Three advantages of electronic text over printed text are (1) teachers and students can change how the text looks—its font, the size of the font, line spacing, word spacing, and margin widths—so that it is more visually appealing to the reader; (2) with the right application, computers and portable devices can read e-text aloud; and (3) e-text files can retain their formatting (boldface headings and subheadings) and can be searched easily.

DAISY: DAISY stands for Digital Accessible Information SYstem. DAISY books are easily navigated and can be searched by chapter, word, bookmark, or section heading. DAISY books have the capability of offering full text and synchronized audio with a synthesized voice, although some offer only audio or only text. They can be played on a computer using specialized applications or on portable DAISY-compatible playback devices.

PDF Files: PDF files, which can be opened with Adobe Acrobat Reader, are the file type that is most often provided by textbook publishers when they are contacted directly. To be read aloud, PDF files must be run through a "virtual scan" using an optical character recognition program such as Kurzweil, and a text-to-speech program is needed to read the files aloud. The newest version of Adobe Reader has a Read Out Loud feature that will read text.

MP3: This is an audio-only format that can be played on a portable device that plays MP3 files or on a computer with an application that plays MP3 files. These files are not searchable. Usually a book in MP3 format will have a separate MP3 file for each chapter.

Large Print: Documents in larger font sizes are sometimes needed for students who have visual impairments. When creating large print files, it is important that images be placed appropriately in the document and that page numbers are assigned consistent with those of the original document.

BRF (Braille Format): BRF files can be opened and read by a device with a refreshable Braille display such as a BrailleNote. These files may need further editing to be embossed and read as a hard copy.

USER PROFILE

Anthony M.

Meet Anthony M.: A graduate of a well-known college in the Northeast, he now works in his field of choice—business. His elementary school teachers would be very surprised to hear this. In the primary grades, Anthony could not read. Although his parents thought he was reading along with them, he was actually listening to them read and then reciting the books from memory. "Functionally I did not know how to read until the fourth grade, and even then it was at a first-grade level. One school district attempted to classify me as mentally retarded," Anthony reports. Eventually he was diagnosed with a perceptual impairment, poor fine motor skills, low mathematical reasoning, and poor spelling ability. In the third grade, he entered a self-contained special education class. "You could tell that the teacher did not have high expectations for any of us," Anthony recalls.

How did he get from being a nonreader to graduating from college? Anthony credits his strong motivation, hard work, and his discovery of scan/read systems. He found using the Kurzweil 3000 helped him immensely with his 12-credit course load. "It was beyond my expectations," he said:

If I were to read a book like *Marketing Principles* [without scan/read], if I were to persevere through all the reading, it would probably take me 2.5 hours to read one chapter. By the time I finished reading the last page of the chapter, I would have forgotten the first part of the chapter and remembered maybe 40 percent of the rest. When using the Kurzweil 3000, it took me half the time to read the chapter, and I'd remember 75 to 80 percent.

I literally had 700 pages of retail management, 980 pages of market research, 650 pages of consumer behavior, and 2,000 pages of econ/stats to read. Reading with the Kurzweil 3000 made it easier for me to digest the information. If I had been trying to read all that without the help of the Kurzweil, I would know just a whole bunch of pieces and it would be difficult. It made a real difference in my comprehension. (Shipon, 2002) ■

TABLE 3.7   Sampling of Text Readers

Product Name	Vendor	Platform	Notes	Web site
ReadPlease & ReadPlease Plus	ReadPlease	Win	Uses AT&T Natural Voices	http://readplease.com
NaturalReader Personal & Professional Versions	NaturalSoft, Ltd.	Win	Uses AT&T Natural Voices	http://www.naturalreaders.com
TextAloud	NextUp	Win	Offers higher quality voices for an additional fee	http://www.nextup.com
GhostReader	ConvenienceWare/ NextUp	Mac	Uses Acapela voices	http://www.nextup.com
EasyReader	Dolphin	Win	Reads DAISY files as well as text & html	http://www.yourdolphin.com
Awesome Talkster	Awesome Talking Library	Win		http://www.awesomelibrary.org/ Awesome_Talking_Library.html
Macintosh OS 10.X—System Preferences: Speech	Apple, Inc.	Mac	Comes with system software on all Macintosh computers	http://www.apple.com/pro/tips/ text_speech.html

Technology Tools to Access Alternate Formats

TEXT READERS.   When reading material is already available as electronic text, such as a Web site or a Microsoft Word document, applications called **text readers** can be used to read the text aloud. Text readers use text-to-speech technology to convert electronic text into spoken audio.

They are ideal for reading aloud articles found on the Web or teacher-made handouts that were created in Microsoft Word. For example, if a teacher has composed a test in Microsoft Word, a student who struggles with reading comprehension could use a text reader to read aloud the test questions (and to proofread his or her answers).

A wide variety of text readers are available, including several free or inexpensive programs that can be downloaded from the Internet (see a sampling in Table 3.7). Some of these are freeware that their developers want to distribute, whereas others are basic versions of more elaborate commercial products, the logic being that once users have tried the bare-bones version, they will be more likely to purchase the higher-quality commercial product. Some text readers highlight the text while reading and offer the ability to adjust the reading speed. In general, text readers priced under $100 offer several refinements over the free versions: They use higher-quality voices and/or offer the user a choice of voices; they offer improved navigation, including the ability to insert bookmarks; some allow the toolbar and icons to be customized; and several have a feature to convert text files to MP3 format for listening on a portable MP3 player.

SCAN/READ SYSTEMS.   Scan/read systems combine the use of a computer, a scanner, optical character recognition software, and speech output to read aloud any printed text while providing a visually enhanced display on a computer monitor. Users of scan/read systems place the pages to be read on a flatbed scanner and click the Scan icon. (Using a document scanner or a high speed scanner instead of a flatbed scanner are faster alternatives.) The information is then converted into electronic text. Scan/read programs then speak the words on the screen while highlighting the corresponding text. This provides a "synchronized auditory and visual presentation of the text" (Hecker, Burns, Katz, Elkind, & Elkind, 2002, p. 1). Optional highlighting in color helps readers keep their eyes on a line of text, while the speech output provides ongoing auditory feedback.

Four of the most popular, full-featured scan/read systems—Kurzweil 3000 (Kurzweil Educational Systems),WYNN (Freedom Scientific), Read and Write Gold (TextHelp), and ClaroRead Plus (Claro Software) offer features that are designed to meet the needs of people who struggle with reading comprehension (see Figures 3.4 and 3.5). The programs offer options to **change the appearance of the visual display** and to **set the reading speed** to match the user's preference. They also offer what Anderson-Inman and Horney (1997) call "**embedding tools**"—a talking dictionary and thesaurus, electronic highlighters to assist students in taking notes and preparing study guides, voice notes, and yellow "sticky notes" for inserting hidden prompts and reminders.

The **talking dictionary** is a good example of how embedding tools can help students who have reading comprehension problems. When a student with reading problems encounters an unfamiliar word, the suggestion to "look it up in the dictionary" is not terribly helpful. Dictionaries, even electronic dictionaries, tend to cram a lot of text onto a single page; the font is quite small and spacing is tight. The student with reading problems often cannot find the word in the dictionary to begin with, and if he or she manages to locate it, reading the small print and understanding it present additional difficulties. Contrast that with the talking dictionaries that are embedded in scan/read systems. The student simply clicks on the unfamiliar word, then clicks on the dictionary icon, and the program immediately displays the dictionary entry for that word and will read it aloud when the student clicks the Read button. In addition, another simple click of the mouse will copy the definition to the computer clipboard so the student can create a customized vocabulary list that can be studied later.

The impact of scan/read applications on the reading performance of postsecondary students with attention disorders was demonstrated in two research studies. Hecker et al. (2002) report that

FIGURE 3.4 Text highlighting feature in WYNN scan/read application.

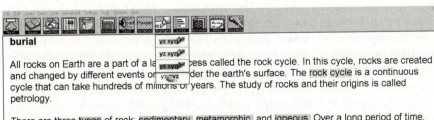

Source: Used with permission from Freedom Scientific.

FIGURE 3.5 In Kurzweil 3000 clicking on a word and then the Look Up Word icon brings up the dictionary screen. The application will read aloud the definition and synonyms.

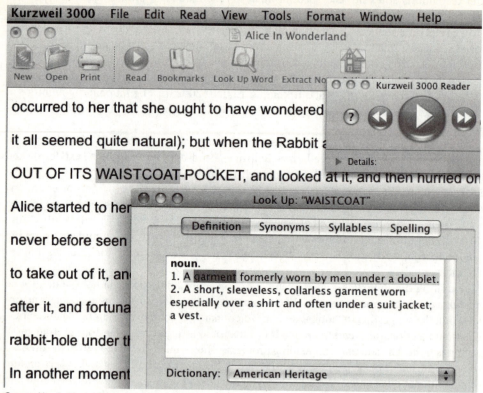

Source: Used with permission from Kurzweil Educational Systems.

when 20 students were trained to use the Kurzweil 3000 program to read assignments in English class and take tests over the course of a semester, they found that scan/read software "allowed the students to attend better to their reading, to reduce their distractibility, to read with less stress and fatigue, and to read for longer periods of time. It helped them to read faster and thereby to complete reading assignments in less time" (p. 243). Results from the Iowa Text Reader Study (Iowa Assistive Technology Text Reader Project, 2008) revealed additional benefits: Students were able to access twice as much information using a scan/read program and showed improved comprehension levels even as the reading difficulty level increased. Improvements were noted on passage comprehension measures and on factual and inferential comprehension questions: "The results demonstrate that students can access the core materials at twice the rate, with understanding at levels of higher thinking, allowing them to work competitively in an inclusion setting" (p. 17).

Horney and colleagues (2009) studied the effects of students using the digital note-taking tools (both text notes and voice notes) embedded in the WYNN scan/read program. Their results showed that students with disabilities in fifth grade made significant gains in reading comprehension when they used the voice notes feature. Using a control group for contrast and pre- and posttests for measurement, the researchers found that the students knew more about the science topics covered after reading and taking digital notes than they did before.

Scan/read programs are powerful tools that can help students with learning disabilities compensate for their reading and study skills problems. However, Anderson-Inman and Horney

Copyright Issues

Providing students who have disabilities with books in alternate formats is often complicated by laws pertaining to copyright. It is illegal, for example, for school personnel to make an electronic version of a textbook with a scan/read program and provide it to several students without first receiving permission from the copyright holder (the author and/or the publisher). Alternate media centers such as Bookshare or Recording for the Blind and Dyslexic require documentation of a print disability to comply with copyright laws. School personnel need to be aware of current copyright law and respect the rights of copyright holders (Langran, Langran, & Bull, 2005).

In general, copyright law exists to protect creativity and the expression of ideas. American copyright law is subject to ongoing interpretation and can be changed at any time by Congress (Langran, Langran, & Bull, 2005). At the time of this writing, two major laws relate to providing accessible instructional materials. Section 107 of the 1976 Copyright Act gives permission to teachers and students to "use copyrighted material legally without the author's permission if it falls under fair use in education" ((Langran et al., 2005, p. 25). **Fair use** is defined as "for purposes such as criticism, comment, news reporting, teaching, ... scholarship or research" (Section 107 of Amendments to Title 17 Since 1976). The law requires a four-factor test to determine if a reproduction qualifies as fair use. For our purposes, the most relevant factor is the *amount* of a work that is to be reproduced. Although there is no formula, the U.S. Copyright Office guidelines suggest that "no more than 10 percent of a published collective work may be employed under fair use guidelines" (Langran et al., 2005, p. 25). The fair use exemption, then, would apply to providing only an article or a chapter in alternate format but not to providing an entire book.

For an entire book, we must look to the **Chafee Amendment**. Passed by Congress in 1996, the Chafee Amendment—Public Law 104–197—establishes a limitation on the exclusive rights in copyrighted works: "The amendment allows authorized entities to reproduce or distribute copies ... of previously published nondramatic literary works in specialized formats exclusively for use by blind or other persons with disabilities" (Library of Congress, 1996). The act defines each of the terms in the previous sentence:

For purposes of this section, the term—

1. 'authorized entity' means a nonprofit organization or a governmental agency that has a primary mission to provide specialized services relating to training, education, or adaptive reading or information access needs of blind or other persons with disabilities;
2. 'blind or other persons with disabilities' means individuals who are eligible or who may qualify in accordance with the Act entitled 'An Act to provide books for the adult blind', approved March 3, 1931 (2 U.S.C. 35a; 46 Stat. 1487) to receive books and other publications produced in specialized formats; and
3. 'specialized formats' means Braille, audio, or digital text which is exclusively for use by blind or other persons with disabilities.

The sidebar Students With Print Disabilities Eligible Under the Copyright Act as Amended provides additional details related to (2).

(1997) emphasize that students need to be *taught* how to use the features in these programs. Their study found, for example, that embedding tools can improve student achievement only if struggling readers are taught to use them properly. Similarly, following their 2009 study on digital note taking, Horney, Anderson-Inman, and colleagues recommend that "future attempts to increase student learning through digital note taking may do well to focus on how to promote effective selection of the main idea" (p. 58). The need to link the use of technology to teaching and to provide training on how to use technology tools is discussed in more detail in Chapter 13.

Although scan/read technology can make any text accessible, scanning printed documents is very time-consuming. Therefore, it is important for teachers to become knowledgeable about Internet sites that provide files of text that are already in electronic format. Most literature that is in the public domain, such as all of Shakespeare's plays, are available for free download from Internet sites such as **Project Gutenberg** (http://www.gutenberg.net). For example, if a high school English class is studying *Hamlet*, instead of scanning the entire play for a student with learning disabilities, the file can be downloaded from the Internet and read aloud using a text reader or a scan/read system. The student benefits from all of the features and embedding tools in the software, but the need for time-consuming scanning is eliminated. Bookshare.org, which is restricted to students who have disabilities, is another rich online resource for e-text (see Sidebar).

Bookshare.org

Bookshare.org is a Web-based system designed specifically to provide accessible books in digital formats to people with disabilities. These digital formats are the DAISY XML-based format for talking books and the BRF format for Braille devices and printers. To download copyrighted books from Bookshare.org, schools and/or individuals with print disabilities must register as a member and provide documentation of the print disability. An array of security protections and digital rights management solutions ensure that these books are available only to authorized users.

Bookshare was awarded a $32 million grant from the U.S. Department of Education to significantly expand the availability of accessible electronic books and the applications needed for reading them. The award has allowed Bookshare to give all K–12, postsecondary, and graduate students with qualifying print disabilities in the United States access to its library without charge. It has also enabled Bookshare to offer a free copy of the text readers *Read Out:Loud Bookshare.org Edition* (Don Johnston) or *Victor Reader Soft Bookshare Edition* (Humanware) to all of its members. The newest option for Bookshare users is an app for the iPad, iPhone and iPod Touch called Read2Go (available from the iTunes App store). Using high quality voices, Read2Go synchronizes the auditory output with word-by-word highlighting of the text. With the availability of this app, students do not need to be tethered to a computer to access the reading supports they need.

NATIONAL INSTRUCTIONAL MATERIALS ACCESSIBILITY STANDARD.   In the most recent reauthorization of IDEA (2004), a provision was added to ease the problem of procuring textbooks in alternate formats. Called the National Instructional Materials Accessibility Standard (NIMAS), this provision was clarified in 2006 when the U.S. Department of Education, Office of Special Education Programs (OSEP) published specific regulations in the *Federal Register*. NIMAS guides publishers in producing digital versions of textbooks that can be easily converted to alternate formats such as those listed in Table 3.6 (National Center on Accessible Instructional Materials at Cast, Inc., 2010). Publishers are now required to use this standard when preparing source files for textbooks and need to provide these files when requested by state and local education agencies. The regulations also reaffirm the responsibilities of state and local education agencies to provide students who have print disabilities with alternate-format versions of textbooks in a timely manner (National Center on Accessible Instructional Materials at Cast, Inc., 2010).

K–12 textbook publishers are now required to prepare NIMAS file sets for deposit in a national repository of digital materials (National Center on Accessible Instructional Materials at Cast, Inc., 2010). Known as the **National Instructional Materials Access Center (NIMAC)**, the repository is hosted by the American Printing House for the Blind. On request, if the file is in its inventory, NIMAC will provide states and local education agencies with the textbook source files that follow the NIMAS standard.

It is important to note that many files in the NIMAC are *not* "student ready." They follow the NIMAS standard, but someone in the state or local school agency needs to convert the NIMAS file into the specific format that a student needs. It is also important to note that the NIMAS standard and the repository are for students in grades K–12 only; they do not apply to college students or adults. A NIMAS Workflow Graphic that provides details regarding the various steps involved in the whole NIMAS cycle can be viewed at http://aim.cast.org/learn/policy/federal/what_is_nimas.

Internet Sites Offering e-Text

Bookshare.org

http://www.bookshare.org

Bookshare.org is a searchable online library that offers more than 70,000 digital books, textbooks, teacher-recommended reading, and periodicals to people with disabilities. Membership is free for all U.S. students with qualifying disabilities. Bookshare also provides free versions of text readers: Victor Reader Soft Bookshare Edition (Humanware) and Read: OutLoud Bookshare Edition (Don Johnston) to its members. A third text reader—Read2Go—is an app for mobile devices; it can be purchased from the iTunes store.

Electronic Text Center at the University of Virginia

http://etext.lib.virginia.edu

The Electronic Text Center's holdings include approximately 70,000 humanities texts in 12 languages. They include classic British and American fiction, major authors, children's literature, American history, Shakespeare, African American documents, and the Bible.

EServer

http://eserver.org

The EServer, formerly at Carnegie Mellon and the University of Washington, is now based at Iowa State University. It contains more than 32,419 works in 45 collections on such diverse topics as contemporary art, race, Internet studies, sexuality, drama, design, gender studies, accessible publishing, and current political and social issues.

Google Book Search

http://Books.Google.com

This repository contains copyrighted books as well as books in the public domain. Books that are protected by copyright may show up in a search, but the full content of the book may not be available for download. This is a growing area of the Internet and the publishing field, and we are likely to see changes in the near future.

Internet Public Library 2

http://www.ipl.org

Internet Public Library 2 (ipl2) is the result of a merger of the Internet Public Library (IPL) and the Librarians' Internet Index (LII) Web sites. The site is hosted by Drexel University's College of

(continued)

Information Science & Technology, which works with a consortium of colleges and universities with programs in information science to maintain it.

Louis Database of Accessible Materials for People Who Are Blind or Visually Impaired

http://www.aph.org/louis.htm

This database includes 200,000 titles in accessible formats including Braille, large print, sound recording, and electronic files from more than 170 agencies throughout the United States.

Project Gutenberg

http://www.gutenberg.org

At the time of this writing, 33,000 public domain books are in the Project Gutenberg Online Book Catalog. Two million e-books are downloaded each month.

SCAN/READ FOR STUDENTS WHO ARE BLIND OR VISUALLY IMPAIRED.   Scan/read technology is essential for students who are blind or visually impaired. Their needs are different from students with learning disabilities—they do not have reading comprehension problems and many are fluent Braille readers—but they face significant barriers in gaining access to printed materials in a timely manner. They often use scan/read systems when they need quick access to print, for example, the morning newspaper, their mail, professional reports, and legal documents. Kurzweil 1000 (Kurzweil Educational Systems) and OpenBook (Freedom Scientific) are two popular scan/read systems designed to meet the needs of people who cannot see printed text. These systems offer many of the same features as WYNN and Kurzweil 3000, but their interface is easier to use for people who cannot see the screen. Tasks that users with learning disabilities do with a mouse, such as navigating through documents, managing documents, or selecting a tool, can be accomplished through the use of "hot keys" and function keys. Although these commands require some memorization, they are far more efficient than using the mouse for users who are blind.

Portable scan/read devices are the newest reading tools for people who are blind or visually impaired. Kurzweil has partnered with the National Federation of the Blind to produce the KNFB Reader Mobile. This product uses applications that place the functionality of a scan/read program into a regular cell phone. Users can take a picture of any printed text; the KNFB Reader Mobile will then convert it to electronic text using optical character recognition software, and then read it aloud using text-to-speech technology. Intel markets a similar portable device called the Intel Reader. At the time of this writing apps for iPhones that serve a similar function are becoming available. ZoomReader (AiSquared) combines the iPhone's camera with OCR, text-to-speech, and options for high-contrast and magnification.

AIM Navigator

The National Center on Accessible Instructional Materials offers an interactive online tool that is designed to help IEP teams make decisions about accessible instructional materials for individual students. Called the AIM Navigator, the tool guides teams through a step-by-step process that addresses four decision points: (1) determining the need for accessible instructional materials, (2) selecting the format that will best meet a student's needs, (3) acquiring the alternate formats, and (4) selecting playback devices and determining needed supports such as training. The AIM Navigator can be accessed at: http://aim.cast.org/experience/decision-making_tools/aim_navigator

The kNFB Reader Mobile is a handheld scan/read device that works on a Nokia cell phone. The user holds the Reader's build-in digital camera over any kind of point—a worksheet, a journal article, or a restaurant menu—and snaps a picture. In seconds the device speaks the contents of the printed document in clear synthetic speech.

Photo courtesy of kNFB Reading Technology, Inc..

Blio eReader

Blio is the latest e-reading innovation to emerge from the partnership of Kurzweil Technologies and the National Federation of the Blind. It offers many of the same features as scan/read applications such as auditory output synchronized with highlighting, a searchable dictionary and thesaurus, and the ability to insert text and voice notes. In addition, books read with Blio maintain the same layout as the printed book, include full-color graphics, and are viewable in a 3D format complete with pages "turning." Publishers can embed video and audio presentations within Blio books. E-books are downloaded from Blio's own online bookstore, which is searchable. Blio is available for Windows computers as a free download. iPhone and Android versions are under development.

Commercial e-Readers

Amazon's Kindle, Sony's Reader, Barnes and Noble's Nook, and Apple's iPad are changing the publishing field. Also known as e-book readers, these e-readers are lightweight portable devices that display the digital content of books, newspapers, and magazines. Most have wireless capabilities for easily downloading of e-books, and most can store hundreds of titles, eliminating the need for a person to carry multiple volumes. Many allow the reader to add annotations and bookmarks. Some are the size of a paperback book so they resemble their hard-print version, whereas others offer a larger screen for more comfortable reading of newspapers and other traditionally larger texts.

(continued)

Apple's iPad uses a touch screen whose size resembles that of a standard book. The iPad runs the same apps as the iPhone, plus those that are designed exclusively to utilize its bigger screen. To use the iPad as an e-reader, users download books through an online store called iBooks, similar to the way users download music and apps through iTunes. The downloaded books then appear on a virtual bookshelf and readers choose the book they wish to read by tapping the book's image on the screen. After a book has been downloaded, its pages can be displayed as a one-page or a two-page view. Fonts can be changed to the user's liking, and graphics and pictures are included. Pages are turned by simply swiping the screen with a finger.

Accessibility and e-Readers:

At the time of this writing, the capability of these commercial e-readers to meet the needs of students with reading disabilities has not been determined. The ability to modify the appearance of text will help some students, but to be most effective, these devices will need to be able to read books aloud. Apple's screen-reading technology called Voice Over (see Chapter 7) is compatible with the iPad but is somewhat awkward to use as a text reader. Amazon built text-to-speech into its Kindle but subsequently allowed publishers to choose whether to make the feature available for individual titles. Without text-to-speech, e-readers will not be accessible to students with learning disabilities or visual impairments who need auditory support. The Kindle 3 added talking menus to make its navigation system accessible to blind users, but the National Federation of the Blind and the Reading Rights Coalition (see sidebar) point out that Amazon's Web browser is still not accessible and no audible signal is provided about the Kindle's battery power. Other disability groups are concerned that e-readers do not permit connection to devices such as trackballs and switches (see Chapter 8), thereby making them inaccessible to users with physical disabilities.

Reading Rights Coalition

The Reading Rights Coalition was established to advocate for access to alternate formats and text-to-speech for people with disabilities so that they will have equal access to books and other printed materials. The coalition believes that "access to the written word is the cornerstone of education and democracy." Its advocacy focuses on ensuring that "new technologies must SERVE individuals with disabilities, NOT impede them." http://readingrights.org

RECORDED BOOKS. In addition to text readers and scan/read applications, other forms of technology can help older students who struggle with reading comprehension. Books-on-tape were available for many years. The books were read aloud by readers and recorded on four-track tapes that had to be played back on special four-track tape recorders.

Today organizations such as Learning Ally (formerly Recording for the Blind and Dyslexic (RFB&D)) have moved from four-track tapes to digital books, which use the DAISY format. The digital books are available on CD or as a download from the Internet. The advantage to digital recordings is that, unlike tapes, they do not have to be navigated in sequential order from beginning to end. Users can start the book at any place, can insert bookmarks at any point, and can easily navigate from one page or chapter to another, or from one bookmark or heading to the next. This ease of navigation is a significant improvement over the rewind–fast-forward guesswork of books-on-tape. It also affords students the opportunity to use prereading strategies to increase their comprehension and learning. One such strategy is SLiCK, short for **S**et up, **L**ook ahead, **C**omprehend, **K**eep it together (Boyle et al., 2002). This strategy is described in the sidebar.

To listen to Learning Ally's digital books, students need one of the following specialized items: a portable CD player such as a Victor Reader Wave, a small device that reads downloaded

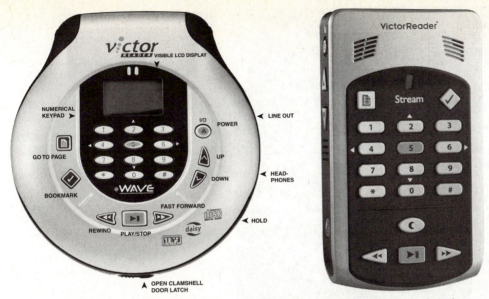

The Victor Reader Wave and the Victor Reader Stream are lightweight portable playback devices for digital books. They can be used with headphones or speakers. Their numeric keypads make it easy for students to navigate by page, chapter, or section. The Wave plays CDs; the Stream plays downloaded audio files.

Photos courtesy of Humanware.

DAISY files such as the Victor Reader Stream, a standard computer equipped with a specialized application available from Learning Ally, or an app for the iPad, iPhone, iPod Touch. It is important to note that for copyright reasons, organizations such as Learning Ally require their members to provide documented evidence of a print disability before they can borrow digital books. (See Sidebar on Copyright Issues.)

SLiCK Strategy for Use With Audiobooks

Boyle and colleagues (2002) explain the SLiCK strategy:

1. The student gets all materials set up: He or she opens the textbook to the correct page, places a SLiCK worksheet on the desk, and loads the CD into the playback device.
2. The student looks ahead through the chapter (both the printed textbook and the audiobook), noting the headings, subheadings, keywords, and vocabulary, in order to think about what is coming up and access prior knowledge about the subject.
3. The student comprehends the text by listening to the audiobook and following along in the text. This step includes pausing the CD to write important points on the SLiCK worksheet and writing a summary of what was learned.
4. The student now must keep it together—must combine the summaries to comprehend the entire reading "to get the bigger picture" (Boyle et al., 2002, p. 54).

Source: Information based on "Reading's SLiCK with New Audio Texts and Strategies," by E. A. Boyle, S. G. Washburn, M. S. Rosenberg, V. J. Connelly, L. C. Brinckerhoff, & M. Banerjee, 2002, *Teaching Exceptional Children, 35*(2), 50–55.

Student reading a book using
an iPod for auditory support.

Photo by Anne M. Disdier

COMMERCIALLY AVAILABLE AUDIOBOOKS.   Commercial bookstores and Web-based businesses that are targeted to the general public are other sources of recorded books. With the popularity of car audio systems, iPads, and MP3 players such as the iPod, listening to recorded books has become a popular activity in our society. People listen to books as they commute, work out in gyms, jog, or just walk around. They borrow recorded books from public libraries, buy them in bookstores, and download them from Web-based services such as Audible.com, Amazon.com, or iTunes. Commercially available recorded books typically focus on bestsellers and popular fiction and nonfiction titles, not on textbooks. However, anecdotal evidence suggests that many teenagers, who do not want to look "different" from their peers, would prefer to listen to an audiobook on an iPod, rather than on a "special" device. For students who do not need to see modified or enhanced text on a computer monitor, these portable audiobooks are an inexpensive, convenient option for school and personal choice reading.

AudibleKids.com, which is geared specifically for children and families, provides audiobooks in MP3 format (http://kids.audible.com). It has a simple interface and offers options to search by age, grade level, or category of children's literature (Animal Stories; Biography and History; Classics and Poetry; Fables, Fairy Tales and Myths; Fiction; Mysteries; Nonfiction; Parenting and Teaching; Sci-Fi and Fantasy; Study Guides and Foreign Language). A search of the category "With Synchronized Images" lists children's books that provide the original illustrations as the application reads the text aloud. In addition to providing audio files, AudibleKids is designed to be an interactive community and to promote the fun of storytelling through audiobooks. Users can listen to books, read and post reviews, and share their favorite books with

Weekly Reader AbleNet Editions

An excellent source of adapted reading materials on current events is the series called *Weekly Reader AbleNet Editions.* Available in both elementary and secondary versions, this series features high-interest/low-level articles on a range of news and nonfiction topics. Each student receives a weekly magazine with access to three levels of adapted content. Levels 1 and 2 include picture symbols placed above words to prompt students who have moderate or severe disabilities. Level 3 does not contain picture prompts and provides more text on each page, but it too provides modified text that is double-spaced and in a larger than usual font. Teachers receive two teacher's guides that present strategies for differentiated instruction, as well as resources and suggestions for additional activities.

others. In collaboration with Reading Is Fundamental, Inc. (RIF), the nonprofit literacy organization, AudibleKids offers several free downloads.

OTHER COMPENSATORY READING TOOLS: ADAPTED BOOKS.   The compensatory tools previously presented are particularly well suited for students who understand material at their grade level when they hear it, even though they struggle with decoding and comprehending written text. Other students, however, have not yet mastered the skills needed to understand grade-level material. These students need additional reading supports and can benefit from another kind of assistive technology.

An estimated 90% of students with multiple disabilities never learn to read above the second-grade level (Koppenhaver & Yoder, 1992). Many students with cognitive disabilities get "stuck" at the emergent literacy level (Erickson, Musselwhite, & Ziolkowski, n.d.). They may listen to stories for enjoyment and participate in reading activities, but they do not progress to being able to read new text independently. Part of the problem has been a lack of appropriate materials, that is, of reading material that is age appropriate, engaging, and written at a level the students can understand (Erickson et al., n.d.). Without such materials, reading development is hampered further because the students do not have many opportunities to read successfully. To break this cycle, these students need reading materials that match their reading abilities and interests, and they need multiple opportunities to read (Erickson et al., n.d.).

Computer technology has proven to be an excellent medium for addressing this problem. A series called Start-to-Finish Books (Don Johnston, Inc.) provides a library of abridged books that are written at lower grade levels but designed for the interests and curricula of higher grade levels (Figure 3.6). Each book is packaged in three formats: a paperback book to read, an audiobook to listen to, and a computer book that provides visual and auditory supports. To help with fluency, the computer book highlights the text as it reads it aloud. The narration is digitized speech, not synthesized, so characters speak with different voices and the reading sounds more like a dramatization than typical computerized voices. This captivates students and involves them in the story. Students can click on unfamiliar words to hear them spoken aloud.

The Start-to-Finish books enable students who are reading on a second- or third-grade level to read a version of *Treasure Island, Huck Finn,* or *Romeo and Juliet.* So if their middle school or high school English class is reading one of these classics, a student whose reading is far below grade level can still enjoy the story and participate in class activities. There are also titles available about sports figures such as Jackie Robinson and Muhammad Ali, and historical figures such as Sacagawea and Rosa Parks. As students' reading skills improve, the series offers another set of titles at the fourth- to fifth-grade reading level.

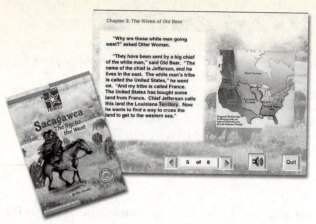

FIGURE 3.6 A sample screen of the computer version of a Start-to-Finish book with the paperback version on the left.

Source: Image provided courtesy of Don Johnston, Inc.

The Start-to-Finish series also includes supplements to textbooks called Core Content. These nonfiction packages provide access to topics covered in middle school and high school curricula, such as evolution (*Adaptation and Change on the Galapagos Islands*) and history (*Fighting Back Against Hitler: Heroes of the Holocaust*). In addition to offering electronic supports, these books have been designed to provide considerate text. Considerate text is written at an appropriate level, is organized in a meaningful way, and provides helpful headings and questions to the reader (Armbruster & Anderson, 1988). It limits the amount of new vocabulary and carefully introduces new words. In the Start-to-Finish Core Content series, for example, all new subject-specific terms are printed in boldface and defined in the glossary. Students can read the book on the computer, following along as the text is highlighted and spoken aloud; they can listen to the audiobook; or they can read the paperback book independently. Curriculum content that was previously inaccessible to students who were poor readers is now accessible through this use of technology.

USER PROFILE

Brian

In a central New Jersey school district, Ms. M is utilizing technology in her special education classroom to enable her students to meet sixth- to eighth-grade curriculum goals. She bases her instructional strategies on current research on brain-based learning, multiple intelligence theories, and differentiated instruction, and technology plays a key role. She has found two products to be particularly helpful when she is working on an alternate proficiency assessment. The following technology applications were successfully utilized in documenting that a student who has low cognitive abilities had achieved all of his goals.

SCAN/READ PROVIDES ACCESS TO CONTENT

For a social studies research project, Brian, an eighth grader who reads far below grade level, was able to gather information on the structure of the U.S. government by having the scan/read program WYNN read selected Web sites to him. He had a copy of the printed worksheet at his desk and a copy saved electronically to WYNN, and he used WYNN to read aloud the fill-in-the-blank questions. He then minimized the electronic worksheet while he researched the answers on the Web.

He returned to the WYNN version of the worksheet to type his answers. WYNN allowed Brian to hear what he had written, edit it if necessary, and check his answers. He then wrote his answers on the printed worksheet. By completing the assignment this way, Brian was able to prove he had comprehended the material, and Ms. M added the worksheet to his Alternate Proficiency Assessment portfolio.

In science, Brian completed a guided research packet on sources of energy. Using WYNN to read aloud Web sites, he researched solar, wind, and hydropower and then prepared a PowerPoint presentation on solar power for the class. For a project on scientists, he researched Thomas Edison and made a brochure about him using the text-to-speech feature of WYNN to edit his work.

WYNN also proved useful when Brian had to complete a timeline assignment. He had been asked to create a timeline about himself to fulfill a requirement in the New Jersey Core Curriculum Standards and to meet one of his cumulative progress indicators. WYNN helped him create the timeline by reading aloud as he typed the events that had occurred in his life. He used WYNN's dictionary and thesaurus features to find the proper spelling and usage of words. Brian also used WYNN to share his work with the rest of the class. He stood in the front of the class and pointed to the various dates and pictures he had created on the poster as WYNN read the electronic version aloud for the rest of the class to hear.

Ms. M had Brian create a personal dictionary. At first, the dictionary contained only personal identifiers such as name, address, and phone number. Brian then used picture cards to indicate what words he would like added to his dictionary, such as pizza, hamburgers, family members' names, and Legos. Words from lessons in the class were also added. Ms. M took a great deal of time to create all of these dictionary pages and make them accessible to Brian. He then used WYNN to listen to the words in the dictionary. He was able to check to see if this was the word he wanted to use when completing class materials or filling out forms.

HIGH-INTEREST/LOW-LEVEL READING MATERIALS PROVIDE ACCESS TO THE CURRICULUM

The second technology product Ms. M found useful in her class was the Start-to-Finish Books Series. She appreciated the variety of subject matter available and the series' ease of use. Since Brian had a particular interest in science, she chose *Liddy and the Volcanoes* and *Hurricane!* for his books. He also chose a Start-to-Finish Book for his personal choice reading, which focused on sports. Brian read along on the screen as the computer read the book aloud. Ms. M used the fill-in-the-blank quizzes at the end of each chapter and other assessment tools to check Brian's comprehension. After his quiz was graded, an option to graph the results was available. Ms. M used this feature to display Brian's progress to him and to provide evidence in his portfolio displaying how he was meeting his cumulative progress indicator. ∎

Source: From "Technology's Contributions to an Alternate Assessment by T. Cordwell, 2006, *TECH-NJ, 17* (1).

USER PROFILE

Carol

Carol is a middle school student who has been receiving special education services since second grade. She is a star soccer player and attends a public school in her hometown. She has been described as having learning disabilities, a central auditory processing disorder, and/or attention deficits. Whatever term you use, the fact remains that she has a very difficult time gaining meaning from text and, as a result, is reluctant to do any reading. In typical teenage fashion, Carol also does not want to "look different," to draw attention to her learning difficulties, so her mother has tried a variety of technology tools to help her succeed in reading.

In the summer before sixth grade, Carol was finally able to enjoy a book when she read *Anne of Green Gables* from the Start-to-Finish series. It was shorter than the original and it was read aloud by the computer, but for the first time Carol understood what she was reading. The following summer, her

(continued)

mother downloaded and reformatted *The Hobbitt* from Bookshare.org, and Carol read it using the scan/read program WYNN. Being tied to a computer was inconvenient, so the following summer (between seventh and eighth grades), Carol chose to listen to the latest Harry Potter book on a portable CD player, following along in the book. During eighth grade, for "personal choice book" assignments she read the Thinking Reader version of *Esperanza Rising.* Then she discovered that she could purchase books from iTunes and downloaded *Heartbeat* (by Sharon Creech) onto her iPod. Now she can listen to age-appropriate books on her iPod, not be tied to a computer, and not look different from the other middle schoolers. ■

Listening to books on mobile devices such as iPads and iPods is becoming a popular compensatory reading strategy. Many programs, including the latest versions of Kurzweil 3000 and WYNN, offer the ability to convert electronic files to MP3 format for this exact purpose.

DECISION MAKING: INSTRUCTIONAL TOOL OR COMPENSATORY TOOL?

Earlier in this chapter, we explained how computer technology can be used to help students *learn to read*. In the last section, we discussed that computers can also be used as a compensatory strategy for students who need to *read to learn* but whose reading skills are inadequate. This section addresses the following questions: How does a teacher *decide* which application of technology to use? *When* does a teacher switch the emphasis from learning to read to using computer technology to help a student read to learn? Edyburn (2003) asks,

> How do we decide if the best course of action is remediation (i.e., additional instructional time, different instructional approaches) versus compensation (i.e., recognizing that remediation has failed and that compensatory approaches are needed to produce the desired level of performance)? When should students be provided with compensatory technologies when they can't read? (p. 18)

In answering this question, Edyburn (2003) finds guidance in the field of occupational therapy. If a student has cerebral palsy and cannot use an arm, a therapist teaches the student alterative ways of completing tasks that require the use of two arms. Compensatory approaches are often used in occupational therapy because with physical disabilities "there are [often] no other ways to complete the task" (p. 19). He parallels this to education: Technology should be considered as a compensatory tool when a student routinely fails "to attain appropriate levels of academic performance" (p. 19). If these students are provided with appropriate compensatory tools, they will "experience success and achieve the functional outcome expected in their academic classes" (p. 20).

The AIM Consortium (National Center on Accessible Instructional Materials at CAST, 2010) recommends the first two years of high school as the ideal time to introduce text-to-speech as a compensatory tool. They identify six characteristics of students that are linked to successful use of text-to-speech for reading: (1) at least average cognitive ability, (2) good listening comprehension skills, (3) reading and writing skills that are significantly below grade level, (4) having received special education services in the past to improve reading and writing skills, (5) at risk for dropping out of high school or not graduating in a timely manner, and (6) a past history of benefitting from human readers such as teacher aides, parents or peers.

FIGURE 3.7 Using technology to adapt text for students who struggle with reading comprehension.

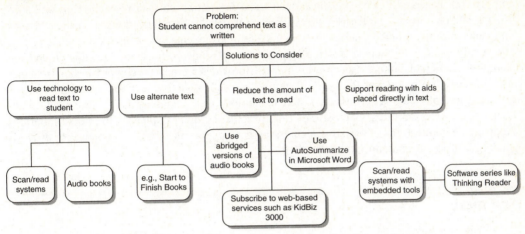

A helpful framework for this decision-making process is provided by Dyck and Pemberton (2002). Although their article focuses on text adaptations and is not specific to assistive technology, the issues they raise are relevant to our discussion. They recommend asking the question, "'Can this student read and understand this text with sufficient speed and accuracy?' If the answer is 'No, the student is struggling with the printed word,' text adaptation should be considered" (p. 29). They provide a decision tree to help teachers select one of six adaptations. We focus on the first four options in the following text and summarize them in Figure 3.7.

The first option to consider for the student who cannot comprehend a text is the substitution of an **alternative text**, "one the student can read and understand but that contains the same content material" (p. 29). Dyck and Pemberton recommend locating substitute books that use considerate text. The technology application presented in this chapter that uses considerate text is the Start-to-Finish Core Content series. This series provides access to core curriculum content for poor readers; it is intentionally designed as a substitute for conventional textbooks.

Next, Dyck and Pemberton suggest asking the question, "Can this student achieve the lesson goal or objective if the **text is read to** the student?" (p. 30, boldface added). They call this "bypass reading" and mention books-on-CD as an example. The Thinking Reader series discussed in this chapter, Bookshare.org and the test reading applications it offers, and scan/read programs such as WYNN and Kurzweil 3000 are also examples of this option; the student experiences the same text as the other students but benefits from being able to *listen* to it.

The third option Dyck and Pemberton discuss is **decreasing the amount** of reading a student is required to complete. This can be done simply by reducing the student's assignment, but other options include using the AutoSummarize feature in Microsoft Word, using abridged versions of books-on-CD, or using the abridged Start-to-Finish Books. The Web-based program KidBiz3000, which was described earlier in this chapter, also reduces the amount of reading for struggling readers.

The fourth option Dyck and Pemberton (2002) recommend is to provide **reading supports**: "Supported reading means placing aids right in the text to make it more interesting and understandable" (p. 32). This is easily done in Blio and scan/read programs such as WYNN and Kurzweil 3000. Talking dictionaries and thesauruses are available at the click of a mouse. Teachers can embed text notes and voice notes in the text that, for example, remind students to look up a word in the dictionary, signify that the next sentence is important, or prompt students to use their reading comprehension strategies. The Thinking Reader series regularly provides prompts for comprehension strategies.

Clearly, regardless of the type of support needed, assistive technology offers multiple means to scaffold reading success. Assistive technology tools can meet the reading needs of students who have disabilities, whether they require remediation or compensation for skill deficits. Appropriate applications of assistive technology can support all of the components of effective reading instruction as identified by the NRP.

Summary

- Reading instruction in grades K–3 focuses on learning to read; that is, learning to identify letters and sounds, decode words, and glean meaning from printed text. By grade 4, students are reading to learn. They are relying on printed text to gain contextual understanding. Instruction focuses on improving comprehension.
- The National Reading Panel identified five areas of reading instruction that are essential for children to learn to read:

  1. Phonemic awareness
  2. Phonics
  3. Fluency
  4. Comprehension
  5. Vocabulary

- The computer can be used as a reading remediation tool by teaching phonological processes, improving decoding skills, and providing opportunities to develop fluency. It improves learning to read by providing systematic, repetitive, and individualized instruction.
- There has been a shift in the format of applications from drill and practice to focusing on strengthening overall reading comprehension strategies using interesting and popular reading materials.
- The Internet offers numerous subscription services that are designed to improve the higher level reading skills of fluency, comprehension and vocabulary. The Internet is also a rich resource for finding reading material that matches students' interests and abilities.
- Students whose reading skills are below grade level benefit from the use of technology as a compensatory tool. Computers and mobile devices can read aloud text and provide access to the curriculum.
- Providing books in alternate formats involves being familiar with different file types, a variety of playback devices— both portable and computer-based, and copyright law.
- Text readers such as Text Aloud, Read Out:Loud, Read2Go and Blio, and scan/read programs such as Kurzweil 3000 and WYNN, offer a variety of tools to increase a student's reading independence and overcome reading difficulties, including a talking dictionary and thesaurus, electronic highlighters for note taking and preparing study guides, voice notes, and sticky notes for inserting hidden prompts and reminders.

Web Resources

For additional information on the topics listed, visit the following Web sites:

Learning to Read
Finding of the National Reading Panel
http://www.nichd.nih.gov/publications/nrp/smallbook.cfm

Great Schools: Learning to Read—Research Informs Us
http://www.greatschools.org/special-education/ LD-ADHD/learning-to-read-research.gs?content=663&page=3

International Reading Association
http://www.reading.org

Reading Rockets: Reading Comprehension & Language Arts Teaching Strategies for Kids
http://www.readingrockets.org

Leveled Reading
http://www.readinga-z.com/guided/index.html

Reading Problems in Students with Learning Disabilities
Georgia Assistive Technology Project
http://www.gatfl.org/learningdisabilitiesguide/readingproblemsdisabilities/readingstrategies.aspx

Assistive Technology Tools for Reading
Great Schools
http://www.greatschools.org/special-education/ assistive-technology/reading-tools.gs?content=948

Phonemic Awareness Instruction
Starfall
http://www.starfall.com

Wilson Reading Program
http://www.wilsonlanguage.com

Orton-Gillingham approach
http://www.orton-gillingham.com

Free demos of phonics software
http://www.riverdeep.com

Intensive Training in Phonological Processes
Fast ForWord
http://www.scilearn.com

Earobics
http://www.earobics.com

Thinking Reader Software Series
www.tomsnyder.com → Reading → Thinking Reader → User Resources

e-Books for Children
BookFlix (Scholastic)
http://teacher.scholastic.com/Products/BookFlixFreeTrial/index.htm

Raz-Kids
http://www.raz-kids.com/

Reading A-Z
http://www.readinga-z.com

Tumblebooks
http://tumblebooks.com

Accessible Instructional Materials and Alternate Formats
National Center on Accessible Instructional Materials
http://aim.cast.org

AIM Navigator
http://aim.cast.org/experience/decision-making_tools/aim_navigator

Text-to-Speech (TtS) and Accessible Instructional Materials (AIM): An Implementation Guide
for Use of TtS and AIM in Secondary Classrooms, April 30, 2010 Update
http://aim.cast.org

Quality Indicators for the Provision of Accessible Materials
http://trueaim.iowa.gov

Accessible Resource Center—British Columbia
http://www.arc-bc.org

National Instructional Materials Accessibility Center
Frequently Asked Questions
http://www.nimac.us/faq_general.html

Scan/Read Software
Claro Read Plus (Windows and Mac)
http://www.claroread.com

Kurzweil 1000 and 3000
http://www.kurzweiledu.com

WYNN
http://www.freedomscientific.com/LSG/products/index.asp

WYNN Tip Sheets
http://www.freedomscientific.com/LSG/products/wynn_tipsheets.asp

Mobile Scan/Read Solutions
kNFB Reader Mobile
http://www.knfbreader.com

ZoomReader
http://mobile.aisquared.com/

Text Readers
Blio e-Reader (Windows)
http://blio.com/

Text Aloud (Windows)
http://www.nextup.com

GhostReader (Mac)
http://www.nextup.com

ReadPlease/ReadPlease Plus (Windows)
http://readplease.com

Awesome Talkster (free; Windows)
http://www.awesomelibrary.org/Awesome_Talking_Library.html

Read Out:Loud—Bookshare Edition (free to Bookshare members; Windows & Mac)
http://www.bookshare.org

Claro Read (Windows and Mac)
http://www.claroread.com

Macintosh Operating System 10.4 and higher includes text reader
http://www.apple.com

Audiobooks
Learning Ally (formerly Recording for the Blind and Dyslexic)
http://www.learningally.org

Speakaboos
http://www.speakaboos.com

Storyline Online (a project of the Screen Actors Guild)
http://www.storylineonline.net

LoudLit.org
http://LoudLit.org

Audio Book Treasury
http://www.audiobooktreasury.com/

Commercial audiobooks
http://www.AudibleKids.com

Adapted Books
Start-to-Finish books
http://www.donjohnston.com/products/starttofinish/library/index.html

News-2-You: Subscription service to online news stories written at beginning literacy levels.
http://www.news-2-you.com/index.aspx

Weekly Reader AbleNet Editions
http://www.ablenetinc.com/

Tool for Making Reading on the Web Easier
Readability: Removes clutter around a Web page's content and allows user to choose a font,
font size, and margin size.
http://lab.arc90.com/experiments/readability

Low-Tech Tools for Reading
Assistive Technology Training Online Project
http://atto.buffalo.edu/registered/ATBasics/populations/Lowtech/reading.php

Suggested Activities

1. *Try out an application that teaches reading skills.* Choose one of the titles in the Thinking Reader series (Scholastic) or a Web-based application that teaches specific reading skills (for example, Riverdeep's Destination Reading or Reading A-Z.). Explore the program thoroughly. Deliberately make wrong answers to see how the program responds and find out what kind of teacher options are available. Does the program teach the reading skills it claims to teach? How would you use this program in your classroom?

2. *Locate and use e-text.* You are an in-class support teacher in a high school English class. The class will be reading Shakespeare's *Romeo and Juliet.* Some of your students read on a fourth-grade level and will not be able to keep up with the reading assignments. Your school has scan/read programs available. Go online and locate e-text versions of the play. Download three different versions, check them for accuracy and style and then choose one to import into SOLO (Don Johnston, Inc.), Kurzweil 3000, or WYNN.

3. *Convert e-text to MP3 format.* Go to http://www.nextup.com and listen to the variety of voices available. Download a trial version of the software program TextAloud (NextUp.com). Use it to listen to a Web page or a Word document. Then convert the file to MP3 format and listen to it again on an MP3 player. Write a narrative commenting on the ease or difficulty of the technical aspects of the task and the implications of this technology for students with disabilities.

4. *Make the reading components of a unit accessible to students with disabilities.*

   a. Select a unit of study for a grade level. It can be a unit that you currently teach, have taught in the past, would like to teach in the future, or one that you have been asked to support by another teacher. Or you can select lesson plans from a Web site, such as www.teachnology.com.

   b. Identify the reading components in the unit (e.g., reading questions on worksheets or quizzes, reading a story, reading nonfiction for preparing a report). Then explain how you would make the reading components accessible to a student who has learning disabilities and a student who has physical disabilities. Be specific. Make sure your recommended solution or solutions match the task and the students' needs. Use a chart like the one that follows to organize and present your information. It will help show the relationship between the specific reading activity and the specific technology solution.

Reading Activity	Adaptations for Student with Learning Disabilities			Adaptations for Student with Physical Disabilities		
	Type of Technology	Product Name & Publisher	Rationale	Type of Technology	Product Name & Publisher	Rationale

5. *Find low-tech solutions for reading.* Add low-tech reading aids to the low-tech writing kit you began in Chapter 2. Go to a local craft store and an office supply store and gather items such as highlighters, highlighter tape, different-sized sticky notes, a page-up paper holder, a cookbook holder, and other items that could be used to support reading.

References

ACHIEVE3000. (n.d.). *Kidbiz3000.* Retrieved June 30, 2010, from http://www.achieve3000.com/article/a3k/index.php?c=2&sc=1

Anderson-Inman, L., & Horney, M. (1997). Electronic books for secondary students. *Journal of Adolescent and Adult Literacy, 40*(6), 486–491.

Armbruster, B. B., & Anderson, T. H. (1988). On selecting "considerate" content area textbooks. *Remedial and Special Education, 9*(1), 47–52.

Assistive Technology Training Online Training Project. (2005). *Low-tech tools: Reading aids.* Retrieved April 27, 2011, from http://atto.buffalo.edu/registered/ATBasics/Populations/LowTech/reading.php

Boyle, E. A., Washburn, S. G., Rosenberg, M. S., Connelly, V. J., Brinckerhoff, L. C., & Banerjee, M. (2002). Reading's SLiCK with new audio texts and strategies. *Teaching Exceptional Children, 35*(2), 50–55.

Dyck, N., & Pemberton, J. B. (2002). A model for making decisions about text adaptations. *Intervention in School and Clinic, 38*(1), 28–35.

Edyburn, D. L. (2003, March/April). Learning from text. *Special Education Technology Practice,* pp. 16–27.

Erickson, K., Musselwhite, C. R., & Ziolkowski, R. (n.d.). *The beginning literacy framework.* Volo, IL: Don Johnston, Inc.

Georgia Assistive Technology Project Tools For Life. (n.d.). Learning Disabilities and Assistive Technologies: Reading. Retrieved May 1, 20011, from http://www.gatfl.org/learningdisabilitiesguide/readingproblemsdisabilities/readingstrategies.aspx

Hecker, L., Burns, L., Katz, L., Elkind, J., & Elkind, K. (2002). Benefits of assistive reading software for students with attention disorders. *Annals of Dyslexia, 52,* 243–272.

Horney, M. A., Anderson-Inman, L., Terrazas-Arellanes, F., Schulte, W., Mundorf, J., Wiseman, S., et al. (2009). Exploring the effects of digital note taking on student comprehension of science texts. *Journal of Special Education Technology, 4*(3), 45–61.

Iowa Assistive Technology Text Reader Project. (2008). *Summary Report of the Iowa Text Reader Studies 2006–2007.* Des Moines, IA: Iowa Department of Education. PDF retrieved May 1, 2011, from http://www.kurzweiledu.com/files/Iowa_Text_Reader_Study_Report.pdf

Iowa Department of Education. (2009). Quality indicators for the provision of accessible materials. Retrieved June 4, 2010, from the Web site of True AIM: http://trueaim.iowa.gov

Koppenhaver, D., & Yoder, D. (1992). Literacy learning of children with severe speech and physical impairments in school settings. *Seminars in Speech and Language, 13*(2), 143–153.

Langran, E., Langran, R., & Bull, G. (2005). Copyright law and technology. *Learning and Leading with Technology, 32*(7), 24–26.

Library of Congress. (1996). *NLS Fact Sheet: Copyright Law Amendment, 1996.* Retrieved June 22, 2010, from http://www.loc.gov/nls/reference/factsheets/copyright.html

Lipson, M. Y., & Wixson, K. K. (1997). *Assessment and instruction of reading and writing disability: An interactive approach* (2nd ed.). New York: Longman.

Meyer, A., & Rose, D. H. (1998). *Learning to read in the computer age.* Newton, MA: Brookline Books.

National Center on Accessible Instructional Materials at CAST, Inc. (2010). *What is the National Instructional Materials Accessibility Standard (NIMAS)?* Retrieved July 21, 2010, from http://aim.cast.org/learn/policy/federal/what_is_nimas

National Center On Accessible Instructional Materials At CAST (2010). *Text-to-Speech (TtS) and Accessible Instructional Materials (AIM): An Implementation Guide for Use of TtS and AIM in Secondary Classrooms, April*

30, 2010 Update. Retrieved May 2, 2011 from http://aim.cast.org/experience/training/aim_implementation_guide

National Reading Panel. (2000). Findings and determinations of the National Reading Panel by topic areas. In *Report of the National Reading Panel: Teaching children to read.* Retrieved May 1, 2011, from the National Institute of Child Health & Human Development Web site: http://www.nichd.nih.gov/publications/nrp/smallbook.cfm

National Reading Panel Subgroup on Alphabetics. (2000). Alphabetics: Part 1, Phonemic awareness instruction. In *Report of the National Reading Panel: Teaching children to read.* Retrieved May 1, 2011, from the National Institute of Child Health & Human Development Web site: http://nichd.nih.gov/publications/nrp/findings.cfm

Northeast and the Islands Regional Technology in Education Consortium (NEIRTEC). (2004). *Technology and teaching children to read.* Retrieved June 1, 2010, from http://www.neirtec.org/reading_report/report.htm#appendixa

Palincsar, A. S., & Klenk, L. J. (1991). Dialogues promoting reading comprehension. In B. Means, C. Chelemr, & M. S. Knapp (Eds.), *Teaching advanced skills to at-risk students: Views from research and practice* (pp. 112–130). San Francisco, CA: Jossey-Bass.

Robin, A. (1998). *ADHD in adolescents: Diagnosis and treatment.* New York: Guilford.

Rose, D., & Dalton, B. (2002). Using technology to individualize reading instruction. In C. C. Block, L. B. Gambrell, & M. Pressley (Eds.), *Improving comprehension instruction: Rethinking research, theory, and classroom practice* (pp. 257–274). San Francisco, CA: Jossey-Bass.

Ross-Kidder, K. (2004). *"Reading disability" or "learning disability": The debate, models of dyslexia, and a review of research-validated reading programs.* Retrieved May 1, 2011, from the LD OnLine Web site: http://www.ldonline.org/ld_indepth/reading/reading_approaches.html

Rothman, R. (2004). Adolescent literacy: Are we overlooking the struggling teenage reader? *Harvard Education Letter, 20*(1), 1–3.

Schulte, A., Conners, C., & Osborne, S. (1999). Linkages between attention deficit disorders and reading disability. In D. D. Duane (Ed.), *Reading and attention disorders* (pp. 161–184). Baltimore, MD: York Press.

Section 107 of Amendments to Title 17 Since 1976, *Copyright laws of the United States.* Retrieved July 28, 2010, from http://www.copyright.gov/title17

Shipon, W. (2002). College student combines motivation and technology to succeed. *TECH-NJ, 13*(1). Retrieved May 1, 2011, from http://www.tcnj.edu/~technj/2002/anthony.htm

Spear-Swerling, L. (2005). *Components of effective reading instruction.* Retrieved June 1, 2010, from http://www.ldonline.org/article/5589

Temple, E., Deutsch, G. K., Poldrack, R. A., Miller, S. L., Tallal, P., Merzenich, M. M., et al. (2003). Neural deficits in children with dyslexia ameliorated by behavioral remediation: Evidence from functional MRI. *Proceedings of the National Academy of Sciences, 100*(5), 2860–2865.

Tom Snyder Productions. (2004). *Thinking Reader teacher's guide.* Watertown, MA: Author.

Wehmeyer, M., Smith, S., Palmer, S., & Davies, D. (2004). Technology use by students with intellectual disabilities: An overview. *Journal of Special Education Technology, 19*(4), 7–21.

Zorfass, J. M., Fideler, E. F., Clay, K., & Brann, A. (2007). Enhancing content literacy: Software tools help struggling students. *Technology in Action, 2*(6), 1–12.

4 TECHNOLOGY TO SUPPORT UNIVERSAL DESIGN FOR LEARNING (UDL) AND DIFFERENTIATED INSTRUCTION

Focus Questions

1. What is the shared goal of universal design for learning (UDL) and differentiated instruction?
2. What are the three basic principles of UDL?
3. How can technology support the principle of multiple means of representation?
4. How can technology support the principle of multiple means of action and expression?
5. How can technology support the principle of multiple means of engagement?
6. What features in Internet browsers can be adjusted to make the Web accessible to students with disabilities?

INTRODUCTION

Previous chapters in this text discussed how assistive technology can support reading, writing, mathematics instruction, and communication. This chapter explores the concept of **universal design for learning** (UDL) and the use of technology to make all curricular areas accessible to the broadest range of learners in today's inclusive classrooms. UDL is "a flexible approach to curriculum design that offers all learners full and equal opportunities to learn. . . . The curriculum is made flexible and customizable so that individuals can learn in ways that work best for them" (National Center on Universal Design for Learning, 2010). UDL seeks to "minimize barriers and maximize flexibility" (Hall, Strangman, & Meyer, 2009, p.7). It overlaps differentiated instruction in that both share the goal of reaching as many students as possible. **Differentiated instruction** asks teachers to "recognize students' varying background knowledge, readiness, language, preferences in learning and interests; and to react responsively. . . . [Its] intent . . . is to maximize each student's growth and individual success by meeting each student where he or she is and assisting in the learning process" (Hall et al., 2009, p.3). Hall et al. (2009) distinguish between the two by describing UDL as a theoretical framework for the design of *curricula* and differentiated instruction as a process of teaching and learning. They point out that the instructional practices recommended by differentiated instruction support the basic principles of UDL. Therefore, this chapter blurs the line between the two and discusses technology applications that support both.

UDL as defined by the federal Higher Education Opportunity Act of 2008

A scientifically valid framework for guiding educational practice that:

(A) provides flexibility in the ways information is presented, in the ways students respond or demonstrate knowledge and skills, and in the ways students are engaged; and

(B) reduces barriers in instruction, provides appropriate accommodations, supports, and challenges, and maintains high achievement expectations for all students, including students with disabilities and students who are limited English proficient.

The flexibility required by UDL is accomplished through the application of three basic principles. These principles state that in their classrooms teachers should do the following:

1 Provide multiple means of representation
2 Provide multiple means of action and expression
3 Provide multiple means of engagement

Each of these guiding principles is discussed below. Figure 4.1 presents a summary called the Universal Design for Learning Guidelines. Readers should keep in mind that although the three principles are presented separately, they overlap and are interconnected. For example, when students are given a choice in how they will demonstrate what they have learned, they are also likely to be more engaged in the activity.

Resource on UDL—CAST.org

CAST is a nonprofit organization that promotes the use of universal design for leaning to expand learning opportunities for all students, including students with special needs. The CAST Web site provides a wealth of resources on UDL, including detailed guidelines on how to develop lessons that are based on the three UDL principles, checkpoints for each guideline, a UDL Systemic Change Tutorial, a UDL Book Builder, a leveled reading series called UDL Editions, a science lab writing site called Science Writer, and a UDL Lesson Builder.

UDL PRINCIPLE 1: MULTIPLE MEANS OF REPRESENTATION

Provide Multiple Means of Representation

No single method is best for teachers to present information to students. Students with sensory impairments (e.g., blindness, visual impairments, deafness, or hearing loss) need information presented in a way that bypasses their disability. Students with blindness or visual impairments need information presented in an auditory or tactile fashion. Students who are deaf or hard of hearing need to receive information visually through text or images. Some students, including many with learning disabilities, learn better when information is presented in a visual manner, rather than solely in a lecture format. These students may understand material better when it is presented in video clips, pictures, charts, or graphs. Other students learn better when material is presented in an auditory fashion, such as through a lecture or audio file or is read aloud. Many

Universal Design for Learning Guidelines

I. Provide Multiple Means of Representation	II. Provide Multiple Means of Action and Expression	III. Provide Multiple Means of Engagement
1. Provide options for perception • Options that customize the display of information • Options that provide alternatives for auditory information • Options that provide alternatives for visual information	**4. Provide options for physical action** • Options in the mode of physical response • Options in the means of navigation • Options for accessing tools and assistive technologies	**7. Provide options for recruiting interest** • Options that increase individual choice and autonomy • Options that enhance relevance, value, and authenticity • Options that reduce threats and distractions
2. Provide options for language and symbols • Options that define vocabulary and symbols • Options that clarify syntax and structure • Options for decoding text or mathematical notation • Options that promote cross-linguistic understanding • Options that illustrate key concepts non-linguistically	**5. Provide options for expressive skills and fluency** • Options in the media for communication • Options in the tools for composition and problem solving • Options in the scaffolds for practice and performance	**8. Provide options for sustaining effort and persistence** • Options that heighten salience of goals and objectives • Options that vary levels of challenge and support • Options that foster collaboration and communication • Options that increase mastery-oriented feedback
3. Provide options for comprehension • Options that provide or activate background knowledge • Options that highlight critical features, big ideas, and relationships • Options that guide information processing • Options that support memory and transfer	**6. Provide options for executive functions** • Options that guide effective goal-setting • Options that support planning and strategy development • Options that facilitate managing information and resources • Options that enhance capacity for monitoring progress	**9. Provide options for self-regulation** • Options that guide personal goal-setting and expectations • Options that scaffold coping skills and strategies • Options that develop self-assessment and reflection

FIGURE 4.1 Universal Design for Learning Principles, Guidelines, and Checkpoints.
Source: Courtesy of David Rose, Cast.

students respond when content is presented in a combination of auditory and visual modes. In the UDL classroom, teachers consider the various ways that students learn and present information in a variety of ways to facilitate learning for the diverse learners within their classrooms.

Various technologies support the principle of multiple means of representation. When information is available in electronic text, it can be read aloud with text-to-speech applications, as discussed in Chapter 3. When text is displayed within word processing applications, its size, color, and font can be changed to meet the needs of individual students. Electronic text in a graphic organizing program can be divided so that only a small amount of information is presented at a time. Information can also be presented via video clips and images downloaded from the Internet. An increasing number of resources present the same information at different reading levels so all students can understand key information at a level that matches their reading ability.

What Multiple Means of Representation Looks Like in a Classroom

The traditional "Chalk and Talk" style of teaching does not meet the criterion of multiple means of representation. Instead, teachers in a UDL classroom use several methods to present key information and concepts to ensure that they meet all their students' learning needs. A combination of lectures, slide show presentations, video clips, and graphic images is typically among these methods. A computer with a video projector delivers the capacity to use a single classroom computer to present any content area material to students in myriad ways. For example, in a sixth-grade science class studying the universe, a teacher can introduce the topic of galaxies by displaying images of different types of galaxies taken by the Hubble Space Telescope (available from the Amazing Space Web site). While these actual images are being displayed, the teacher can verbally highlight the critical features of each type. With relative ease, the teacher can switch between the projected image and a word processing or graphic organizer program to capture important information about the distinguishing features of each galaxy discussed. Thus, students who learn best by listening are supported by the verbal explanation; visual learners are supported by the graphic images, as are those who learn best from a combination of auditory and visual delivery of information.

Far better than notes written on a traditional whiteboard or chalkboard, information captured in a word processing application can be saved, printed, e-mailed, posted on the class Web site, read aloud with text-to-speech applications, or converted to an MP3 format for listening later. If the information is captured in a graphic organizer program such as Inspiration that has the flexibility to display a diagram or a text-based outline, students' individual preferences can easily be accommodated.

One increasingly popular and available technology for supporting multiple means of representation is the **interactive whiteboard**. An interactive whiteboard is a large display surface, similar in appearance to a typical whiteboard. It is connected to a computer that has associated software installed. With the use of a projector, any information that is displayed on the computer monitor—text, still images, sound, video—is displayed on the interactive whiteboard. Here is where the "interactive" comes in. The interactive whiteboard functions like a giant touch screen. Simply touching it with your finger, a special pen, or other device (depending on the particular brand) causes the computer to respond as if the mouse were clicked at that particular spot, and with the swipe of a finger an item can be dragged to another spot. Teachers can stand right next to the interactive whiteboard and focus their attention on the students and content delivery, rather than looking down to operate a computer. With the touch of their fingertip, they can deliver engaging, multimedia-enhanced, interactive lessons. Writing notes, creating diagrams, drawing figures, or performing other writing tasks is done with "digital ink"; the writing or markings appear and can even be saved, but no real ink is transferred to the whiteboard. Information about two leading whiteboard manufactures who concentrate on education is included in Web Resources at the end of the chapter.

Continuing our example of the study of galaxies, teachers can project onto an interactive whiteboard a Web browser and a choice of narrated video clips about galaxies. A search of the word *galaxy* at the Hulu Web site turns up hundreds of results. Teachers can use the drop down arrows under Show and select How the Universe Works to find video clips on the shape of galaxies and how galaxies are born. Selecting the show SpaceRip yields more relevant, engaging video clips. Alternately, teachers can search the Discovery Channel for free video clips; those who work in schools that subscribe to Discover Education Streaming (formerly United Streaming) have even more videos at their disposal. By enabling teachers to present information in so many vivid ways, interactive whiteboards help them address the needs of students who "find text difficult as the only mode of communication" (Somekh et al., 2007, p. 5).

Features specific to interactive whiteboards are beneficial for students who need options to help with memory and the transfer of information because they may not immediately grasp new information. Teachers can elect to have the interactive whiteboard application capture what is written along with the accompanying spoken explanations. Students then have the option to re-play the lesson—seeing both the written notes as they are added and hearing the teacher's expla-nation. This is supportive of students with attention issues or auditory processing issues who may miss parts of lessons. It is beneficial for any student who needs repeated exposure to material in order to comprehend it, as well as for students who have missed lessons because of absences.

In addition to providing textbooks in hard copy, the UDL classroom also provides **elec-tronic versions of textbooks**. When these are available from the publisher as a standard option, the electronic versions is made available to all students and they can choose to read in their preferred format. Those who choose the electronic text version are able to customize the visual presentation by changing the size, style, and color of the font along with the background color of the page. They are also able to adjust the line spacing and page margins to match their read-ing preferences. Electronic text gives students who are auditory learners, struggling readers, or nonreaders the option of listening to the textbook read aloud on the computer with text-to-speech applications (see Chapter 3). Alternately, the electronic text can be converted to an MP3 format, giving students the option of listening to the textbook away from a computer on an MP3 player.

The array of graphic, audio, video, and text-based resources on the Internet is a treasure trove supporting multiple means of presentations. Many Web sites provide text-based information that is inaccessible to students because of the visual display or because students are struggling readers or nonreaders. Readily available technologies, discussed next, address these barriers so all students can benefit from Internet resources that supplement or replace textbook readings.

Readability, a free utility that is added to the Bookmark or Favorites toolbar in a user's Web browser (e.g., Internet Explorer or Firefox), removes distracters such as advertisements and displays the remaining text-based information in a format specified by the user. Options that are customizable are font size and style, line spacing, and margin width. Figure 4.2a shows a Web page as normally displayed in Mozilla Firefox. Figure 4.2b shows the same page displayed using Readability for a reader who needs wide margins and narrow lines of text so that eye tracking across a line of text is reduced.

Students who are struggling readers or nonreaders can use a number of free or commercial applications to listen to Web pages read aloud. Several word prediction programs (see Chapter 2) such as WordQ and Co:Writer 6, read aloud text in several applications, including Web pages, as do scan/read systems such as Kurzweil, WYNN, and Read & Write Gold (see Chapter 3). Information on free programs that will read Web pages is provided in Table 4.1.

UDL PRINCIPLE 2: MULTIPLE MEANS OF ACTION AND EXPRESSION

Provide Multiple Means of Action and Expression

Writing is commonly used as the primary means of measuring student learning. Students are required to engage in numerous handwriting activities—completing worksheets, writing reflec-tions, composing essays, and taking tests—to demonstrate their knowledge. Although having students compose handwritten responses is an efficient method of obtaining information in a rel-atively short amount of time, it does not accurately reflect *all* students' learning. For many stu-dents, the handwriting component limits their ability to demonstrate their proficiency. Teachers in the UDL classroom realize that students can demonstrate their learning through multiple

FIGURE 4.2a Web page (http://www.caineassociates.com) viewed without modification in Firefox.

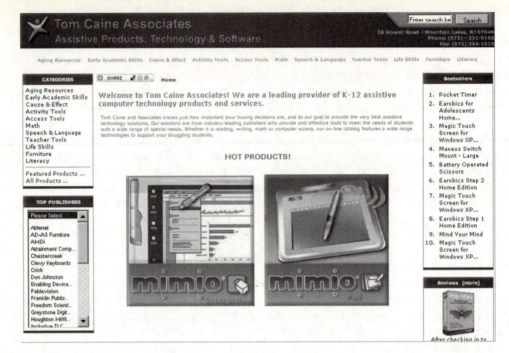

Source: Courtesy of Tom Caine and Associates.

FIGURE 4.2b The same Web page viewed using Readability settings for a reader who is easily distracted by visual clutter.

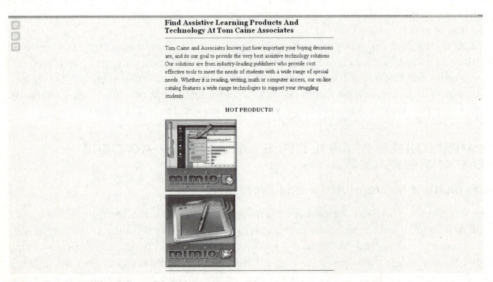

Source: Courtesy of Tom Caine and Associates.

TABLE 4.1   Free Web Page Readers

Product Name	Publisher	Platform	Web site/Availability
NaturalReader	NaturalSoft, Ltd.	Win	http://www.naturalreaders.com
Awesome Talkster	Awesome Talking Library	Win	http://www.awesomelibrary.org/Awesome
CLiCk, Speak	CLC World	Win	http://clickspeak.clcworld.net/

means of action or expression, not solely through handwriting. These teachers recognize that the essential element is student learning and that there are many ways for students to demonstrate learning, which may or may not involve handwriting.

Technology offers several options that allow students to demonstrate what they know even if they have difficulty with written expression. Many of the same technology tools that support the UDL principle of multiple means of representation also support the principle of multiple means of expression and action. In the following section, readers will see how technology can be used to provide students with options that allow them to capitalize on their strengths.

What Multiple Means of Action and Expression Look Like in a Classroom

In the UDL classroom, teachers appreciate the differences among students' abilities, learning styles, talents, and preferences. They realize that the use of pencil and paper is only one of the ways to assess student achievement. Consider a sixth-grade social studies class that has been studying the Civil War. The teacher wants to assess the students' understanding of its causes. Alternatives to handwriting an essay could include composing and editing essays on computers using (1) a word processing application alone, (2) a word processing application with text-to-speech for auditory feedback (see Chapter 2 for additional information on text-to-speech applications), (3) a graphic organizing application such as Inspiration to help with planning and organization, or (4) a word processing application that offers scaffolding such as wordbars or word banks (e.g., WriteOnline or Clicker 5).

Since the teacher's main concern in this Civil War assignment is to gauge students' understanding of the war's causes— not to assess their writing skills—there are several alternatives.

netTrekker, an Academic Search Engine for Differentiated Instruction Supports UDL

One obstacle to using Internet-based activities in the classroom is the risk that students will digress and end up virtually anywhere on the Web. Although school filtering software blocks successfully much unwanted content, it does not screen for age, grade level, or appropriateness or reduce the volume of results returned when commercial search engines such as Bing or Google are used. A fifth grader searching Google for information on the Revolutionary War will be faced with more than 8 million results. To counteract this problem, many school districts subscribe to an academic search engine such as netTrekker (Thinkronize, Inc.). Established and monitored by educators, netTrekker offers Internet content that is prescreened and organized by five readability levels (see Figure 4.3). Teachers can target their search results to find grade-level content at an appropriate reading level for every child in their class. This means that all children—regardless of their reading level—can read about the topic of study and participate in class discussions and activities. An important feature that sets netTrekker apart from other academic search engines is that it offers a read-aloud feature (text-to-speech). It automatically reads highlighted text out loud for students who need additional reading support.

FIGURE 4.3 Sample netTrekker screenshot. Notice the "read aloud" icon on the bottom right.

Source: Courtesy of netTrekker.com

Students who are visual learners can search the Internet and compile a collection of relevant graphic images or videos to which they must add meaningful captions and/or annotations. (In the menu bar on the Google home page, a click on Images or Videos will return results that are only images or only videos.) However, not all images or videos in the results can be used legally, many will be protected by copyright and students need to be made aware of copyright infringement issues. To avoid copyright violations, another option is to direct students to conduct their image searches at Web sites that contain only images or videos that students are free to use. Figure 4.4 provides a sampling of these image and video search Web sites.

Once students have completed their collection of images and/or videos, they select the way they would like to present them to demonstrate their knowledge. Using Inspiration, the graphic organizer program discussed in Chapter 2, students can construct a diagram, map, or outline with embedded images and videos. Students can utilize Inspirations' Presentation Manager to generate automatically slide presentations of their diagram, map, or outline, including images and video. Students who do not have access to Inspiration can insert their images and videos into a multimedia presentation tool such as PowerPoint. Inserting written or recorded audio descriptions and/or explanations can serve to further document the students' depth of understanding.

Students with Internet access may find that creating an interactive poster, or Glog, at Glogster EDU is the best way to showcase their knowledge. Once teachers complete the free registration for Glogster EDU Basic, they can request login names and passwords for up to 100 students. Students can then log in from any computer with an Internet connection and create a virtual poster. They can add sound, video, text, images, graphics, and wallpaper to their Glogs. Glogster EDU gives teachers control over the activities of their class and provides a private, secure place

FIGURE 4.4 Sources for Free Images and Video Clips

A Community–Indexed Photo Archive

More than 27,000 photos and images in the public domain.
http://gimp-savvy.com/PHOTO-ARCHIVE

FreeFoto.com

More than 130,721 images with 177 sections organized into 3,585 categories.
http://www.freefoto.com

Pics4Learning

Includes thousands of images contributed by teachers, students, and amateur photographers.
http://pics4learning.com/

morgueFile

Collection of high–resolution digital stock photography.
http://www.morguefile.com/

Freestockfootage.com

QuickTime preview clips can be downloaded for free; higher resolution clips must be purchased.
http://www.freestockfootage.com/

for students to create and save their work. Glogster EDU Premium, available for a monthly or yearly fee, offers management and control features as well as creativity tools beyond those available in EDU Basic. Figure 4.5 shows the opening template of a Glog in Glogster EDU with a clear, uncluttered interface that makes it easy to use for students with a broad range of abilities.

FIGURE 4.5 Opening template in Glogster EDU Basic

Source: Reproduced with permission of Glogster EDU

Subscription-Based Web Services that Support Multiple Means of Engagement

The following Web sites offer thousands of media resources that are matched to state standards. The sites can be searched by subject and grade level so teachers can easily find relevant materials. Although the sites charge a subscription fee to access their entire collections, all of them offer free sample activities or time-limited free trials.

BrainPOP http://www.brainpop.com

> Provides thousands of engaging animated videos that illustrate curriculum content in every subject area. Subscription options include BrainPOP Jr. (K-3), BrainPOP, BrainPOP Español, and BrainPOP ESL.

Discovery Education Streaming (formerly United Streaming) http://streaming.discoveryeducation.com

> Provides more than 200,000 content specific video clips matched to state standards.

Learn 360 http://www.learn360.com

> A media-on-demand service that provides video clips, speeches, images, and songs and options for class blogs and discussion boards.

Rand McNally Classroom http://education.randmcnally.com/education/

> Offers more than 1,800 maps, games and lesson plans for conducting engaging geography and social studies lessons.

UDL PRINCIPLE 3: MULTIPLE MEANS OF ENGAGEMENT

Provide Multiple Means of Engagement

When students are interested and/or invested in an activity, topic of study, materials being used, or other elements of lesson, they are more attentive and motivated (Meyer & Rose, 1998). Experienced teachers know that little learning takes place if students do not attend to the content and concepts being presented. Finding one activity, one topic, one material, or one of any element of an educational experience that will engage a classroom full of learners with diverse backgrounds, abilities, skills, talents, and interests is not likely. For this reason, teachers need to apply the third principle of UDL, provide multiple means of engagement.

Prensky (2001) refers to today's K–12 students as "digital natives" because "they have spent their entire lives surrounded by and using computers, videogames, digital music players, video cams, cell phones, and all the other toys and tools of the digital age" (p. 1). Fortunately, many of these technologies are the key to gaining and holding students' attention, and they offer a platform to provide multiple means of engagement.

What Multiple Means of Engagement Looks Like in a Classroom

Teachers in the UDL classroom understand that "one size does not fit all." They understand that to engage the broadest range of learners possible, they must supplement the use of traditional classroom materials (e.g., textbooks, novels, and reference materials) with the technology with which digital natives are so familiar and comfortable.

Picture a ninth-grade literature class undertaking the task of reading Shakespeare's *Romeo and Juliet*. Some students will embrace the traditional play, written in Elizabethan English, perhaps finding it charming or enjoying a challenge. Without even opening the cover, some students will be turned off just by the looks of the volume. Other students might be willing to read the play until they encounter the unfamiliar language. The amount of text may overwhelm some students, and other students just will be unable to understand the text at all. Each of these types of students can be engaged in the UDL classroom.

A low-tech means of engaging many of the students might be to use *Classical Comics*, which are classic literature titles published in a comic book format at three different reading levels. The appearance alone may increase engagement of some students. Each title of *Classical Comics* is published in three versions of text—original text, "plain text," and "quick text." Original text, as the name implies, uses the exact words of the author. Plain text translates the words into modern English to facilitate understanding. Quick text uses modern English but reduces the amount of text presented, making it both faster and easier to read. Figure 4.6 illustrates the three different versions of text from *Romeo and Juliet*.

FIGURE 4.6 Romeo and Juliet from *Classical Comics* showing three levels of text

Original Text

Plain Text

Quick Text

Source: Reproduced with permission of Classical Comics

For students who are more engaged when they listen rather than read, the traditional version of *Romeo and Juliet* can be downloaded free of charge from a variety of sources and students can then use text-to-speech applications to listen to it on a computer. Or the text can be converted to MP3 format and transferred to students' MP3 players for a portable option. Another portable option is to borrow a recorded version from Learning Ally (formerly Recording for the Blind and Dyslexic). (See Chapter 3 for a discussion of text-to-speech and sources of alternate formats.)

To be able to engage in and understand *Romeo and Juliet*, other students may need to listen to a simplified version of the text in modern English. These students' needs and preferences can be accommodated as well. The Start-to-Finish series by Don Johnston, Inc. provides a version of this title with text written at an elementary reading level. The text can be listened to on a CD and viewed on a computer as it is read aloud. (See Chapter 3 for additional information on Start-to-Finish Books.)

UDL Editions by CAST is a free literature resource that teachers find engages and supports many of their students. It offers a free version of textHelp that allows students to hear the text that is displayed on the screen being read aloud and permits highlighting in a choice of colors. With the click of the mouse, the highlighted information can be displayed in a separate window in a color-sorted list that can be copied to the clipboard and pasted into another document and saved or printed. UDL Editions support reading comprehension with "Stop and Think" prompts, which offer varying levels of support—maximum, moderate, or minimal. Figure 4.7 shows the opening screen for *About Coyotes*.

A powerful technology tool for motivating and engaging students is the interactive whiteboard. In addition to enhancing the presentation of information and capturing teachers' notes electronically, interactive whiteboards offer novel ways for students to interact with curriculum content. Because the touch screen interface is so direct and simple to use, students can manipulate drawings, images, and text with ease. Math lessons in fourth grade are a good example. When teaching students how to calculate the area of a circle, square, rectangle, and parallelogram, a teacher can download SmartBoard-based lessons from the Smart Technologies Web site that provides relevant problems with premade, colorful shapes for several students

FIGURE 4.7 Sample UDL Editions by CAST showing the three levels of support and the textHelp toolbar that offers text-to-speech and highlighting

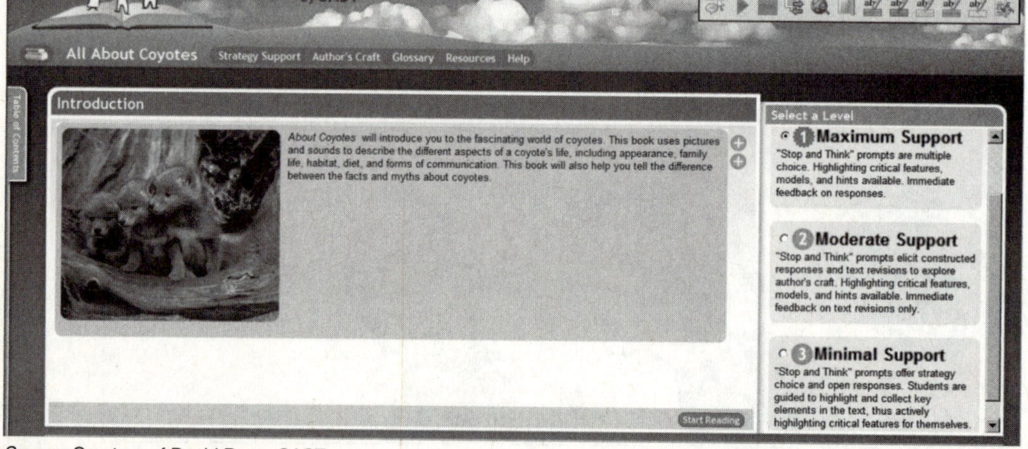

Source: Courtesy of David Rose, CAST.

FIGURE 4.8 An interactive lesson on using a protractor to measure angles presented on a SmartBoard.

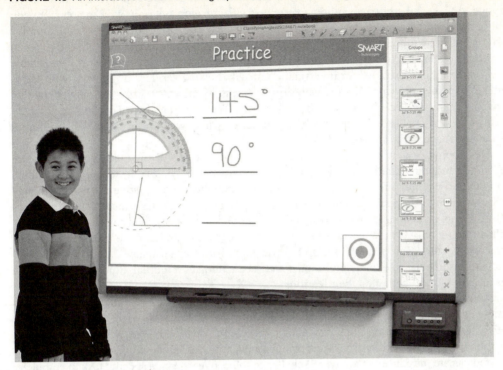

Source: Photo courtesy of Smart Technologies, Inc.

to solve at one time (Smart Technologies, 2010). An on-screen ruler can be moved around for taking measurements. Some activity templates include a check-your-answer feature. By providing clear, colorful images and enabling students to manipulate lesson materials, the interactive whiteboard engages students who are visual and/or kinesthetic learners and/or students who have attention issues.

Many Web 2.0 tools support the principle of multiple means of engagement. **Wikis** and **blogs** can provide an authentic purpose for reading, researching, and writing about topics. Web-based wikis are collaborative in nature; visitors to the wiki can add, delete, or change the content, and the wiki keeps track of everyone's contribution (TeachersFirst, 2010). The collaborative nature of wikis allows all students to take an active part in the development of content, with each student contributing according to his or her abilities. In the science class studying galaxies introduced earlier, students who are better writers and understand the concepts well may contribute the bulk of text-based information initially. Students who are more creative or artistic may develop diagrams or graphic images illustrating the different types of galaxies and supporting the concepts presented in the text. Other students may locate Web sites related to the content presented and provide links to those Web sites. The engagement of each student is promoted when students self-select the elements on which to work. Additionally, contributing to a collaborative project can be less threatening than needing to complete a project independently.

Teachers in K–12 schools can safeguard and control the content of students' wikis by taking advantage of the free services provided for K–12 classroom teachers by Wikispaces.

This service, Wikispaces for Educators, offers free wiki hosting along with the options to allow everyone to view and edit pages; allow everyone to view pages, but only wiki members to edit them; or allow only wiki members to view and edit pages. This last option makes collaborative efforts accessible within a safe and secure environment.

Educators are encouraged to investigate a variety of wiki hosting services as well as how to use wikis in the classroom. An investigation of wiki hosting services might start with viewing the Wikipedia entry for "Comparison of wiki farms." This entry discusses the general and technical features of Web farms, which are basically Web hosting sites. Teachers seeking information on ways to use wikis creatively and effectively may want to investigate the resources provided by TeachersFirst's Wiki Walk Through.

Developing content collaboratively in a wiki may not appeal to students who are more independent and individualistic. When students want to control what is presented to the public, express their own opinions or viewpoints, or demonstrate their own creative talents, blogs may be a better choice. Blogs are usually created and maintained by an individual. Blogging gives students the opportunity to create a document for a public audience, which can be more motivating than writing only for the teacher. In the social studies class studying the causes of the Civil War, students could, for example, set up blogs arguing for or against states' right to secede, or they could assume the role of an abolitionist and use the blog as a journal. Students can also use blogs as a tool for reflecting on their learning.

Another highly engaging activity that is based on the Internet is the inquiry-based activity known as **WebQuests.** WebQuests are teacher-designed activities in which most or all of the resources provided for students are available on the Web (Dodge, 2007). A WebQuest's components follow the same structure as a lesson plan: introduction, task, process, evaluation, and conclusion. Students are introduced to an overall challenge (objective), given a specific task to complete, provided with specific links to visit, told how their work will be assessed, and asked to reflect on their performance. The distinguishing feature of WebQuests is that students are presented with a specific challenge to solve using *preselected* Web links. Students are *not* sent on a virtual scavenger hunt where they spend unproductive time searching for information and can become "lost" on the Web or distracted from the task at hand. Rather, the teacher selects appropriate links that he or she knows will provide the information the students need to complete the WebQuest challenge.

Bernie Dodge (2007), the inventor of WebQuests, highlights their critical attributes:

A real WebQuest
- is wrapped around a doable and interesting task that is ideally a scaled-down version of things that adults do as citizens or workers.
- requires higher-level thinking, not simply summarizing. This includes synthesis, analysis, problem solving, creativity, and judgment.
- makes good use of the Web. A WebQuest that isn't based on real resources from the Web is probably just a traditional lesson in disguise. (Of course, books and other media can be used within a WebQuest, but if the Web isn't at the heart of the lesson, it's not a WebQuest.)
- isn't a research report or a step-by-step science or math procedure. Having learners simply distilling Web sites and making a presentation about them isn't enough.
- isn't just a series of Web-based experiences. Having learners go look at this page, then go play this game, then go here and turn your name into hieroglyphs doesn't require higher level thinking skills and so, by definition, isn't a WebQuest.

WebQuests are typically designed to be worked by small, cooperative groups of students, promoting collaboration and communication. Because WebQuests are highly customizable (the task, process, evaluation criteria, and resources are set and selected by teachers), they can be created, or modified, to provide appropriate levels of challenge for all students. The WebQuests Web site at San Diego State University maintains a searchable database of more than 2,500 WebQuests that teachers can download. The site also offers QuestGarden, a subscription-based add-on that provides step-by-step directions for creating WebQuests, as well as additional examples. The QuestGarden site supports attaching documents in Inspiration, Microsoft Word, and PowerPoint to WebQuests.

WEB ACCESSIBILITY

In the excitement about the promise of UDL and supportive Internet resources, it would be easy to overlook the fact that the content of some Web sites may be inaccessible to students. Chapters 7 and 8 discuss making the computer itself accessible to a broad range of users, including those with disabilities. This discussion focuses on the visual and auditory presentation of Web pages, the manner in which information is presented, and the abilities necessary for navigating and interacting with the content.

As with computer access, it is a good idea to consider features that are built into operating systems and applications before moving to specialized solutions. The most frequently used Internet browsers (applications used to access and display Web pages) offer features to make them easier to use by individuals with disabilities. Popular Internet browsers such as Internet Explorer, Firefox, Safari, Opera, and Google Chrome all allow users to override the text size and font specified by Web page designers to accommodate individual users' needs; this is especially helpful for students with visual impairments and some students with learning disabilities. Users of these browsers can also change the font color and background color to meet their needs and preferences. (Google Chrome users must install the free extensions Color Change and Chrome Theme in order to be able to do so.) Being able to select the background and font colors is beneficial for users who need high contrast due to visual impairments, those with color blindness, and those who are able to read more easily with particular text and background colors.

Each of the browsers also affords the ability to zoom in to take a closer look at elements on the screen or to zoom out to make the image smaller. This is another feature that makes Web pages accessible to students with visual impairments. A screen shot of Internet Explorer's zoom feature is found in Figure 4.9.

The World Wide Web has become a highly multimedia environment, which makes it difficult for students with visual impairments or blindness and students who are deaf or hard of hearing to get the full meaning of a Web page. Information presented visually such as pictures, videos, and charts, rather than in text, is inaccessible to students who cannot see the images. Web page designers can increase the accessibility of Web pages by providing written descriptions of images and transcripts for videos. This text-based information can be made accessible when it is read aloud by various applications.

Students who are deaf or hard of hearing are not able to access information that is conveyed through sound. With the proliferation of video clips on the Web, it is essential that teachers pay attention to the need for **captioning**. CaptionTube is a free utility that enables users to add closed captions to any YouTube video. After the video is imported into YouTube, the user plays the video and adds captions as needed. When all the captions have been added, the user

FIGURE 4.9 Zoom feature in Internet Explorer.

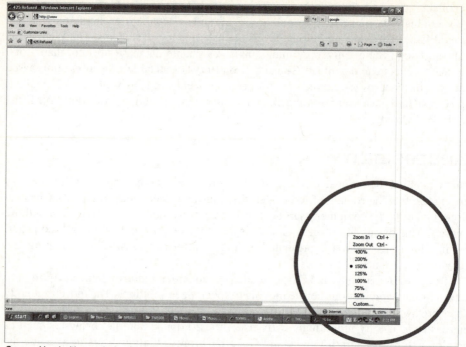

Source: Used with permission from the Center for Assistive Technology and Inclusive Education Studies (CATIES), The College of New Jersey.

exports the captions and then uploads them to his or her YouTube account. The videos remain hosted on YouTube, and CaptionTube creates a bookmark. CaptionTube then streams the videos from their original location and syncs them with the captions.

If a browser's options and preferences fail to make Web pages sufficiently accessible, assistive technology tools such as screen magnification applications and screen readers (see Chapter 8) can increase accessibility. Web pages can be enlarged to match users' preferred viewing sizes, and Web page elements such as pictures, text, navigation bars, and tables can be identified via speech output. However, despite utilization of these technology tools, barriers may continue to inhibit Web page access due to the underlying coding of the pages. If a Web page does not conform to recommended accessibility standards, even sophisticated

World Wide Web Consortium (W3C)

The W3C is an international consortium devoted to leading the World Wide Web to its full potential. To achieve its mission, one of the primary goals of W3C is to make the Web "available to all people, whatever their hardware, software, network infrastructure, native language, culture, geographical location, or physical or mental ability" (http://www.w3.org/Consortium/mission). The W3C develops Web standards and guidelines to assist Web site developers with the creation of accessible Web pages. Figure 4.10 provides a brief overview of the W3C guidelines.

FIGURE 4.10 W3C Guidelines for Web Accessibility.

The W3C publishes a handy reference titled *Quick Tips to Make Accessible Web sites* that offers the following suggestions for accessible Web design:

Images and animations. Use the **alt** attribute to describe the function of each visual.

Image maps. Use the client-side **map** element and text for hotspots.

Multimedia. Provide captioning and transcripts of audio, and descriptions of video.

Hypertext links. Use text that makes sense when read out of context. For example, avoid "click here."

Page organization. Use headings, lists, and consistent structure. Use **CSS** for layout and style where possible.

Graphs and charts. Summarize or use the **longdesc** attribute.

Scripts, applets, and plug ins. Provide alternative content in case active features are inaccessible or unsupported.

Frames. Use the **noframes** element and meaningful titles.

Tables. Make line-by-line reading sensible. Summarize.

Check your work. Validate. Use tools, checklist, and guidelines at http://www.w3.org/TR/WCAG

Adapted from *Quick Tips to Make Accessible Web sites,* by the W3C, 2001. Retrieved from http://www.w3.org/WAI/quicktips/

screen readers will not be able to make the page accessible. Teachers need to be careful in their selection of Web pages to use for instructional activities so that all students can access the information.

An issue related to Internet access is access to information on school district Web sites. Many school districts post important information such as report card distribution dates, parent-teacher conference dates, and emergency closings on their sites. Increasingly, teachers are making information such as homework assignments and test dates available to students and their families by posting information on their class Web sites. If school district Web sites do not conform to the W3C accessibility standards, students with disabilities or their parents or guardians with disabilities may be denied access to the information. We strongly recommend that teachers bring the Internet access needs of students with disabilities and the W3C standards to the attention of their district technology coordinators.

Educators who embrace UDL principles will find that incorporating technology into their teaching is a powerful way to enhance the learning of all of their students. They will discover that many students, with and without disabilities, will be able to participate and engage in learning activities and demonstrate their knowledge through technology in ways that were not evident before. By having access to a range of educational and instructional technology solutions in the classroom, many students will be able to access the regular education curriculum and complete assigned tasks. This may lead to a reduced need to provide specialized technology solutions designed to meet the specific needs of a particular student who has disabilities.

USER PROFILE

Using Yahoo! to Improve Student Achievement

Ms. M. teaches students with intellectual disabilities, ages 14 to 21. The students are enrolled in a high school transitional education program, and instruction focuses on functional academics, communication, social skills, and transition behaviors. Most of the general education students in the high school use the Internet to locate resources for school projects, find directions, communicate with one another, and communicate and socialize with peers in other communities throughout the world. Ms. M. realized that using the Internet independently and accessing Internet resources were important goals for her students as well, and she set out to teach them these functional, age-appropriate skills.

Ms. M. selected Yahoo! (http://www.yahoo.com) as their Internet portal because membership is free and its appearance and functionality are readily customiz-able using the My Yahoo! feature. She has taught her students to navigate to the Yahoo! Web site, log in, retrieve and send e-mail, explore specific Web sites, and engage in assigned Web-based activities. She uses selected Yahoo! services to teach her students specific skills, all of which increase their independence.

For example, the students practice their reading and writing skills, as well as their social and communication skills, when they use e-mail and Yahoo! Greetings to create and send e-cards to classmates, their teachers, and others (http://www.yahoo.americangreetings.com/index.pd). They use Yahoo! Calendar (http://calendar.yahoo.com/) as a time management tool and memory jogger. Students can set event e-mail reminders for upcoming appointments, tasks, special occasions, and assignment due dates, among other things. They use Yahoo! Maps (http://mapsyahoo.com/) to get directions, which provides a real-life example of the importance of learning your address, an opportunity to practice typing their address, and practice in map-reading skills. The students practice functional skills for leisure purposes as well when they use Yahoo! They can view movie trailers and look up show times and locations using the search engine.

Ms. M. evaluates her students' achievements through performance-based assessments, quizzes, direct observations, portfolios of students' e-mails, and students' self-assessments. Using Yahoo! has indeed moved her students closer to their transition goals, and 2 years after integrating Yahoo! into her students' educational programs, she is confident she made the right decision ■

Summary

- UDL is a flexible approach to curriculum design that reduces barriers in instruction by providing opportunities for students to learn in whatever way works best for them. The basic principles of UDL complement the instructional practices recommended by differentiated instruction.

- The three UDL principles state that in their classrooms teachers should provide (1) multiple means of representation, (2) multiple means of action and expression, and (3) multiple means of engagement.

- Multiple means of representation: In the UDL classroom, teachers present information in a variety of ways — not solely through "chalk and talk" — to facilitate learning for the diverse learners within their classrooms.

- Technologies that support the principle of multiple means of representation include electronic text, text-to-speech, graphics, video presentations, interactive whiteboards, and Web page readers.

- Multiple means of action and expression: In the UDL classroom teachers recognize that there are many ways for students to demonstrate learning besides the traditional writing assignment and they provide alternative means of assessing student knowledge.

- Technologies that support the principle of multiple means of action and expression include the use of word processing, graphic organizing, text-to-speech, and word prediction applications to provide writing supports; the use of search engines to locate appropriate images and/or videos combined with the use of a presentation application such as PowerPoint or Inspiration's Presentation Manager for the creation of a multimedia presentation; and the use of an online poster site such as Glogster to create an electronic poster.

- Multiple means of engagement: Teachers in a UDL classroom know that students are more attentive and motivated to learn when they are interested and/or invested in an activity or topic, and using the latest technology is an effective way of engaging them in learning.

- Technologies that support the principle of multiple means of engagement include interactive whiteboards, wikis, blogs, and WebQuests.

- For students to benefit from Web-based activities, teachers must make sure the Web sites they use, including their schools' Web sites, are accessible to students with disabilities.

- Popular Internet browsers offer features that make the browsers easier to use by individuals with disabilities.

- World Wide Web Consortium (W3C) publishes standards and guidelines to assist Web site developers with the creation of accessible Web pages.

Web Resources

Overviews of Universal Design for Learning
National Center on Universal Design for Learning
http://www.udlcenter.org/aboutudl/udlguidelines

Differentiated Instruction and Implications for UDL Implementation
by T. Hall, N. Strangman, and A. Meyer
http://www.cast.org/publications/ncac/ncac_diffinstructudl.html

Multiple Means of Representation
Amazing Space
http://amazing-space.stsci.edu/

Creating Classrooms for Everyone: How Interactive Whiteboards Support Universal Design for Learning
http://bcudl.pbworks.com/f/interactivewhiteboardsanduniversaldesignforlearningjan20.pdf
Smart Technologies Educator Resources
http://www.education.smarttech.com/ste/en-US/Ed+Resource/
ActivClassroom by Promethean
http://www.prometheanplanet.com/en/
Hulu
http://www.hulu.com/
Discovery Education Streaming
http://streaming.discoveryeducation.com/
Readability
http://lab.arc90.com/experiments/readability/

Multiple Means of Action and Expression
Inspiration's Presentation Manager
http://www.inspiration.com
Glogster EDU
http://Edu.glogster.com
netTrekker
http://www.nettrekker.com/us/product-information/main

Multiple Means of Engagement
Classical Comics
http://classicalcomics.com/
UDL Editions by CAST
http://udleditions.cast.org/
TeachersFirst Wiki Walk-Through
http://www.teachersfirst.com/content/wiki/
Wiki Spaces for Educators
http://www.wikispaces.com/site/for/teachers
Tutorials on creating WebQuests and a searchable database of WebQuests created by others
http://webquest.sdsu.edu/
WebQuest Design Process
http://webquest.sdsu.edu/designsteps/index.html

Web Accessibility
Accessibility in Internet Explorer 8
http://www.microsoft.com/enable/products/ie8/default.aspx
Accessibility Features in Firefox
http://www.mozilla.org/access/features
CaptionTube
http://captiontube.appspot.com/
World Wide Web Consortium (W3C)
http://www.w3.org/
Examples of Inaccessible Web Design
http://www.c-net.us/inaccessible-website-examples

Suggested Activities

1. *Investigate lesson plans and activities available for an interactive whiteboard.* Go to one of the following Web sites:
Promethean: http://www.prometheanplanet.com/en/resources/
SmartBoard: http://exchange.smarttech.com
StarBoard: http://resourcecenter.hitachi-software.de/us
Pick a grade level and content area and find an appropriate whiteboard activity. Describe how this resource will allow you to meet the needs of different learners.

2. *Explore Readability.* Go to http://lab.arc90.com/experiments/readability. Follow the instructions to install Readability in your Web browser. Explore how different settings affect the appearance of Web pages. How could this help your students?

3. *Create an electronic poster in Glogster EDU Basic.* Go to http://edu.glogster.com. Browse through sample posters to see the possibilities, then click on Try to Create Yours, and experience the process of making one yourself. Discuss how your students might respond to this method of expression.

4. *Check out UDL Editions.* Go to http://UDLeditions.cast.org. Choose a title and explore the different ways of reading it. How could this electronic resource help your students?

5. *Evaluate WebQuests.* Bernie Dodge has developed a WebQuest to introduce teachers to this instructional model. Go to http://webquest.org/index-resources.php and select the A WebQuest about WebQuests. In a small group, evaluate each WebQuest listed according to the roles described in the posted instructions. Discuss criteria for a good WebQuest based on your evaluation.

6. *Use the Microsoft Word 2010 Accessibility Checker.* Word 2010 includes a new accessibility checker that allows you to check for accessibility problems. To run the accessibility checker, select File → Info → Check for Issues → Check Accessibility. For more information about document accessibility, go to http://webaim.org/techniques/word

7. *Learn how to add an alternative tag ("alt tag") to an image in Microsoft Word.* Go to http://webaim.org/techniques/word/#alttext and follow the instructions to add an "alt tag" to an image.

References

Dodge, B. (2007). *Creating WebQuests*. Retrieved July 31, 2010, from http://webquest.org/index-create.php

Hall, T., Strangman, N., & Meyer, A. (2009). *Differentiated instruction and implications for UDL implementation*. Retrieved July 28, 2010, from http://www.cast.org/publications/ncac/ncac_diffinstructudl.html

Meyer, A., & Rose, D. H. (1998). *Learning to read in the computer age* [Electronic version]. Retrieved July 28, 2010, from http://www.cast.org/publications/books/ltr/index.html

National Center on Universal Design for Learning. (2010). *About UDL: Learn the basics.* Retrieved July 30, 2010, from http://www.udlcenter.org/aboutudl/udlguidelines

Prensky, M. (2001). Digital natives, digital immigrants part 1. *On the Horizon, 9*(5). Retrieved July 28, 2010, from http://www.marcprensky.com/writing/Prensky%20-%20Digital%20Natives,%20Digital%20Immigrants%20-%20Part1.pdf

SMART Technologies. (2010). *Notebook lesson activities, grades 4–6, math.* Retrieved August

1, 2010, from http://www.education.smarttech.
com/ste/en-US/Ed+Resource/Lesson+activities/
Notebook+Activities

Somekh, B., Haldane, M., Jones, K., Lewin, C.,
Steadman, S., Scrimshaw, P., et al. (2007).
Evaluation of the primary schools whiteboard
expansion project—Summary report. Education
& Social Research Institute: Manchester

Metropolitan University. Retrieved July 29,
2010, from http://partners.becta.org.uk/upload-
dir/downloads/page_documents/research/white-
boards_expansion.pdf

TeachersFirst. (2010). *Wiki Walk-Through.*
Retrieved July 31, 2010, from http://www.
teachersfirst.com/content/wiki/

5 | COMPUTERS AND THE INTERNET TO TEACH MATH

Focus Questions

1. Why are good educational applications effective teaching tools for students who have disabilities?
2. What features of educational applications are likely to accommodate individual preferences and meet the needs of students with a wide variety of disabilities?
3. What key questions should be considered when selecting educational applications to meet students' goals and objectives?
4. What kinds of educational applications can be used to address automaticity/math fact fluency?
5. What kinds of technology tools can be used to address visual-spatial or motor control difficulties?
6. What kinds of educational applications can be used to teach math concepts, math skills, and problem solving?
7. What kinds of low-tech and mid-tech adaptations can assist students with disabilities in completing math assignments?

INTRODUCTION

Computers have become as commonplace in the classroom as pencils and notebooks, and their presence has expanded the options available to teachers of students with disabilities. In Chapter 2, the computer was discussed as a tool for enhancing writing; Chapter 3 discussed the computer as a tool for reading; this chapter explores how using computer technology can enhance instruction in mathematics for students with disabilities. The term *instruction* refers to teaching—reinforcing or assessing students' abilities to understand concepts or demonstrate skills. The emphasis of this chapter is using the classroom computer as a tool to teach math concepts to students who have disabilities. Many textbooks are devoted entirely to using instructional technology or educational technology in classrooms, and this chapter is not intended as a substitute. Rather, it explores specific technologies that can facilitate learning math, increase engagement and participation, and build independence for students with disabilities. The computer is an extremely flexible tool that can enhance all students' learning. It can provide students at all levels with myriad meaningful learning experiences.

ADDRESSING THE NEEDS OF STUDENTS WITH DISABILITIES

Students with disabilities who need extended practice and repetition especially can benefit from using the computer. Educational applications are particularly promising for helping these students master needed skills because they can be customized to meet individual needs, provide sufficient repetition, and systematically present materials (Wehmeyer, Smith, Palmer, & Davies, 2004). Well-constructed educational applications "allow teachers to provide students with repeated practice opportunities, an unlimited number and variety of examples, and focused individual feedback" (Ayres & Langone, 2005).

Students who have difficulty with memory, auditory processing, visual perception, language, internal motivation, or attention often find it challenging to attend to a task that is without stimulation (Carroll, 1993, as cited in Wehmeyer et al., 2004, and Hickson, Blackman, & Reis, 1995). It is therefore essential to engage such students in interesting and motivating ways. Computer use in the classroom can provide students with external motivation and keep them engaged (Brown, Miller, & Robinson, 2003). Educational applications can present information in the ways in which students learn best, and teachers can select applications that have features that match students' individual needs.

Students with disabilities can benefit from computer use in the classroom; however, there are significant issues that need to be considered for successful implementation. The term **educational applications** is used in the ensuing discussion to encompass both software programs and interactive Web-based activities. The following section identifies specific features of educational applications that promote learning in students with disabilities, criteria for selecting educational applications, and various technology tools that address the specific challenges students with disabilities encounter with learning mathematics.

DESIRABLE FEATURES OF EDUCATIONAL APPLICATIONS

Although the needs of each student are unique, there are general characteristics of educational applications that assist a broad spectrum of students. The work of Wehmeyer et al. (2004) identifies features that are likely to accommodate individual preferences as well as meet the needs of students with a wide variety of disabilities. The following features are recommended:

- Simplified screens and instructions
- Consistent placement of menus and control features
- Graphics along with text to support nonreaders and early readers
- Audio output , e.g., spoken instructions and auditory feedback
- Accessibility by a variety of methods
- Ability to set pace and level of difficulty
- Appropriate and unambiguous feedback
- Easy error correction

Simplified screens and instructions are beneficial for a variety of reasons. When the visual presentation is clear and uncluttered, students can easily discern the important elements and identify where they should focus their attention. Students are not distracted or confused by graphics and animations that are not integral to their learning. Simplified instructions allow students who struggle with receptive language, following multiple-step directions, or other learning issues to understand what needs to be done for successful interaction with the educational application.

Consistent placement of menus and control features makes it easier for students to know which menu to access or where to point and click to engage appropriately with the learning activity. This reduces the complexity of working with activities so students are able to devote their energy and concentration to the content of the activity, increasing the potential for learning.

Graphics provided along with text enable nonreaders and early readers to engage successfully with computer-based learning activities. The picture cues can provide the scaffolding needed by struggling readers. The graphics give students an opportunity to access important content despite difficulty reading directions or text-based navigation controls.

Audio output provided by educational applications allows students who are struggling or nonreaders as well as students who are strong auditory learners to access content and benefit from spoken instructions and frequent, relevant feedback. Auditory output can be understood more easily because it bypasses reading weaknesses and addresses the students' strengths. Students can spend their energy and cognitive resources on learning concepts, adjusting their strategies, and incorporating feedback provided as they continue to interact with the applications.

When educational applications are *accessible by a variety of methods* (i.e., by either the keyboard or the mouse or with alternate computer access methods [see Chapter 8]), they can be used effectively by a greater number of students. Those students who can easily use both a mouse and a keyboard can access most educational applications. However, when *only* the mouse or *only* the keyboard can be used, students with disabilities may find their access restricted or precluded altogether.

Pace can be considered as the speed at which students are expected to respond to or initiate interaction. Students who find it difficult to execute a quick response benefit from adjustable response rates; these can provide sufficient time for them to demonstrate mastery of the content, rather than measuring their speed of response. Pace can also be considered as the speed of progression from one concept to another or from one level of difficulty to another. Students who need extended practice benefit from being able to control the speed at which the program advances. This enables them to develop, practice, and master the skills associated with one concept or at one difficulty level before moving on. Being able to set the level of difficulty allows students to enter educational applications at the most appropriate level and makes the activities usable by students at different levels. When educational applications allow the user to control both the pace and the level of difficulty, they are accessible to a more diverse range of students.

Appropriate and unambiguous feedback is an important feature of educational applications for all students, but it is especially important for students with special needs. When feedback is provided to inform students whether an answer is right or wrong (e.g., in an educational application that provides practice on math facts), it is imperative that the feedback be delivered clearly and in a manner that students will understand. For students who have difficulty reading or those who are nonreaders, auditory feedback or graphic feedback—provided separately or combined with print-based feedback—are good choices. For example, when a student enters the correct answer, appropriate feedback would be auditory feedback saying, "That's correct. You're on a roll," displaying a picture of "thumbs up," or doing either one while displaying the text "Correct. $3 + 4 = 7$." When the feedback is meant to inform students that their answer is incorrect, it is important that it be done clearly, but with kindness and sensitivity. Simply displaying or speaking the message "Wrong" delivers feedback that may be perceived as harsh. It may diminish students' interest and motivation over time.

Another consideration for appropriate feedback is that the feedback for correct answers should always be more stimulating and rewarding than the feedback for incorrect answers. If not, it can lead to confusion and misunderstanding. Students may not realize that an enhanced response is due to making an error. Additionally, they may intentionally enter wrong answers because it is more interesting and entertaining to do so.

Feedback that indicates only that an answer is correct or incorrect is not as meaningful as explanatory feedback, which provides information that will help students to be successful on future items. Explanatory feedback is designed to help students understand why an answer is incorrect and why an alternate answer is correct. This type of feedback is more likely to lead to transfer of knowledge to novel situations (Moreno, 2004).

Easy error correction: The nature of an application's error correction can be a decisive factor in a student's success or failure. For myriad reasons, students may wish to change their initial input. When input is accepted immediately, students have no opportunity to change answers or correct mistakes. Additionally, if error correction is overly burdensome (e.g., time consuming or confusing), students with disabilities may not be able to make changes efficiently or effectively. This may create the mistaken impression that a student does not understand or has not mastered certain concepts or content.

Understanding the implications of the various features in educational applications is a first step for teachers; the next crucial step becomes selecting the features that are best suited to students' needs. Although there are many factors to consider when selecting educational applications for particular students, the primary considerations should be that the learning activities naturally fit instructional goals or objectives and that they meet the interests of the students. Educational applications should not be a forced fit; it is imperative to match them to the students and not vice versa. Teachers should employ a user-centered approach when selecting educational applications, matching them to the students' IEP goals to keep students on target with the curriculum.

Key questions to consider when selecting educational applications to help meet students' goals and objectives include the following:

- What is the intended outcome of the use of the educational application? For example, is it meant to strengthen math skills in problem solving or is it meant to build speed and accuracy with basic math facts?
- Is the educational applications likely to fulfill its stated purpose? For example, if the stated purpose of the activity is to build problem-solving skills, does it provide the explanatory feedback needed to do so or simply assess whether or not problems are solved correctly?
- Can the educational applications be used as an alternative to traditional classroom activities to enhance students' participation? For example, will students learn as effectively using online math manipulatives [LB3]as they would using traditional manipulatives?

Teachers should select educational applications with specific outcomes in mind. Some educational applications support student learning in several areas of math and at several levels of achievement. Some focus on a specific math topic, only one aspect of a topic, or on only one achievement level. If there is a cost associated with the educational application (e.g., purchase price or subscription fee), then teachers must be able to justify the intended outcomes for using the educational application prior to requesting that funds be expended. This will increase the likelihood that the educational application will meet the needs of the students and decrease the chances that it was acquired simply because it was affordable or had an attractive visual display.

Furthermore, students' interests must be considered. If the educational application matches students' interests, they will be more apt to dedicate their attention to it. When students find learning activities meaningful and interesting, including those that are computer-based, they spend more time on task and are more likely to meet learning objectives.

Given the previous discussion about how to select educational applications and the numerous options available, it may seem like a daunting task to make an appropriate selection. However, it need not be so. Figure 5.1 offers an easy, user-friendly checklist for guiding the evaluation of educational applications. It represents a synthesis of the previous discussion and emphasizes the match between students' individual needs and specific features of educational applications. It can be used as a quick tool for evaluating the appropriateness of any educational application.

FIGURE 5.1 Quick Guide for Selecting Educational Applications.

What is the goal or purpose of computer use?

❑ Providing an alternative means of completing schoolwork, participating in classroom activities, or demonstrating knowledge

❑ Teaching basic concepts and academic skills

❑ Providing practice with basic concepts or academic skills

❑ Using as a tool for writing (mechanics), prewriting, and composition

❑ Providing opportunities to think critically and solve problems

❑ Finding information on the Internet or other reference tools

❑ Using for play, leisure, or for exploring interests

❑ Self-expressing or making choices

❑ Practicing basic concepts (such as colors, shapes, and classification)

❑ Encouraging emergent literacy (developing language, developing an interest in written language, etc.)

❑ Other _____

Content of the educational application

❑ Does it match the goal or purpose of computer use?

❑ Does it match the students' interests?

Matching student needs

❑ Young children and nonreaders or struggling readers benefit from speech output (spoken instructions).

❑ Children with attention difficulties need software whose feedback, reinforcement, and visual presentation are not distracting.

❑ Children with perceptual problems need uncluttered screens and clear, easily readable fonts.

❑ Children with visual impairments often need speech output.

❑ Children with physical and/or cognitive disabilities need programs in which speed of response or input is not essential.

Flexibility of educational application

❑ Can the visual display be customized for student's individual needs?

❑ Can sound or music be turned off?

❑ Can levels be selected or modified?

❑ Can specific content be selected?

❑ Can speed and reaction time be modified?

Ease of use: Should be both easy to use and simple to customize.

Source: Adapted from "Content Software Makes the Grade," by D. A. Newton, A. G. Dell, and A. M. Disdier, 1998, *Exceptional Parent, 20(12).* Adapted with permission.

We recommend strongly that teachers try educational applications before adopting them. Many vendors offer free trials for 15 days or 30 days, and trial versions are often fully functioning versions of the educational application (they are time limited, meaning they will cease to work after a certain period or will no longer be accessible on the Web). Some trial versions may lack some of the functions available in purchased versions; users may not be able to save, print, or enable options such as record keeping. Many Web-based applications are available for free; however, some Web sites require users to pay subscription fees. When available, trial versions of Web-based applications that require a subscription fee are usually accessed by completing a registration process at the vendor's Web site. Teachers should take advantage of demo versions, free trials, and free subscription offers because the best way to determine whether educational applications are appropriate is to try them out firsthand.

SELECTING EDUCATIONAL APPLICATIONS: FOCUS ON MATH

Achieving fluency and automaticity with important information; visual-spatial organization (e.g., aligning digits for computation); understanding math concepts such as number sense, time, measurement, and money; and solving word problems are all difficult for students with math disabilities to master. Technology solutions that address these problem areas will be discussed in the following section. Not all of the features presented earlier will be found in all of the technology resources provided; teachers must use their professional judgment to determine which features are essential for each individual student. Exemplars of educational applications that offer features that are especially supportive of students with disabilities are presented for each common problem area, along with general educational applications that can also be beneficial for students with disabilities.

Automaticity and Fluency

Foundations for Success: The Final Report of the National Mathematics Advisory Council (2008) defines *automaticity* of basic skills as "the fast, accurate, and effortless processing of content information" (p. 30). Automaticity is also referred to as *math fact fluency* (National Council of Teachers of Mathematics, 2000). Computational fluency—being able to efficiently and accurately carry out procedures to solve computation problems—relies heavily on automaticity with basic number facts. Figure 5.2 illustrates what is meant by math fact fluency and computational fluency.

Students are expected to achieve computational fluency with addition and subtraction of whole numbers by the end of third grade, which requires automaticity with basic addition and subtraction facts by that time. By the end of fifth grade, students are expected to achieve computational fluency with multiplication and division of whole numbers, which requires automaticity with basic multiplication and division facts. Both automaticity and computational fluency with whole numbers, fractions, decimals, and percentages, which are the critical foundational elements for success with more advanced math, are expected by the end of seventh grade (National Panel, 2008).

Meeting these benchmarks is difficult for many students. The National Mathematics Advisory Panel (2008) found that despite the critical role that automaticity plays in math success, "Few curricula in the United States provide sufficient practice to ensure fast and efficient solving of basic fact combinations and execution of the standard algorithms" (p. 26). Meeting these benchmarks is

FIGURE 5.2 Definitions of math fact fluency and computational fluency.

The National Council of Teachers of Mathematics (NCTM) Principle and Standards of School Mathematics (2000) indicate that students should develop both math fact fluency and computational fluency.

Math fact fluency means being able to quickly and accurately recall the answers to problems such as the following:

$$3 + 4 = \quad 12 - 3 = \quad 4 \times 5 = \quad 12 \div 4 =$$

Computational fluency refers to having efficient and accurate methods for computing that are based on well-understood properties and number relationships. This means a student is able to quickly and correctly solve problems such as the following. Math fact fluency supports computational fluency.

$$\begin{array}{r} 71{,}623 \\ -46{,}795 \end{array} \qquad \begin{array}{r} 908 \\ \times\,320 \end{array} \qquad 68\overline{)5372}$$

even more problematic for students with disabilities who need even more instruction, practice, and reinforcement than their typical peers; have difficulty remembering as many facts as their typical peers; fail to transfer the math facts to long-term memory; and have difficulty retrieving quickly those math facts that have been transferred (Geary, 1999; Hasselbring, Lott, & Zydney, n.d.).

Considering that students who fail to develop math fact fluency are at a disadvantage when it comes to developing computational fluency and understanding higher order mathematics concepts (Hasselbring et al., n.d.), the panel's (2008) finding that some students with math disabilities will never become completely fluent is equally important.

Low- and mid-tech tools such as addition and multiplication charts and calculators help compensate for a lack of automaticity. Compensation is essential because automaticity "frees up working memory for more complex aspects of problem solving (National Math Advisory Panel, 2008, p. 30). Assistive technology, which frees students from trying to figure out basic math facts, enables them to devote their cognitive resources to learning higher order content.

Murray, Silver-Paculla, and Helsel (2007) provide guidance regarding when to allow students to use calculators. Their decision-making process, which is based on the question "What is the primary purpose of the activity?," is especially appropriate for students with disabilities. If the purpose is to practice computational skills, then, obviously, the use of calculators is not indicated. If the purpose of the activity is problem solving, exploring number patterns, working with data, or other such higher-order activities, then the use of calculators is indicated.

TECHNOLOGY-BASED ACTIVITIES THAT ADDRESS AUTOMATICITY/MATH FACT FLUENCY. This section focuses on educational applications that address automaticity because of the key role that automaticity plays in achieving math success. Educational applications that promote success with other facets of mathematics, including computational fluency, are addressed in a subsequent section titled Math Concepts, Skills, and Problem Solving.

Math focused educational applications provide opportunities for targeted practice to foster development of math fact fluency. Students' practice time is well spent when activities afford frequent encounters with the facts they have not yet mastered. Time on task and attention can be increased when the practice is presented in engaging and motivating activities. Following is a sampling of technology resources that can help build automaticity.

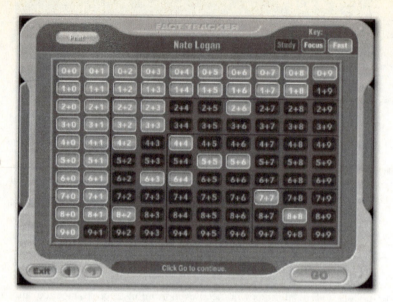

FIGURE 5.3a FASTT Math. Fact grid screen for a typical math-delayed student.

FIGURE 5.3b FASTT Math customizable settings.

	Default Setting	Additional Options		Reasons to Change the Setting
Problem Format	Horizontal	Vertical	Mixed	Give students practice viewing problems in another format.
Problems per Session	70	60	50	If a student has trouble completing sessions quickly or is struggling and becoming frustrated before finishing the session.
Response Time Limit (in seconds)	1.25	1.50	1.75	Modify for students who consistently have trouble mastering facts in less than 3 or 4 sessions.
Language	English	Spanish		ELL support for Spanish speakers.
Program Audio	On	Off		Turn off audio if it becomes distracting to students. Students can also turn sound off or on from within the software.
Narration Support	Off	On		Turn on to enable students to hear problems read aloud as they are presented.
Text Contrast	Regular	High Contrast		Provides high contrast for screen text for visually impaired students.

Source: Reprinted with permission from Tom Snyder Productions.

FASTT Math (Fluency and Automaticity through Systematic Teaching with Technology; Tom Snyder)is a math intervention program that helps students acquire math fact fluency (Figure 5.3a). The program assesses students' command of basic facts by measuring response time and then generates customized activities based on the results. Students progress through the customized series of activities to strengthen memorization of facts and eliminate the need to rely on counting strategies to solve problems. Teachers can monitor students' progress via reports that the program can generate at the student, class, grade, and school levels. Figure 5.3b shows how teachers can customize FASTT Math's options and explains the typical reasons for changing the settings.

Timez Attack (Big Brainz) focuses solely on multiplication facts, teaching the 2 to 12 times tables. Timez Attack, produced by the team that created Sony Playstation games, engages students in a high-tech video game environment featuring high-quality graphics. A free Base Version is available for download, and a Full Version can be purchased. Both versions are fully functional; however, the Full Version includes additional game environments such as Machine World and Lava World that offer variety and may make the program more appealing over time.

The ArithmAttack can be played online or downloaded free to your computer and played off-line with Microsoft Internet Explorer. With ArithmAttack, students can practice basic addition, subtraction, multiplication, and division facts. Customized problem sets are easily generated by setting the highest and lowest numbers to use so students' practice can be targeted to their particular areas of need.

Arcademic Skill Builder math games are designed to help develop automaticity in addition, subtraction, multiplication, division, integers, fractions, and ratios. There are multiplayer (one to four players) and single-user games; all are played online and feature several customizable features. For all games, users can set custom number ranges to provide targeted practice on specific areas of need. Multiplayer games can be public or private, with private games requiring players to enter a password in order to play. Single-user games allow users a measure of control over the speed of the game—slow, normal, fast. All games can be played by clicking on answers with the mouse; typing the number of the button that displays the correct answer (three or four buttons depending on the game); or using the left, right, and up arrow keys.

A limited number of keys are required to control the games so they easily could become accessible to students who are unable to use the standard keyboard or mouse. An alternate keyboard (e.g., IntelliKeys), alternate mouse (e.g., trackball or joystick), a scanning array for single switch use, or a programmable switch interface that accommodates up to four switches can make these games accessible for students with physical disabilities. (See Chapter 8 for information on these alternate methods of computer access.)

Visual-Spatial or Motor Control Difficulties

Students with disabilities may experience difficulty with writing numbers, aligning digits in computation problems, and creating visual representations (e.g., shapes or angles) for a number of reasons. Often the difficulties have their roots in fine motor control or visual spatial issues. Regardless of the cause, the manifestation of the problem is often written work that is hard to read or illegible; problems to be computed that have digits written in the wrong place-value position; or geometric figures that vary slightly from the accepted representation to totally unrecognizable. Depending upon the degree to which students exhibit these difficulties, it may be difficult or impossible for them to demonstrate their level of achievement or mastery of concepts.

Some students with motor control or visual-spatial issues may not be able to understand and interpret their own written work. When these students are required to copy math problems from a book, whiteboard, or blackboard the result may be handwritten problems that they themselves cannot read or problems that have been copied with digits in the wrong place value position. Therefore, even when students may have achieved automaticity with number facts they may not be able to arrive at a correct final answer.

As students progress in math, the type and complexity of their math writing increases significantly. They must solve problems with numbers of greater value, which requires writing and aligning longer strings of numbers. They must write numbers as fractions, decimals, and percents and draw and label lines, angles, and two- and three-dimensional figures. To solve advanced math equations students need to be able to write combinations of letters, symbols, and numbers, including subscripts and superscripts. For students with visual-spatial difficulties these types of notations can present huge obstacles to being successful in math.

EDUCATIONAL APPLICATIONS THAT ADDRESS VISUAL-SPATIAL AND MOTOR CONTROL DIFFICULTIES.   Educational applications that minimize the handwriting demands of math work are especially helpful for students with visual-spatial difficulties. Several of these math applications are presented next.

MathPad (Cambium Learning) is a talking math worksheet program that enables students to perform arithmetic computations with whole numbers on the computer in much the same way they would using pencil and paper. Students with fine motor difficulties can demonstrate their skill simply by using the keyboard or clicking the mouse, and students with severe disabilities can utilize MathPad's scanning feature (see Chapter 8 for discussion of scanning for computer access). MathPad displays just one problem at a time, and the digits that are supposed to be in each place (e.g., ones' place, tens' place, hundreds' place) are properly aligned. Customizable speech output can help students with visual impairments and students who have reading problems; it may also increase the attention of students who are easily distracted. A feature allows students to easily show regrouping (formerly referred to as borrowing or carrying) when performing calculations so teachers can target the specific levels of addition, subtraction, multiplication, or division at which students need practice (see Figure 5.4). Teacher-generated problem sets can be

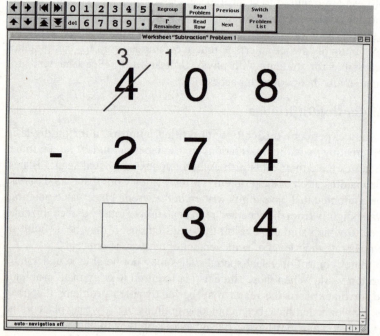

FIGURE 5.4 MathPad's regrouping feature.

Source: Imagery provided courtesy of Cambium Learning Technologies

solved directly on the computer and students can receive immediate feedback. When assigned problem sets are completed and printed, all of the steps of the problem will appear on the printout, not just the answers. Teachers can then review the work and identify where in the computation process any mistakes are being made, just as they would for students completing work with pencil and paper. (Problem sets can also be printed out as worksheets for students who are able to solve the problems in the traditional pencil-and-paper mode; the teacher must then provide all feedback.) MathPad is beneficial for students who have difficulty working with pencil and paper due to poor fine motor skills, students who need speech output, students who have difficulty setting up problems so digits are aligned properly, students who require immediate feedback, and students who are more motivated and engaged in academic tasks when using the computer.

MathPad Plus (Cambium Learning) extends all of the features of MathPad to arithmetic computations with fractions and decimals (Figure 5.5). It provides several additional features to support student success. Students have the option of viewing the problems represented as pie charts, fraction bars, or decimal grids; these representations can increase the students' understanding, especially those who are visual learners. Students' understanding of fractional relations may be enhanced by being able to manipulate problems directly on the screen. This is an especially important feature for students who are unable to handle the manipulatives that are often used in math instruction.

FIGURE 5.5 MathPad Plus showing a fractions problem using pie charts.

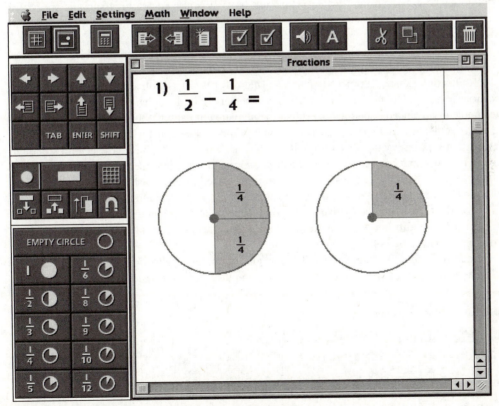

Source: Imagery provided courtesy of Cambium Learning Technologies

Virtual Pencil (VP) Arithmetic (Henter Math) is an educational application designed for students who are, in the words of the publisher, "pencil impaired" (i.e., unable to operate a pencil effectively). Students who are pencil impaired could include those who are blind or have motor impairments or learning disabilities that interfere with writing. VP Arithmetic makes addition, subtraction, multiplication, and division with whole numbers, fractions, and decimals accessible to students with disabilities. Similar to MathPad, VP Arithmetic allows students to solve problems in much the same way they would using pencil and paper, including performing and showing intermediate steps. The application offers speech feedback in a manner that makes it functional for students who are blind. The extensive speech feedback reads problems and provides enough information so students who cannot see the problem can understand the position of digits and can navigate to where they need to be. VP Arithmetic also features a tutorial mode in which "the tutor" informs the student as to where he or she is in the problem, what steps need to be done to solve it, and if desired the answer. In test mode, teachers can password-protect files, disable the tutorial features, and ensure that the work produced demonstrates students' knowledge.

Virtual Pencil (VP) Algebra extends most of the features of VP Arithmetic so students with disabilities can solve algebraic equations. VP Algebra reads equations using correct math terminology such as *square root of, quantity squared*, and *exponent*. Speech feedback allows students to navigate to any point in the equation and provides the information needed to understand their position within the equation. Students can manipulate complicated equations and can copy and paste portions to be solved separately and then reinsert them into the original equation. Password-protecting VP Algebra files prevents them from being altered by students.

Number Navigator (Oats Project) does not have specialized features such as speech or scanning, but for those who need a simple "math processor" (an application for creating mathematical expressions or equations) to enter and solve basic math problems on the computer, this free program may be a good solution. Colors, fonts, and font sizes are customizable.

Microsoft Word, the popular word processing program, can also be used as a math processor. Microsoft Equation Editor, an object available in Microsoft Word as well as other Microsoft Office applications, enables students who have difficulty with handwriting but have good mouse control to create simple or advanced equations in correct mathematical notation. Numerous symbols are provided and are entered via a mouse click. (Equation Editor is included in the Microsoft Office bundle, but it must be purposefully installed or it will not show up when Insert Object is selected.) Although Microsoft Equation can be used to create equations, completing the intermediate steps used to solve them may be a cumbersome task, especially at more advanced levels. To show their work, students need to use Drawing toolbar items such as the line tool and text box (Figure 5.6 and Figure 5.7).

For students in advanced math classes, MathType (Design Science) may be a better choice. MathType offers additional symbols to create a wider variety of equations and the ability to enhance equations using color coding.

Scientific Notebook (MacKichan Software) is a high-end application that is designed to do more than allow users to write equations on the computer; it is designed for *solving* equations.

FIGURE 5.6 Microsoft Equation toolbar.

Source: Microsoft product screen shot reprinted with permission from Microsoft Corporation.

FIGURE 5.7 Mathematical expressions and equations typed in Microsoft Word using the Microsoft Equation toolbar.

$$\frac{1}{2} + \frac{3}{4} = 1\frac{1}{4} \quad \sqrt{4} \quad \frac{3}{10} \div \frac{2}{15} = \frac{1}{15}$$

This program provides students who have disabilities the opportunity to participate in advanced math classes. Students can work with calculus, vector calculus, transformations, and matrices, among other topics.

Meanders' Annotator provides a solution to handwriting problems in geometry. It is also an add-on tool that works in Microsoft Office. When geometry problems are presented in Microsoft Word, Meander's Annotator enables students to draw on diagrams, record legible markings such as congruent angles and parallel lines on geometric figures, and plot lines on XY graphs.

Math Input Panel in Windows 7

In previous version of Windows, math notes could be written with a tablet PC and stylus, but they could not be manipulated or read aloud because they were stored as an image file. Windows 7 provides a new Math Input Panel that allows math equations to be handwritten into a program and then converted to a text-based math equation.

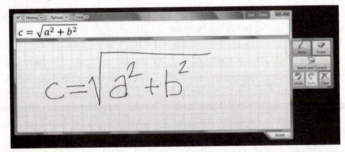

Math equations are written into the Math Input Panel using the tablet and stylus setup as before. When the student is ready to insert it into Microsoft Word, the equation will be recognized as MathML or Mathematical Markup Language. MathML is an application that is used on many Web pages and in high-end math applications such as Math Type and Scientific Notebook because it maintains the structure of equations.

When converting to MathML, the program maintains the accuracy of both the visual presentation of the equation and its meaning. This is especially significant for students who use screen readers or other playback software to read math embedded in text. For example, a^2 will be read as "A to the second power," rather than "A two."

Students with disabilities who rely on speech recognition to operate a computer can perform basic arithmetic and advanced mathematics using MathPad By Voice or MathTalk/Scientific Notebook (Metroplex Voice Computing, Inc.), respectively. Both applications require Dragon Naturally Speaking (Nuance), a voice recognition program. Students can input math calculations into the computer by voice and then print their work to be handed in just like their peers (see Figure 5.8).

FIGURE 5.8 MathTalk/Scientific Notebook (Metroplex) solving a calculus problem.

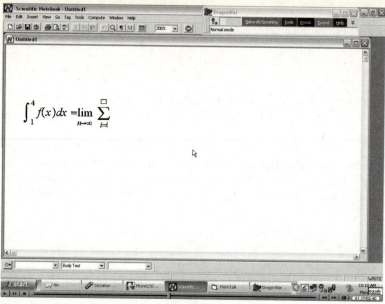

Source: Image courtesy of Metroplex Voice Computing, Inc.

Efofex Software: Empowering Students With Disabilities

The Efofex Software math products are educational applications written for teachers by teachers to make mathematics teachers' jobs easier. The four programs—FX Draw, FX Equation, FX Graph, and FX Stat—provide computerized ways to construct geometric figures, write equations, create graphs, and produce statistically correct images, respectively. Serendipitously, the company's owners found that their applications also make math accessible to students with special needs who find it difficult to write equations and create math-related graphics with standard tools. For many years, Efofex Software has been donating its educational applications to students with documented disabilities. The company remains committed to helping students with disabilities and has formalized this practice in the Em^{Power} Program. Through this program, subject to conditions, Efofex will provide registration codes free of charge for all its products to any student whose disability makes mathematics and science materials difficult to produce.

Figure 5.9 provides basic information about the math computation applications discussed in the preceding text.

Math Concepts, Skills, and Problem Solving

The National Mathematics Advisory Panel (2008) states, "Understanding core concepts is a necessary component of proficiency with arithmetic and is needed to transfer previously learned procedures to solve novel problems" (p. 25). The panel defines proficiency as "students should understand key concepts, achieve automaticity as appropriate (e.g., with addition and related subtraction facts), develop flexible, accurate, and automatic execution of the standard algorithms, and use these competencies to solve problems (p. 22). That is, for students to be successful in math, in addition

FIGURE 5.9 Math computation applications for students with disabilities.

Application	Publisher	Level	Description
MathPad	Cambium Learning Technologies http://www.cambiumtech.com	Grades K–2	A talking arithmetic worksheet program for basic operations (whole numbers only). Lines up math problems automatically (vertically or horizontally) and prompts students for regrouping.
MathPad Plus	Cambium Learning Technologies http://www.cambiumtech.com	Grades 3–8	Extends the features of MathPad to fractions and decimals. Problems can be viewed as pie charts, fraction bars, or decimal grids.
Virtual Pencil Arithmetic	Henter Math http://www.hentermath.com	Elementary	A program for working through basic operations of whole numbers, fractions, and decimals. When paired with screen reading software, it provides speech feedback on positions of digits for students who are blind. Tutorial mode can be turned on or off.
Virtual Pencil Algebra	Henter Math http://www.hentermath.com	Middle and above	Extends the features of VP Arithmetic to algebraic equations. Reads mathematical symbols and describes position of digits within the equations (when used with screen reading software).
MathTalk/ Scientific Notebook	Metroplex Voice Computing, Inc. http://www.mathtalk.com	Middle and above	Must be used with Dragon Naturally–Speaking (voice recognition software). Student speaks math problems at any level—from prealgebra to algebra, trig, calculus, statistics, and graduate-level math. Offers graphing capabilities.

to automaticity, they need to develop both fluency with the execution of procedures and a thorough understanding of mathematical concepts. They must be able to use all three—automaticity, fluency, and conceptual understanding—to become effective problem solvers.

The literature reviewed by Maccini and Gagnon (2000) supports the use of manipulatives as an effective instructional practice for all students, including students with disabilities. These hands-on experiences can help students with disabilities understand abstract math concepts. However, many students with physical disabilities are unable to access concrete manipulatives. Others may be in classrooms that do not have access to the wide variety of manipulatives related to the range of math concepts addressed in a course, there may not be enough of a given type of manipulative for each student to have individual experience, or the time devoted to using manipulatives may be insufficient to develop conceptual understanding.

Both concrete and virtual manipulatives are effective for building mathematical relationships and connections toward conceptual understanding (Anstrom, n.d.). Virtual manipulatives are widely available, especially on the Web, to provide students with disabilities an opportunity to develop conceptual understanding. In fact, a wealth of educational applications are available to assist with the development of skills and concepts needed to succeed in mathematics. Along with commercial and free applications, "Web-based activities offer teachers and parents options that are free, and teachers with limited budgets can find multiple sites to meet the needs of students with varied abilities[LB7]" (Murray et al., 2007, p. 2). The following section directs readers to a sampling of resources that provide opportunities for additional engagement, practice, and instruction with mathematical concepts and skills; educational applications targeted at general education students that contain features to support students with disabilities; and educational applications designed to make math accessible to students with disabilities.

EDUCATIONAL APPLICATIONS THAT ADDRESS MATH CONCEPTS, SKILLS, AND PROBLEM SOLVING.   To benefit students, educational applications, including virtual manipulatives, must be connected clearly to the concepts being developed and must be matched to students' developmental levels (Maccini & Gagnon, 2000). In addition to guidelines presented earlier in this chapter, the match between concepts and developmental level must be kept in mind as teachers select educational applications for students with disabilities.

To support the development of math concepts for students in Grades K–12, virtual manipulatives are available at a number of Web sites. An excellent resource is the National Library of Virtual Manipulatives maintained by Utah State University. Users can navigate the site by category —Number & Operations, Algebra, Geometry, Measurement, or Data Analysis & Probability—and/or by grade levels preK–2, Grades 3–5, Grades 6–8, or Grades 9–12.

Figure 5.10 shows base 10 blocks being used to model grouping in addition. Students who need extended practice, visual representations of concepts, and/or interactive activities can benefit from the resources available at Illuminations, a Web site maintained by the National Council of Teachers of Mathematics. This site offers numerous online activities that support the development of math concepts for students in Grades K–12.

Computing Technology for Math Excellence provides explanatory information related to using virtual manipulatives. The section titled Manipulatives on the Web provides an extensive, annotated list of virtual manipulative Web sites. The active links bring the user directly to the selected Web site.

Teachers looking to build the math skills of students Grade preK–8 can find links to excellent resources at Internet 4 Classrooms (http://www.internet4classrooms.com).This free Web portal is designed to assist anyone who wants to find high-quality, free Internet resources to use in classroom instruction and to reinforce specific subject matter areas at home.

FIGURE 5.10 Virtual Manipulatives Web site showing base 10 blocks addition.

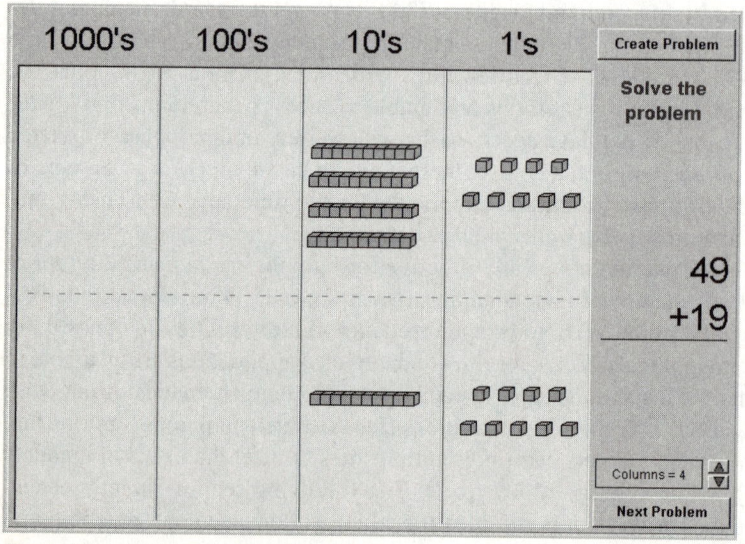

Source: Printed with permission of MATTI Math.

Students studying advanced probability and statistics may find the Virtual Laboratories in Probability and Statistics to be a useful resource. Kyle Siegrist, the principal author of the site and a member of the Department of Mathematical Sciences at the University of Alabama in Huntsville, provides expository text to help students understand the basic theories of probability and statistics. Accompanying applets (small Java-based applications) provide dynamic, interactive means to demonstrate the mathematical theories presented.

Math Playground provides a wealth of resources to support learning math concepts, skills, and problem solving. Free, online math activities are provided in the categories of Math Games, Word Problems, and Logic Puzzles. Thinking Blocks is one of the activities found in the Word Problems section. It provides practice with solving addition, subtraction, multiplication, division, and ratio multistep word problems. Students can check their work after each step and receive feedback.

Conceptua Math (http://www.conceptuamath.com) focuses on fractions and offers a variety of tools for teachers to use to enhance their whole class instruction. The company's online application, Conceptua® Fractions, covers fraction topics typically taught in grades 2–7. It provides visual models that are accompanied by spoken text to facilitate independent use by students who are struggling readers. Conceptua® Fractions includes formative assessments and captures student data, enabling teachers to monitor students' progress and make appropriate instructional decisions.

Destination Math (Houghton Mifflin Harcourt Learning Technology) targets the development of skills in math reasoning, conceptual understanding, and problem solving for students in Grades K–12. The use of animation and audio output helps keep students engaged. Student success is supported with explicit step-by-step instructions and opportunities to practice problem-solving skills. A full Spanish version called Destino Matematicás is available to support students who are English Language Learners.

EDUCATIONAL APPLICATIONS FOR TEACHING FUNCTIONAL MATH SKILLS.   Some publishers offer math applications designed specifically for students with cognitive disabilities whose curriculum focuses on the teaching of functional skills. For example, Attainment Company offers a variety of applications that cover topics such as computation, money and time. These programs provide support to non-readers through voice prompts and graphic cues. For some applications, IntelliKeys overlays are available to make the program accessible to students who need to use this programmable alternate keyboard. (See Chapter 8.)

AUTHORING APPLICATIONS.   Authoring applications are those programs that allow teachers to add their own content to create customized activities. They can be used to create learning opportunities for students with disabilities for whom a computer is an absolute necessity, as well as for those students who are simply more engaged and attentive when working on the computer. Authoring programs expand learning opportunities for students who need auditory output, students who are unable to use handwriting to practice skills and demonstrate knowledge, students who are unable to manipulate materials (e.g., arranging objects into arrays as an introduction to multiplication), and students who rely on the computer for access to the curriculum but whose needs cannot be met with "out-of-the-box" applications. With the appropriate authoring program, teachers can create learning activities that are engaging, correlate to the general education curriculum, and support the success of all students.

Authoring applications vary in complexity. Programs such as Macromedia's Flash that are targeted for Web page developers and for other commercial users require computer skills beyond those possessed by most classroom teachers. However, other authoring programs are available that are designed to be used by teachers to create curricular activities that are accessible using a variety of alternate input methods. Applications fitting into this last category are the focus of the following discussion. The use of such authoring programs may require teachers to develop new technical skills; however, these skills can be mastered easily by teachers who have general computer proficiency. Most authoring applications provide detailed tutorials that are invaluable for novice users. Of course, mastering any new skill takes time and practice, and teachers will find that the longer they work with a specific authoring application, the quicker they will be able to create custom activities.

With an appropriate a authoring application, learning activities can be created in any curricular area, including math. A program such as Clicker 5 (Crick Software) allows users to create a range of activities. For example, teachers can create what Crick Software calls "hit and happen" activities for a student who is working on learning the numbers and counting. With a click of the mouse, three circles can appear with a corresponding text label, "three circles," along with an auditory message such as, "One, two, three. There are three circles." For a young student who will not attend to bland circles, the image could be teddy bears, dump trucks, or whatever image will hold the student's interest. For an older student, the image could be age-appropriate items such as sports cars, musical instruments, or dollar bills. Subsequent clicks of the mouse could bring up four circles, then five circles, and so on, with accompanying text and auditory feedback. Clicker 5's talking word processing function can be used to read aloud word problems to students who are struggling or nonreaders.

Classroom Suite 4 (Cambium Learning) is another authoring application that teachers can use to create numerous types of accessible learning activities. Learning activities designed to meet the needs of individual students can be created "from scratch" using the creativity tools, or teachers can opt to modify premade activities that are provided in the template library.

Crick Software and Cambium Learning both provide helpful venues for teachers to share their teacher-created materials. Rather than always having to design original activities, teachers can search Crick Software's Learning Grids Web site or Cambium's IntelliTools Classroom Activity Exchange to see if someone else has created an activity that can be downloaded and used as is or modified to meet the needs of their own students.

Low-Tech and Mid-Tech Adaptations for Teaching Math

The assistive technology continuum is relevant to the teaching of math, just as it is to the teaching of writing and reading. Manipulatives, which have been standard instructional materials for years, are a good example of low-tech aids. Many other products are available to help students understand and master basic math concepts. Onion Mountain Technology markets fraction rubber stamps, a manipulative number line, laminated addition and multiplication tables, and a special ruler that has multiple transparent overlays to help students understand the relationships between the different units of measure. Large calculators with oversized buttons are useful for students who lack fine motor control. Talking calculators can help students with learning disabilities check their work by reading aloud every keystroke that the student enters. Talking calculators are also needed by students with visual impairments. See 'n' Solve calculators show the entire math problem on the screen, which enables students to see their work as they solve computation problems with whole numbers and/or fractions. For students who are learning functional math, easy-to-use mid-tech devices are available. The "coin abacus" and "coin-u-lator" contain keys that are shaped and sized just like coins; they are designed to teach basic money counting. Other calculators offer practical features such as automatically calculating tax and tips.

An oversized calculator with large buttons is an example of a mid-tech tool for math.

Source: Courtesy of Onion Mountain Technology.

Summary

- Myriad educational applications, interactive Web-based activities, and applications specially designed for students with disabilities offer opportunities to make the general education mathematics curriculum accessible to students with a wide range of disabilities.
- The computer can be a patient tutor, providing instruction or repetitive practice in an engaging and motivating manner.
- With the proper educational application, students who cannot use pencil and paper effectively can use the computer to acquire skills and demonstrate their knowledge. They can even use the computer to perform math computation and calculations at a basic or an advanced level.
- In order for the computer to be an effective instructional tool, teachers need to carefully select educational applications and Web sites for student use. They need to be certain that the educational applications they choose align with the curriculum and move students toward meeting their educational goals. That is, the activities should not be merely fun and engaging, but meaningful and educationally relevant.
- Educational applications are available that address automaticity and math fact fluency, visual-spatial and motor control difficulties, and math concepts, math skills and problem solving.
- Authoring applications designed to meet the needs of students with disabilities afford teachers an opportunity to create activities with customized content that are accessible using the standard keyboard and mouse or built-in accessibility features.

Web Resources

Enhancing Instruction with Computers
Kathy Schrock's Guide for Educators
http://school.discoveryeducation.com/schrockguide/

Eduscapes
http://eduscapes.com/

Reviews of Educational Applications and Apps

Superkids
http://www.superkids.com

Education World
http://www.educationworld.com/a_tech/archives/edurate.shtml

Guide to First Class Learning Software
http://www.learningvillage.com

Educational Applications that Teach Math

FASTT Math
http://www.tomsnyder.com

Timez Attack
http://www.bigbrainz.com/

ArithmAttack
http://www.dep.anl.gov/aattack.htm

Arcademic Skill Builder
http://www.arcademicskillbuilders.com/

A+ Math
http://www.aplusmath.com

Visual Fractions
http://www.visualfractions.com

Mrs. Glosser's Math Goodies
http://www.mathgoodies.com

Attainment Company
http://www.attainmentcompany.com

Educational Applications that Address Motor Control Issues in Math

MathPad and MathPad Plus (Windows only)
Cambium Learning Technologies
http://www.cambiumtech.com/

Virtual Pencil Arithmetic and Virtual Pencil Algebra
http://hentermath.com

MathType
http://www.dessci.com/en/products/mathtype

Scientific Notebook/Scientific Word
http://www.mackichan.com/

Meander's Annotator
http://www.themeanders.com

Efofex and Em^{Power}
http://www.efofex.com/empower.php

Educational Applications: Math Concepts, Skills, and Problem-Solving

National Library of Virtual Manipulatives
http://nlvm.usu.edu/en/nav/vlibrary.html

Number Navigator (Oats Project)
http://www.oatsoft.org/Software/NumberNavigator

Illuminations from the National Council of Teachers of Mathematics
http://illuminations.nctm.org/ActivitySearch.aspx

Computing Technology for Math Excellence
http://www.ct4me.net/math_manipulatives.htm#Manipulatives

Internet 4 Classrooms
http://www.internet4classrooms.com

Virtual Laboratories in Probability and Statistics
http://www.math.uah.edu/stat

Math Playground
http://www.mathplayground.com

Destination Math
http://hmlt.hmco.com/DM.php

Easy-to-Use Authoring Applications for Teachers
Clicker 5
http://www.cricksoft.com/uk/products/clicker

Classroom Suite
http://www.cambiumtech.com

Learning Grids
http://www.learninggrids.com

Cambium's IntelliTools Classroom Activity Exchange
http://www.intellitools.com

Low Tech Tools for Math
Onion Mountain Technology
http://www.onionmountaintech.com

Suggested Activities

1. *Review an educational application or app for the iPad.* Choose one of the applications or apps listed in the previous section or on one of the sites listed. Learn the application thoroughly—this means you need to use it several times, change the settings/preferences/options, deliberately make errors, and so on. Write a review of the application using Figure 5.1 as a guide. Use the following headings: Title, Publisher, Web site address, Cost, Notable system requirements, Purpose (Goals), Structure, Special features, Strengths, Weaknesses, and Summary. Share these in class or on a class discussion board.

2. *Explore Virtual Manipulatives.* Visit the Web site of the National Library of Virtual Manipulatives (http://nlvm.usu.edu/en/nav/ vlibrary.html). Click on one of the math strands—Number & Operations, Algebra, Geometry, Measurement, or Data Analysis & Probability. This will display the complete list of activities for each grade range. Identify a manipulative that appears in more than one grade range and explore it in each of the ranges. Be sure to click on the Activities button to explore all the activities available for each grade range. Which state or local curriculum standards are supported by the virtual manipulative you explored? How might the virtual manipulative be integrated into a classroom to enhance students' learning?

3. *Generate a TECHMATRIX*: Access the TECHMATRIX at http://www.techmatrix.org and click on Advanced Search. Select Math as the Content Area, Middle School for Grade

Level, Teacher as the Role, Specific Learning Disability as the IDEA Disability Category, and Opportunities to Learn Concepts for Learning Support. Click Go. Generate a matrix by clicking Compare All Products Found once the search results are returned. Explore the matrix to compare product features. Change the search criteria and generate additional matrices according to your interests and needs.

4. *Add to your portfolio.* Use a search engine (e.g., Google [http://www.google.com] or Yahoo [http://www.yahoo.com]) to locate educational resources, applications and apps for teaching math. Conduct searches using phrases such as "Web sites for teaching math" and "online math activities," and "iPad apps for learning math." Explore the sites/applications identified by your search. Then add a selection of resources that are most relevant to your area of professional practice to your portfolio.

References

Anstrom, T. (n.d.). Supporting students in mathematics through the use of manipulatives. Washington, D.C.: Center for Implementing Technology in Education. Retrieved June 13, 2010 from http://www.cited.org/library/resourcedocs/ Supporting Students in Mathematics Through the Use of Manipulatives.pdf

Ayres, K., & Langone, J. (2005). Evaluation of software for functional skills instruction: Blending best practice with technology. *Technology in Action, Technology and Media Division, 1*(5), 1–8.

Brown, A., Miller, D., & Robinson, L. (2003). Teacher-directed software design: The development of learning objects for students with special needs in the elementary classroom. *Information Technology in Childhood Education*, (1), 173–186.

Geary, D. C. (1999). *Mathematical disabilities: What we know and don't know.* Retrieved May 11, 2011 from the Learning Disabilities Online Web site: http://www.ldonline.org/article/5881

Hasselbring, T. S., Lott, A. C., & Zydney, J. M. (n.d.). *Technology-supported math instruction for students with disabilities: Two decades of research and development.* Retrieved November 20, 2006, from the Center for Implementing Technology in Education Web site: http://www.cited.org/library/ resourcedocs/Tech-SupportedMathInstruction-FinalPaper_early.pdf

Hickson, L., Blackman, L. S., & Reis, E. M. (1995). *Mental retardation: Foundations of educational programming.* Boston, MA: Allyn & Bacon.

Maccini, P., & Gagnon, J. C. (2000). Best practices for teaching mathematics to secondary students with special needs: Implications from teacher perceptions and a review of the literature. *Focus on Exceptional Children*, 32 (5), 1–22.

Moreno, R. (2004). Decreasing cognitive load for novice students: Effects of explanatory versus corrective feedback in discovery-based multimedia. *Instructional Science,32* (1), 99–113.

Murray, Silver-Pacuilla, & Helsel, . (2007). Improving Basic Mathematics Instruction: Promising technology resources for students with special needs. *Technology in Action,.* 2(5), 1–8.

National Council of Teachers of Mathematics. (2000). *Principles and standards of school mathematics.* Reston, VA: Author.

National Council of Teachers of Mathematics. (2004). *Principles and standards of school mathematics* (Appendix: Table of Standards and Expectations). Retrieved May 11, 2011 from http://www.nctm.org/standards/content. aspx?id=16909

National Mathematics Advisory Council (2008). Final Report of the National Mathematics Advisory Council. Washington, D.C.: U.S. Department of Education. Retrieved May 11, 2011 from *http://www2.ed.gov/about/bdscomm/ list/mathpanel/report/final-report.pdf*

Newton, D.A., Dell, A. G., & Disdier, A. M. (1998). Content software makes the grade. *Exceptional Parent, (28),* 12.

Wehmeyer, M., Smith, S., Palmer, S., & Davies, D. (2004). Technology use by students with intellectual disabilities: An overview. *Journal of Special Education Technology, 19*(4), 7–21.

6 | ASSISTIVE TECHNOLOGY TO ENHANCE COMMUNICATION

Focus Questions

1. What kinds of obstacles do students who are hard of hearing face in a typical classroom?
2. What practices should a teacher follow if she or he has a student in class who uses an assistive listening system?
3. What is hearing assistive technology and how can it help students who are hard of hearing?
4. Why is Internet technology considered "an instrument of liberation" by people who are deaf or hard of hearing?
5. What kinds of obstacles do students who cannot speak face in school?
6. What is augmentative communication, and why is it important?
7. What does the TASH Resolution on the Right to Communicate say?

INTRODUCTION

Being able to communicate your thoughts, feelings, and ideas is absolutely critical to being successful in school and the workplace. Being able to understand other people's communication attempts is equally essential. For people who cannot hear speech or people who cannot express themselves through speech, technology offers an exciting range of solutions. In this chapter, we discuss assistive technology tools that can enhance communication between students with disabilities and their teachers and peers. We introduce the areas of hearing assistive technology, which helps students who are hard of hearing, and augmentative communication, which helps students who cannot speak.

THE IMPORTANCE OF COMMUNICATION—PART 1

Computer technology "meant the beginning of the end of my isolation—isolation from other people," writes Hank Kisor, a Chicago journalist who is deaf (1990, p. 152). Kisor continues, "The microchip is probably the greatest aid to communication the twentieth century has … provided" (p. 225). E-mail, real-time chats, and instant messaging "enable me to 'talk'…with the hearing world at large…. To me they were truly an instrument of liberation" (p. 230).

The feeling of isolation Kisor refers to is common among people who are deaf or hard of hearing (Andrews, Leigh, & Weiner, 2004; Steinberg, 2000; Stinson & Foster, 2000). A student who cannot hear a teacher's question will not be able to answer the question or communicate his or her understanding of the subject matter. A student who cannot hear a fellow student's comment in class or at the lunch table will not be able to carry on a conversation or enjoy a social interaction. If your hearing has ever been diminished by an ear infection or a bad head cold, you may have some idea of the isolation caused by an inability to hear clearly.

Problems Students Who Are Deaf or Hard of Hearing Have with Communication

Before we discuss technology tools for students who are deaf or hard of hearing, it will be helpful to briefly define *deaf* and *hard of hearing*. Although they are similar, there are important differences between the terms, and these differences affect the usefulness of specific technology tools.

STUDENTS WHO ARE DEAF.   Students who are deaf have little or no functional hearing (DO-IT, 2004). They usually are not highly skilled or comfortable with speaking, and they communicate primarily through sign language. (American Sign Language [ASL] is one common form of sign language, but it is not the only form.) These students require a sign language interpreter to communicate with nonsigners and to participate in school activities.

STUDENTS WHO ARE HARD OF HEARING.   Unlike students who are deaf, students who are *hard of hearing* do not typically use sign language. They usually can understand speech through a combination of personal hearing aids, which amplify sounds, and their skills in lip-reading. Students who are hard of hearing may have some speech impairments, but they can usually speak well enough to be understood. In recent years, increasing numbers of children who are hard of hearing have had cochlear implants surgically inserted in their inner ears (Northeast Technical Assistance Center [NETAC], 2000; see Sidebar); with appropriate training, these implants are significantly increasing the hearing abilities of students who are hard of hearing.

Communication Problems in School

Students who are hard of hearing often have difficulty following lectures, particularly if the acoustics of the room are poor or if the teacher speaks quietly, quickly, or unclearly (DO-IT, 2004). Although their hearing aids may be adequate in one-on-one conversations, the poor acoustics of many classrooms (caused by cement floors and walls, noisy heating and cooling systems, and lack of soft materials to absorb sound) lessen the hearing aids' effectiveness for understanding lectures: "Whereas a young adult with normal hearing may experience a mild awareness of room reverberation and background noise, it may not significantly reduce the intelligibility of the spoken message for that student. For the person using a hearing aid, however, such conditions form an acoustic barrier to listening" (Warick, Clark, Dancer, & Sinclair, 1997).

Exacerbating the problem of poor acoustics is the need for teachers to move around a classroom. If a teacher turns his or her back to the class—to write on the blackboard, for example—the student who is lipreading can no longer hear the lecture. Similarly, if the teacher looks down while demonstrating a science lab activity, the student who reads lips cannot see the teacher's face. Class discussions and video presentations are two other classroom activities that present difficulties to students who are hard of hearing.

Cochlear Implants

Cochlear implants are miniature electronic devices that are surgically implanted in the inner ear (the cochlea) to improve useful hearing. They are designed to bypass cochlear hair cells that do not work and to provide direct stimulation to the auditory nerve. Cochlear implant users will have, in addition to the miniature implant itself, a tiny microphone, a signal processor (older models are worn on a waistband; newer models use tiny behind-the-ear units), and a small signal coupler (transmitter and receiver). The microphone picks up sounds and sends them to the processor, which selects and codes the sounds. The coded sounds are then sent through the skin to a transmitting coil that converts them to electrical impulses, and the implanted electrode array stimulates the auditory nerve.

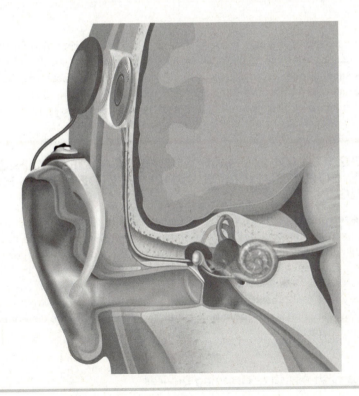

Source: Courtesy of Advanced Bionics.

Supporting Students Who Use Assistive Listening Devices: Guidelines for Teachers

1. Become knowledgeable about the assistive listening device. Request training from an audiologist and/or manufacturer of the system.
2. Discuss how the assistive listening device will be used with the student ahead of time.
3. Position the microphone carefully. It should not be near a noise source such as an overhead projector. It should be 3 to 5 inches from the teacher's mouth.
4. Consult with an audiologist about optimal positioning of the receiver or speakers.
5. Inform the entire class about how the assistive listening device will be used in classroom instruction. Remind students to speak one at a time. Be sure to repeat questions and comments from other students. When possible, pass the microphone/transmitter from student to student.
6. Try to face the student in case he or she relies on visual cues to aid understanding.
7. Use the assistive listening device for audiovisual presentations.
8. Perform a listening check with the equipment regularly. Establish and follow a regular maintenance routine and schedule.

Source: From *The Role of Assistive Listening Devices in the Classroom* (NETAC Teacher Tipsheet Series), by Northeast Technical Assistance Center, 1998, Rochester, NY.

Outside the classroom, students who are deaf and hard of hearing also face obstacles in trying to communicate with their teachers and peers. Understanding speakers in face-to-face situations such as small-group discussions and social situations is hampered by the presence of background noise and several people talking at once. Communication over distances is problematic because deaf and hard of hearing students are usually not able to use standard telephones.

TECHNOLOGY TOOLS THAT ADDRESS COMMUNICATION PROBLEMS FOR STUDENTS WHO ARE DEAF OR HARD OF HEARING

Hearing assistive technology is the term for assistive technology that helps people who have hearing losses. It includes **alerting devices** that indicate the presence of sound in the environment, such as smoke detector indicators, shaking alarm clocks, and baby cry signalers. Hearing assistive technology also includes **adaptations for telephones**. Tables 6.1 and 6.2 provide examples of these kinds of assistive technology. This chapter, however, focuses on hearing assistive technology that can enhance students' communication in the classroom. (Specialized applications of technology that are used for note taking for students who are deaf or hard of hearing are discussed in Chapter 2.)

Hearing Lectures with Assistive Listening Devices

Called "binoculars for the ears" (SHHH, 2006), **assistive listening devices** (ALDs) help reduce the effect of an "acoustically unfriendly room" (Warick et al., 1997). They catch a desired sound

TABLE 6.1	Alerting Devices for People Who are Deaf or Hard of Hearing
Device	**Function**
Alarm clock with flasher or strobe light	A light or bright strobe flashes when the alarm clock goes off.
Shake Awake travel alarm clock	Placed under a pillow, this vibrates to wake up the user.
Alarm clock with flash and vibrator	Can use either the flashing light or vibrator or both simultaneously.
Door beacon	When someone knocks at the door, the beacon flashes.
Wireless strobe door chime	The door chime sets off a strobe light.
Smoke detector with strobe light	A powerful strobe light flashes when the smoke detector is activated. It can also be connected to a bed vibrator.
Baby cry signaler	It emits a strobe light or vibrates a bed when a baby cries.
Blink receiver	A strobe light flashes when hooked to a unit of your choice.
Super phone ringer	This rings the phone very loudly; it can be used in conjunction with amplified telephones.
Phone flasher	A light flashes when the phone/TTY rings.
Silent call wireless alerting system	This is an integrated system that can alert a person to the activation of any one of a number of common household devices. It can be connected to a strobe light, vibrator, or a regular household lamp and can be used in various locations of a house. The advantage is that this system can indicate the presence of a sound at places other than where the sound occurred, and it can be set to use different patterns to differentiate types of sounds.

Source: From "Assistive Technology for People Who Are Deaf and Hard of Hearing," by J. Dodds, 2003, *TECH-NJ, 14*(1).

(the teacher's voice, for example) as cleanly as possible and amplify it for students who are hard of hearing. ALDs help these students by

- Minimizing background noise such as chairs moving, fan motors whirring, and students talking
- Overcoming the weakening effect of sound traveling through air
- Reducing the effect of poor room acoustics (SHHH, 2006)

Providing a high-quality listening environment is known to have a major impact on the academic performance of students who are hard of hearing (NETAC, 1998).

ALDs do not replace hearing aids. Hearing aids are worn all day long and amplify all sounds in a student's environments. ALDs, on the other hand, are used when it is important to amplify a specific voice such as a teacher's. By placing a microphone close to the speaker's mouth, ALDs provide the most advantageous ratio between the intensity of speech and the level of background noise (NETAC, 1998). They also eliminate echoes. An ALD can be used along with hearing aids or as a stand-alone unit.

TABLE 6.2	Telecommunication Devices for People Who are Deaf or Hard of Hearing
Device	**Function**
Amplified telephone	This allows the user to adjust the volume and control the tone, for example, boosting the treble or bass on a stereo.
Portable phone amplifier	This small gadget fits over a telephone handset. It can be taken and used anywhere.
TTY (also known as a TDD—Telecommunication Device for the Deaf)	Equipped with a keyboard and small visual display, a TTY enables users to type their messages and send them over telephone lines. Two deaf people using TTYs can communicate with each other directly.
Relay service	If the person on one end of a phone call uses a TTY and the person on the other end uses a regular (speaking) telephone, the services of a relay operator are needed. When the TTY user types, the relay operator speaks the message to the telephone user. When the telephone user speaks, the relay operator types the message to the TTY user. To comply with the Americans with Disabilities Act, all telephone companies now provide this service free of charge.
Video relay	Many deaf people who communicate via sign language prefer video relay technology. Using a webcam (camera) and a high-speed Internet connection, a video of a deaf person signing is transmitted to a sign language interpreter who translates the signs into speech for the intended hearing person. Two sign language users can use the video technology to communicate with each other directly, without the need for a relay operator. (See User Profile in sidebar.)
Pocket Speak-and-Read Portable VCO (Voice Carry Over)	For people who cannot hear on the phone but have use of their voice and prefer to use their voice, this device slides on the telephone handset and provides a screen readout as a TTY does. The call must be placed through a relay service.
Text messages on commercial cell phones	Text messaging provides a telecommunications method for people who are deaf or hard of hearing that does not require specialized equipment or the involvement of a third party.

Types of Assistive Listening Devices

FM SYSTEM.   With a personal FM system, the teacher wears a wireless lavalier microphone clipped to his or her lapel or blouse and a small transmitter worn on a belt or waistband. The student wears a small receiver and some kind of coupling device—usually headphones, ear buds, or a direct connection to his or her hearing aid. Special cables are available to connect with the hearing aids of students who have cochlear implants. When the teacher speaks, an auditory signal is broadcast to the FM receiver worn by the student. The student hears the amplified teacher's voice either through headphones or directly through the hearing aid. The wireless unit is battery operated, portable, and unobtrusive.

INFRARED SYSTEM.   Infrared ALDs have similar components to FM systems (microphone, transmitter, and receiver), but they use infrared light waves for transmission instead of FM radio waves. Infrared technology is used in everyday devices such as remote control units for televisions and garage door openers. The advantage to infrared systems is that there is minimal distortion and internal amplifier noise in its signal so the sound quality can be superior to that of FM systems. Infrared

Michael L.

Michael L. was diagnosed with bilateral sensorineural hearing loss at 16 months of age. Living close to the Jersey shore all his life, he loves to be home over the summer so he can take advantage of its proximity to the water. He loves going to the boardwalk, running on the beach, or just hanging out with friends. Michael is also an avid soccer player. He played four years of varsity soccer while attending the National Technical Institute for the Deaf at the Rochester Institute of Technology pursing his BS in social work. He has traveled all over the world playing soccer for the USA Deaf Soccer Team, including the first ever Deaf World Cup tournament in Patras, Greece.

Michael's primary means of communication is American Sign Language (ASL). When he is not in the presence of another sign language user or when he wants to communicate with someone at a distance, he has found two kinds of technology to be indispensable: a T-Mobile Sidekick cell phone (http://www.sidekick.com/sidekick-demo.aspx) and a video phone.

T-MOBILE SIDEKICK FOR TEXTING AND SIPRELAY

When he is on the go, Michael relies on his T-Mobile Sidekick. With its full QWERTY keyboard and 2.6-inch display, he can easily send and receive text messages, just like any cell phone user. The added advantage for Michael is that he can use text messaging to communicate with a hearing person if he is in a situation without a sign language interpreter,

such as at a restaurant or in a store. Additionally, the Sidekick can use a Sorenson program (http://www.sorensonvrs.com) called SIPRelay (www.siprelay.com/what_is.aspx), which is a free download that acts as an intermediary between Michael and a hearing person. Michael connects to the SIPRelay server on his Sidekick, types a text message and the phone number of the person he wants to reach, and an operator calls the number and reads the message. Michael uses this method to order a pizza or call family or friends.

VP-200 VIDEO PHONE WITH VIDEO RELAY SERVICE

A second piece of technology that Michael uses is a video phone called the VP-200, which works with the Sorenson Video Relay Service (SRVS). This service offers similar, but better, services than the SIPRelay. The SVRS connects to a regular television set and uses a high-speed Internet connection to relay video. Michael uses the VP-200 to connect to a sign language interpreter who then translates his signs orally over the phone for the intended hearing person. This is especially helpful for Michael when he is at home and wants to communicate with a hearing person without texting. Additionally, Michael can contact someone directly without the relay service if the person also has a VP-200. In this arrangement, both parties sign to each other and can see the other's signing. If a person has a laptop with a webcam, they can also be contacted directly. The video relay technology makes it

possible for deaf people to communicate just as immediately as hearing people do on a telephone.

Michael prefers using the VP-200 whenever possible. Unlike using a TTY or his Sidekick, communication using this system is immediate and he can speak in his own language. The service is available to Michael 24 hours a day, and he can use it to place emergency phone calls.

When on a call, the monitor shows two different videos at the same time. The first video displayed is that of the person being contacted. In the opposite corner, a second video is displayed of Michael that shows how he is being received by the person connected with him. This is important because it helps Michael check the room lighting and his position in front of the camera.

What makes this system so effective is that it is a *video* relay service as opposed to a typed relay service. Since Michael's primary language is ASL, he can communicate with people more efficiently through his own language. Michael explained how this use of technology allows people who are deaf or hard of hearing to experience all the benefits of technology while still embracing Deaf culture[AD16]. For these reasons, he highly recommends video relay technology for people who are deaf or hard of hearing. ■

Source: Adapted from "Text Messaging and Video Relay: Innovative Communication Options," by K. A. Ahrens, 2009, *TECH-NJ, 20*, pp. 7 & 12. Retrieved from http://www.tcnj.edu/~technj/2008/TECHNJ2009/TechnologyfortheDeaf.htm

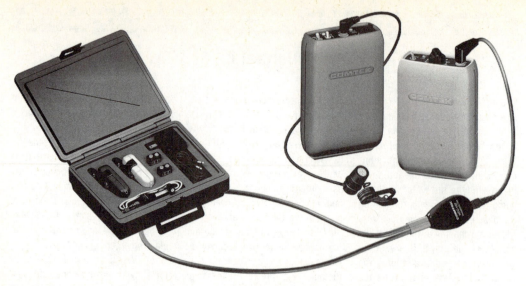

The teacher wears the lavalier microphone and transmitter, and the student wears the receiver.

Source: Photo courtesy of Cantek, Inc.

USER PROFILE

Nicole (14-year-old high school student)

The students in Mr. D.'s world history class are annoyed with his co-teacher for not grading a project they did weeks ago. The class leader thinks of a way to show disapproval and comes to the front of the room to propose her plan to the rest of the students. After addressing the group, the leader turns to Nicole, who is sitting in the front row. She confirms that Nicole heard the idea and is in agreement. Nicole has a hearing impairment. Although this disability sometimes limits a student's participation in the classroom, Nicole is not excluded from the protest being planned, neither is she ever left out of classroom activities. Her inclusion is due, in part, to

her classmates' awareness of her disability and her teachers' positive attitudes. Equally important, she stays involved with the help of an FM system. Because Nicole's classroom has two teachers, a daisy chain system is set up with multiple transmitters. Mr. V. wears one transmitter while Mr. D. wears both a transmitter and receiver. Mr. V.'s voice is sent to Mr. D.'s receiver. In turn, his transmitter passes the sound along the chain to Nicole's receiver.

There are several advantages to this setup: (1) Although Nicole lipreads, she misses a lot of information with lipreading alone. (2) Lipreading does not capture the in-

flection in a speaker's voice. (3) The co-teachers are free to move around the classroom; with an FM system it is not necessary for them to face Nicole at all times or stand close by in order for her to hear them. (4) Nicole can hear the soundtrack on videos that are shown in class by simply having a teacher place the FM system microphone close to the monitor. (5) The FM system's ability to minimize background noise is especially helpful for Nicole because her school has an open layout, which tends to be very noisy. ■

Source: Adapted from "FM System, C-Print Assist Hard-of-Hearing Student in High School," by T. Spadafora, 2003, *TECHNJ, 14* (1), p. 4.

transmission is also private because, unlike the FM signal, light cannot travel through walls. This is why theaters and courtrooms prefer infrared ALDs to FM systems. Schools, however, tend to not use infrared ALDs because they require a direct line of sight between teacher and student, with no physical objects in between, and the teacher needs to limit his or her movement around the classroom.

INDUCTION LOOP SYSTEM.   Induction loop systems use electromagnetic waves for transmission and work directly with hearing aids. A wire is looped around the perimeter of a space such as a classroom or school auditorium. Sounds are picked up by the teacher's microphone, amplified, and sent through the loop, creating an invisible magnetic field. A telecoil (called a T-switch) in the student's hearing aid serves as a receiver and picks up the signal from the loop. The hearing aid then reconverts this signal into sound, amplifies it, and feeds it directly into the student's ear (NETAC, 1998).

SOUNDFIELD AMPLIFICATION SYSTEM.   A soundfield amplification system broadcasts the teacher's voice through loudspeakers that are mounted on the walls or ceiling. A speaker can also be placed directly next to a student. Other components of the soundfield amplification system are a microphone and transmitter worn by the teacher. This kind of system has been successfully used with students who have attention deficit disorders and central auditory processing disorders. It helps them filter out distracting background noise and focus on the teacher's voice (Boswell, 2006).

Table 6.3 lists the advantages and disadvantages of these four systems. It is important to note that the effectiveness of all ALDs can be affected by a number of factors. The quality of the

TABLE 6.3   Summary of Assistive Listening Systems

Device	Advantages	Disadvantages
FM system	• Student can sit and face anywhere within the system's range. • System can be used inside or outside (not affected by light).	• Potential confidentiality issues: The sound broadcast may carry through walls. • Possible electrical interference.
Infrared system	• Privacy is protected because the broadcast signal is secure within the room. • Sound quality can be superior to FM systems.	• There must be a direct line of sight between teacher and student; they must face each other directly with no physical objects in between. • Teacher needs to limit movement around the classroom. • Not effective in direct sunlight.
Induction loop system	• Can be used by anyone with a hearing aid without requiring another piece of equipment for the listener. Users can simply switch their hearing aids to T-switch mode.	• Requires permanent installation. • Possible electromagnetic interference from nearby power transformers, heavy equipment, etc.
Soundfield amplification system	• Serves the entire classroom; all students benefit from the amplification.	• Helpful only for mild or moderate hearing losses.

microphone used can improve or degrade the sound quality, as can the quality of the coupling device—headphones, T-switches, and cochlear implant patch cords (SHHH, 2006). Providing adequate training, of both the student and the teacher, is also a critical factor (NETAC, 1998). If a student indicates that an ALD is not working (or if a teacher suspects a problem), simple troubleshooting techniques should include checking for a dead battery or a break in the wiring, making sure the system has been turned on, checking for interference, and checking to see whether the student's hearing aid's T-switch has been turned on.

Interacting with Teachers and Peers Outside Class

An important part of learning often involves interacting with teachers and fellow students outside class. Before the advent of computer technology, students who were deaf or hard of hearing were at a significant disadvantage. Today common computer applications such as e-mail, instant messaging, chat rooms, discussion boards, blogs, and Skype present convenient alternatives for communicating with teachers and fellow students. They avoid the issue of hearing completely. As Kisor (1990) writes, "Computer chatting was a staggering revolution in communications. For the first time I could participate in group talks without worrying about whether people could understand my speech … and whether I could follow the bouncing ball of conversation among a large number of people" (p. 251).

Similarly the revolution in cell phone technology has freed people who are deaf and hard of hearing from the struggles of using the telephone. Text messaging, once an exotic add-on to cell phone plans but now a widely used feature, provides a mainstream alternative to specialized telecommunication devices for the deaf (TDDs, also know as TTYs). It offers a new independence for people who are deaf or hard of hearing because they can now carry a lightweight, easy-to-use cell phone with them anywhere and can communicate directly with anyone who also has text messaging activated on his or her cell phone (Schindler, 2003).

THE IMPORTANCE OF COMMUNICATION—PART 2

Have you ever had laryngitis or another illness that took away your ability to speak? Or have you ever been in a foreign country in which nobody understood your speech? If so, you will have had some experience with the frustration and powerlessness of being voiceless. Bob Williams (2000), a disability advocate who cannot speak due to cerebral palsy, expresses it this way: "The silence of speechlessness is never golden. We all need to communicate and connect with each other…. It is a basic human need, a basic human right" (p. 248). This intense hunger to communicate is strikingly conveyed by Ruth Sienkiewicz-Mercer, a woman with quadriplegia cerebral palsy. Although Ruth cannot walk, feed, or dress herself, these physical limitations do not compare with her inability to speak: "Without a doubt, my inability to speak has been the single most devastating aspect of my handicap. If I were granted one wish and one wish only, I would not hesitate for an instant to request that I be able to talk, if only for one day, or even one hour" (Sienkiewicz-Mercer & Kaplan, 1996, p. 12).

Problems Students with Physical Disabilities or Autism Have with Communication

Many students who have physical disabilities such as cerebral palsy cannot speak. They do not have the oral motor control necessary to articulate words and sentences. One estimate is that

41% of the school-aged population with cerebral palsy has some speech problems, with 22% being reported to have no understandable speech (Blackstone, 1993). *Dysarthria* is the technical term for speech disorders that are due to the inability of the oral motor muscles to move to their proper positions because of neuromotor control issues (Stuart, 2002). Dysarthria has been reported in 88% of children with athetoid cerebral palsy, and in 52% of those with spastic cerebral palsy (Blackstone, 1993). Although speech therapy can help some children with mild dysarthria develop some functional speech, many will never develop intelligible speech.

Another group of students who cannot speak have neurological disabilities such as autism. Communication problems are one of the defining characteristics of individuals with autism (Wing, 1996). Although they do not have physical disabilities and some may be able to recite television commercials or sing songs by rote, many students with autism have *dyspraxia*, which is an interruption in the ability to program the position of the speech musculature (Stuart, 2002). They do not have the motor planning skills necessary to express themselves meaningfully.

Problems Resulting from Communication Problems

How can students actively participate in class activities if they cannot speak? How can they demonstrate knowledge and understanding if they do not speak? How can they make choices, express their opinions, reveal their interests if they cannot speak? How can they socialize and develop friendships if they cannot speak? Bob Williams (2000), an augmentative communication user himself, highlights the serious problems of not being able to speak:

> If I could not express myself clearly and accurately [with my augmentative communication device], I could not tell my physician and others how I feel or describe the health problems I may be having. Similarly, I could not let others know what I know or what I am capable of learning. Nor could I go to work or vote. (p. 250)

Unfortunately, many people in our society—including education professionals—tend to equate an inability to speak with an inability to think (Williams, 2000). They often hold very low expectations for children who cannot speak and, as a result, do not offer challenging educational opportunities. Williams expresses it best:

> Why are so many people consigned to lead lives of needless dependence and silence? Not because we lack the funds, nor because we lack federal policy mandates needed to gain access to those funds. Rather, many people lead lives of silence because many others still find it difficult to believe that people with speech disabilities like my own have anything to say or contributions to make. (p. 250)

The inability to communicate often leads to intolerable frustrations that, in many students with autism or severe cognitive disabilities, lead to temper tantrums, screaming, biting, hitting, and self-abusive behaviors (Carr et al., 1994; Durand, 1993). This connection between communication frustrations and challenging behaviors has received increasing attention in the last 25 years. A major component of current educational programs for students with autism involves strategies for teaching functional communication skills as alternatives to challenging behavior (Koegel, Koegel, & Dunlap, 1996). Because many students with autism have dyspraxia, functional communication for them often involves augmentative communication systems.

TECHNOLOGY TOOLS THAT ADDRESS COMMUNICATION PROBLEMS FOR STUDENTS WHO CANNOT SPEAK: AUGMENTATIVE COMMUNICATION

Having the power to speak one's heart and mind changes the disability equation dramatically. (Williams, 2000, p. 249)

One of the most powerful applications of computer technology has been the development and ongoing refinement of devices that can speak. The technical term for this technology is **alternative and augmentative communication** (AAC), which is shortened for convenience to **augmentative communication**. Simply put, augmentative communication is "about helping individuals who cannot speak to interact with others" (Beukelman & Mirenda, 2000, p. 13). Augmentative communication systems serve as an *alternative* to speech for people who cannot talk. The word *augmentative* is emphasized because we all—whether we can or cannot speak— also use other, nonverbal means to communicate with others. For example, we all use facial expressions, gestures, and body language when we communicate. Augmentative communication systems are designed to "augment" whatever existing communication a person has. Blackstone (1993), a leading researcher, summarizes the benefits of augmentative communication: "For a person with a severe motor impairment who does not speak, communication… is the key that unlocks the door, … letting the individual *Out* and the rest of the world *In*. It is language that truly connects one human to the other" (p. 4).

Rick Creech

Rick Creech, who has cerebral palsy, offers a simple way for students to get a hint of what it feels like to be unable to speak:

Go to a party and don't talk. Play mute. Use your hands if you wish but don't use paper and pencil…. Here is what you will find: people talking; talking behind, beside, around, over, under, through, and even for you. But never with you. You are ignored until finally you feel like a piece of furniture. (Musselwhite & St. Louis, 1988, p. 104)

Augmentative communication systems can be *unaided* or *aided*. **Unaided** systems use only a person's body for communication. Sign language is a good example of an unaided system. A person does not need to carry anything with him or her; the communication system (sign language) is always available in every environment. In contrast, **aided** systems involve the use of an external piece of equipment to convey a message. An alphabet board is an aided communication method. So are assistive technology–based systems. An inconvenience of aided systems is that they must be transported by the user, and they may present problems in inclement weather. However, unlike sign language, aided systems have the advantage of being easily understood by most listeners (Stuart, 2002).

Anthony Arnold

My name is Anthony Arnold, and I'm from North Dakota. I was born on May 22, 1977. Right before birth, I had a lack of oxygen in my brain, which is needed for normal development. Due to this, I have cerebral palsy, which affects my whole physical body and my speech abilities. I now use a power chair and an augmentative communication device to gain independence.

Before my first communication board, I pointed at sales fliers and objects in my house to communicate with my family. I know sometimes my parents got frustrated by my pointing and their having to guess, but I feel it also offered them some encouragement. It helped them realize that I did know something.

EARLY COMMUNICATION BOARDS

From this discovery, my parents went to a rehab clinic to meet with my team and suggested developing a communication board that could be easily understood by anyone. It took my parents some time to sell my therapists on this idea. During this time I also began to attend to preschool, which helped create some interaction between other children and me. This built more interest in communication board use and led to more communication boards with more symbols.

By the time I reached elementary school I had a communication board with almost 100 symbols on it. I knew more parts of speech than most five-year-olds. I was easily making 10 or more word sentences. This usually frustrated people trying to follow my hand movements (it wasn't easy to read as fast as I was building a sentence). From watching my progress with communication boards and realizing that there was no more physical room to put 200 words on a board, my parents and therapists started researching other methods. At that time, the Prentke Romich Company was just introducing the *Touch Talker*. Here was a portable device with a computer-generated voice, one of the first available in 1984. It was a wonderful and dependable device, so we decided to rent one for a trial period and eventually bought it.

INDEPENDENCE THROUGH TECHNOLOGY

When I first received my *Touch Talker*, I remember that was the happiest day of my childhood. I finally had a way of communicating without having somebody always there reading my board. During this time I was seen by two speech-language pathologists who were truly dedicated to working with my parents and teachers to build my vocabulary and my interest level for using the device.

Anthony, who has cerebral palsy, uses the Pathfinder (Prentke Romich Company) to communicate. *Courtesy of Roberta Arnold. Reprinted with permission from Anthony Arnold.*

I would say that during my early teenage years was when I began to realize how much my *Touch Talker* (and then my *Liberator*) helped me gain independence. I wanted to help others receive what I had already received thanks to many people, including my parents. So I made a career goal of working for the Prentke Romich Company (PRC) or another place where I could use my knowledge and experiences to help.

THE DREAM JOB

I began working for PRC as an Ambassador, traveling to conferences to display the powers of the *Liberator* (the successor to my *Touch Talker*). I still do that today. After seeing the success of the Ambassador program, PRC developed the Remote Troubleshooter Program for the Technical Service Department. I answer technical service calls about PRC's augmentative communication devices at night and on weekends when the company is closed. I feel we have had great success with this program. I have been doing it for five years now, and I love it....

I recently commissioned a painting of all of my communication boards. ...Excerpts from my speech follow:

One of the things I most like about this painting is that it shows that communication development doesn't just happen over night, which is a common misconception. I received my first communication board with six pictures on it at the age of two. Now I'm 27, using the most advanced communication device we have available today (*Pathfinder*), and within these years, I have used a number of different communication boards and augmentative communication devices. ■

Source: From "Augcom User Helps Others as a Troubleshooter for Prentke Romich Company," by A. Arnold, 2003, *TECH-NJ*, *14*(1), p. 14.

The commissioned painting of the progression of Anthony's communication boards.
Source: Photo by Anthony Arnold.

UPDATE

Anthony Arnold in 2010

I recently upgraded to an ECO™2 from an ECO-14. I chose to go with an ECO2 primarily because I like the fact that it has more memory, which allows for faster computing. The ECO-14 was a wonderful communication device, but I always felt that I was missing out on something, the faster processing the better, especially in this day and age. Another benefit is the option of having built-in WiFi capabilities without needing anything externally sticking out. The WiFi capabilities are always on and ready to go, and I can access a network anywhere I might be.

I enjoy the new icons and skins now available on the ECO2. As an augmentative and alternative communicator, we don't want to be left out and if other devices have newer icons why shouldn't we. I give PRC a lot of credit for listening to this request!

Another feature I appreciate is the Bluetooth capabilities allowing for interfacing with a cell phone. I have advocated for cell phone features for years, and they're finally here! My family and friends enjoy knowing I have a cell phone I can access at all times. ■

Source: From "Update: ECO2" by Anthony Arnold, retrieved from http://www.prentrom.com/eco/anthony-arnold/

Listservs for Augmentative Communication Users

Anthony Arnold highly recommends joining the ACOLUG (Augmentative Communication OnLine Users Group) listserv to learn more about augmentative communication and to exchange ideas with augmentative communicators, family members, college students, and professionals. ACOLUG is hosted by Temple University's Institute on Disabilities (http://listserv.temple.edu/archives/ACOLUG.html). Voice for Living is a blog on augmentative communication issues that is hosted by the company Dynavox Mayer-Johnson (http://www.voiceforliving.com).

The profile written by Anthony Arnold, an augmentative communication user, introduces many of the basic principles of augmentative communication. Augmentative communication devices can range from low tech to high tech. Anthony's first communication board, when he was a toddler, was simply a few pictures mounted on a piece of wood (low tech). He pointed to what he wanted, and an adult who was present would "read" his request. This low-tech board was expanded to more than 100 picture symbols that were arranged categorically on a laminated, foldout display. Today he uses a high-tech device called an ECO-2 (Prentke Romich), which offers unlimited vocabulary, a high-quality computer-generated voice, strategies for increasing his speed of communication (called "rate enhancement"), wireless access to the Internet, and seamless interface with a cell phone.

Augmentative communication techniques existed before computer technology was widely available (e.g., Anthony's early picture board), but computer technology has led to an explosion of options, features, and communication power. Applications such as Boardmaker (Mayer-Johnson) have greatly simplified the process of creating picture boards for teachers, parents, and speech therapists. When selecting a system, augmentative communication users can choose to use a picture-based system, text-based system, or a combination of the two. They can choose a male or female voice, an adult's voice, or a child's voice. Even inexpensive devices (less than $300) can now speak aloud with a good-quality voice. Speech output on a device enables an augmentative communication user to gain attention (e.g., "Mrs. T., I need help!") and to communicate more elaborate messages more quickly. (The Go-Talk Express 32 in the photo on page 154 is an example of a device that is picture-based and provides speech output.) For his job as an augmentative communication troubleshooter, Anthony stores pre-programmed answers and instructions on his ECO-2 and accesses them when he is talking to a customer by simply pressing a few keys.

Which augmentative communication system is the best? No single device is appropriate for all students. Students have different needs and strengths that change over time (Beukelman & Mirenda, 2000). The augmentative communication system chosen for a student must match that particular student's abilities, communication needs, motor skills, daily environments, and personal preferences. For example, a child who walks and runs needs an augmentative communication system that will not break easily. This was not a concern for Anthony, who uses a wheelchair for mobility; his first high-tech device was heavy and fragile, but it was mounted securely to his wheelchair tray. A young child or a child with developmental disabilities who cannot read or spell needs an augmentative communication system that uses photographs or picture symbols and not words. Anthony is a high school graduate with solid reading skills; although he uses a picture symbol system because it is fast, he needs a spell mode option when he wants to communicate something that is not represented by his picture symbols, or when he is programming his device.

GoTalk Express 32
Courtesy of Attainment Company.

Gus Estrella

Gus Estrella (2000), a graduate of the University of Arizona who has cerebral palsy, describes one way his computerized augmentative communication system enhanced his life:

> When I finally had a more powerful VOCA [voice output communication appliance] … I started to have real conversations with people whom I had always wanted to talk…. My father was one person that I had always wanted to have a conversation with, but there was always a barrier. Finally that barrier was broken! Now we were able to carry on a real conversation without needing someone to translate my grunts into real words! We were able to talk about women…. Plus we were able to talk about all the beers we had the night before at the football game, without my mother knowing what we really did. Now we could have our little secrets that would drive my mother nuts! (p. 37)

The decision-making process in selecting and setting up an augmentative communication system for a student is complex. It must involve a team of people—at a minimum, a speech-language pathologist, the student, the parents, and the classroom teacher. Usually a physical or occupational therapist is part of the team to help with issues related to motor skills. Many factors must be considered, including the communication demands of the student's various environments, the student's language development, the student's motor abilities, and the student's personal preferences. One study of augmentative communication evaluations reported that in a pool of 64 individuals with cerebral palsy, a total of 17 different types of augmentative communication devices were recommended (LaFontaine & DeRuyter, 1987). These included low-tech picture boards and word boards, and 13 different types of electronic devices. Half of the individuals in this study were able to use a finger to access their augmentative communication system; those who could not point with a finger used a variety of other access methods such as chin pointers, joysticks, optical indicators, and switches for scanning. Chapter 11 provides additional information on decision making for augmentative communication.

Several times in his profile Anthony mentions his speech-language therapists, teachers, and parents, which highlights the importance of training and support. Simply providing a student with the latest, most dazzling augmentative communication devices is not enough. Augmentative communication will not make a difference in students' lives unless schools provide

- **Training:** on strategies for communication and on how to use the specific device
- **Support:** ongoing and timely technical support
- **Practice:** multiple opportunities for the student to communicate with the device in all of his or her environments (Estrella, 2000)

Bob Williams (2002) points to the importance of providing access to augmentative communication to *all* individuals who cannot speak, calling for a transformation of attitudes and expectations:

> Every person, regardless of the severity of his/her disabilities, has the right… to communicate with others, express everyday preferences and exercise at least some control over his or her daily life. Each individual, therefore, should be given the chance, training, technology, respect and encouragement to do so. (2002, p. 2)

Specific strategies for classroom teachers to provide this kind of support are the focus of Chapter 12.

TASH Resolution on the Right to Communicate

The right to communicate is both a basic human right and the means by which all other rights are realized. All people communicate. In the name of fully realizing the guarantee of individual rights, we must ensure:

- that all people have a means of communication which allows their fullest participation in the wider world;
- that people can communicate using their chosen method; and
- that their communication is heeded by others.

Where people lack an adequate communication system, they deserve to have others try with them to discover and secure an appropriate system. No person should have this right denied because they have been diagnosed as having a particular disability. Access to effective means of communication is a free speech issue.

Originally adopted November 1992; revised December 2000.

Source: Information from "TASH Resolution on the Right to Communicate," by TASH, 2002, *TASH Connections, 25*(5).

Summary

- Students who are hard of hearing have difficulty following classroom instruction due to poor acoustics, classroom layout, and teacher style. They are also at a serious disadvantage during social interactions.
- Hearing assistive technology, a category of assistive technology that helps people who have hearing losses, can help students who are hard of hearing by amplifying specific sounds while minimizing background distractions. A variety of assistive listening devices are available to meet specific needs.
- Common Web-based applications such as e-mail, instant messaging, chat rooms, discussion boards, blogs, and Skype have made the computer "an instrument of liberation" for people who are deaf or hard of hearing because they open avenues of communication that do not rely on hearing or speaking.
- Text messaging on cell phones is similarly liberating for people who are deaf or hard of hearing.
- Students who lack the ability to speak are at a serious disadvantage in school: They are unable to express ideas and opinions, participate in class discussions, demonstrate what they have learned, and engage in social situations.
- Augmentative communication is defined as a way to supplement an individual's method of communication to assist comprehension. It is, for some, essential in making themselves understood and for conveying clear messages to a variety of audiences.
- Augmentative communication devices range from low tech to high tech; selecting a system that matches a student's needs is a complex process that must involve a team of professionals, as well as the student and family.
- Augmentative communication increases an individual's independence and opens the door to numerous opportunities.
- See Table 6.4 for a summary of technology tools that enhance communication.

TABLE 6.4	Summary of Technology Tools That Enhance Communication		
Communication Goal	**Technology Tools**	**Sample Products**	**Who Benefits?**
Hearing lectures and class discussions	Assistive listening devices	Phonak Personal FM System Phonic Ear Soundfield Amplication System	Students who are hard of hearing; students who have attention deficit disorder or central auditory processing disorder
Interacting with faculty and peers outside class	TTY/TDD Text messaging e-mail Online discussion boards Video phone with video relay service	Ameriphone Available in cell phone plans Any commercial e-mail program Any online course system VP-200 with Sorenson Video Relay Service	Students who are deaf or hard of hearing
Participating in class activities, expressing yourself, making choices, interacting with others, demonstrating your knowledge	Augmentative communication systems	ECO-2 Vanguard Plus Springboard Lite Dynavox V & Vmax Go-Talk 20+	Students who cannot speak (e.g., students with cerebral palsy or students with autism)

Web Resources

For additional information on the topics listed, visit the following Web sites:

Cochlear Implants
National Institute on Deafness and Other Communication Disorders
http://www.nidcd.nih.gov/health/hearing/coch.htm

Alerting Devices
Soundbytes
http://www.soundbytes.com/Visual_Alerting_Systems.html

Relay Services
Sorenson Video Relay Service
http://www.sorensonvrs.com

SIPRelay Service
http://www.siprelay.com/what_is.aspx

Assistive Listening Devices
Comtek
http://www.comtek.com/assistive.html

Williams Sound
http://www.williamssound.com/home.aspx
American Speech, Language and Hearing Association
http://www.asha.org/public/hearing/treatment/assist_tech.htm
Sound-Field Systems Guide for Classrooms in Alberta
http://www.infrastructure.gov.ab.ca/docType486/Production/soundfieldguide.pdf

Augmentative Communication
International Society for Augmentative and Alternative Communication (ISAAC)
http://www.isaac-online.org/ie

Vermont Communication Resource Guide (2003) (Updated April 2010)
Download PDF from
http://www.ddas.vermont.gov/ddas-publications/publications-dds/publications-dds-default-page

Perspectives of Augmentative Communication Users
Gus Estella's Distinguished Lecture
http://www.aacinstitute.org/Resources/PrentkeLecture/1997/GusEstrella.html
Rick Creech's Distinguished Lecture
http://www.aacinstitute.org/Resources/PrentkeLecture/2004/RickCreech.html
Success Stories from Prentke Romich
http://www.prentrom.com/success/
Success and News Stories from Dynavox
http://www.dynavoxtech.com/success/default.aspx

Autism and Communication
Communication Interventions for Children with Autism
http://www.autismnetwork.org/modules/comm/aac/index.html

Suggested Activities

1. *Research a personal perspective.* Read *I Raise My Eyes to Say Yes* by Sienkiewicz-Mercer and Kaplan (1996). Then write a short paper discussing the following: (a) How significant was Ruth's inability to speak? How did it affect her life? (b) How has Ruth's story affected your attitude, expectations, and/or teaching practices toward students who are nonspeaking?

2. *Investigate assistive devices for people who are deaf or hard of hearing.* Locate a demonstration center near you that provides assistive devices for people who are deaf or hard of hearing. These centers are often funded by state agencies or organizations focused on hearing impairments. If you cannot visit a center, explore Web sites such as Gallaudet University's LeClerc Center at http://clerccenter.gallaudet.edu/x17217.xml, DeafWeb Washington at http://www.deafweb. org/assist.htm, or *TECH-NJ* at http://www. tcnj.edu/~technj/2003/dodds.htm. What kinds of assistive devices are available that help people who are deaf or hard of hearing carry out daily living activities independently?

3. *Research cochlear implants.* Write a short research paper on cochlear implants. How long have they been available? Who is the latest group to receive them? How are children who have cochlear implants being educated? What is the controversy surrounding cochlear implants?

4. *Investigate the function of cell phones and personal digital assistants.* Conduct an

interview with a person who is deaf or hard of hearing to find out what technology tools he or she uses: cell phone, text messaging, instant messaging, and so on. What specific activities is this technology enabling the person to do?

References

Andrews, J. F., Leigh, I. W., & Weiner, M. T. (2004). *Deaf people: Evolving perspectives from psychology, education, and sociology.* Boston, MA: Allyn & Bacon/Pearson Education.

Arnold, A. (2010). Update: ECO2. Retrieved May 25, 2010, from http://www.prentrom.com/eco/anthony-arnold/

Arnold, A. (2003). Augcomm user helps others as a troubleshooter for Prentke-Romich Company. *TECH-NJ, 14*(1). Retrieved May 26, 2010, from http://www.tcnj.edu/~technj/2003/arnold.htm

Beukelman, D. R., & Mirenda, P. (2000). *Augmentative and alternative communication: Management of severe communication disorders in children and adults* (2nd ed.). Baltimore, MD: Brookes.

Blackstone, S. (1993). Clinical news: AAC for people with CP. *Augmentative Communication News, 6*(5).

Boswell, S. (2006). Sound field systems on the rise in schools: Improved test scores cited as benefit. *The ASHA Leader, 11*(7), 1, 32–33.

Carr, E. G., Levin, L., McConnachie, G., Carlson, J. I., Kemp, D. C., & Smith, C. E. (1994). *Communication-based intervention for problem behavior: A user's guide for producing positive change.* Baltimore, MD: Brookes.

DO-IT. (2004). *Disabilities, opportunities, internetworking, and technology.* Retrieved May 26, 2010, from the Faculty Room Web site: http://www.washington.edu/doit/Faculty/

Dodds, J. (2003). *Assistive technology for people who are deaf and hard of hearing. TECH-NJ, 14*(1). Retrieved May 26, 2010, from http://www.tcnj.edu/~technj/2003/dodds.htm

Durand, V. M. (1993). Functional communication training using assistive devices: Effects on challenging behavior. *Augmentative and Alternative Communication, 9,* 168–176.

Estrella, G. (2000). Confessions of a blabber finger. In M. Fried-Oken & H. Bersani (Eds.), *Speaking up and spelling it out* (pp. 31–45). Baltimore, MD: Brookes.

Kisor, H. (1990). *What's that pig outdoors? A memoir of deafness.* New York: Penguin Books.

Koegel, L. K., Koegel, R. L., & Dunlap, G. (1996). *Positive behavioral support: Including people with difficult behavior in the community.* Baltimore, MD: Brookes.

LaFontaine, L., & DeRuyter, F. (1987). The nonspeaking cerebral palsied: A clinical and demographic database report. *Augmentative and Alternative Communication, 3,* 153–162.

Musselwhite, C., & St. Louis, K. (1988). *Communication programming for persons with severe handicaps.* Austin, TX: Pro-Ed.

Northeast Technical Assistance Center. (1998). *The role of assistive listening devices in the classroom* (NETAC Teacher Tipsheet Series). Rochester, NY: Author.

Northeast Technical Assistance Center. (2000). *Serving deaf students who have cochlear implants* (NETAC Teacher Tipsheet Series). Rochester, NY: Author.

Schindler, C. (2003). Text messaging: More than just an add-on to cell phone plans. *TECH-NJ, 14*(1). Retrieved May 26, 2010, from http://www.tcnj.edu/~technj/2003

Self Help for Hard of Hearing People. (2006). *Facts on hearing loss.* Retrieved May 26, 2010, from http://www.hearingloss.org/learn/factsheets.asp

Sienkiewicz-Mercer, R., & Kaplan, S. B. (1996). *I raise my eyes to say yes.* West Hartford, CT: Whole Health Books.

Spadafora, T. (2003). *FM system & C-Print™ assist hard-of-hearing student in high school. TECH-NJ, 14*(1). Retrieved May 26, 2010, from http://www.tcnj.edu/~technj/2003/cprint.htm

Steinberg, A. (2000). Autobiographical narrative on growing up deaf. In P. E. Spencer, C. J. Erting, & M. Marschark (Eds.), *Essays in honor of Kathryn P. Meadow-Orlans: The deaf child in the family and at school* (pp. 93–108). Mahwah, NJ: Erlbaum.

Stinson, M. S., & Foster, S. (2000). Socialization of deaf children and youths in school. In P. E. Spencer, C. J. Erting, & M. Marschark (Eds.), *Essays in honor of Kathryn P. Meadow-Orlans: The deaf child in the family and at school* (pp. 191–209). Mahwah, NJ: Erlbaum.

Stuart, S. (2002). Communication: Speech and language. In M. L. Batshaw (Ed.), *Children with disabilities* (5th ed., pp. 229–241). Baltimore, MD: Brookes.

TASH. (2002). TASH resolution on the right to communicate. *TASH Connections, 28*(5).

Warick, R., Clark, C., Dancer, J., & Sinclair, S. (1997). Assistive listening devices. In R. Stuckless, D. Ashmore, J. Schroedel, & J. Simon (Eds.), *A report of the National Task Force on Quality of Services in the Postsecondary Education of Deaf and Hard of Hearing Students*. Rochester, NY: Northeast Technical Assistance Center (NETAC), Rochester Institute of Technology, National Technical Institute for the Deaf. Retrieved May 26, 2010, from the Northeast Regional Center Web site: http://netac.rit.edu/publication/taskforce

Williams, B. (2000). More than an exception to the rule. In M. Fried-Oken & H. Bersani (Eds.), *Speaking up and spelling it out* (pp. 245–254). Baltimore, MD: Brookes.

Williams, B. (2002). Preface. *Vermont communication resource guide*. Retrieved May 26, 2010, from the Division of Developmental Services Web site: http://depts.washington.edu/augcomm/03_cimodel/commind1_intro.htm

Wing, L. (1996). *The autistic spectrum: A guide for parents and professionals*. London, England: Constable.

PART 2

ACCESS TO COMPUTERS

CHAPTER 7

Providing Access to Computers: Using What You Have

CHAPTER 8

Assistive Technology for Computer Access

CHAPTER 9

Issues in Selection of Access Method(s)

7 | PROVIDING ACCESS TO COMPUTERS: USING WHAT YOU HAVE

Focus Questions

1. What universal design features facilitate computer access for students with disabilities? What are the characteristics of students for whom the specific features may be appropriate?
2. What additional operating system features are provided for users with disabilities, and what are the characteristics of students for whom these specific features may be appropriate?

INTRODUCTION

In Chapters 1 through 6, you read about how computers have the capacity to help students with disabilities participate in educational, social, and leisure activities. In order to participate in these activities students must be able to use a computer. Many students with disabilities will be able to use a computer effectively simply by taking advantage of adjustments and settings readily available within their computer's operating system.

This chapter focuses on universal design features and other accessibility features provided in operating systems that are relevant to students with disabilities. Not every feature is applicable to every student, nor is a particular feature appropriate for every student with a particular disability; computer access solutions must be decided on a case-by-case basis according to each student's specific needs and preferences (see Chapter 9). Thus, as we discuss features in this chapter, we match them with the characteristics of students for whom they might be appropriate, rather than with disability categories.

The computer operating systems that dominate preK–12 educational environments are Macintosh OS and Microsoft Windows; consequently, discussion focuses on these two systems. Operating systems are continually updated, which has led to an inconsistency in versions that are installed on computers in schools. Because it is not possible to address each operating system version, only Macintosh OS X and Microsoft Windows 7, the latest versions, are referenced in the sections that follow.

By making laptop computers available in a range of sizes, computer manufacturers adhere to the principles of universal design.

Photo by Ellen C. Farr.

UNIVERSAL DESIGN

As explained in Chapter 1, the computer industry has adopted the concept of universal design that was first introduced in the fields of architecture and design. Wanting to sell as many computers as possible, the industry recognized the commercial value of designing operating systems that are usable by as many people as possible. This means people who are new to computers, as well as expert users; people who use computers for enjoyment at home, and those who use them in the workplace; young people who have good eyesight; and people older than 40 who need reading glasses. In this section, we will discuss how the second principle of universal design, flexibility in use, has been incorporated in operating systems and how this benefits students with disabilities.

Flexibility in Use

The first guideline for the principle of flexibility in use encourages designers to make products that provide choice in methods of use. The developers of the most recent computer operating systems have adhered to this guideline, and it is manifested in having the choice of using either the mouse or the keyboard to control the computer. Being able to operate a computer solely using the keyboard may be surprising to many. Using the mouse to control and navigate computers is so common, comfortable, and familiar that many people assume it is the *only* option. However, both Macintosh and Windows operating systems offer keyboard shortcuts that provide access to all functions directly from the keyboard. For example, in Windows 7 an item can be permanently deleted by pressing Shift + Delete, rather than by using the mouse to drag the item to the Recycle Bin and then having to select the option to "Empty the Recycle Bin." Table 7.1 provides other examples of keyboard shortcuts in Windows 7.

Having the option to use the keyboard instead of the mouse provides computer access for users who find it difficult or impossible to control a mouse. This includes students with fine motor control difficulties, limited range of motion, or visual impairments that interfere with seeing or tracking the mouse pointer on the computer screen. An important consideration for students who use keyboard shortcuts is that this method places a considerable cognitive load on the students. They must remember a large number of keyboard shortcuts, and they must be able to read and understand a keyboard shortcut reference list so they can locate seldom used or forgotten commands.

TABLE 7.1	Sample Keyboard Shortcuts in Windows 7
Maximize a window	Windows key + Up Arrow ⇑
Snap to the left side	Windows key + Left Arrow ⇐
Snap to the right	Windows key + Right Arrow ⇒
Peek (quick preview of a program)	Windows key + T

Computers can also be controlled by voice. Both Windows 7 and Mac OS X v10.6 Snow Leopard allow users to speak commands into a microphone to have the actions performed. This feature is called Speech Recognition in Windows and Speakable Items in Mac OS X. Users can launch programs, open and close windows, and access menus solely by speaking the proper commands. Students with motor control issues, muscle weakness or fatigue, as well as students with vision impairments may benefit from speech recognition. As with the use of keyboard commands, those who operate the computer via speech recognition must be able to remember the commands and be able to read a reference list of common commands.

In addition to having a choice over how to input into a computer, Mac users can make a choice regarding their computer's **output** (i.e., how information is presented to the user). The Mac's System Preferences offers the option of text-to-speech—that is, having any text read aloud when it is highlighted and a designated key sequence is pressed. Users also have the option of setting the speaking rate. This feature is especially helpful for users with reading disabilities and attention deficits.

The second guideline for the principle of flexibility in use calls for designers to **accommodate left- and right-handed users**. Both the Macintosh one-button mouse and the Microsoft two-button mouse are suitable for this purpose. Because Macintosh computers use a one-button mouse, a student can simply position the mouse on the side of the keyboard that is most convenient. At first glance, the Microsoft two-button mouse may not seem to be designed for left-handed users because the left button controls the major mouse functions, a design suited for right-handed users. However, the functions of the two buttons can be switched using the Mouse Properties Control Panel in the Windows 7 operating system (see Figure 7.1). When the button functions are switched and the mouse is positioned to the left side of the computer, students can use their left index fingers on the right button, which now controls the major mouse functions. Thus, both the one-button mouse and the two-button mouse accommodate left- and right-handed users, and both mice meet the needs of students who may have only a left hand or who can control only left-hand movements well enough to use the mouse.

The third guideline of the principle of flexibility in use suggests that designers take into account variations among the precision and accuracy of computer users. Both the Macintosh and Windows operating systems incorporate this guideline by providing the means to **enlarge the size of icons**. Enlarged icons are easier to see and the larger surface areas make them easier to target with the mouse. Both operating systems also allow users to adjust the speed of the mouse. Slowing down the speed at which the mouse pointer moves may facilitate accurate targeting of icons, menus, or other items. Larger icons and a slower mouse speed, used alone or in combination, make it possible for some students with disabilities to use a computer without the need to add specialized devices. These two options may be helpful for students who have hand-eye coordination problems, visual impairments, hand tremors, mild motor control issues, or cognitive disabilities.

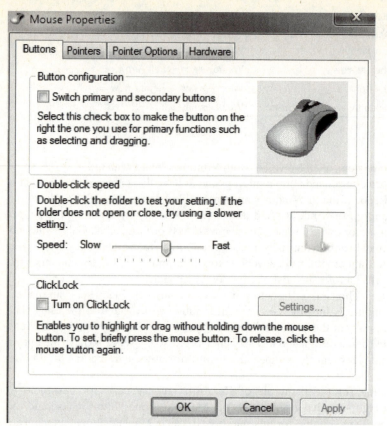

FIGURE 7.1 Mouse properties control panel in Microsoft Windows XP.

Source: Microsoft product screen shot reprinted with permission from Microsoft Corporation.

The final flexibility-in-use guideline advises designers to provide **adaptability to the user's pace**. This guideline is incorporated in computer operating systems in a variety of ways and is exemplified by the control users have over certain mouse and keyboard features. In both Macintosh and Windows operating systems, users can adjust the speed at which the mouse pointer moves and the speed at which the button must be pressed to register a double-click. Slowing the mouse pointer speed may assist students who have difficulty with visual tracking; students who find it difficult to execute small, precise mouse movements; and students who need to look at the mouse while they move it and then need time to look up to the monitor to see where the mouse pointer is located. Increasing the speed at which the mouse pointer moves may benefit those with a limited range of motion as the mouse pointer will move a greater distance with each movement. Students who control the mouse pointer through the use of mouse emulators (alternative devices used to perform mouse functions; see Chapter 8) benefit from being able to select the mouse pointer speed that best meets their needs. Slowing down the double-click speed (i.e., increasing the amount of time between the two mouse clicks) may be helpful for students who have fine motor control issues.

Being able to make adjustments to the **keyboard repeat rate** is another illustration of adaptability to a user's pace. Users can adjust the delay before a key will start repeating and how fast it repeats once it starts. Increasing the delay before a key begins to repeat makes the computer more accessible for students who have fine motor control or other issues making it difficult to release a key after it has been selected. Slower repeat rates also benefit students who need to look at the keyboard as they type and have difficulty raising their heads to verify typing accuracy.

Table 7.2 provides a summary of the guidelines associated with the principle of flexibility in use, features, and the characteristics of students for whom the features may be beneficial. Remember that no operating system feature can meet the needs of every student with the

TABLE 7.2	Operating System Features Adhering to Flexibility-In-Use Principle	
Flexibility-in-Use Guideline	**Operating System Features**	**Student Characteristics**
Provide choice in method of use	Control computer with mouse or keyboard	Keyboard use supports students who have • Poor fine motor control • Limited range of motion • Difficulty in visually tracking mouse pointer
	Receive information by reading (monitor) or listening (text-to-speech)	Text-to-speech supports students with reading disabilities or attention deficits.
Accommodate left- and right-handed users	One-button mouse; functions of the two-button mouse can be switched	Able to use only one hand or has better control with one hand
Take into account variations in precision and accuracy of mouse use	Enlarged icons	Low vision Visual perceptual issues Hand-eye coordination problems Hand tremors Poor fine motor control Cognitive deficits
Adaptability to user's pace	Set speed of mouse travel	**Increase** mouse speed for students with limited range of motion
	Set timing for double-click	**Decrease** mouse speed for students with
	Set keyboard repeat delay	• Visual tracking difficulty • Poor fine motor control
	Set keyboard repeat speed	• Difficulty raising head to monitor the movement of the mouse pointer
		Increase repeat delay for students with • Poor fine motor control • Difficulty raising head to check for typing accuracy

characteristics listed in this table, and that these features may also benefit students with characteristics not mentioned.

Each of the four guidelines of the flexibility-in-use principle has resulted in operating system features that positively impact computer access for students with disabilities. These features
were developed to increase usability and meet the needs of the general public, not just users
with disabilities. However, certain features are incorporated into operating systems especially to
enable people with disabilities to use the computer; these are discussed in the following section.

ACCESSIBILITY FEATURES FOR USERS WITH DISABILITIES

The accessibility statements of Apple Inc. and Microsoft Corporation emphasize that these produc-
ers of the two major computer operating systems are committed to promoting computer access
for individuals with disabilities (Apple Inc., n.d.; Microsoft, n.d.). Both companies have built a
variety of special features into their operating systems specifically to increase the usability of their
products by people with physical disabilities, vision impairments or blindness, and hearing impairments or deafness. Most, but not all, of the accessibility features can be accessed through what
Macintosh OS X refers to as **Universal Access** and Windows 7 refers to as **Ease of Access Center**
(see Figure 7.2). Although the specific features may differ, there are many similar accessibility
supports in both operating systems. For example, both provide screen magnification that can be
beneficial to users with visual impairments. Both magnify the entire image on the screen, allow the
user to adjust the level of magnification, and offer high-contrast settings (white on black and color
inversion). However, Windows 7 also provides a lens-mode, which is an option to magnify only
a portion of the screen surrounding the mouse pointer (similar to a magnifying glass). Lens-mode
enables users to see which part of a display is being magnified and is especially helpful for Internet
browsing when users may be looking for a specific link or piece of information on a page.

Keyboard Modifications and Mouse Control

Readily available keyboard modifications, used alone or in various combinations, can increase
students' productivity and eliminate much of the frustration associated with using the standard
keyboard and mouse. These modifications may eliminate the expense of purchasing specialized
equipment and avoid drawing undue attention to students' disabilities through the use of that
equipment. Many students with disabilities will be able to engage in computer-based activities
using the same computer components as their typical peers.

STICKYKEYS.   StickyKeys allows students to press keys sequentially to execute functions that
typically require pressing the keys simultaneously. With StickyKeys activated, the modifier keys
(Shift, Control, Alt, Windows Logo) respond as if they were being held down until the next non-
modifier key is pressed. StickyKeys combined with keyboard shortcuts enables students who are
able to press only one key at a time to control applications and operating system functions. For
example, a student who has cerebral palsy and types with only one finger can use the keyboard
shortcut Control+S to save his or her document or Control+P to print the document. He or she
would not be able to execute either of these commands without the use of StickyKeys.

SLOW KEYS.   Slow Keys increases the amount of time a key must be depressed before registering a keystroke so that brief keystrokes will be ignored. This facilitates effective keyboarding for
students who have difficulty releasing a key once they have applied pressure or students who may

FIGURE 7.2 MouseKeys.

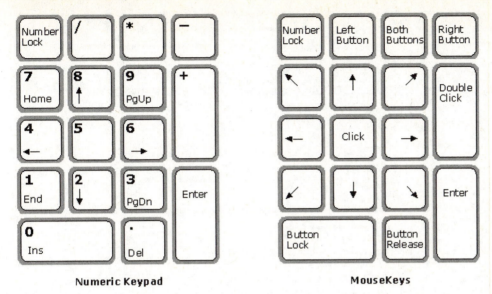

Numeric Keypad   MouseKeys

unintentionally put pressure on keys as their hands travel from one key to the next. Slow Keys is especially useful in increasing productivity by eliminating the frustrating sequence of typing too many letters, unintentionally erasing too many letters while trying to correct the original mistake, then retyping the desired letter. Students who may benefit from activating Slow Keys include those with hand tremors, muscle weakness or fatigue, and poor fine or gross motor control.

MOUSEKEYS.   MouseKeys is an accessibility feature that allows users to direct the mouse pointer and execute all mouse functions using the keyboard's numeric keypad (Figure 7.2). Both the speed at which the mouse pointer travels and accelerates are adjustable to meet individual needs. MouseKeys gives students who can use a keyboard successfully, but not a mouse, the ability to direct the mouse pointer, click, double-click, and drag directly from the keyboard. They do not ever have to move the mouse.

Keyboard modifications and mouse control that are enabled via Universal Access or Ease of Access Center (see Figure 7.3) enhance computer accessibility whether used alone or in combination with additional adjustments made through the keyboard and mouse control panels. Considering the possible combinations of keyboard and mouse modifications and adjustments, it is easy to see that the needs of many students may be met by determining the appropriate configuration of features available within computer operating systems.

Despite employing the modifications and adjustments already discussed, some students may continue to experience difficulty using the standard keyboard. If these students are able to use a mouse or an alternate pointing device such as a dowel grasped in a fist or a hands-free mouse (see Chapter 8), they may be able to utilize the onscreen keyboards offered by both Mac OS X and Windows operating systems. **Onscreen keyboards**, which place an interactive image of the keyboard on the monitor, allow students to select a key by moving the mouse to the desired key and clicking on it. See Figure 7.4. In the Windows 7 operating system, users can also select a key by hovering over it, that is, by keeping the mouse pointer on the image of the key

FIGURE 7.3 Ease of Access control panel in Microsoft Windows 7.

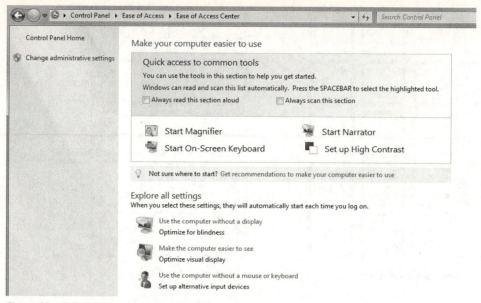

Source: Microsoft product screen shot reprinted with permission from Microsoft Corporation.

FIGURE 7.4 On-screen keyboard in Windows 7.

Source: Microsoft product screen shot reprinted with permission from Microsoft Corporation.

for a designated period of time. This enables users with limited motor control to access the on-screen keyboard.

In Windows 7, users can choose a keyboard layout by selecting Standard Keyboard or Enhanced Keyboard, which changes the number of keys available. Users can also resize the Windows 7 onscreen keyboard and keys, enlarging them to see them better and/or to improve the accuracy of selection. In addition, the Windows 7 onscreen keyboard provides word prediction (see Chapter 2) in a row above the function keys. All of these features enable users with some kinds of physical disabilities (such as muscular dystrophy or spinal muscular atrophy) improved access to computers.

Those students who are unable to use a mouse or alternate pointing device may still be able to utilize the Windows 7 onscreen keyboard by using scanning, which requires the ability to press only one key, such as the space bar or mouse, or a single switch (see Chapter 8 for a discussion of scanning and single switches). Once scanning is activated, one row of the keyboard will be highlighted at a time. Pressing the space bar will select a row; pressing it again will scan individual keys within the row; pressing it one more time will select that key. Although this is a slow input method, scanning makes computers accessible to students with even the most severe physical disabilities.

Modifications for Students with Sensory Impairments

Several features are available to make the computer easier to use for students who are blind or visually impaired and students who are deaf or hard of hearing. Many of these features are available through Universal Access and Ease of Access Center. For some users, activating these features enhances computer accessibility and eliminates the need for additional assistive technology hardware or software (see Chapter 8). For other users, these features will be part of a computer access solution that includes the use of additional assistive technology products.

HARD OF HEARING AND DEAFNESS.   Computers emit beeps, tones, and voiced messages to alert users to a variety of events; students who are hard of hearing or deaf may be unable to hear these sounds. Both Mac OS X and Windows 7 provide accessibility controls to replace auditory prompts and signals with **visual signals**, icons, or captions. So, for example, when a dialog box that requires a user's attention is displayed and the user tries to do something without responding to the message, rather than just emitting a beep to remind the user that he or she must make a selection, there can also be a spoken alert or a visual signal such as a flashing caption bar, window, or desktop.

VISUAL IMPAIRMENTS OR BLINDNESS.   Students with visual impairments often require a higher visual contrast and font size than the standard computer display provides in order to make text clearly discernible. This situation can be remedied using Universal Access or Ease of Access to apply a **high-contrast color scheme**—black background with white lettering, or white background with black lettering. Selecting the high-contrast display option presents files, folders, program names, and menu bar items in a large font in the selected color scheme. The display settings apply not only to the desktop, but to programs as well. So, for example, if a student chooses a black background and white text, the menu bars of every program will use that high-contrast color scheme.

Both Mac OS X and Windows 7 provide **screen magnification**, which enlarges the image on the monitor, to make the computer more accessible for users with low vision. The magnification ranges and options available within the operating systems vary (e.g., the maximum degree of magnification and size of magnification area), and features need to be carefully explored and configured to meet a student's screen magnification needs. It is important to remember that as the magnification level is increased, a smaller portion of the whole image is visible at one time. This may not interfere with understanding text-based items, but it may make it difficult to comprehend graphic images. Being able to **enlarge the mouse pointer** is another feature built into operating systems that helps students with visual impairments.

Both Macintosh OS X and Windows 7 provide **voiced feedback** to help students who have visual impairments or blindness use computers. The voice feedback can read everything on the screen: menu bars and menu items, icons, and dialog boxes, as well as text. Although both systems provide voiced feedback, just as with other accessibility items, the manner in which the voiced feedback is provided is different from one system to the other.

Narrator, the screen reader in Windows 7, offers users three options for speech feedback. Every key the user selects is spoken aloud when Echo Users' Keystrokes is chosen. To hear system messages, users must select Announce System Messages; Announce Scroll Notification informs the users whenever the screen scrolls. Users can customize voice settings by selecting the speed, volume, and pitch of the speech feedback. A default voice is available within the operating system, and if users have other voices installed on their computers, they have the option of using those voices.

VoiceOver, the screen reader in the Mac OS, is a full-featured screen reading program that provides functionality found in many commercial programs. (See Chapter 8.) Users can set the speed, volume, and pitch of voices, as well as select from the range of voices provided in Mac OS. VoiceOver users can assign specific voices to different functions and can navigate using keyboard equivalents. VoiceOver provides support for refreshable Braille display devices and provides users who are blind or visually impaired with access to the Apple iPad.

Finding the appropriate combination of general operating system and accessibility features is an important step in providing access to computer-based educational, recreational, and leisure activities. These features alone may be enough to meet the computer access needs of students with disabilities; however, they may need to be combined with assistive technology devices and/ or other applications. Keep in mind the operating system features presented in this chapter as you read Chapter 8. The success of specialized assistive technology devices often depends on the proper adjustments of the system features presented in this chapter.

Summary

- The concept of universal design is that products and environments should be usable by as many people as possible without the need for special adaptations.
- Of the seven principles of universal design, flexibility in use is most applicable to this discussion of computer design as it relates to students with disabilities. Programs adhering to this principle provide a variety of methods of use; accommodate right- and left-handed users; and provide for flexibility among the precision, accuracy, and pace of computer users.
- Additional operating system features in both Windows 7 and Macintosh OS X that adhere to the flexibility-in-use principle provide additional support for students with disabilities. Both offer important adjustments such as keyboard and mouse control, voice feedback, and display options to assist users with disabilities in completing tasks more easily.

Web Resources

For additional information on the topics listed, visit the following Web sites:

Keyboard Shortcuts
Microsoft Windows 7
http://windows.microsoft.com/en-US/Windows7/Keyboard-shortcutsMacintoshOSX

Macintosh OSX
Macintosh OSX http://support.apple.com/kb/HT1343

Windows 7 Accessibility Features
Ease of Access Center
http://windows.microsoft.com/en-us/windows7/products/features/accessibility

Macintosh OS X Accessibility Features
Universal Access
http://www.apple.com/accessibility

Suggested Activities

1. *Add to your portfolio.* Visit the Microsoft Web site (www.microsoft.com) and enter the phrase "Ease of Access" in the search box. Review the resources located, and then select relevant resources to add to your portfolio. Next, visit the Apple Inc. Web site (www.apple.com) and enter the phrase "Universal Access" in the search box. Review the resources identified and then select relevant resources to add to your portfolio.

2. *Use mousekeys.* Log in to a desktop computer running a Windows or Macintosh operating system. Turn on MouseKeys through the Accessibility Control Panel (Windows 2000 or XP), Ease of Access Center (Windows Vista or Windows 7), or Universal Access in System Preferences (Macintosh OS X). Set aside the mouse and use the numeric keypad instead to control the mouse. (Refer to Figure 7.2 for information on which keys correspond to specific mouse movements.) Open a browser, use MouseKeys to navigate to Favorites or Bookmarks, and select a Web site. Explore the site by using MouseKeys to follow links. If you prefer, navigate to the address bar and enter a URL. Open the Mouse Control Panel to change the speed of the mouse, and experiment with different mouse speeds. After a minimum of 10 minutes, turn off MouseKeys and write a two-page paper describing your experience

with this feature and the insights you gained from this activity.

3. *Use high contrast.* In Windows 7 locate the Ease of Access control panel. Select Optimize visual display, and then select Choose a High Contrast theme. Explore the various High Contrast themes by clicking on the image. Create a table detailing the features of the various High Contrast themes (In Windows 2000 or Windows XP locate the Accessibility Options through the Accessibility Control Panel. Explore the various High Contrast settings by selecting different settings and clicking Apply to activate them.).

4. *Explore universal design.* Explore the universal design publication list of the Center for Universal Design at North Carolina State University, http://www.design.ncsu.edu/cud/pubs_p/pud.htm. Read at least four of the case studies in the section titled "Case Studies on Universal Design." Then write a two-page paper identifying the case studies you read and discussing the impact universal design has on people with disabilities and others.

5. *Use the ease of access center.* Use the Microsoft Ease of Access Center to see how to configure the computer to meet individual user needs. From the Start menu, select Control

Panel and then Ease of Access Center. Read the information and select different options for each scenario. Keep a written record of your choices and record the result of these changes. Repeat this procedure at least two more times. When you have finished experimenting with the Ease of Access Center, write a two-page paper discussing your experience and what types of individuals might find the Ease of Access Center most helpful. Submit the narrative along with your written records of questions, answers, and changes that were made.

References

Apple Inc. (n.d.). *Accessibility statement*. Retrieved May 11, 2011 from http://www.apple.com/accessibility

Microsoft. (n.d.). *Accessibility Today* Retrieved March 6, 2010, from http://www.microsoft.com/enable/today.aspx

8 | ASSISTIVE TECHNOLOGY FOR COMPUTER ACCESS

Focus Questions

1. What is the assistive technology continuum, and what is its significance?
2. What are the major types of alternative keyboards, and what are the characteristics of students for whom each type would be appropriate?
3. What are the major types of mouse emulators, and what are the characteristics of students for whom each type would be appropriate?
4. How can alternative input and output devices make the computer accessible for students with vision impairments and blindness?

INTRODUCTION

Chapter 7 presented operating system features that can be adjusted to provide computer access to students with disabilities; however, some students require additional adaptations to be successful computer users. As stated in Chapter 1, the assistive technology that facilitates computer access for these students exists on a continuum from low tech to high tech (Blackhurst, 1997). This chapter presents technology covering the full range of the **assistive technology continuum** beginning with the low-tech end. This is the point at which technology consideration should begin, progressing to mid-tech and high-tech solutions only if a student's needs remain unmet. This chapter presents only suggestions or guidelines. With assistive technology there are no hard and fast rules; the most appropriate device must be determined through careful evaluation and actual usage. Principles guiding the selection process are discussed in Chapter 9.

LOW-TECH ADAPTATIONS FOR COMPUTER USE

Low-tech adaptations use no electronic components and are relatively low-cost items. Universal design features and accessibility features discussed in Chapter 7 have increased computer accessibility and have replaced the need for some low-tech adaptations such as devices to physically hold down the Shift or other modifier keys. However, low-tech assistive technology devices such as keyboard labels, selecting/pointing devices, keyguards, moisture guards, magnifying lenses, and

TABLE 8.1	Low-Tech Adaptations for Computer Access	
Low-Tech Adaptations	**Types**	**Student Characteristics**
Keyboard labels	Larger letters	Have visual/perceptual issues
		Have low vision
	High-contrast colors	Have low vision
	Braille	Blind
		Braille reader
	Blank	Have cognitive deficits
		Have visual/perceptual issues
		Have attention issues
Selecting/Pointing devices	Handheld dowel	Can control upper extremities but are unable to isolate a finger
	Mouthsticks	Cannot use hands but have good head control
	Chinsticks	
	Headsticks	
Keyguards	Acrylic or metal	Need targeting assistance
		Use selecting/pointing device
		Need wrist support
Moisture guards	Transparent—long-term use or disposable	Have a tendency to spill and/or drool
	Printed with key labels	Have visual/perceptual issues
		Have low vision

equipment to position computer components still play a vital role in providing computer access for individuals with disabilities. Table 8.1 lists low-tech adaptations, features, and the characteristics of students for whom the devices may be beneficial.

Keyboard Labels

Some students have difficulty using the standard keyboard because they cannot see the letters, numbers, and symbols on the keys. The standard keyboard can be customized to meet individual needs by affixing a variety of self-adhesive **keyboard labels**. Labels with larger letters and higher contrast (e.g., white letters on a black background) may meet the needs of students with visual-perceptual difficulties or those with low vision. Tactile labels with Braille markings make the computer keyboard accessible for students who are blind and are Braille readers. Blank keyboard labels can be used to cover nonessential keys, making the keyboard less confusing and visually distracting. Blank labels may make the keyboard more accessible for students with cognitive deficits and those with visual-perceptual or attention issues.

Selecting/Pointing Devices

Some students who have physical disabilities cannot isolate a finger or use their hands at all to press a single key on the standard keyboard. **Selecting/pointing devices** make that possible. These devices may be controlled by movements of the hand/arm, head, or foot. Mouthsticks, headsticks, and chinsticks are controlled by head movements. Both headsticks and chinsticks require a head-piece to hold the selecting/pointing device in position. These devices may be purchased from

Jade

Jade is a 9-year-old girl with cerebral palsy. An assistive technology evaluation was requested by her school district. Reports indicated that a variety of assistive devices had already been tried, but nothing worked. When Jade tried to use an alternative keyboard, she hit more than one key. She could isolate and point her index finger to some degree, but when she selected a letter, her other fingers invariably pressed other keys as well. She was unable to curl her other fingers tightly enough to avoid the unintentional keystroke. When Jade grasped an ordinary marker in a loose fist, she was able to select only one letter at a time. This was the first part of her computer access solution; however, she could not consistently select the key she wanted. When a keyguard was affixed to the keyboard, Jade's accuracy increased significantly. The combination of a keyguard with a pointing/selecting device gave Jade a reliable method of accessing the computer and, therefore, access to a wealth of educational opportunities.

Person typing with a low-tech dowel and keyguard.
Photo by Tammy Cordwell

commercial vendors, but they are often homemade using dowel rods of varying lengths and diameters with a protective cover on the end that comes in contact with the keyboard; pencil erasers or plastic end caps, such as those used for wire shelving are frequent choices. Items such as a thick marker, pencil, or short pieces of dowel rods may also be used as handheld selecting/pointing devices. A special grip may need to be fashioned to accommodate an individual's ability to grasp the device. Generally, students who benefit from selecting/pointing devices are those who can control their upper extremities but are unable to point a finger to select a key or students who have good head control, but limited ability to use their upper extremities. At times a dowel rod affixed to a shoe may be an effective selecting/pointing device for someone with good foot/leg control but poor upper body control. Sometimes a selecting/pointing device is the only assistive technology needed; at other times, it is just one part of the computer access solution.

Keyguards

Keyguards are acrylic or metal covers with holes that are placed atop the computer keyboard; generally, there is a corresponding hole for each of the keys. Keyguards, either ready-made or custommade, increase typing accuracy. Students using a selecting/pointing device or those with poor fine motor control may find it easier to target specific, individual keys because the holes allow only one key at a time to be pressed. Students who experience hand or arm fatigue can rest their wrist on the keyguard when selecting keys and, if necessary, slide their hands across the keyguard to get from one key to the next. The keyguard prevents unintended keystrokes from registering.

   Some students may benefit from custom-made keyguards that have holes for only the keys needed to interact with a given software program. Students with cognitive deficits may experience greater success interacting with the computer program if only the specific keys they need to use are accessible. This type of custom-made keyguard may also facilitate more efficient computer use for some students using selecting/pointing devices.

Moisture Guards

Moisture guards, also known as keyboard protectors or keyboard skins, are flexible, polyurethane covers that fit over the keyboard to protect it from moisture, dirt, dust, or other damaging substances. Moisture guards can be completely transparent, allowing the lettering on the keys to show through, or they may incorporate large-print, high-contrast key labels. Most moisture guards are designed for long-term use, but disposable moisture guards are available as well. Students who drool or have a tendency to spill or drop things may require a moisture guard to facilitate successful computer use. The type of moisture guard that is most appropriate will depend on the specific characteristics of the student and whether multiple users have access to the keyboard. For example, a moisture guard designed for long-term use with high-contrast key labels would be appropriate for the keyboard of a computer owned by a student with multiple disabilities who drools and has low vision. However, if this student is using a classroom computer, which has a keyboard that is frequently shared with other students, then it may be more hygienic to put high-contrast labels directly on the keys and use a transparent, disposable keyboard skin.

ALTERNATE INPUT: MOUSE ALTERNATIVES

Macintosh OS X and the Windows Operating System feature a graphical user interface (GUI). The GUI operating systems make computer use easier for the general public. Users do not have to memorize and type in computer commands; they can simply position the mouse pointer on what they desire and click or double-click to execute commands. However, for computer users with physical disabilities who have difficulty with fine motor control or those who have vision impairments or blindness and cannot see the mouse pointer or the onscreen graphics, controlling the mouse often presents a challenge.

As discussed in Chapter 7, one possible solution to accessing operating system commands is to use keyboard shortcuts in place of a mouse. However, there are many reasons why keyboard shortcuts will not meet the needs of all students: (1) Remembering operating system shortcuts can be extremely challenging or impossible for many students. (2) Once students have accessed the application that they want to work with, they may discover that the program does not respond to keyboard shortcuts or only certain features are available with keyboard shortcuts. (3) Students who use a wide variety of applications face the difficult task of recalling the keyboard shortcuts specific to each program. (4) Keyboard shortcuts, without the aid of a screen reading application, fail to serve the needs of students who cannot use a keyboard or who cannot clearly see images on the monitor. This section discusses mouse alternatives, also called mouse emulators, that enable students with physical disabilities to use their most reliable, controllable movements to direct the mouse pointer. (Special applications designed to meet the needs of students with vision impairments and blindness are discussed in the sections on screen magnification and screen readers.)

Trackballs

Unlike a computer mouse that must be moved across a horizontal surface, a **trackball** remains in one place. To move the mouse pointer, a ball, which is housed in the stationary base, is rotated; the mouse pointer moves in response to the rotation of the ball. Trackballs usually have

This adapted trackball has a keyguard and separate buttons for left click, right click, double click, drag, x/y lock and speed.

Reprinted with permission from Traxsys Input Products.

one to three buttons positioned near the ball that function just like mouse buttons (Webopedia, 2001). They are available in a variety of shapes and sizes to meet a wide range of individual needs and can be operated with a thumb, finger(s), the palm of the hand, a foot, or other body part. Most trackballs are designed to make computing tasks faster or more convenient for the general public, but these trackballs also may be appropriate for individuals with disabilities. Other trackballs are designed *especially* for individuals with disabilities, and these are the focus of this discussion.

Although each feature of a trackball is important in determining its appropriateness for students with disabilities, the size of the roller ball and the position or protection of the buttons are foremost concerns. Trackballs can be divided into three categories according to their size: (1) mini-trackballs, (2) standard trackballs, and (3) large trackballs. Mini-trackballs work well for users with very good fine motor control and for those who have a very limited range of motion (e.g., a student with muscular dystrophy). The Mini-Trackball (IBS Electronics) is a good example; the entire trackball measures just 1 inch by 2 inches so the ball that needs to be rotated is quite small and can be manipulated with the movement of a single finger. Standard trackballs require a greater range of motion than mini-trackballs but can be operated with a whole hand, a fist, a single finger, or a selecting/pointing device such as a headstick. Large trackballs, such as BIGtrack (Keytools) with a 3-inch roller ball, may be appropriate for younger students, those with poor fine motor control in their upper extremities, and those who use a foot to operate the trackball.

The position of the buttons on the trackball makes a trackball accessible or inaccessible to students with disabilities. The buttons must be positioned so the student can easily reach and press them, but not in a position that subjects them to unintentional presses. In fact, as you will see in the following discussion, accessibility and protection of the buttons are key features that distinguish trackballs designed for users with disabilities from those designed for the general public.

As noted previously, keyguards are useful for students who experience hand or arm fatigue because they can rest their wrist on the keyguard when selecting keys without initiating unintentional key presses. The same technology can be applied to protecting the buttons of a trackball: A keyguard for a trackball, which also may be referred to as a handguard or fingerguard, has holes that allow students to rotate the ball and to access the buttons when they are ready to press them. To use a trackball with a handguard, such as the Roller II or Roller Plus trackballs by Traxsys, students need to have adequate range of motion. If students are able to isolate a finger or use a selecting/pointing device, they can reach into the holes and press the buttons that execute a left click, right click, or the drag lock feature.

Switch-adapted trackballs (e.g., the Tracksys Roller II and Roller Plus discussed earlier) address difficulties students may have with pressing the buttons to execute mouse functions. Sometimes the buttons are too small, sometimes they are not in a position that students can reach, or students may not be able to isolate a finger or use a pointing device to reach buttons that are protected by a handguard. Switch-adapted trackballs have receptacles into which switches can be connected. (See section on Single Switches for Scanning and Morse Code.) Once connected, each switch executes a different mouse function (e.g., right click, left click, double-click, or drag-lock). Students need to be able to access multiple switches to use switch-adapted mice. The switches need to be positioned so they are easy to press with either the same body part that is used to move the roller ball or other body parts.

The buttons on some switch-adapted trackballs remain active when the switches are connected, whereas in others the buttons are deactivated when the switches are connected. Deactivating the buttons eliminates unintentional presses and may be helpful when trying to teach trackball/mouse skills; the switches can be presented only when the mouse pointer has reached the desired position.

This may be especially valuable when working with students who have cognitive impairments, students who might perseverate on pressing buttons, or students with attention issues.

Joysticks

Joysticks are similar to trackballs in that they provide a stationary base; however, in place of a ball set into the base, joysticks offer a moveable handle that is perpendicular (or almost perpendicular) to the base. Joystick handles do not need to be moved very far to direct the mouse pointer to any spot on the computer monitor, so they may be a good solution for students who have limited control of their fingers and hands.

The accessibility and protection of the buttons are key to usability of joysticks, just as they are for trackballs. Buttons must be positioned so they are not accidentally pressed while moving the joystick handle but are still within reach of the student. A keyguard can facilitate joystick use by making it possible for students to rest their hands on the base without activating any of the buttons.

Several joysticks—such as SAM (Switch-Adapted Mouse) Joystick (RJ Cooper & Associates) and Tracksys Joystick—offer features geared toward enabling students with disabilities to control the mouse pointer. **Adapted joysticks** may include one or more of the following features: special handles to accommodate different grasping abilities, keyguards to prevent accidental clicking, a click-lock button so the button does not need to be held down while moving the handle in order to "drag," and switch receptacles that provide switch access to button functions. Adapted joysticks may be plug-and-play (simply plug them in and they are ready to go), or software may need to be installed so the computer will translate the joystick movements and button presses into mouse movements and button clicks.

Student who has a physical disability accessing a computer with an adapted joystick.

Photo by Deborah A. Newton

Touch Screens

Touch screens, also called touch windows, provide computer input by a direct touch to the computer monitor. These are commonplace in today's society; they are used at information kiosks, automated teller machines (ATMs), smart phones, and iPads. Touch screens may be integrated (not added on) into the monitor just like those we see in the community. However, there are also touch screens that can easily be added to existing monitors. The TouchWindow by Riverdeep is an add-on touch screen available to fit either 15-inch or 17-inch monitors. Touch screens are a direct, almost intuitive way to interact with the computer—you reach out and touch what you want to select. It is the directness and intuitiveness of touch screens that make them an appropriate computer input device for many young children, students with severe disabilities, and students with autism. They are often used to establish cause and effect, that is, to teach students that what they do has a direct result: A simple point causes the computer to react. With good motor control, touch screens can be used to access a wide range of special education applications. The advent of the iPad and comparable tablet computers has led to the development of numerous apps that are accessed via touch alone.

Head-Pointing Systems

Just as head-controlled pointing devices (e.g., headsticks and mouthsticks) can provide access to the standard keyboard, head-controlled devices can be used to position the mouse pointer and access all mouse functions. For mouse control, however, the devices are high tech—the opposite end of the assistive technology continuum. They are sophisticated electronic devices that are relatively expensive.

Head-pointing systems are available for both desktop and laptop computers. Typically, one component of the system sits on top of the computer monitor, and the student wears the other component. The location of the wearable component depends on the specific system. The device on top of the monitor tracks the movement of the student's head from the signals it receives from the wearable component. The wearable component may be a type of headset or a piece of special reflective material (usually a dot) placed on the forehead, the rim of eyeglasses, or the brim of a hat. Infrared or optical sensors detect the position and movement of the reflective material.

A head-pointing system, like a standard mouse, requires the student to execute a left click, right click, and/or a double-click. The mouse clicks can be accomplished by activating a switch with some part of the body or with a special application that interprets dwelling (remaining at a certain spot for a specified length of time) as a click. Students using a head-pointing system are likely to use an on-screen keyboard for word processing. On-screen keyboard programs are available with dwell selection options; users select letters by holding the mouse pointer on the letters for a predetermined amount of time.

Head-pointing systems are an option for students who cannot use their hands for operating the mouse, including students with muscular dystrophy and spinal cord injuries, among others. Being able to see and follow the movement of the mouse pointer on the monitor and having good head control are essential prerequisites for using a head-pointing system. Students must be capable of moving their heads in small increments for precise positioning and keeping their heads still when necessary. (As a result, most students with cerebral palsy are not candidates for head-pointing systems.) Students also must be able to manage multiple programs simultaneously, including combinations of dwell-clicking software, an on-screen keyboard, and computer applications such as word processing programs or Internet browsers.

USER PROFILE

Dylan

Like most 10-year-old boys, Dylan speaks a different language with his tech savvy peers, complete with sound effects and animation. He blasts through asteroids hurling through space on his laptop. He talks of DragonFable, dual discs, high scores, next levels, and release dates for the newest Sony PlayStation games. Currently a fifth grader, he zips through the halls of his elementary school driving his Permobil power chair. His mobility is significantly compromised due to contractures from a physical disability, but he can maneuver his chair skillfully and "stop on a dime" with the use of a small cork ball that he controls with lip and chin movements. Assistive technology has also enabled him to be a full participant in his classroom—*after* extensive problem solving.

TECHNOLOGY NEEDS CHANGE AS DYLAN GETS OLDER

In third and fourth grade, as the demands of writing and revising daily papers increased, it became evident that his early assistive technology—a mouth stick and page turner—were not meeting his needs. He could copy only eight words per minute and he began to slip behind his peers. The constant "catch up" placed undue demands upon him. Once one problem was addressed and solved, another immediately presented itself. His team tried providing him with the classroom's desktop computer, but the setup required him to face the wall with his back to his peers and the teacher.

After a few weeks of borrowing and exploring several technology options, his school acquired a Dell Inspiron 1510 laptop, a SmartNav hands-free mouse, and a HP 4150 all-in-one scanner. Dylan quickly learned how to use the on-screen keyboard with his SmartNav and progressed to typing 20 words per minute.

SMARTNAV HANDS-FREE MOUSE WITH ON-SCREEN KEYBOARD

The SmartNav camera is mounted in the fold of the laptop between the screen and keyboard, the mouse is secured with a custom splint to his right footrest, and Dylan wears a SmartNav reflective dot on his forehead. After moving his head to place the cursor on a desired letter on the on-screen keyboard, he selects it by right-clicking with the big toe of his right foot. His speed improved with the use of macros and WordQ (QuillSoft) word prediction software. The scanner allowed us to scan individual pages for homework and save them to a jump drive or memory stick that went back and forth from school to home. An extra set of books was provided for home use to reduce the need to transport them, and all software being used at school was provided for his home computer. This combination of technology tools resulted in Dylan being able to sit with his peers, complete his writing assignments in a timely fashion, and enjoy being an active member of his fifth-grade class.

Source: Alternate Format Provides Access to Curriculum for Elementary School Student, by Marge Walsh, *TECH-NJ, Vol. 20*, pp. 3–4. Reprinted with permission.

Eye-Gaze System.

Eye-gaze systems track the movements of students' eyes to direct the mouse pointer. Eye-gaze systems use an infrared-sensitive video camera, or several cameras, to determine where a student is looking and then position the mouse pointer at that spot. Most systems provide on-screen grids or on-screen keyboards that the user looks at to select letters, words, or computer functions. Depending on the eye-gaze system, clicking is accomplished by using a switch, dwelling/hovering, or blinking the eye.

Using eye movement to direct the mouse pointer can provide computer access for people who have no reliable muscle movements except good voluntary control over their eyes. Students who have muscular dystrophy, spinal muscular atrophy, high-level spinal cord injuries, or brainstem strokes (which can result in "locked-in syndrome") are candidates for this access method. To be successful with an eye-gaze system, students must have adequate vision and must be able to control their eye movements, including moving them in small increments and focusing on one spot; they cannot have continuous, uncontrolled head movement. Eye-gaze system users must be able to understand and manage simultaneously the system and the computer applications they are using.

Table 8.2 lists mouse alternatives, features, and the characteristics of students for whom the devices may be beneficial.

TABLE 8.2   Mid-Tech to High-Tech Mouse Alternatives

Mouse Alternatives	Types	Student Characteristics
Trackballs	Mini-trackballs	Have good fine motor control but a limited range of motion
	Standard trackballs	Have a greater range of motion
		Have moderate fine motor skills
		Have good gross motor skills
	Large trackballs	Are young
		Have poor fine motor skills
		Operate the trackball with feet
	Adapted trackballs	Have poor fine motor skills
		Need to rest wrist on a keyguard
Joysticks	Software that converts game joystick input to mouse control	Can control a standard game joystick
	Adapted joysticks	Need to use switches to click
		Need a keyguard
		Need to operate the joystick with a body part other than hand
Touch screens	Integrated touch screens	Are young
		Need to learn cause and effect
	Add-on touch screens	Need a direct, intuitive interface
Head-pointing systems	Headset and reflective dot	Cannot use hands
		Can see and follow the movement of the mouse pointer
		Have excellent head control
Eye-gaze systems	Camera(s) on monitor and eyeglasses or goggles	Cannot use hands or head
		Can control eye movements
		Can keep head completely still

ALTERNATE INPUT: ALTERNATIVE KEYBOARDS

Many times the word *keyboard* invokes an image of the standard computer keyboard with the keys approximately 1/2-inch square and a QWERTY (named for the first six letters of the top row of letters) arrangement. The standard QWERTY keyboard works well for most students; however, many students with disabilities are unable to use the standard keyboard and alternatives must be found. A wide variety of alternative keyboards make the computer accessible to almost every student. These keyboards fall into the major categories of expanded keyboards, mini-keyboards, one-handed keyboards, and on-screen keyboards. Each of these categories is discussed in detail in the following text, including the students for whom each type of keyboard is most appropriate.

Expanded Keyboards

Expanded keyboards, also referred to as enlarged or oversized keyboards, are exactly what they sound like—keyboards that offer a larger surface area than the standard keyboard. They are beneficial to students with poor fine motor control who need a large target area to execute an accurate keystroke whether they are using their hand, foot, or typing aid. To be successful with expanded keyboards, students must have a range of motion sufficient to access all the keys.

Expanded keyboards differ from one another in overall size, key size, keyboard layout, and functionality. Despite variations in the overall size of expanded keyboards, as well as the size of the keys, they are all larger than conventional keyboards and offer keys that are larger than standard keys. Expanded keyboards are available with either the QWERTY layout or an alphabetical layout. For example, the BigKeys Keyboard (Greystone Digital Inc.), which has 1-inch square keys, must be ordered with either a QWERTY or alphabetical layout. However,

IntelliKeys with ABC overlay installed. The math overlay, Internet overlay and set-up overlay are below.

Source: Imagery provided courtesy of Cambium Learning.

flipping the switch on the back of the keyboard will activate the other layout. Users can either put keyboard labels on the keys to reflect the new layout or pop off the keys and reposition them.

Other expanded keyboards come with sets of overlays, which are preprinted keyboard layouts that can be easily substituted for the standard QWERTY overlay. IntelliKeys (Cambium Learning) is a popular expanded keyboard that uses overlays. Students can use the overlay that most closely meets their needs. Teachers can tweak standard overlays or create customized overlays using an application called Overlay Maker 3. (See Customizable Keyboards section.) Selection of the optimal layout depends on many factors, including the student's cognitive ability, prior familiarity with the QWERTY layout, educational applications being used, and a student's desire to use keyboards similar to those their typical peers use.

One difference in keyboard functionality is the tactile and/or auditory feedback that a student receives when making a keystroke. An expanded keyboard may function similarly to a standard keyboard, and students will be able to feel the key move downward when they press on it. This provides tactile feedback indicating a key has been selected. Other expanded keyboards feature a flat surface. Pressure on the key registers a keystroke but there is no movement of the key, so no tactile feedback is received. Students must watch for the computer output, such as a letter typed into a document, or listen for auditory feedback to be sure a keystroke has registered. Other differences in functionality are discussed in the section on Customizable Keyboards.

Mini-Keyboards

Mini-keyboards, as the name implies, are keyboards that are substantially smaller than the standard keyboard. In general, mini-keyboards are beneficial for students with motor impairments that (1) restrict their range of motion, making it difficult or impossible to access all the keys on the standard keyboard and (2) have good accuracy within a narrow range of motion. Conditions that fit these characteristics are usually neuromuscular ones such as muscular dystrophy and

Tash USB Mini-Keyboard.
Courtesy of AbleNet, Inc.

spinal muscular atrophy. Mini-keyboards may also be effective computer input devices for students who have use of only one hand (see the section One-Handed Keyboards).

These keyboards differ from one another in overall size, key size, keyboard layout, and functionality. In comparison to the standard QWERTY keyboard, mini-keyboards are smaller in both overall size and the size of the keys. They are available in the QWERTY layout and also in frequency-of-use layouts, which place the letters used most often toward the center of the keyboard. Selection of the appropriate layout must be made on a case-by-case basis depending on the needs of the individual student. Students already familiar with the QWERTY layout may prefer to continue to use it. However, students who are just learning to keyboard may have no preference and would be open to a frequency-of-use layout that increases the speed of text entry or reduces fatigue.

Some mini-keyboards function in the same way as a standard keyboard—that is, keys must be physically depressed. Other mini-keyboards offer a pressure-sensitive membrane surface that responds to very light pressure. There is even a mini-keyboard that requires no pressure at all; to operate the Magic Wand Keyboard (In Touch Systems), students touch the keyboard with the accompanying hand wand or mouth wand. Tactile and auditory feedback varies from one mini-keyboard to the next. Those keyboards that do not require physically depressing a key will usually provide an auditory tone that signals a keystroke has registered.

One-Handed Keyboards

A variety of keyboard options are available for those who have good finger dexterity but use of only one hand. As previously mentioned, a mini-keyboard is one option; other one-handed keyboarding options include half-QWERTY keyboards, one-handed Dvorak keyboards, and chorded keyboards. Each type of keyboard provides full keyboard functionality and is designed to permit students to type without having to look at the keyboard. To use a half-QWERTY keyboard (Matias Corporation), students must have good dexterity in one hand. They place this hand on the home row keys just as they would if they were going to touch-type in the traditional manner. The letters that are typically typed with that hand are typed as usual. To type the letters that are typed with the other hand, the student holds down the spacebar and the keyboard is remapped and responds as if the keys on the other side of the keyboard are being pressed. Each key on the keyboard is capable of entering two different letters, one when the key is pressed alone and another when it is pressed in conjunction with the spacebar. For example, a student using her right hand would use the right index finger in the home row position to type a "j." To type an "f," the key that is in the home row position for the index finger of the left hand, the student would use her thumb to hold down the spacebar and use her index finger on the same key that types a "j" because when the spacebar is held down, that key becomes the "f" key.

Half-QWERTY keyboards can have the physical appearance of a standard keyboard and serve the needs of both left-handed and right-handed typists; the student simply uses the appropriate side of the keyboard (see Figure 8.1). Half-QWERTY keyboards are also available that are just the half of the keyboard that the user requires. In the classroom setting, for a computer that is shared among all the students, the full keyboard may be the better option because it can be used by two-handed typists as well as students who use keyboard with one hand. Aside from being able to share the computer more easily, the keyboard has a more typical appearance, which is important to many students.

The **Dvorak keyboard layout** places the most frequently used keys in the home-row position. Access to a Dvorak keyboard layout can be provided in a variety of ways (see Figure 8.2). First, there are Dvorak keyboards that are hardwired and replace the standard keyboard; no

FIGURE 8.1 Half Keyboard.
The Half Keyboard allows one-handed touch-typing with the left hand. Users simply hold down the space bar with their thumb to type the keys normally typed with the right hand.

Source: Used with permission from Matias.com.

FIGURE 8.2 Dvorak keyboard

software is needed. A hardwired keyboard is a good solution for students needing to use computers in more than one location. Students can bring their keyboards with them, plug them in, and be ready to go. Next, there are keyboards with keys labeled to represent the Dvorak layout that require installing software in order for the keyboard to function. The least costly option for one-handed typists is using one of the Dvorak keyboard layouts that are available free of charge from

Microsoft and Apple Inc. In addition to the Dvorak layout designed for two-handed typists, there are Dvorak keyboard layouts for typists who use only the left hand and for typists who use only the right hand. In both of the one-handed layouts, the keys are arranged to facilitate touch-typing. If this method is selected, the keys on the standard QWERTY keyboard will need to be relabeled, perhaps by using stick-on key labels.

Chorded keyboards have an appearance that is markedly different from standard keyboards. Rather than presenting the array of keys found on a typical keyboard, a chorded keyboard has very few keys. Chorded keyboards are available for either the left hand or right hand. Students place a finger on each of the main keys on the keyboard, and their fingers remain in the same position, except for the thumb. The thumb is used to press several different keys. All of the functions of the standard keyboard are available from the chorded keyboard by pressing the keys in various combinations, analogous to playing musical chords. Each letter is formed by pressing the correct combination of keys. Good dexterity is needed for chorded keyboarding as well as good memory skills because the user must remember the various key combinations.

On-Screen Keyboards

On-screen keyboards, such as Discover:Screen 2.0 (Madentec Limited), WiVik (Bloorview Kids Rehab), or Click-N-Type (Lake Software), place an image of the keyboard on the computer monitor. Letters and functions are selected by clicking on them with a mouse or any of the mouse emulators (mouse alternatives) discussed previously. Once students position the mouse pointer on the key they want, they simply click the mouse to select it. If they are unable to click a mouse, dwell selection is frequently an option; when the mouse pointer is positioned on a letter and allowed to remain, or dwell, on the key for a user-defined amount of time, a keystroke registers. (As shown in Chapter 7, Windows 7 also offers an on-screen keyboard.)

On-screen keyboards provide computer access for students who do not have the motor skills necessary to use the keyboard but can control a mouse or mouse emulator such as a joystick, trackball, or a head-controlled mouse (see mouse alternatives already discussed). They also help students who have difficulty visually refocusing when they transfer their attention from the monitor to the keyboard.

Customizable Keyboards

Customizable or programmable keyboards can be configured to meet students' individual needs; that is, the keyboard can be told what text to enter or what commands to execute when keys are pressed. So, for example, a single key could be programmed to enter a letter, word, phrase, sentence, or more with one stroke. The closing to a letter, space for a signature, and the author's typed name could be entered—all with a single keystroke. There are three basic types of customizable keyboards: (1) standard QWERTY-type keyboards with additional programmable keys, (2) customizable keyboards utilizing interchangeable overlays, and (3) customizable on-screen keyboards.

Just like the standard QWERTY keyboard, standard customizable keyboards come with a fixed number and placement of keys. These keyboards vary in the number of keys that can be programmed and in the placement of the programmable keys. To register keystrokes, students must be able to depress the keys.

Customizable keyboards that employ interchangeable keyboard layouts (e.g., IntelliKeys) will usually come with a variety of preprinted, preprogrammed overlays. If one of the supplied

Danny

Danny, a high school student, illustrates the value of an on-screen keyboard. Danny's right hand was severely burned in a fire. During the healing process, he was wearing a pressure bandage to help reduce scarring, and because he was right handed, he was unable to write. Although this was a temporary problem, Danny needed a way to take notes and keep up with his schoolwork until he could use his right hand again. During an assistive technology assessment, Danny tried various standard and alternative keyboards but had a great deal of difficulty locating the letters he wanted. This made typing with his left hand slow and arduous. An on-screen keyboard was presented during the assessment, and Danny was able to locate the keys he wanted quickly. Despite the pressure bandage, he was able to control a mouse with his right hand and could quickly and easily navigate from key to key. An on-screen keyboard was just what he needed.

overlays is appropriate for a student, the overlay is simply placed on the keyboard. Special coding on the overlay may allow it to be recognized automatically or the user may have to let the keyboard know which overlay is being used. (The manner in which this is done depends on the specific keyboard.) Companion software such as Overlay Maker 3 for IntelliKeys empowers teachers to create their own layouts that can be configured precisely to meet the needs of individual students. Teachers can create customized overlays "from scratch" or make alterations to the standard overlays provided. In addition to being able to specify the text or computer commands that are sent to the computer when a key is selected, the number, size, spacing, and position of the keys are customizable as well.

On-screen customizable keyboards are simply on-screen keyboards (as already discussed) that can be adapted to the needs of individual students. The degree to which these keyboards can be customized varies greatly. Most on-screen keyboards are customizable to some degree, providing the flexibility to change such characteristics as the key size, color, and font. Many offer a variety of on-screen layouts from which to choose and the ability to tailor those to student needs (e.g., Discover:Screen by Madentec). The most customizable onscreen keyboards provide options for changing the size, color, font, number, function, placement, and auditory feedback of the keys; they also provide the option of editing a provided keyboard or creating a custom keyboard from scratch. As with programmable keyboards, the keys of some on-screen keyboard arrays can contain words, phrases, sentences, or computer commands.

Students who can use a standard keyboard but need to be able to complete a limited number of tasks or enter a limited number of selected words, phrases, or sentences with a single keystroke might find a standard-type programmable keyboard useful. Students for whom an expanded keyboard may work with just a few alterations are good candidates for keyboards with interchangeable, customizable overlays. These keyboards are also appropriate for students with cognitive deficits who might benefit from using a keyboard featuring only the keys they need to operate a particular program (e.g., the numbers in order from 1 to 10). Students with learning disabilities who find the standard keyboard too visually confusing or distracting may be more successful with an overlay that eliminates keys they would seldom, if ever, use (e.g., the F keys, Print Screen, Scroll Lock, Pause/Break).

There are several advantages to having a keyboard with a broad range of customizable features. Most important, it is possible to tailor the keyboard to a student's individual needs. In

Math overlay on the
IntelliKeys

Photo by Tammy Cordwell; used with permission of Cambium Learning.

classrooms where students have differing computer access needs, a customizable keyboard may be able to meet the needs of a number of students.

Several points must be considered when choosing a customizable keyboard. First, the students are the users of the finished product. Most likely a teacher, therapist, parent, or other person will need to customize the keyboard for the student, so time must be devoted to learning how to make the modifications. The second consideration is that finding just the right settings requires time and patience, of both the teacher's and the student's. The adage "If at first you don't succeed, try, try again" is fitting. It may take many adjustments and much fine-tuning to get things just right. Table 8.3 lists alternative keyboards, features, and the characteristics of students for whom the devices may be beneficial.

Single Switches for Scanning and Morse Code

Some students who have severe physical disabilities do not have enough motor control to use any of the access methods discussed previously. If, however, they can reliably control a single movement such as flexing a fist, turning a head to one side, or pressing a foot, they may be able to access a computer using a single switch with scanning. To understand single-switch scanning, it is necessary to understand how the terms *switch* and *scanning* are used in this context.

TABLE 8.3   Mid-Tech to High-Tech Alternative Keyboards

Alternative Keyboard	Types	Student Characteristics
Expanded keyboards	QWERTY layout	Have poor fine motor control
		Need a large target area
		Are familiar with the QWERTY layout
		Want a layout similar to typical peers
	Alphabetical layout	Have poor fine motor control
		Need a large target area
		Are young
		Have cognitive deficits
		Are unfamiliar with the QWERTY layout
	Overlays	Have poor fine motor control
		Need a large target area
		Require nonstandard layout (e.g., numbers overlay)
		Share a keyboard with students who have different needs
Mini-keyboards	QWERTY layout	Have restricted range of motion
		Can use only one hand
		Have good targeting skills
		Are familiar with the QWERTY layout
		Want a layout similar to typical peers
	Frequency-of-use layout	Have restricted range of motion
		Can use only one hand
		Have good targeting skills
		Need to increase keyboarding speed
		Are willing to learn frequency-of-use layout
One-handed keyboards	Half-QWERTY	Have good dexterity in one hand
		Are familiar with the QWERTY layout
	One-handed Dvorak	Have good dexterity in one hand
		Are willing to learn Dvorak layout
	Chorded keyboards	Have good dexterity in one hand
		Have no, or almost no, range of motion
		Can remember the chords
On-screen keyboards		Cannot use a keyboard
		Can control a mouse or mouse emulator

Alternative Keyboard	Types	Student Characteristics
		Find it easier to locate keys on-screen than on a keyboard
Customizable	QWERTY keyboards with programmable keys	Can use a standard keyboard
		Need access to a limited number of customized tasks or commands
	Customizable-interchangeable overlays	Need modifications to standard overlays
		Have cognitive deficits
		Find the standard keyboard too confusing or distracting
		Benefit from overlays customized to match particular educational tasks or specific computer programs
	Customizable on-screen keyboards	Cannot use a keyboard
		Can control a mouse or mouse emulator
		Find it easier to locate keys on-screen than on a keyboard
		Need modifications to provided layouts
		Have cognitive deficits
		Find the standard keyboard too confusing or distracting

Single switches are hardware devices that send signals to the computer to emulate various computer inputs such as a mouse click or an Enter command. Switches come in a wide variety of shapes and sizes and can be activated by almost any deliberate action. Many switches are activated by being pressed with hands, feet, elbows, heads, or other body parts. Other switches are activated in a variety of ways including pulling, squeezing, blinking an eye, or sipping and puffing.

Scanning refers to a selection method in which a highlighter moves from item to item in an on-screen array provided by an application. Figure 8.3 shows an on-screen array in Discover Envoy (Madentec Limited). The student watches the highlighter as it moves from item to item. When the highlighter is on the item that the student desires, the student activates the switch to select the item. The computer then performs as if it received conventional input (i.e., as if the keyboard or mouse had been used). On-screen arrays can be used to do anything a keyboard or mouse can do, including accessing operating system functions, surfing the Internet, and entering text into word processing or other applications.

An interface device of some type is needed to connect the switch to the computer. The device may be designed solely for the purpose of accommodating use of a switch (usually referred to as a **switch interface**) or may be a mouse, joystick, or other item through which a switch may be connected. The interface device, along with the application providing the on-screen array, determines the way the computer responds to switch activations. For example, switch activation

Sample switches from AbleNet, Inc.

Courtesy of AbleNet, Inc.

may cause the computer to respond as if the mouse button had been clicked, the Return key had been pressed, a letter key had been pressed, or a sequence of keys had been pressed to enter a computer command or string of text, or a variety of other responses.

Several applications are programmed to support single-switch scanning and provide on-screen scanning arrays. Many on-screen keyboards (discussed previously) have a scanning option. All these applications come with at least one premade array, usually a representation of the standard QWERTY keyboard, and many come with multiple arrays. Some applications allow for extensive modifications to premade arrays, whereas others allow none, or only minor modifications. Applications offering the most flexibility provide the means to create completely original, custom arrays.

Speech output is typically offered by scanning programs. In auditory scanning mode, the item name or another cue is spoken aloud as it is highlighted to inform the user of the content *before* he or she makes a selection. Auditory scanning may be beneficial to students who have vision impairments, reading problems, or cognitive issues, along with severe physical disabilities. Auditory feedback, which can be used alone or in combination with auditory scanning, is provided *after* a user makes a selection to confirm that the item selected was the one intended.

Other features also vary from application to application. One variation is the way in which an array is scanned. Some programs allow the user to control whether the application scans (highlights) column-by-column, row-by-row, item-by-item, or some combination of these. Although most applications allow some control of the scanning speed, the degree of control of response time varies. Many programs offer a choice between automatic and step scanning. **Automatic scanning** mode, as implied by the name, moves the highlighter automatically from item to item with just one switch activation. **Step scanning** requires many more switch activations; the switch must be activated *each time* the user wants to move the highlighter.

As with other alternative computer access devices, it is a student's individual characteristics and needs that determine which switch and application(s) are most appropriate. A student who is unable to use his or her hands reliably might have better head control. Capitalizing on this strength, a switch could be positioned for activation by tilting the head to the side, tipping the head back, or tipping the head forward—whatever motion is most accurate and easiest to

FIGURE 8.3 The Discover Envoy (AbleNet) scanning array. First groups of letters are highlighted. After the user selects a letter group, the program scans each individual letter.

Source: Courtesy of AbleNet, Inc.

accomplish. If this student has good vision and good response time, an application with premade arrays allowing minimal modifications might meet the student's needs. However, if the student has a visual impairment, the on-screen scanning application would need to offer auditory scanning and/or an enlarged array.

Most on-screen scanning applications are used in conjunction with another computer application. To word process a report, for example, a student could use the on-screen scanning array to select letters that are then entered into whatever word processing application the student is using. The word processing application responds just as if the text had been entered from the keyboard. Students who use scanning often increase their rate of text entry by using word prediction, discussed in Chapter 2.

Single-switch scanning is an important access method because it is often the *only* means of computer access available to individuals with severe physical disabilities. However, it can be extremely slow. For students whose physical disabilities limit them to use of a single switch but who have high cognitive abilities and good memories, a faster option may be **Morse code**. Some switch interface devices allow users to enter text and computer commands using Morse code. An application is usually needed to translate the code into computer input, but a device such as the Darci USB (WesTest Engineering) is a plug-and-play Morse code computer access device—no separate application is needed. All Morse code software programs accept input from just one

USER PROFILE

Pintoo

Clear, bright, dark eyes peer at the cursor as it moves across the computer screen in highly selective and controlled increments. Noticing me, the young man pauses, smiles, and says, "Hello, I'm Pintoo. I'm happy to see you." I introduce myself and glance at the journal entry on the screen; it tells of my anticipated arrival and our interview.

Although he has difficulty moving due to athetoid cerebral palsy, Pintoo turns toward me by maneuvering his lean frame with a wriggling kind of motion. He explains that he and his speech therapist are refining the settings on his new computer. "I like this a lot," he says. He accesses the computer using a sip and puff switch. Used in

connection with an interface called Discover:Switch (originally by Don Johnston Inc., now marketed as Discover Envoy by AbleNet), it enables Pintoo to input into his computer with single-switch scanning, in lieu of a keyboard.

FIRST SCHOOL EXPERIENCE AT AGE 9

Pintoo has come a long way in his short time at this school. Born in India, he spent his first 8 years at home with his family, whose dominant language is Gujarati, a dialect of Hindi. Pintoo credits watching TV for his fluency in English. He speaks Gujarati as well. Attending school for the first time when his family moved

to the United States, he has demonstrated incredible academic achievement. In only one year's time, he has advanced to second-grade levels in math and reading.

SINGLE-SWITCH SCANNING WITH WRITE:OUTLOUD AND CO:WRITER

Pintoo's computer enables him to complete his schoolwork with relative ease. His teacher and speech-language therapist have taught him to use Co:Writer (Don Johnston Inc.), the word prediction program, with Write:OutLoud (Don Johnston Inc.), the talking word processing program. Using his sip and puff switch (a switch that is activated by either a

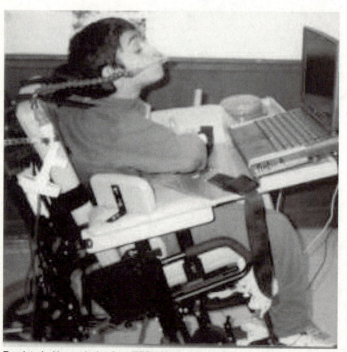

Pintoo, who has quadriplegia cerebral palsy, operates his computer using single-switch scanning and a sip and puff switch.

Reprinted with permission from TECH-NJ.

sip or puff into a tube positioned by the user's mouth) and a scanning array from Discover:Switch (originally by Don Johnston Inc., now marketed as Discover Envoy by AbleNet), he activates the switch by puffing when the desired letter is highlighted. When scanning is used in conjunction with Co:Writer, selecting the letter "p," for example, presents a list of predetermined words beginning with that letter. Co:Writer then scans the list of words. When the scan reaches the word he wants, Pintoo puffs the switch again, and the word is entered into the word processing document. To speed things up, Pintoo and his teachers or therapists have added custom lists of frequently used words and expressions to the Co:Writer dictionary.

When working to determine Pintoo's best access method, his teacher and therapist found that he utilizes a sip and puff switch better than voice-activated software. He speaks clearly and is able to use voice commands with the computer, but his voice is not strong enough for extended work on the computer, and using speech recognition tired him quickly. Although his current setup is adequate, he is always on the lookout for new and better access tools. Reflecting on his many experiments with various computer input devices, he explains, "You have to try everything."

TECHNOLOGY OFFERS POWER AND CONTROL

Pintoo's teacher shares that he is strong in math and written expression. Pintoo beams with pride as he tells me that he uses Big:Calc (Don Johnston Inc., no longer available) for math. Pintoo adds, "I take things home that I've done at school during the day, too." A quick glance at his computer's directory indicates sizable files. Pintoo also enjoys current events. He explains, "I want to read the news online. I'm getting a modem so I can get online. I want to send e-mail to the president, governor, and others who can help people." What is the impact of this assistive technology on Pintoo? "The computer gives me a feeling of power and control over what I'm doing. I want to go to college and be a doctor."

Source: From "Assistive Technology Promotes Rapid Academic Advances," by G. Quinn, 1998, *TECH-NJ, 9*(1), 3–6.

---

switch that is used to enter both dots and dashes; the amount of time the switch is activated determines whether a dot or dash is entered. Some applications will accept input from two, or even three, switches, which is beneficial for students who cannot control the timing of switch presses to enter dots and dashes from just one switch. With two switches, one switch is used to enter dots and the second to enter dashes. After a prescribed amount of time, if no additional dots or dashes are entered, the code is considered complete and sent to the computer. Using three switches eliminates timing as a requirement for successful use of Morse code; the third switch is used to signal that the code is complete and should be sent to the computer.

Not all students who can use switches can use Morse code for access to the computer. There is a heavy cognitive demand for Morse code users; they must be able to remember the codes for all of the computer commands, as well as the entire alphabet. If a student is unable to control the timing of switch activations and needs to use two or three switches, then he or she must be able to reliably activate each switch, a difficult (or impossible) task for many switch users.

Speech Recognition

Speech recognition, also called **voice recognition**, technology permits a user to speak into a microphone to operate the computer or to create text. Speech recognition applications must be installed on the computer so spoken words can be translated into computer commands or text. The emphasis in this chapter is on using speech recognition to provide access to the computer and computer applications for people with disabilities. Chapter 2 addressed the use of speech recognition to help with written expression. Although there is repetition of some information here, readers who desire a thorough understanding of the applications of speech recognition technology for students with disabilities need to read both chapters.

Students who are unable to use a computer with their hands, for reasons such as muscular dystrophy, cerebral palsy, or spinal cord injuries, but are able to speak may find speech recognition technology an option for computer access. One way of classifying speech recognition systems is based on the way the user speaks, with a pause between each word or with a natural speech pattern. These applications are termed *discrete speech programs* and *continuous speech programs*, respectively. **Discrete speech applications** require the user to pause briefly, approximately one-tenth of a second, between each word. **Continuous speech applications** require users to produce a steady stream of words, pausing only between phrases or sentences. The needs and abilities of the individual student determine which type of program is more appropriate.

The earliest speech recognition applications utilized discrete speech, but discrete speech applications are increasingly hard to find. They are usually the better choice for hands-free computer operation so that when control over the operating system is a priority, a discrete speech application, such as DragonDictate Power Edition (Dragon Systems) may be required. DragonDictate can launch and close applications, access menus, select items in dialog boxes, control the mouse, and execute most computer functions without ever having to use the mouse or keyboard.

Discrete speech applications are more accurate than continuous speech applications for students whose articulation of words varies from the standard (Alliance for Technology Access [ATA], 2000), and for those who are able to speak only one word at a time; consistency in pronunciation is more important than precise articulation. The speech recognition application can be trained to recognize words the way students say them, but they must say the word the same way every time.

Continuous speech applications focus more on speed and accuracy of text entry than does total hands-free computer use (ATA, 2000). They are a good choice when increased text output is a priority and students are capable of speaking continuous streams of words, because word processing rates using continuous speech applications surpass those of discrete speech applications. Many continuous speech applications also provide some degree of control over operating system features and may provide mouse control as well. Although continuous speech applications offer increased speed and accuracy for typical computer users, they work against students who must speak one word at a time. The initial training requires students to speak phrases or sentences so the students' voices can be matched to the voice models on which the speech recognition is based. This is impossible for some students with physical disabilities. Speaking continuous streams of text increases accuracy because the program can analyze the context in which a word is spoken. For example, the words *possible* and *passable* might be confused if spoken alone. When spoken in the phrase "as soon as possible," the program would analyze the other words in the phrase and know that the speaker most likely said *possible*. Students who can speak only one word at a time are at a disadvantage with such applications.

Another way in which speech recognition applications are categorized is speaker-dependent and speaker-independent. **Speaker-dependent programs** are designed for a single user who proceeds through a process to train the voice files, which continue to develop as the programs are used. This type of program can be advantageous for users who have speech differences because it will adjust to the way in which a particular user says the words. **Speaker-independent programs**, on the other hand, are designed to be used by many different people. Their voices will be compared against many voice models . There may be no training required or only an abbreviated training process. Drawbacks to speaker-independent systems are that there may be smaller vocabulary sets from which to draw, and they are less likely to accurately recognize words spoken by students with speech differences.

Many factors must be considered when deciding to use a speech recognition application. The applications typically require fast computer processing speeds and lots of memory (both

RAM and ROM). This means they will not run smoothly on older computers. However, human resources, more than technical issues, will ultimately determine whether speech recognition is a successful access solution. Students and school personnel must make a commitment to training the voice files and working with the application in an appropriate way. They need to correct errors in the prescribed manner to build the voice file because uncorrected errors and errors improperly corrected can degrade the voice file, resulting in decreased accuracy. Students must be patient and able to handle frustration. They will need to interrupt their work in other applications (e.g., word processing) to do necessary training and correcting, and interruptions may be frequent, at least initially. Students also must be able to work with the computer operating system, the speech recognition application, and other applications simultaneously. For example, when using speech recognition to work with a word processing application, students need to understand and manage the functioning of both programs. They need to know what the word processing program is capable of doing and the commands they must speak to get the program to do what they want (e.g., select sections of text, apply styles and formats, or create tables). Simultaneously, they need to work with the speech recognition application and when errors occur, be able to determine whether they are due to what they said (e.g., having spoken the wrong command) or to inaccurate recognition of what they said. This determines the approach to resolving the problem. The User Profile on Megan M. Part 2 (see sidebar) describes how a person with no use of either hand uses speech recognition as a computer access method.

Environmental factors impact success with speech recognition and must be given careful consideration. Obviously, students must speak aloud to utilize speech recognition technology. This may cause distractions to others in a classroom setting. It may also make it impossible for students to keep their work private until they are ready to share, to record confidential information such as journal or diary entries, or to answer questions during class assessments such as tests and quizzes. The noise produced by other students engaged in typical classroom activities may interfere with the accuracy of recognition. Using a noise-filtering microphone or placing students away from the noisiest locations in the classroom can help increase accuracy; however, students will achieve optimal accuracy when using speech recognition in a quiet environment. Note that separating students from their peers to increase the accuracy of recognition runs counter to principles for inclusive education.

USER PROFILE

Megan, Part 2

In Chapter 2, you were introduced to Megan M., who has no use of her hands and who taught herself how to use speech recognition for writing. Megan also uses Dragon NaturallySpeaking for accessing her computer. She speaks keyboard equivalents for typing, tabbing, and entering and deleting text, as well as for opening and closing programs and files. For example, when capitalizing a letter, instead of hitting the Shift key with the corresponding letter, Megan says "Shift key" and then the corresponding alpha character to capitalize. Essentially any key on the keyboard can be spoken and understood by Dragon as a keyboard function.

Most people are familiar with this dictation ability of voice recognition technology, but many are unaware of the power voice recognition holds for navigating around the computer screen by emulating

(continued)

FIGURE 8.4 Mouse navigation in Dragon NaturallySpeaking

To use MouseGrid:

1 Say *"MouseGrid"* to place the MouseGrid™ over the full screen (as in this example) or say *"MouseGrid Window"* to place it over the active window.

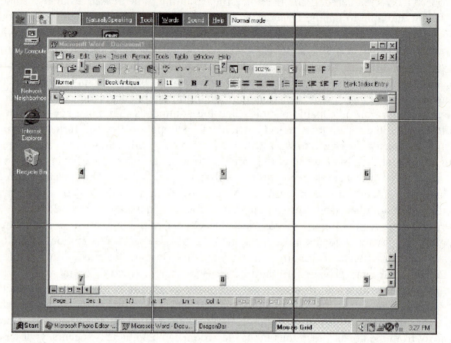

The mouse motion commands

Here is a summary of the available mouse motion commands.

SAY	THEN A DIRECTION	THEN A SPEED (OPTIONAL)
Move Mouse	Up	Fast
Mouse Move	Down	Faster
Drag Mouse	Right	Much Faster
Mouse Drag	Left	Very Fast
	Upper Left	Slow
	Lower Left	Slower
	Upper Right	Much Slower
	Lower Right	Very Slow

Source: Reprinted with permission from *TECH-NJ.*

mouse commands. Megan controls her mouse using a function within Dragon called MouseGrid. MouseGrid enables her to separate the screen into nine quadrants. As each quadrant is selected, it becomes a smaller quadrant, making the movement of the mouse extremely precise (see Figure 8.4). As Megan fires out numbers, she is essentially breaking down the computer screen into mini-quadrants so she can target her mouse click accurately.

An important part of Megan's speech recognition setup is the microphone she has chosen to use. It is called an array microphone and offers two important advantages. It has a noise-canceling feature that allows background noise not to interfere with the dictation. Megan finds this feature essential because she constantly listens to music through her computer while working. Another benefit of an array microphone is its position. Instead of requiring a headset, an array microphone sits below the computer monitor and sends a listening beam. This enables Megan to work on her computer at any time without having to rely on an assistant to place the headset on her head. With this combination of assistive technology—speech recognition and an array microphone—the only assistance Megan needs is someone to turn on her computer at the beginning of the day.

Megan explains the impact of the technology on her life:

> Assistive technology helps me communicate and function independently through several different mediums: instant messaging, text messaging, writing, e-mail, live chats, etc. It has given me control in many areas of my life. Ultimately, voice recognition software will contribute greatly towards my obtaining a successful career in the future. This technology enables me to accomplish things that would be virtually impossible to accomplish on my own. There is no way I would have all the success I've had, and will continue to have, without this technology.

Source: Adapted from Schindler (2005).

ALTERNATIVE OUTPUT OPTIONS

Screen Magnification

It is common educational practice for students who are blind or visually impaired to be taught to touch-type in the early grades. This eliminates the need to see the keyboard when typing. However, students who have visual impairments may not be able to see the computer monitor clearly enough to be able to read text, menus, icons, and so on. These students will likely benefit from screen magnification. As the name implies, **screen magnification** provides an enlarged view of text, images, and the entire desktop on the computer monitor. There are various ways to accomplish screen magnification. This section discusses the two most common methods—physical magnifying lenses and screen magnification applications.

Low magnification powers, from just over $1\times$ up to $3\times$, can be achieved with physical magnifying lenses. Magnification lenses are available in a variety of sizes to accommodate the most common computer monitor sizes. Depending on the particular product, lenses attach directly to the computer monitor or are freestanding, positioned just in front of the monitor.

For students who need greater magnification, physical magnifying lenses are not adequate. Instead, commercial **screen magnification applications** provide up to $32\times$ magnification power. The Windows 7 screen magnification feature can be set to magnify up to 1600%. Screen magnification applications offer several options and display modes. Some applications magnify the full-screen image so only a portion of the original, unmagnified view is visible at any time. To view more of the image, the student needs to move the mouse or use keyboard commands to bring another section of the image into view. Other applications show the typical, unmagnified view at all times, but magnify the area directly under the cursor or mouse pointer. Again, the student needs to move the cursor or mouse pointer to get a magnified view of another part of

Using a video magnifier this student, who is visually impaired, is able to read a newspaper.

Photo by Katherine Gabry

FIGURE 8.5 ZoomText window: The Magnifier tab in ZoomText displays toolbar controls for the application's magnification features.

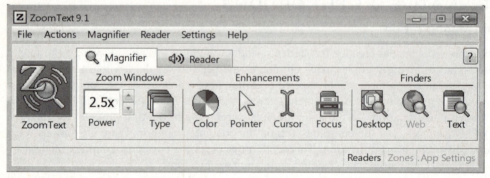

Source: Printed with permission of Ai Squared.

the screen. Full-featured applications provide a range of options that may include inverting or changing colors to provide high contrast, adjustable size or placement of the magnification area, a choice of enlarged mouse pointers and cursors, pointer locator features, options for controlling the way in which the magnified area is brought into view, and screen reading (voice output), which is discussed in the following section. Figure 8.5 shows toolbar controls in ZoomText (Ai Squared).

The higher contrast and larger text and graphics that screen magnification technology provides promote successful computer access for students with low vision. Screen magnification may also be helpful to some students with learning disabilities. Enlarged text is frequently an adaptation for students with perceptual impairments, so screen magnification may help them work more successfully with the computer. Each student's unique characteristics and needs must be considered when selecting screen magnification technology, either lenses or software. When selecting screen magnification applications, ample time must be devoted to finding the optimal settings for color, magnification power, and speech output, if required.

Screen Readers

Screen-reading applications provide auditory output for most or all of the elements that are visible on a computer monitor. Full-featured screen readers speak the contents of dialog boxes and menus, identify toolbar buttons and the presence of graphic images, alert users to new windows, and speak the text found in word processing documents and other applications. In addition to spoken output, some screen-reading programs provide screen magnification and/or support for Braille output (discussed in the next section). Spoken output and Braille output options help meet the needs of students with vision impairments ranging from low vision to blindness.

Screen-reading programs utilize the operating system keyboard commands discussed in Chapter 7, as well as commands specific to the screen-reading applications themselves. For example, application-specific commands direct the screen reader to begin speaking, stop speaking, speak toolbar buttons, or speak the names of desktop icons. These commands enable students to navigate through documents and control the screen-reading application, other applications, and the operating system.

Screen readers are customizable to meet individual needs. Customizable speech output features allow adjustments to such characteristics as the rate, pitch, amount of text spoken when commanded to read (called "verbosity"), and the way the program speaks while a student is typing. In some programs, specific commands can be created to execute user-specified functions to make computer use more convenient or to work with nonstandard computer applications. Programs that offer customizable features are useful for meeting the changing needs of a single student or meeting the needs of more than one student.

Refreshable Braille

Refreshable Braille is one of the ways that some screen-reading programs output information about what appears on the computer monitor. A **refreshable Braille display** (RBD) is a separate device that sits in front of the keyboard (or is built into some Braille note takers). Refreshable Braille is similar to traditional Braille embossed on paper in that it uses raised dots to indicate letters, contractions, punctuation, and other elements of writing, and students read it the same way—by moving their fingers across the lines. However, there are two important differences: Traditional Braille uses six-dot cells to produce a character, whereas refreshable Braille uses eight-dot cells. The extra dots are specific to the computer, indicating such items as cursor location or special formatting. The most important difference between Braille embossed on paper and refreshable Braille is that refreshable Braille is dynamic rather than static. In a refreshable Braille device, a series of pins raises and lowers in response to electronic signals to form the dot pattern in each cell. As the student moves through a document, either adding new text or reading existing text, the pins reconfigure, or refresh, to reflect the new information. For example, an RBD device might show the Braille characters for the first line of text from a page in an electronic book. After a student reads the first line and the cursor advances, the pins refresh to display the Braille equivalent for the next line.

Various manufacturers produce RBDs for use with laptop or desktop computers. The size of the display varies with price. An 80-cell RBD is capable of displaying the Braille translation for one line of computer text. Forty-cell RBDs need to refresh twice to display one line of computer text, and 20-cell RBDs need to refresh four times. Regardless of the number of cells, most RBDs are positioned under the keyboard with only the part that the user reads sitting directly in front of the keyboard.

RBDs are incorporated into many Braille note-taking devices. Note takers are similar to handheld computers; they are small, portable, lightweight devices with either a Braille or QWERTY keyboard. Depending on the model, students can monitor and review their work through speech output, refreshable Braille, or both. When connected to computers that have screen-reading programs, note takers with refreshable Braille will function as RBDs for the computer.

RBDs can facilitate successful computer use for students who are blind and read Braille. Depending on the needs of the students, RBDs may be used alone or in conjunction with speech output from a screen-reading program. Some students with vision impairments or blindness may benefit from simultaneously listening to and reading the material, just like some of their sighted peers.

Braille Embossers

Braille printers, known as **Braille embossers**, make the output from word processing and data entry efforts accessible in hard-copy format to students who read Braille. Using a Braille embosser, students can check the accuracy of their own work. However, having access to a Braille embosser is not comparable to having an RBD that provides real-time access to information. Refreshable Braille gives students feedback while they are creating text, which provides an opportunity to make on-the-spot corrections, whereas Braille embossers provide a hard copy of the finished product.

Whether students need alternative or adapted computer input, output, or both, the search for solutions to access issues begins at the low-tech end of the assistive technology continuum and capitalizes on what students are able to do. The focus is on students' strengths, not their weaknesses. Some issues for consideration were presented in the previous discussion, along with suggestions for students for whom various input and output solutions might be appropriate. However, the match between student needs and assistive technology must be made on a case-by-case basis. Each student's needs must be considered individually and a decision made only after the student has had an opportunity to use the assistive technology in his or her natural environment. The following chapter provides information that will help guide this decision-making process.

Summary

- Assistive technology that facilitates computer access for students with disabilities exists on a continuum from low tech to high tech. Low-tech solutions include keyboard labels, selecting/pointing devices, keyguards, and moisture guards.
- Alternatives to navigating with a mouse for students who do not have the fine motor dexterity needed to use a mouse include keyboard shortcuts, trackballs, joysticks, touch screens, head-pointing systems, and eye-gaze systems.
- Alternatives to regular keyboards for students who do not have the fine motor dexterity needed to use them include expanded keyboards, mini-keyboards, one-handed keyboards, on-screen keyboards, customizable keyboards, single-switch scanning, Morse code, and speech recognition.

- Alternatives to the traditional visual output (i.e., computer screen) are needed for students who are blind or visually impaired. These alternatives include screen magnification, screen readers, refreshable Braille displays, and Braille embossers.

- There are advantages and disadvantages to each of these input and output methods. The match between students' needs and assistive technology solutions must be carefully considered.

Web Resources

For additional information on the topics listed, visit the following Web sites:

Low-Tech Adaptations for Computer Access
Hooleon Corporation
http://www.hooleon.com

InfoGrip, Inc.
http://www.infogrip.com

Mouse Alternatives
Assistive Technology Training Online Project (ATTO)
http://atto.buffalo.edu
→ ATBasics → AdaptingComputers → MouseOptionsReturn

SmartNav
http://www.naturalpoint.com/smartnav

TrackerPro
http://www.ablenetinc.com

Eye-Gaze Tracking System
http://www.eyetechds.com/

Alternate Keyboards
Inclusive Design Research Centre: OCAD University
http://idrc.ocad.ca/index.php/resour ces/technical-glossary/32-alternative-keyboards

IntelliKeys
http://www.intellitools.com/programpage_intellikeys.html

On-Screen Keyboards
DiscoverPro, Discover Screen, Discover Envoy
http://www.ablenetinc.com

Dvorak Keyboard Layout
http://www.dvorak-keyboard.com

Switches
Ablenet, Inc.
http://www.ablenetinc.com

SEN Switcher: Developing Switch Skills
http://www.northerngrid.org/index.php/component/content/article/81-sen/271-sen-switcher

Darci USB: Morse Code Computer Access
http://www.westest.com/darci/usbindex.html

Speech Recognition
Inclusive Design Research Centre at OCAD University
http://idrc.ocad.ca/index.php/resources/technical-glossary/50-voice-recognition

Introducing Speech Recognition in Schools: Using Dragon Naturally Speaking
http://www.scribd.com/doc/15420204/11dragon-naturally-speakingteachers-traininguser-manuals

Assistive Technology for Students with Visual Impairments
National Federation of the Blind's Technology Resource List
http://www.nfb.org/nfb/Technology_Resource_List1.asp?SnID=887575

The Screen Magnification Home Page
http://www.magnifiers.org/index.shtml

Texas School for the Blind and Visually Impaired
http://www.tsbvi.edu/technology/at-overview.htm

Braille and Braille Technology
American Foundation for the Blind
http://www.afb.org/braillebug/braille.asp

Suggested Activities

1. *Add to your portfolio.* Use a search engine (e.g., Google or Yahoo!) to locate Web sites related to assistive technology for computer access. Explore the sites and add to your portfolio the sites you think will be most valuable.

2. *Create a computer user profile.* In Chapter 1, you were asked to observe or interview a person with a disability and to write a short paper discussing the benefits of assistive technology for this person. Conduct a follow-up observation or interview with this individual, this time focusing on the technical details of the assistive technology.

   a. *Means of access:* What movements does the person use to access the computer?

   b. *Applications:* List the titles of applications used. Provide a brief description of each program and how it is used.

   c. *Hardware:* Describe the hardware used. Include the brand of computer, peripherals, adaptive inputs, and adaptive outputs. Include clear descriptions of what the assistive devices do.

   d. *Setup:* If relevant, describe how the person is positioned to use the computer. (What kind of seating is used? Where is the equipment placed? etc.)

   e. *Effectiveness:* How effective are the person's attempts at using the computer? Is the person accomplishing his or her goals?

3. *Use single-switch scanning as an access method.* Write a three-or four-sentence "autobiography" using both hands on a regular keyboard. Then type the same paragraph using single-switch scanning with an array of your choice. If using the on-screen keyboard in Windows, from the Settings menu set the Typing mode to "Joystick or key to select" to enable scanning using the spacebar. If using IntelliTalk, you can choose a QWERTY, ABC, or Frequency on-screen keyboard and you can set the program to use the mouse for "dedicated scanning." How did the two input methods compare? Discuss the benefits and drawbacks to single-switch scanning. What features affect speed and accuracy? What are the implications for training? If you could, how would

you modify the scanning array to meet your students' needs?

4. *Simulate a visual impairment.* Download and install the Visual Impairment Simulator (VIS) available at http://www.cita.uiuc.edu/software/vis/ on a computer running Windows. Launch VIS and read the Help file before beginning. Select an item under Impairment and use the mouse to access the Start menu, launch an application of your choice, and use it for few minutes. Exit the program, and then select the next Impairment. When you have experienced each condition in the Impairment list, write a three-page reflection about the experience. Be sure to comment about the most challenging aspects of using the computer with the simulated visual impairments, any solutions you discovered to make computer use easier, and the emotions you experienced. In addition to the narrative, create a document (e.g., table or bulleted list) identifying each of the simulated visual impairments in VIS and suggestions for assistive technology that might make computer use easier for students with visual impairments.

References

Alliance for Technology Access. (2000). *Computer and Web resources for people with disabilities* (3rd ed.). Alameda, CA: Hunter House.

Blackhurst, A. E. (1997). Perspectives on technology in special education. *Teaching Exceptional Children, 29*(5), 41–48.

Quinn, G. (1998). Assistive technology promotes rapid academic advances. *TECH-NJ, 9*(1), 3–6.

Schindler, C. (2005). Voice recognition provides independence for Ramapo College student. *TECH-NJ,* 6(1), Retrieved July 12, 2010, from http://www.tcnj.edu/~technj/2005/ramapo.htm

Webopedia. (2001). *Trackball.* Retrieved July 28, 2010, from http://www.webopedia.com/TERM/t/trackball.html

9 ISSUES IN SELECTION OF ACCESS METHOD(S)

Focus Questions

1. What are the essential characteristics (quality indicators) of the process of assistive technology *consideration*?
2. What are the seven hallmarks of exemplary assistive technology assessments?
   a. Who should be on an assistive technology team?
   b. What information needs to be gathered before the discussion turns to specific technology tools?
   c. Why is a trial use of technology so important?
   d. What kinds of supports need to be provided for assistive technology to be successful?
3. What are the Education Tech Points for assistive technology planning?
4. What are the four parts to the SETT Framework?
5. Why is data collection an important part of the assistive technology assessment process?
6. What are some helpful guides to assistive technology assessment and decision making?

INTRODUCTION

Chapter 8 presented an extensive array of assistive technology options that make computers accessible to students with a broad range of disabilities. These options have expanded greatly in the past 10 years and continue to grow and improve; new products are developed and existing products are enhanced each year. Although it is easy to be captivated by the latest technology, impressed by perceived potential, and carried away with visions of student success, it is essential to remember that it is not the technology itself, but the student himself or herself who must be the focus of any attempt to identify appropriate assistive technology:

> The overarching objective during the assessment process is to keep the learner's strengths and abilities squarely at the forefront of the assessment and to use these to ameliorate potential difficulties in the classroom. If the assessor loses sight of the learner and becomes too enamored of "gee-whiz" technology … then the learner … may not find much of a functional use for the assistive technology device. (Beigel, 2000, p. 239)

This chapter on assistive technology decision making is based on this fundamental concept: It is imperative to match the technology to the student, not the other way around.

CONSIDERATION OF ASSISTIVE TECHNOLOGY DURING IEP DEVELOPMENT

The Individuals with Disabilities Education Act (IDEA) mandates that teams responsible for developing the IEP for students with disabilities consider each student's need for assistive technology devices and services. However, there is no clear-cut definition of *consider*, and the process varies greatly from state to state, district to district, and sometimes even school to school. Ideally, the student's goals and objectives are reviewed by the team, and a discussion ensues regarding the need for assistive technology to help meet these goals. The effectiveness of this discussion directly relates to the assistive technology knowledge of those involved in the process; IEP team members must be aware of the range of options along the assistive technology continuum (i.e., low tech to high tech—see Figure 1.2) in order to adequately consider students' assistive technology needs. Figure 9.1 directs the reader to resources that provide information on the full range of available assistive technology solutions.

Helpful guidelines for considering assistive technology have been developed by the QIAT Consortium (pronounced "quiet," an acronym for Quality Indicators for Assistive Technology). Comprised of assistive technology professionals and other stakeholders throughout the country, the QIAT Consortium has established sets of quality indicators to ensure the delivery of effective assistive technology services. Figure 9.2 presents the Quality Indicators for Assistive Technology Consideration.

When informed IEP teams consider a student's need for assistive technology (AT), they reach one of three conclusions: (1) No AT is needed—the AT the student is currently using meets his or her needs, (2) certain types of AT should be tried, or (3) they cannot make a determination without more information or assistance (Gierach, 2009).

Decision making related to computer access, as well as other assistive technology needs, may occur during the consideration process, but when the team members do not have the knowledge or skills to make an appropriate decision, an in-depth assistive technology assessment may be needed. Such an assessment is one of the AT services to which students are entitled under the IDEA (see Chapter 1). Reed (2004) notes that the major differences between "consideration" and

FIGURE 9.1 Resources for Considering Assistive Technology Across the Continuum from Low Tech to High Tech.

Continuum of Consideration	University of Kentucky Assistive Technology (UKAT) Project http://edsrc.uky.edu/www/ukatii/resources/WATI_Continuum_of_Consid.pdf
Assistive Technology Consideration Quick Wheel	Technology and Media (TAM) Division, Council for Exceptional Children (CEC) http://www.tamcec.org/publications/planning-tools/
TAM Technology Fan: Assistive Technology Considerations for Academic Success	Technology and Media (TAM) Division, Council for Exceptional Children (CEC) http://www.tamcec.org/publications/technology-fans/
A Resource Guide for Teachers and Administrators About Assistive Technology	WATI (Wisconsin Assistive Technology Initiative) http://www.wati.org/content/supports/free/pdf/ATResourceGuideDec08.pdf

FIGURE 9.2 Quality Indicators for Consideration of Assistive Technology Needs.

1. Assistive technology devices and services are considered for all students with disabilities regardless of type or severity of disability.

2. During the development of the individualized educational program, the IEP team consistently uses a collaborative decision-making process that supports systematic consideration of each student's possible need for assistive technology devices and services.

3. IEP team members have the collective knowledge and skills needed to make informed assistive technology decisions and seek assistance when needed.

4. Decisions regarding the need for assistive technology devices and services are based on the student's IEP goals and objectives, access to curricular and extracurricular activities, and progress in the general education curriculum.

5. The IEP team gathers and analyzes data about the student, customary environments, educational goals, and tasks when considering a student's need for assistive technology devices and services.

6. When assistive technology is needed, the IEP team explores a range of assistive technology devices, services, and other supports that address identified needs.

7. The assistive technology consideration process and results are documented in the IEP and include a rationale for the decision and supporting evidence.

Source: QIAT Consortium. (2005). *Quality Indicators for Assistive Technology Services: Research-based update.* Retrieved July 12, 2010 from http://natri.uky.edu/assoc_projects/qiat/qualityindicators.html

"assessment" are in the duration, complexity, and need for new information. Another important difference is the assistive technology expertise of the professionals involved in these processes.

HALLMARKS OF EXEMPLARY ASSISTIVE TECHNOLOGY DECISION MAKING AND ASSESSMENT

Just as with assistive technology consideration, assistive technology assessment is not a uniform and clearly defined process. However, the field is enriched by the development of several models that guide assessment. Utilizing one of the decision-making guides discussed later in the chapter is not essential for successful assistive technology assessment. What is essential is that assessment and decision making include seven elements that are the hallmarks of exemplary assistive technology assessments:

1. Use of a *team* approach
2. Focus on the *student's* needs and abilities
3. Examination of the specific *tasks* to be completed
4. Consideration of relevant *environmental issues*
5. *Trial use* of assistive technology tools
6. Providing necessary *supports*
7. Viewing assessment as an *ongoing process*

Each of these elements is discussed in detail in the following sections.

Use of a Team Approach in Assistive Technology Assessment

Assistive technology can benefit students with disabilities in a number of different ways, including enhancing speech and communication, mobility, ability to perform activities of daily living, and providing access to educational and vocational opportunities. No individual can be expected to single-handedly meet students' needs in all areas because of the unique skill set each in area required. Indeed, simply keeping abreast of new technology in these areas is a daunting task. Utilizing a team approach to assistive technology assessment, however, mitigates the need for one person to know everything—a virtually unattainable goal—and increases the chances of finding appropriate AT solutions.

Occupational therapists, physical therapists, and speech language pathologists often have a wealth of assistive technology information and expertise as it relates to their individual fields. Working together rather than individually, they are more likely to meet a student's assistive technology needs. **Occupational therapists**, whose expertise includes fine motor skills, may be the most knowledgeable about technology that assists students who struggle with the mechanics of handwriting. **Physical therapists**, who specialize in posture and mobility, may be most skilled at identifying technology for mobility-related issues, such as power wheelchairs. **Speech-language pathologists** are the professionals most likely to be aware of technology that aids expressive and receptive communication.

Some schools or districts include a professional designated as an **assistive technology specialist** on the team. This specialist may have the broadest assistive technology knowledge base, perhaps encompassing the technology in each of the other disciplines. However, this does not diminish the significance of contributions from other team members. The insights they provide pertaining to discipline-specific issues can be invaluable. For example, if an alternative keyboard is suggested for trial by a student, the occupational therapist on the team can help determine the optimal positioning so the keyboard can be accessed in a manner that is least likely to cause problems from stress or strain. If that keyboard is to be used to access a computer-based augmentative communication system, then the team's speech-language pathologist can offer valuable insights regarding vocabulary selection and arrangement of items.

Other essential members of the team are the **parent(s)** and the **student** (Wahl & Haugen, 2005). Family members are the ones with the most intimate knowledge of the student, in addition to being the ones most vested in the student's future success. They may have priorities that differ from, yet are equally as important as, those of educational personnel. It may be necessary for family members to support the use of assistive technology outside the school environment. They will be willing to do so only if they are in agreement with the purpose and choice of technology; there must be no conflict with family values and culture (Parette & McMahan, 2002). (See Chapter 12 for a discussion of cultural issues in assistive technology selection and use.) Likewise, students' opinions and feelings about the technology must be solicited; these are key to acceptance and use. If the technology does not appear to offer benefits desired by the student, or the student has not been involved in the selection process, there is an increased risk of technology abandonment (Riemer-Reiss & Wacker, 2000). If the technology makes the student feel stigmatized, self-conscious, or otherwise socially ill at ease, it is likely to be used very little or abandoned entirely (Newton & Petroff, 2005). Including students in the decision-making process can prevent such negative outcomes.

A useful publication for actively involving students in the AT assessment process with an emphasis on self-determination is *Hey! Can I Try That? A Student Handbook for Choosing and Using Assistive Technology* (Bowser & Reed, 2001). This handbook, written in a manner that supports and encourages self-determination, provides information and asks guiding questions to help students determine what needs they would like to address with assistive technology, and it encourages students to bring these ideas to the attention of the IEP team.

A student's **teacher** or teachers must also be part of the team. Teachers have a considerable amount of information about their students that other team members may lack. Within the school environment, they may be most familiar with students' work habits and behavioral

USER PROFILE

Marshall

Marshall is a ninth-grade student who struggles with reading. He is able to decode many words, but his efforts at decoding are so resource intensive that he has little left over to make sense of what he reads. Marshall needs an assistive technology solution to help him comprehend printed material so he can be successful in his classes. Certainly this entails making meaning from his textbooks, but it could also mean being able to understand what is printed in reference books and on worksheets, handouts, and tests. Beyond paper-based materials, Marshall also needs to be able to access and comprehend Internet resources.

Marshall continues to receive reading remediation instruction. When classroom instruction focuses on word recognition, phonics, or word attack skills, Marshall does not need text-to-speech software because the goal is to improve his decoding skills, not read for meaning. He says he does not need to have a text-to-speech program or scan/read system available during reading class as the material is read aloud by the teacher or classmates. At home, however, when he needs to read and understand a novel, read in the content areas, or research topics on the Internet, he needs assistive technology to be independent and successful. A scan/read system was recommended to provide auditory access to print-based materials. A system that reads Web pages was recommended so Marshall has access to the same wealth of information that is available to his typical peers.

Marshall attends his local high school for part of the school day and participates in three academic classes. He spends his afternoons at a vocational-technical school. In each location, Marshall needs to be able to take notes and complete written assignments. A portable word processing device (e.g., Neo) is a good choice for him. He will be able to easily transport this device from school to school. He will also be able to get through the school day without having to worry about dead batteries or being able to replace the batteries as needed with standard, reasonably priced batteries. ■

characteristics, tasks that need to be completed, activities in which students need to participate, and environments in which students function. These pieces of information contribute substantially to a successful assessment; indeed, they are among the hallmarks of exemplary assistive technology decision making/assessment and are discussed in more detail in the following text.

Focus on Student Needs and Abilities

An assistive technology assessment must always be **student centered**, identifying the technology to meet students' individual needs; never should the available technology drive the assessment. Accordingly, the goals for the technology assessment derive from the general tasks the student needs to perform in school—for example, reading for information in the content area, accessing information from the Internet, completing expository or creative writing assignments, or finding a way to use the computer (Chambers, 1997; Lueck, Dote-Kwan, Senge, & Clarke, 2001; Reed, 2004).

Once goals based on student need have been identified, the student's current abilities must be explored. It is important to base assistive technology solutions on student strengths—what students *can* do rather than simply on what they are unable to do. Among the questions you might ask are the following:

- Is the student an auditory, visual, or kinesthetic learner?
- Does the student have good phonetic and/or decoding skills?

- Is the student able to remember numerous keyboard shortcuts?
- Can the student control a mouse?
- Does the student have good control of at least one body part, and if so, which one?

Remember, it is important to build on strengths to minimize or overcome deficits.

Examination of Tasks to Be Completed

The focus on the student looks at the general tasks the student needs to complete, such as reading textbooks or writing papers. Examination of tasks to be completed looks more closely at the specifics of the tasks, at all of the steps involved in completing a certain task. Reading a book, for example, involves more than simply decoding the words. At a minimum, it also involves turning the pages and using reading comprehension skills, those skills necessary to make sense of the words that have been decoded. Using a computer involves more than being able to accurately hit the keys on a keyboard and target items with a mouse. The user must also be able to launch programs and remember the commands for specific software programs, among other things.

Consideration of Relevant Environmental Issues

The environments in which a student functions must be carefully examined. One significant issue is the variety of places a student frequents during the school day and whether the student engages in educational tasks at home. There are several options for meeting a student's needs in multiple locations. One option is to provide a portable device such as a laptop computer that can travel with the student from location to location. Another option is to have duplicate technology available in each location in which it is needed. For example, since students complete a lot of reading at home, a student with a visual impairment might be provided with a video magnifier at home as well as one in school. Students might have a variety of assistive technology

USER PROFILE

Meredith

Meredith is a seventh-grade student who has some gross motor movement in her right arm and hand, and good fine motor control in her left hand. She is unable to write legibly to demonstrate her knowledge or to participate in classroom activities such as creative writing and note taking. Being able to produce legible written text is the general task that needs to be accomplished.

Word processing is an obvious solution for producing legible written work. However, the word processing task has to be carefully

analyzed. In addition to simply being able to accurately target and select specific keys, Meredith needs to be able to type capital letters, punctuation marks, and the symbols above the number keys. Many of these require the use of two hands—one to hold down the Shift key and the other to press the key with the desired character. Using a computer program for word processing requires Meredith to be able to use the mouse to select menu items or use keyboard shortcuts (which typically require pressing at least

two keys simultaneously) to access important functions such as formatting, saving, and printing. For many students, the component tasks of word processing must be taken into account, but they generally do not pose a problem; however, because Meredith can use only one hand for keyboarding, each component task may present a challenge.

Considering Meredith's abilities and needs, and the identified task, it is apparent that at least part of the technology solution involves StickyKeys or MouseKeys. ■

solutions that meet their needs in different locations. A student who depends on augmentative communication, for example, may use a high-tech system such as an ECO2 (Prentke Romich) in the classroom and at home, a smaller durable voice output device such as a GoTalk (Attainment) in gym class, and a laminated communication wallet in swim class at the community pool.

Mid- and high-tech assistive technology devices require a power source. Extra batteries need to be stored or recharged in a convenient location so that fresh batteries are readily accessible when needed. Assistive technology that must be plugged into an electrical outlet impacts where a student must be situated (i.e., in close proximity to the outlet). Electrical outlets positioned on walls necessitate placing students on the periphery of the classroom. Should this be the case, there are three priorities when arranging the furniture in the classroom: (1) Students must be able to easily navigate to the specific location, 2) access to the electrical outlet should be unobstructed, and 3) the placement should not isolate students from their peers. If a student's classroom does not have accessible power outlets, then the technology chosen needs to run adequately on batteries.

In addition to physical environments, the decision-making process must also consider attitudinal environments. The attitudinal environments in which students function significantly impact the success or failure of assistive technology implementation. Teachers, therapists, family members, caregivers, and others must encourage and support the use of the technology as a tool that facilitates student success in achieving educational goals. It is not meant to and does not provide an "unfair advantage" over typical peers. Rather, assistive technology provides students with a means of accessing curriculum content, engaging in learning opportunities, and expressing what they know in a manner that capitalizes on their strengths.

Collaborative and collegial attitudes among educational professionals support successful assistive technology implementation. Research demonstrates that learning from knowledgeable colleagues is an important source of technology knowledge building (Lewis, 1997). Educational professionals must also support and collaborate with family members. Sharing information about positive assistive technology experiences, problems encountered, problem resolution, and other related questions and concerns among all stakeholders opens important lines of communication. Sharing information about assistive technology use in school and at home develops a collective body of knowledge that is more likely to support the student's technology use. Collaborative and collegial attitudes ensure that no one needs to feel isolated and unsupported or needs to reinvent the wheel when problems arise. When education professionals and family members support one another, they are better able to meet the needs of the assistive technology user.

Trial Use of Assistive Technology

When only written documentation is considered, many students and their technology needs may appear to be similar. It is easy to fall into the trap of assuming that assistive technology that is beneficial for one student will be beneficial for all students. However, there is no way to know if specific technology will meet a student's needs until that student has an opportunity to try it. **Trial use** refers to a time period in which a student experiments with the recommended technology, preferably in his or her natural environment(s). Sometimes it is immediately obvious that the technology solution is effective, whereas other times an extended trial period of 6 to 8 weeks or longer may be necessary. The length of the trial period depends on many factors, including the complexity of the technology and the extent of training required for the student and those who support the student in using the technology, based in part on entering knowledge or skill levels and student characteristics (Chambers, 1997). The Quality Indicators for Evaluation of the Effectiveness of Assistive Technology (QIAT Consortium, 2005) highlight the importance of conducting observations of the student with the trial technology using formal data collection techniques to document technology use/nonuse and data analysis to monitor changes in a student's performance that result from the implementation of assistive technology services.

AT Data Collection

The following Web sites provide helpful resources to assist in collecting data for assistive technology decision making:

- Keys to Success: Assistive Technology Data Collection—Evaluating Effectiveness. PowerPoint presentation developed by Michigan's Assistive Technology Resource.
  http://mits.cenmi.org/Portals/4/Documents/Training/DataCollection.ppt
- How Do You Know It? How Can You Show It? Manual to Guide and Support IEP Teams in the Development of Appropriate Data Collection Strategies to Evaluate the Effectiveness of Assistive Technology.
  http://dpi.wi.gov/sped/pdf/at-know-it-show-it.pdf
- The National Assistive Technology in Education Network provides a variety of downloadable data collection forms in Microsoft Word.
  http://www.natenetwork.org/manuals-forms

It may be necessary for a student to develop prerequisite skills before it is possible to determine if the assistive technology will be beneficial. If computer-based technology seems to be a likely solution and the student has no computer skills, time and training need to be devoted to developing basic computer competency before determining if the technology can be used successfully. A student may need to develop keyboarding skills before it is possible to determine if assistive technology will be beneficial. For students whose handwriting is slow and laborious, using a computer-based word processing program or portable word processing device can ease the burden and increase the rate of text entry. An initial assessment may determine whether these students can use the computer or a portable device as well as whether they are open to the idea of word processing. However, until they have sufficiently developed their keyboarding skills it is impossible to make a meaningful comparison between handwriting speed and keyboarding speed.

Another purpose for an extended trial is determining the feasibility of actually using assistive technology in the student's natural environment. There are numerous reasons why technology that may appear to meet students' needs during a brief trial in an assessment may not work as well for students in their "real lives" in classrooms and at home. Time constraints and other organizational issues may cause insurmountable problems. Students may be reluctant to use the technology in all environments, at times because of the presence of peers. They may be reluctant to use it when they feel it segregates them from peers or is intrusive and labels them as "special education" students. Newton (2002) found that students may refuse to use technology that is made available only to special education students but may enthusiastically embrace the same technology when it is available to all students. Newton and Petroff (2005) report that students may reject using assistive technology in the classroom solely because they do not consider it to be age appropriate.

Providing Necessary Supports

Deciding on the appropriate technology is just the beginning of the process for utilizing assistive technology for accessing educational opportunities. Lack of technical support and training have been identified as major barriers to technology implementation by numerous researchers (Gruner et al., 2000; McGregor & Pachuski, 1996; Wessels, Dijcks, Soede, & DeWitte, 2003). Therefore, it is critical that **training and technical support** receive due attention. Education professionals cannot integrate and support the use of assistive technology if they are unfamiliar with what it does, how it works, or how to troubleshoot basic problems.

Technical problems are not unusual. Reported technical problems include software conflicts, especially with programs that require speech engines for voice output; hardware and software conflicts; and computers not meeting the minimum system requirements for applications to run effectively (Newton, 2002; Newton & Petroff, 2005). Assistive technology, like all technology, will need repairs and maintenance from time to time. Technical support needs to be readily available to resolve problems and maintenance issues quickly. Students must have ready access to functioning assistive technology to make progress toward meeting their IEP goals and objectives.

The successful use of assistive technology requires appropriate **training** for students and those who support their use of it. Students must learn to use the technology fluently before they can be expected to use it to support their academic achievement. To be an independent AT user, a student must have skills in four different but complementary areas: operational skills, functional skills, strategic skills and social skills (Behnke & Bowser, 2010). **Operational skills** are the technical skills that are needed for operating the device. A student must know how to turn a device on and off, select the appropriate icons or keys, and use basic commands. **Functional skills** involve knowing how to do the tasks for which the device is intended and how to use the AT tool to help with that task, such as writing or expressive communication. **Strategic skills** involve the ability to decide which tool or strategy to use for a specific activity and knowing when to use and not use an AT device. **Social skills** in the context of assistive technology involve knowing how to use the technology appropriately around other people. A student may need to learn how to be courteous with a device or may need to help others understand why the student needs it. These four types of skills must be part of a student's assistive technology training program.

Training is equally important for teachers, other staff who interact with the AT user, and parents. Many teachers and education professionals report feelings they have not received enough training to adequately meet the technology needs of their students (McInerney, Osher, & Kane, 1997; Office of Special Education Programs, 2000). Often, parents and family members have no training or experience with recommended technology. Training that builds competence and confidence of students, family members, and education professionals is essential.

At times, the supports necessary for successful assistive technology use are a matter of logistics. This includes making sure that the technology is available when and where it is needed. Arrangements may need to be made for transporting the device from classroom to classroom or from home to school and vice versa if the student cannot transport it independently. Logistical issues must be addressed when using scan/read systems or obtaining accessible materials from organizations such as Recording for the Blind and Dyslexic (RFB&D) or Bookshare.org. The materials students need must be scanned, downloaded, formatted, and/or ordered in advance of when they are scheduled to be used; materials must be readily available in accessible format when they are needed. These implementation issues are discussed in more detail in Chapter 13.

Technical support, training, and logistical issues must be carefully considered. Best practice calls for using an **assistive technology implementation plan** to focus attention on all aspects of technology support. As part of the implementation plan, "it is important to identify who is responsible for monitoring each aspect of the implementation of an assistive technology plan" (Bowser, 1991, as cited in Bauder, Lewis, Gobert, & Bearden, 1997, p. 33). Specifying responsible parties helps all those involved know what they are accountable for and increases the chances that the plan will be successfully implemented.

Viewing Assessment as an Ongoing Process

An assistive technology assessment is not an end point; rather, it should be viewed as the beginning of a new cycle. Once the technology has been decided on, provided, and supported, the adequacy of the technology must be continually monitored. It is important to periodically re-examine the student's characteristics, tasks to be accomplished, and environments in which the student functions because these may change over time. The assistive technology solutions that initially met a student's needs may become inadequate or inappropriate.

The Quality Indicators for Evaluation of the Effectiveness of Assistive Technology (QIAT Consortium, 2005) point out that assistive technology assessment must be a "dynamic, responsive, ongoing process that is reviewed periodically. . . Scheduled data collection occurs over time and changes in response to both expected and unexpected results. Data collection reflects measurement strategies appropriate to the individual student's needs. Team members evaluate and interpret data during periodic progress reviews."

Technological advances and innovations continuously provide new and improved assistive technology solutions. The technology that most effectively met a student's needs at one point in time may be supplanted by newly available technology, which may provide greater independence, ease of use, or more flexibility. Students for whom no assistive technology solutions can be identified initially may realize even greater benefits from technological advances and innovations; the technology necessary to meet their needs may become available over time. When assessment is an ongoing process, follow-up services ensure that assistive technology keeps pace with students' changing needs and that they benefit from the most recent developments.

RESOURCES TO GUIDE ASSISTIVE TECHNOLOGY CONSIDERATION AND ASSESSMENT

A major obstacle to effective assistive technology implementation has been education professionals' lack of knowledge about assistive technology (Gruner et al., 2000). Responding to this situation, some states have established assistive technology resource centers that provide technical support and training to local education agencies and clear guidelines for technology assessments. Their Web sites offer a variety of helpful resources on consideration and assessment of assistive technology needs. (See Table 9.1.)

Whereas some school districts employ their own assistive technology teams that conduct assessment, others do not. If your district does not, the resources in Table 9.2 may help you locate a qualified professional to conduct assistive technology assessments.

TABLE 9.1   Online Resources for Assistive Technology Consideration and Assessment

Assistive Technology Project	Web site for Resources
Wisconsin Assistive Technology Initiative (WATI)	http://www.wati.org
Georgia Project for Assistive Technology (GPAT)	http://www.gpat.org
Oregon Technology Access Program (OTAP)	http://www.otaporegon.org

TABLE 9.2	Online Resources for Locating Assistive Technology Assessment Professionals
Alliance for Technology Access (ATA) Centers	http://www.ataccess.org
RESNA Credentialed Assistive Technology Service Providers	http://www.resna.org/PracInAT/CertifiedPractice/Directory/Practitioners.html
State Tech Act Programs	http://www.resna.org/taproject/at/statecontacts.html
State Occupational Therapy Associations	http://www.aota.org/featured/area6/links/LINK03.asp

Quality Indicators for Assessment of Assistive Technology Needs

Some states provide assistive technology manuals that include assessment guidelines; other states leave the establishment of these guidelines in the hands of local education agencies. Regardless of whether assessment guidelines are set by the state or local education agencies, they should conform to the standards of best practice in AT assessment articulated in the Quality Indicators for Assessment of Assistive Technology Needs, presented in Figure 9.3. These indicators highlight desired characteristics of an assessment process, but they do not recommend or endorse a specific assessment procedure.

FIGURE 9.3 Quality Indicators for Assessment of Assistive Technology Needs.

1. Assistive technology assessment procedures are clearly defined and consistently used.
2. Assistive technology assessments are conducted by a multidisciplinary team that actively involves the student and family or caregivers.
3. Assistive technology assessments are conducted in the student's customary environments.
4. Assistive technology assessments, including needed trials, are completed within reasonable timelines.
5. Recommendations from assistive technology assessments are based on data about the student, environments, and tasks.
6. The assessment provides the IEP team with documented recommendations about assistive technology devices and services.
7. Assistive technology needs are reassessed by request or as needed based on changes in the student, environments, and/or tasks.

Source: QIAT Consortium. (2005). *Quality Indicators for Assistive Technology Services: Research-based update.* Retrieved July 22, 2010, from http://natri.uky.edu/assoc_projects/qiat/qualityindicators.html

Assistive Technology Decision-Making Guides

Various models and frameworks for technology decision making are available to facilitate consideration of assistive technology and assistive technology assessment. In this textbook, we refer to these collectively as decision-making guides. The following section discusses several popular decision-making guides that appear frequently in the literature and are among the most widely known and utilized. Figure 9.4 presents other decision-making guides that readers are encouraged to explore.

FIGURE 9.4 Assistive Technology Decision-Making Guides.

Considering Assistive Technology for Students with Disabilities including Assistive Technology Consideration Checklist from Georgia Project for Assistive Technology
http://www.gpat.org/resources.aspx?PageReq=GPATConsider

CIRCUIT Evaluation Kit: Curriculum ties, Independence, Responsibility, Choice, Universal design, Incentive, Toolbox
http://www.onionmountaintech.com/item.php?id=605

Dynamic Assistive Technology Evaluation (DATE) from Texas Assistive Technology Network (TATN)
http://www.texasat.net/default.aspx?name=trainmod.evaluation

EvaluWare
http://www.assistivetech.com/corporate/products/evaluware.aspx

FEAT: Functional Evaluation for Assistive Technology
http://www.nprinc.com/assist_tech/feat.htm

University of Kentucky Assistive Technology (UKAT) Toolkit
http://serc.gws.uky.edu/www/ukatii/

Education Tech Points for Assistive Technology Planning

Rather than presenting an assessment protocol, the Education Tech Points (Figure 9.5) defines six points at which assistive technology needs to be considered (Bowser & Reed, 1995). Education Tech Points 1 and 2 occur during the processes of referring and evaluating students for eligibility for special education services. The major question at the referral stage is whether

FIGURE 9.5 Education Tech Points for assistive technology planning.

Education Tech Point 1—Initial Referral Questions Assistive technology questions at the referral stage center on the specific problem that the student is experiencing and whether simple, readily available assistive technology utilized in the classroom might provide enough support that referral to special education would not be necessary.

Education Tech Point 2—Evaluation Questions Questions for the evaluation team include whether the student can be evaluated accurately without assistive technology and what types of assistive technology might enhance the student's performance on the evaluation.

Education Tech Point 3—Extended Assessment Questions Generally understood to mean a trial period, questions to be addressed relate to what specific tasks the student needs to be able to do and what, if any, assistive technology could possibly help. Needs to incorporate a focus on the specific environments in which the student functions.

Education Tech Point 4—IEP Plan Development Questions The school district must determine if assistive technology is needed for the child to receive a free appropriate public education (FAPE).

Education Tech Point 5—Implementation Questions Implementation questions focus on responsibility for day-to-day operations. This includes questions such as who will make sure the equipment is up and running, what will happen when it needs repair, and what will the district provide in the interim if it is going to seek outside funding to purchase a device (Bowser, 1995).

Education Tech Point 6—Periodic Review Questions IDEA requires the periodic review of each student's IEP. This review should include evaluation of the effectiveness of the assistive technology solutions in the child's plan.

Source: From "Education Tech Points for Assistive Technology Planning," by G. Bowser and P. Reed, 1995, *Journal of Special Education Technology, 12*(4), 325–338.

FIGURE 9.6 SETT Framework.

Questions under each section are expected to guide discussion rather than be complete and comprehensive in and of themselves.

The Student
- What is the functional area(s) of concern? What does the student need to be able to do that is difficult or impossible to do independently at this time?
- Special needs (related to area of concern)
- Current abilities (related to area of concern)

The Environments
- Arrangement (instructional, physical)
- Support (available to both the student and the staff)
- Materials and equipment (commonly used by others in the environments)
- Access issues (technological, physical, instructional)
- Attitudes and expectations (of staff, family, others)

The Tasks
- What *specific* tasks occur in the student's natural environments that enable progress toward mastery of IEP goals and objectives?
- What *specific* tasks are required for active involvement in identified environments?

Analyze the information gathered on the student, the environments, and the tasks to address the following questions and activities:

The Tools
- Is it expected that the student will not be able to make reasonable progress toward educational goals without assistive technology devices and services?
- If yes, describe what a useful system of assistive technology devices and services for the student would be like.
- Brainstorm tools that could be included in a system that addresses student needs.
- Select the most promising tools for trials in the natural environments.
- Plan the specifics of the trial (expected changes, when and how tools will be used, cues, etc.).
- Collect data on effectiveness.

Revisit the SETT Framework information periodically to determine if the information that is guiding decision making and implementation is accurate, up-to-date, and clearly reflects the shared knowledge of all involved.

Source: Zabala, J. S. (2005). Ready, SETT, go! Getting started with the SETT Framework. *Closing the Gap, Vol. 23*, No. 6, pp. 1–3.

the provision of appropriate assistive technology might negate the need for special education evaluation and possible classification. At the evaluation stage, the basic question is whether technology is needed to obtain accurate evaluation results.

Education Tech Point 3 focuses on identifying appropriate assistive technology through extended trial use. Points 4 through 6 emphasize the need to provide the supports necessary for student success. The first support component, Education Tech Point 4, occurs during the development of the IEP. It is at this point that needed assistive technology devices and services are incorporated into the IEP and education agencies become legally bound to supply them. Education Tech Points 5 and 6 relate to short- and long-term follow-up, respectively. These are especially important because "merely prescribing a specific device or piece of equipment does not necessarily enhance or enable an individual to perform basic life skills" (Lueck et al., 2001, p. 22). The devices must be used and supported. Relatively soon after a student is provided with assistive technology, implementation problems, such as technical difficulties and additional training needs, must be identified and resolved. The tasks students need to perform change over time, as do their environments. Therefore, students' assistive technology needs must be periodically reviewed to ensure they continue to receive the free appropriate public education (FAPE) to which they are entitled.

SETT Framework

The SETT framework (introduced in Chapter 1) evolved from the work of Dr. Joy Zabala, a leader in the field of assistive technology. It derives from her efforts to answer an often asked question, "What is the best assistive technology?" Zabala found that the answer to this seemingly simple question is the not-so-simple "It depends." Extensive experience revealed to Zabala that the best technology depends on the individual *S*tudent; the *E*nvironment(s) in which the student functions, and the specific *T*asks that the student needs to accomplish. It is only after these first three areas are explored that the best *T*ools can be determined.

The SETT Framework, shown in Figure 9.6, is not an assessment protocol; rather, it provides a general structure for exploring the four major areas of concern regarding the provision of assistive technology. Within each area, specific guiding questions are provided or issues are raised to assist those who are charged with considering students' assistive technology needs. The SETT Framework intentionally puts tools (assistive technology) last, emphasizing the importance of keeping the focus on the student, where the student functions, and the tasks the student needs to accomplish. In this manner, technology decisions remain student focused; meeting a student's needs, not the technology, is predominant. The SETT Framework is an iterative process; the student's characteristics, environments, and tasks need to be periodically revisited to ensure previously identified assistive technology remain appropriates and additional technology is provided as needed.

A free publication from the Wisconsin Assistive Technology Initiative (WATI) is especially helpful in explaining how the SETT Framework can be utilized as the basis for AT assessment (Gierach, 2009). Called *SETT in Action: Assessing Students' Needs for Assistive Technology (ASNAT) 5th Edition*, this resource manual includes chapters that discuss assessment in specific areas of need, for example, access to computers, writing, and reading. Suggestions to consider for the student, environment, and tasks related specifically to the chapter's topic are provided, helping inform and focus the information-gathering stage of the assessment process.

Another comprehensive resource is the Web site of Special Education Technology: British Columbia (SET-BC). Its *Physical Access Technologies—A Guide for School-Based Teams* (2009) is a seven-module series with narrated slide shows and supporting print-based materials. Each module is dedicated to a specific type of assistive technology (e.g., keyboard options, pointing options, switches, and scanning options) and provides information about the relevant assistive technology and special considerations, as well as a section on matching students' needs or characteristics to technology features to facilitate selection of the most appropriate technology option. Each module concludes with an excellent example of how the SETT Framework was used to arrive at assistive technology solutions for SET-BC clients.

Any assistive technology assessment, in addition to featuring the seven hallmarks of AT assessment mentioned earlier, should include the following three steps: information gathering, decision making, and a plan for followup and/or training (Gierach, 2009). (See Figure 9.7 for an example of the SETT Framework for decision making.) The first three components of the SETT Framework—student, environment, task—are valuable parts of the information-gathering phase of assessment. The last area—tools—serves as a starting point for decision making by identifying the assistive technology that IEP team members believe warrants exploring with students. The assistive technology must be tried with students, and data must be collected

FIGURE 9.7 Example of the SETT Framework for Decision Making.

Student Scenario—**Keyboard**—Collaborative Consideration of AT Devices and Services

Part 1: Consideration of Student Need

Student: Jacob

Perspective: Writing challenges due to physical and cognitive impairment; reading challenges due to cognitive delays

Examining Current Conditions to Consider Educational Need

Student	Environment	Tasks
Jacob has severe intellectual impairment, cerebral palsy, autism, and epilepsy. Impaired mobility, spasticity.	Jacob spends most of his time in the school resource room.	Language Arts & Literacy:
Fine motor control and gross motor control are compromised; it's difficult for Jacob to hold a pencil or turn a page. He has a hard time seeing or choosing letters on a standard keyboard.	He has a full-time [paraprofessional]. He attends high school in a small community. The school and home collaborate on Jacob's program, trying to coordinate efforts and equipment as much as possible.	• To create 3-word sentences • Learn to independently spell his name • Practice letter and word recognition • To access literature at his level
He is responsive, energetic, and enthusiastic; has good sense of humor; enjoys school environment and being with teachers and other students.		Life Skills: • Jacob is learning to write a grocery list to take shopping. • Jacob is learning to appreciate stories, and the team uses a number of social stories with him.
Knows his schedule, can engage in many activities and focus on a task for a substantial period of time.		
His vocabulary continues to increase; he's learning to link words in a simple written or oral sentence.		
Although Jacob knows a few sight words, he is not able to read independently.		
One of the team's goals is for Jacob to learn to spell his name independently.		
Most of Jacob's learning is assisted; his writing is often hand-over-hand.		
Jacob's curriculum is focused on life skills.		

Part 2: Assistive Technology Solution—Jacob

• Jacob's team decided that a desktop PC and Clicker 5, accessed with a large keys keyboard and touch screen, was the best solution for him.

• Jacob's [paraprofessional] sets up Clicker grids with both pictures and words (or letters) on the cells. Jacob alternates between both of his access methods, typing with the large keys when he recognizes the letters he wants, and touching the screen when he recognizes only the picture cue. Jacob likes to use the keyboard when he wants to add words not included in the grids. The team encourages Jacob to type with the large keys because the keys are easier for him to recognize, target, and hit than those on a standard keyboard. The team chose a QWERTY layout instead of an alphabetized layout because the goal is for him to be familiar with a standard keyboard. At home, Jacob does similar tasks using the same type of keyboard and without a touch screen. The team believes that it's important for Jacob to know both access methods, as he will not always have the option of a touch screen once he leaves school.

- He is learning to spell his name and knows a few other sight words. With assistance, Jacob completes his shopping list, prints it out, and goes shopping with his [paraprofessional]. He takes his work home to show his family.
- Jacob has become more independent by producing his own shopping list—he enjoys his SET-BC computer time and is proud of his work.

Source: Physical Access Technologies—A Guide for School-Based Teams (2009). Module Six—Physical Access Technologies—Switches and Scanning Options, pp. 46–47. By Special Education Technology—British Columbia (SET-BC), retrieved June 9, 2010, from http://www.setbc.org/setbc/access/access_physical_technologies.html

Student Scenario—**Switches**—Collaborative Consideration of AT Devices and Services

Part 1: Consideration of Student Need

Student: Meaghan

Perspective: Writing and communication challenges

Examining Current Conditions to Consider Educational Need

Student	Environment	Tasks
Meaghan has cerebral palsy, spastic quadriplegia. She has some control over her right hand and the left side of her head.	Grade 7 classroom is large and airy.	Language Arts:
Her speech is very soft and halting; there are many sounds that she cannot produce.	Meaghan has a very supportive classroom teacher.	• To write a short poem (six to eight stanzas long) about being in Grade 7
She cannot read regular size print (needs 72 point or larger).	The support worker is very comfortable with Meaghan's technology.	Personal Growth and Development:
She can spell the first three or four letters of many of the words in her spoken vocabulary.	Meaghan requires extensive support throughout the day from the support worker.	• To write two or three paragraphs about her power wheelchair
Her expressive writing resembles that of an eight-year old.	Meaghan is an outgoing youngster and popular with her classmates.	
Fatigue and response rate are huge concerns when Meaghan is speaking or writing.		
Meaghan cannot complete assignments with pencil and paper, keyboard or mouse.		
IEP goals include allowing her to participate as much as possible in classroom activities, improving her speech, writing a daily journal.		
She loves the Canucks, Hannah Montana, and her wheelchair.		

(continued)

Part 2: Assistive Technology Solution—Meaghan

- After several years and several communication systems, Meaghan's team has found an access method that allows her to communicate effectively with those in her home and school environments.
- Meaghan uses two switches to control her laptop. With her head switch, she moves the mouse pointer on her computer screen and with her hand directly activates a switch to make selections.
- For her writing, Meaghan uses Speaking Dynamically Pro (SD-Pro www.mayer-johnson.com). With SD-Pro, Meaghan is able to move to any area on the screen array and choose any single item in the selected area.
- To increase her writing output, Meaghan uses the word prediction option in SD-Pro. As she chooses the letters that begin a word, the word prediction software tries to guess the correct word ending. For example, when Meaghan "types" the letter "h" followed by the letter "o," the word prediction software creates a list of words beginning "ho," including "hockey," "home," "house," and "hold."
- SD-Pro is set up so that Meaghan can hear an auditory preview of each item in a scanning array. Following the auditory preview, Meaghan can select an item by hitting her hand switch or move to the next area by hitting her head switch.
- Her team reports that this particular combination of physical access technologies and communication software allows Meaghan to create her own unique messages that let her

Source: Physical Access Technologies—A Guide for School-Based Teams (2009). Module Six—Physical Access Technologies—Switches and Scanning Options, pp. 46–47. By Special Education Technology—British Columbia (SET-BC), retrieved June 9, 2010, from http://www.setbc.org/setbc/access/access_physical_technologies.html

and analyzed before final decisions are made. Next, training and follow-up issues, critical for successful implementation of promising assistive technology hardware and software, must be addressed. At a minimum, this implementation planning must include training needed by students, parents, and others who will support the use of assistive technology; timetables for accomplishing each task; and identification of the individuals responsible for each task.

Summary

- A plethora of assistive technology options exist, yet selection must be based on student needs, not availability of technology.
- Federal law mandates that IEP teams consider whether a student would benefit from assistive technology. In order for this consideration to be effective, teams should employ a method that includes the seven elements that are hallmarks of exemplary assistive technology decision making and assessment:

  1. A team approach should be used. Occupational therapists, physical therapists, speech-language pathologists, assistive technology specialists, teachers, parents, and the student all contribute their expertise and unique perspectives. Working together, assistive technology solutions are apt to be more appropriate than solutions developed with less input.

  2. The focus should be on students' needs and abilities. The selection of assistive technology should address specific goals and be based on a student's strengths.

  3. The tasks a student needs to complete should be considered in detail and assistive technology selected that would enhance the student's ability to successfully complete the tasks.

4. Consideration should be given to relevant environmental issues such as portability and whether or not access to a power supply is required. The attitudinal environment must also be considered. Assistive technology use will be more successful when those supporting the student understand and appreciate that the technology is a tool that facilitates student success in achieving educational goals.

5. A trial use of assistive technology is necessary to determine if the assistive technology is appropriate. At times, an extended trial may be needed. Time and consideration must be given to a potential learning curve when introducing new technology.

6. Sufficient technical support and training must be provided for students and all persons involved in supporting students' use of the technology.

7. Assistive technology assessment should be considered an ongoing process to address students' changing needs, abilities, and environments and ensure that they benefit from advances in technology.

- Assistive technology resource centers can provide training and technical support and offer guidelines to support technology assessments.
- Quality Indicators for Assistive Technology Consideration and Assistive Technology Assessment are available.
- There are a variety of assistive technology decision-making guides. Among the most widely known are Educational Tech Points for Assistive Technology Planning, and the SETT Framework. Both include the seven hallmarks of exemplary assistive technology assessment.

Web Resources

For additional information on the topics listed, visit the following Web sites:

Assistive Technology Teams
Assistive Technology Teams: Many Ways to Do It Well
National Assistive Technology in Education Network (NATE Network)
http://www.natenetwork.org

Assistive Technology Assessment
Special Education Technology British Columbia: Alternate Access Technologies: A Guide for School-Based Teams. Download PDF from
http://www.setbc.org/Download/LearningCentre/Access/alt_acc_tech.pdf

Trial Use of Assistive Technology
NATE Network: Data Collection Forms
http://natenetwork.buffalo.edu/products.htm

WATI: Extended Assessment of Assistive Technology Needs
http://www.wati.org/AT_Services/extendedassess.html

Assistive Technology Decision-Making Guides
Quality Indicators for Assessment of Assistive Technology Needs
http://natri.uky.edu/assoc_projects/qiat/qualityindicators.html

Education Tech Points
http://www.wati.org/AT_Services/edutech.html

SETT Framework
http://atto.buffalo.edu

SET-BC Physical Access Technologies
http://www.setbc.org/setbc/access/access_physical_technologies.html

Suggested Activities

1. *Add to your portfolio.* Visit the QIAT Web site (http://www.qiat.org). Review the Quality Indicators for Assistive Technology Services by clicking on the link "Quality Indicators." Add a copy of the Quality Indicators to your portfolio.

2. *Use the SETT framework.* Using a SETT form like the one below to complete the section on technology tools for the following student:

   Student: Bradley is a 6-year-old boy in first grade. He is nonverbal, cannot use a pencil or other writing tools, and is unable to use a standard keyboard or mouse. Bradley controls his wheelchair by using a joystick with his right hand. He has a delightful personality, no visual or perceptual impairments, and at least average cognitive ability.

   Environment: Bradley is included in a general education first-grade classroom in his neighborhood school.

   Tasks: Bradley needs a means of completing daily assignments and demonstrating his knowledge related to early reading and writing.

3. *Conduct a parent interview.* Interview the parent(s) of a student who uses assistive technology for computer access. After you have completed the interview, compare the answers with the information provided in this chapter regarding the role of the parent and trial use of assistive technology. Prepare a three- to five-page paper that summarizes the parental responses and your comparison. Ask the following questions as well as questions that have been approved by your instructor:

   a. What professionals were involved in making the decision regarding the assistive technology that was appropriate for your child?

SETT Framework for Assistive Technology Decision Making

Student	Environment(s)	Tasks	Tech Tools
Bradley 6 years old, in first grade, nonspeaking, cannot use a pencil or other writing tool, not able to use a standard keyboard or mouse, controls his wheelchair with a joystick with his right hand; has a delightful personality, no visual or perceptual impairments, at least average cognitive ability	Is included in a general education first-grade classroom in his neighborhood school	Needs a means of completing daily assignments and demonstrating his knowledge related to early reading and writing	

b. Did your child get to try the assistive technology before a final decision was made? If so, how long did he or she use it before the final decision?

c. Were you involved in the decision-making process? If so, in what ways were you involved?

References

Bauder, D., Lewis, P., Gobert, C., & Bearden, C. (1997). *Assistive technology guidelines for Kentucky schools.* Frankfort, KY: Kentucky Department of Education. Retrieved June 17, 2011 from http://www.education.ky.gov/KDE/Instructional+Resources

Behnke, K., & Bowser, G. (2010). Supporting transition of assistive technology users. *Journal of Special Education Technology, 25*(1), 57–62.

Beigel, A. R. (2000). Assistive technology assessment: More than the device. *Intervention in School and Clinic, 35*(4), 237–243.

Bowser, G., & Reed, P. (1995). Education TECH points for assistive technology planning. *Journal of Special Education Technology, 12*(4), 325–338.

Bowser, G. & Reed, P. (2001). *Hey! Can I Try That? A Student Handbook for Choosing and Using Assistive Technology.* Retrieved May 20, 2011 from http://www.educationtechpoints.org/manuals-materials/hey-can-i-try-that

Chambers, A. (1997). Consideration: A detailed look … Has technology been considered? *Closing the Gap, 17*(4).

Gierach, J. (Ed.). (2009). *Assessing students' needs for assistive technology (ASNAT): A resource manual for school district teams* (4th ed.). Milton, WI: Wisconsin Assistive Technology Initiative. Retrieved July 2, 2010, from http://www.wati.org/content/supports/free/pdf/ASNAT5thEditionJun09.pdf

Gruner, A., Fleming, E., Carl, B., Diamond, C. M., Ruedel, K. L. A., Saunders, J., et al. (2000). *Synthesis on the selection and use of assistive technology* (Final report). Washington, DC: U.S. Department of Education.

Lewis, R. B. (1997). Changes in technology use in California's special education programs. *Remedial and Special Education, 18*(4), 233–234.

Lueck, A. H., Dote-Kwan, J., Senge, J. C., & Clarke, L. (2001). Selecting assistive technology for greater independence. *RE:view, 33*(1), 21–33.

McGregor, G., & Pachuski, P. (1996). Assistive technology in schools: Are teachers ready, able, and supported? *Journal of Special Education Technology, 13*(1), 4–15.

McInerney, M., Osher, D., & Kane, M. (1997). *Improving the availability and use of technology for children with disabilities* (Final Report). Washington, DC: Chesapeake Institute of the American Institutes for Research.

Newton, D. (2002). *The impact of a local assistive technology team on the implementation of assistive technology in a school setting.* Unpublished doctoral dissertation, University of Cincinnati.

Newton, D., & Petroff, J. (2005, January). *What happens after the evaluation?* Paper presented at the Assistive Technology Industry Association Conference, Orlando, FL.

Office of Special Education Programs. (2000). *Promising practices in technology: Supporting access to, and progress in, the general curriculum.* Washington, DC: U.S. Department of Education.

Parette, P., & McMahan, G. A. (2002). What should we expect of assistive technology? Being sensitive to family goals. *Teaching Exceptional Children, 35*(1), 56–61.

Physical Access Technologies—A Guide for School-Based Teams (2009). Module Six—Physical Access Technologies—Switches and Scanning Options, pp. 46–47. By Special Education Technology—British Columbia (SET-BC), retrieved June 9, 2010, from http://www.setbc.org/setbc/access/access_physical_technologies.html

QIAT Consortium (2005). *Quality Indicators for Assistive Technology Services: Research-based update.* Retrieved July 22, 2010, from http://natri.uky.edu/assoc_projects/qiat/qualityindicators.html

Reed, P. (2004). *The W.A.T.I. Assessment Package: Assistive Technology Assessment.* Oshkosh, WI: Wisconsin Assistive Technology Initiative.

Riemer-Reiss, M., & Wacker, R. (2000). Factors associated with assistive technology discontinuance among individuals with disabilities. *Journal of Rehabilitation, 66*(3), 44–50.

Wahl, L., & Haugen, K. (2005). Selecting technology: What products are best for me? In Alliance for Technology Access (Ed.), *Computer resources for people with disabilities: A guide to assistive technologies, tools and resources for people of all ages* (4th ed., pp. 58–89). Alameda, CA: Hunter House.

Wessels, R., Dijcks, B., Soede, M., & DeWitte, L. (2003). Non-use of provided assistive technology devices, a literature overview. *Technology and Disability, 15*, 231–238.

Zabala, J. S. (2005). Ready, SETT, go! Getting started with the SETT Framework. *Closing the Gap, 23*(6), 1–3.

AUGMENTATIVE COMMUNICATION

10 | SELECTING AND DESIGNING A STUDENT'S AUGMENTATIVE COMMUNICATION SYSTEM

Focus Questions

1. Are there any prerequisites to augmentative communication?
2. What are the myths and realities surrounding augmentative communication?
3. Who must be involved in the selection and design of a student's augmentative communication system?
4. What are the primary considerations involved in selecting and designing a student's augmentative communication system?
5. What are the three major components of an augmentative communication system that must be determined during the selection process?

INTRODUCTION

Over the past several decades, the use of augmentative or alternative communication systems (referred to as augmentative communication in this text) increasingly has become a solution for many people with disabilities who in the past would not have been able to participate fully in school, the workplace, or the community (Downey & Hurtig, 2003). Students who are nonspeaking or unable to express themselves effectively through spoken language are the candidates for augmentative communication systems.

As defined in Chapter 6, *augmentative communication* is a term used to describe a wide range of solutions to difficulties in communication. These solutions are considered "**aided**" when they include the use of a device such as a language board or talking computer, or "**unaided**" when they involve the use of pointing, facial expressions, or sign language. Augmentative communication systems may be based on low-, mid-, or high-tech solutions, or a combination of all three, but it is essential to include the individual's personal approach to expressing him- or herself in the system. For example, some people who have difficult-to-understand speech may use a voice output computerized device for communicating complex messages but use facial expressions, a nod, or single-word approximations for simple responses to questions. Other people may use a language board to point to specific pictures that represent words or ideas but also respond to yes/no questions using gestures. The sidebar presents the perspective of an adult augmentative communication user on the benefits of combining low-, mid-, and high-tech approaches.

Confessions of a Multimodal Man

Call me fickle, I've never been loyal to one communication mode. I'll use anything that seems most efficient in a given situation. Like when I am going to the movies, I know I'm not going to spend a lot of time chatting up the ticket seller, so before I leave home I use my computer to print up a sign that says what movie I want a ticket for. I flash that at the ticket seller when I get to the theatre. It's just a whole lot quicker.

Becoming a parent has forced me into situations I never dreamt I'd be in. Who knew I'd be going to PTA meetings, parent-teacher conferences, or having to deal with such things as play dates?

Then there's the whole youth culture thing. My son, who's grown now, exposed me to the wonderful world of Eminem and Snoop Dogg. Now with my daughter, I'm having to deal with such people as Brittany Spears and those tycoons, Mary-Kate and Ashley. I would never choose any of these people to be in my social network. It's been quite an experience for a guy who grew up listening to the music of the 30s and 40s.

My favorite communication mode is e-mail. E-mail really levels the social playing field for me. It lets me present who I really am without all the annoying visual distractions of the in-person Michael Williams. I use e-mail to conduct business, negotiate contracts, make dates with friends, and foment cultural mischief. I find e-mail much more comfortable than the telephone, which I find extremely slow and frustrating.

I use the Liberator, LightWRITER, and a printed letterboard every day at various times during the day. Why do I need three devices? Isn't one sufficient? In a word, no.

If I didn't have the Liberator, I wouldn't be here talking with you today. However, you'll notice the Lib is big and awkward, and if you could lift it, you'd discover it has a considerable weight factor to it. I carry the Lib on my lap, and it's very hard on my knees. I can feel your puzzled eyes boring through this page. You want to know why I don't mount the Liberator on my damn wheelchair. The short answer to this question is, I don't want to mount the Liberator on my damn wheelchair! Okay? Call me silly, but I don't want tons of assistive technology dripping off my chair. Its scares people off to see all that technological firepower coming at them. You think I'm kidding about this? I'm deadly serious about this.

There's a more important reason I don't mount the Lib on my wheelchair. Sitting here, I may look very disabled, but actually I have quite a bit of functionality in my body. I can transfer in and out of my wheelchair by myself fairly easily. This allows me to do some very important personal things without the help of other people. Things like go to the bathroom. Have you tried to negotiate your way into a public bathroom stall with a big, old communication device mounted on a wheelchair? You may get in the stall, but how do you get from your wheelchair onto the throne without falling on your ass as you

Michael Williams with his Liberator (Prentke Romich).

Courtesy of Attainment Company

Source: From *Why I Use More Than One Communication Device,* by Michael B. Williams, presentation at California State University–Northridge's 20th Annual International Conference "Technology and Persons with Disabilities," March 16, 2005, Los Angeles, CA. Reprinted with permission.

hold onto the grab bar and gingerly attempt to swing past your communication device and lower yourself onto the seat? And that is why I don't mount the Liberator on my wheelchair!

Here's another thing to ponder: Observe the size of the Liberator. Notice its rather large footprint. Now imagine you have a really hot date and you want to book a table at a swank restaurant. How big a table do you book? If you book a table for two, one of you ain't gonna eat, or one of you ain't gonna talk, because the Liberator soaks up too much table space. If you book a table for three, you risk igniting the ire of the maitre d'. Either way, your evening is a bust, and your budding relationship is down the tubes.

I can feel your puzzled eyes boring through the page again. You're asking yourselves, What would Michael Williams do at a critical time like this? Well, I'll tell you what I'd do. I'd use either one of these handy-dandy augmentative communication tools. The letterboard lies nicely next to you on the table. Its basic black contributes an additional touch of suaveness to an already elegant dining ambiance. The letterboard, however, also provides a slightly more intense conversational experience. Your partner watches intently as your hand glides slowly across the smooth surface of the letterboard. Your long, lean finger languishes lovingly over each letter as it slowly constructs linguistic meaning out of chaos.

Don't care for such intensity? Try this LightWRITER. It's small, it's simple, it's elegant. And yes, ladies and gentlemen, it provides the perfect atmosphere for a conversation while dining. It sits primly on the corner of the table. Your partner need only flick a glance to the screen now and then to see what you are saying. And you have the added assurance that if your partner misses something, you need only push the talk button at the end of your thought and the LightWRITER will say it for you. And that, ladies and gentlemen, is why I use more than one communication device.

In order to realize success for an individual who is nonspeaking, an augmentative communication system must be carefully designed for use within the student's natural environments. Therefore, this chapter will present the critical issues in the decision-making process of selecting the appropriate components of a student's augmentative communication system, the implications for implementation, and the importance of ongoing evaluation and system modification. In addition, the roles of educational personnel, students' families, and the students themselves are presented within a structure of collaborative teaming for assessment and implementation.

Sample mid-tech augmentative communication devices.

Courtesy of Attainment Company

Student using an augmentative communication system while doing schoolwork.

Kevin J. Cohen. Used with permission.

An augmentative communication system must reflect the basic features of any traditional method of communication. That is, it must provide the user with the ability to (1) construct a message using symbols, (2) deliver that message to another person (receiver), and (3) further respond to the receiver in a timely manner. In other words, an augmentative communication system must enable the user to initiate or sustain a conversation with another person. The profiles of augmentative communication users included in this chapter illustrate the variability in systems while showing the consistency in the basic components of any model. Each of these augmentative users effectively and efficiently incorporates their innate abilities to communicate within a system of aided and unaided augmentative communication solutions. They have systems that are well constructed to meet their individualized needs. How were these systems designed? What factors were considered?

The following section presents a recommended protocol for the process of selecting and designing augmentative communication systems that expands on the basic elements of the SETT Framework that was presented in Chapter 9.

USER PROFILE

Julie

Julie is a fourth-grade student in a general education classroom who receives special education supports and services. She was born with a congenital condition, uses a motorized wheelchair, and is nonspeaking. Julie uses an augmentative communication system that consists of three methods of communication: (1) unaided; (2) aided, low-tech; and (3) aided, high-tech. Her unaided methods include a yes/no gesture and some intelligible single-word responses; the aided, low-tech method she uses is a simple call button that enables her to get people's attention; and the aided, high-tech method she uses is a computerized voice output device that she accesses with a dowel that she grasps in her fist. The voice output device uses a symbol system that is capable of producing any word or phrase with a reduced number of keystrokes. This symbol system, in which the user selects a predetermined sequence of items to retrieve a complete word, phrase, or sentence, is called an *encoded system* (Dowden & Cook, 2002). ■

CONSIDERATIONS IN SYSTEM SELECTION AND DESIGN

The initial steps in the selection and design of an augmentative communication system begin with a recognition that a student requires and can benefit from enhanced methods of communication. Although professional dogma in the past declared that only certain people were the candidates for augmentative communication systems, it is now believed that regardless of an individual's disability or the severity of that disability, *all* people with communication difficulties can achieve enhanced communication abilities through the use of augmentative communication (Hourcade, Everhart-Pilotte, West, & Parette, 2004; Kroth & Bolson, 1996). Individual differences and abilities inform the selection and design process, especially as it relates to the complexity of some devices, but *all* nonspeaking students should be given the benefit of augmentative communication consideration. Current practice reflects the position that the only prerequisite to communication is **opportunity**. In other words, every student who is nonspeaking or presents difficulty in using speech that cannot be easily remediated is a candidate for consideration.

Myths and Realities

Waiting for so-called prerequisites to develop is the only one of many misconceptions that have negatively affected services to students with disabilities who are nonspeaking. Table 10.1 lists other common myths and provides accurate information to counter these myths. Teachers need to be aware of these realities so that they can provide appropriate supports for students who are—or soon will be—augmentative communication users in their classes.

TABLE 10.1 Myths and Realities About Augmentative Communication		
Myth	**Reality**	**Reference**
Augmentative communication will inhibit an individual's further development of speech and therefore must be used only as a last resort.	Augmentative communication does *not* inhibit an individual's further development of speech and, in some cases, may actually enhance speech development.	Daniels, 1994; Finch & Romski, 2004; Schlosser, 2003
Specific levels of cognitive abilities are required prior to using augmentative communication devices.	There are no readiness criteria for teaching communication. Waiting for students to "be ready" only prevents the further development of needed communication skills.	Kangas & Lloyd, 1988; Van Tatenhove, 1987
A student must present specific adaptive behavior skills such as eye contact and a well-defined point before augmentative communication may be considered.	Readiness criteria based on behavioral characteristics are unsupported by the research and should not apply to the augmentative communication consideration process.	Beukelman & Mirenda, 2005
Augmentative communication requires some level of literacy skill prior to consideration.	Augmentative communication devices can be used as a source of support or scaffolding in the educational process and can provide a means to further develop literacy skills.	Hetzroni, 2004; Erickson 2000; Musselwhite & King-DeBaun, 1997

Who Should Assess? Collaborative Team Assessment Approach

The process for selecting and designing an augmentative communication system for a student involves the coordinated efforts of a team of professionals, parents, and the student. It is critical that decisions regarding system selection and design use a broad range of information (Beukelman & Mirenda, 2005). Therefore, a team that represents a variety of relevant disciplines and has knowledge of the student must be convened. The team members may vary depending on the needs of the specific student. For example, in the profile presented earlier, Julie's team includes an occupational therapist to help with fine motor issues related to her accessing the call button and the high-tech device with a stylus.

In addition to these individualized team members, all augmentative communication assessment teams must include the following: (1) a professional, such as a speech-language therapist, who is trained and experienced in augmentative communication assessment and applications; (2) the student; (3) his or her parent(s) or family members; and (4) the teacher(s) or other professionals involved in the student's everyday school, community, or work environment. These four core categories are essential to ensure the identification of a successful augmentative communication system; other members may be added to the team if they have specialized knowledge or expertise related to the specific student. Without the participation of these team members, the resulting system will be poorly designed and difficult or impossible to implement. The following user profile illustrates the problems that can arise when appropriate team members are not included in the assessment process.

When teachers or other professionals familiar with the student are not included in the decision-making process, it is more likely that the augmentative communication system will not be appropriate to the school setting and that school personnel will not have an understanding of the implementation features of the system. A comparable situation occurs when school staff does not adequately involve the parent(s) or family in the assessment process. This often results in the development of communication systems that may not transfer well to the home environment, the one in which the student spends most of his or her time. Further, when the student's ideas and preferences are not considered in the assessment process, the result may be technology abandonment (Grady, Kovach, Lange, & Shannon, 1993). In this case, the student abandons the use of the devices and resorts to more familiar but less effective forms of communication. Therefore, it is critical to recognize that the selection and design of an augmentative communication system must reflect a collaborative team approach and must include the student and people who are familiar with the student. Table 10.2 lists possible collaborative team members and their functions.

USER PROFILE

John

John is a 7-year-old boy with cerebral palsy who is nonspeaking. His parents arranged to have him evaluated for augmentative communication at a hospital-based assistive technology assessment center. Although they accompanied him to the evaluation, no one from John's school program attended the evaluation. The assessment results recommended a complex augmentative communication system that used auditory scanning and a head switch for activation. Unfortunately, when the recommendation was provided to the school, several problems were apparent. First, the auditory scan feature was loud and disruptive to the other students in John's general education classroom, and there was no option for using headphones. Second, John's head switch was in a position that may have seemed appropriate at the assessment center but was incongruent and in opposition to his physical therapist's goals for positioning. ■

TABLE 10.2 Possible Collaborative Team Members	
Augmentative Communication Team Member	**Function**
Student	Provides input regarding successful existing methods of communication, personal preferences, and ease of use
Teachers	Provide input regarding classroom environment and daily and communication needs in the curriculum
Parent(s) and family members	Provide input regarding home environment, family activities, and communication needs at home and in the community
Professional who is trained and experienced in augmentative communication assessment and applications	Provides input regarding the student's communicative status and function; knowledgeable about augmentative communication systems and features
Occupational therapist	Provides input regarding the student's fine motor abilities and sensory challenges
Physical therapist	Provides assistance and support for the gross motor and seating or positioning needs of the student
Information technology support person	Provides advice about and technical assistance in connecting augmentative communication devices to computers, the school's network, and the Internet and serves as a troubleshooter for implementation
Peer of the student	Provides input to the appropriateness and function of augmentative communication system from an age-appropriate perspective

A collaborative team is characterized by people working in concert to achieve a common goal, using an interdependent process in which there is parity, shared resources, and respect for one another's disciplines (Snell & Janney, 2000). This form of teaming represents a transdisciplinary approach in which members contribute and integrate their knowledge to select and design an individualized augmentative communication system. It allows for role differentiation between disciplines that are defined by the situation, rather than by discipline-specific characteristics (Bruder, 1994). For example, although the speech-language therapist is the expert in communication, it is the teacher who implements the augmentative communication system routinely in the classroom, so the team may decide that the teacher will be the person to introduce the new system and its new vocabulary to the student. The speech-language therapist remains an important team member but releases his or her direct service role to the teacher.

Other characteristics of the augmentative communication team are that the assessment process must be viewed as ongoing and team members must communicate regularly with each other. Finally, the collaborative assessment team must place the student in a central and active role in decision making. Regardless of the student's abilities or challenges, he or she must be involved in every step of the process and must be a major contributor to all decisions.

How Should the Team Assess? Features of the Collaborative Assessment Process

In Chapters 1 and 9, a framework for assistive technology decision making—the SETT Framework (Zabala, 2005)—was presented. The SETT Framework begins with describing the student and his

TABLE 10.3   Participation Model for Collaborative Team Assessment
• Assessment of a student's current communication patterns • Assessment of a student's needs across daily routines • Identification of access barriers within the natural environment • Determination of future communication needs in these environments • Selection and design of an augmentative communication system • Evaluation of the efficiency and effectiveness of the augmentative   communication system (ongoing)

Source: Information from *Augmentative and Alternative Communication* (3rd ed.), by D. R. Beukelman and P. Mirenda, 2005, Baltimore: Paul Brookes Publishing.

or her environments. When applied to augmentative communication, the SETT Framework then focuses on the student's attributes that are related to communication, including the demands for communication in the environment. The **communication demands** are the tasks that are identified within each of the environments, such as answering questions in class or greeting and interacting with peers. After considering student characteristics, environments, and the communication demands of those environments, the team then moves to consider the technology tools—that is, augmentative communication solutions that best match the individual student. These tools are the specific high-tech, mid-tech, or low-tech augmentative devices that will be identified for trial. In summary, the SETT Framework reminds the team to keep the student (*S*tudent) at the center of the assessment process and to consider the demands of the student's environments (*E*nvironments) and daily activities (*T*asks). Only after the *S, E* and first *T* have been considered, should the team move to the second T—technology tools, which in this case refers to augmentative communication tools.

Features of the Process of Selecting Augmentative Communication Systems

The approach to assessment for augmentative communication has evolved over the past several decades. Currently, students are assessed by teams who work collaboratively from the early stages of selection and design, through implementation, and finally to evaluation of the efficiency and effectiveness of the system. The **communication needs model** developed by Beukelman, Yorkston, and Dowden (1985) has been refined to reflect a systematic collaborative process, which they refer to as the **participation model** (Beukelman & Mirenda, 2005). The participation model is a collaborative assessment approach that requires a multiphase assessment process, as outlined in Table 10.3, and uses consensus building as a central feature of the process. It begins with the assessment of a student's current communication patterns and needs across daily routines, and it continues with the identification of access barriers within the natural environment. Next, future communication needs are discussed; only then is the selection and design of a system undertaken. This is followed by the team's ongoing evaluation of the efficiency and effectiveness of the system.

The use of a collaborative team approach that is future oriented prevents the static nature of some augmentative communication systems. There must be ongoing recognition that students' communication needs change and evolve to meet the demands of new environments. As students grow, their augmentative communication systems need to transform to meet new challenges and situations.

What Components Must Be Identified? Symbols, Vocabulary, and Access Method

In determining the best augmentative communication solution, the collaborative team must determine the most appropriate components of the student's system. This section focuses on three major decisions that need to be made at this point in the assessment: the **symbol system** to be used to represent vocabulary, the specific **vocabulary**—or messages—the student will express with the system, and the method by which the student will **access** the system. Decisions regarding these three components are guided by the following questions:

- To what extent can the student access symbolic language? What kinds of symbols are most understandable to the student?
- What messages would the student most likely need and want to express to others?
- What parameters and challenges does the student present regarding access to the use of augmentative communication devices? Which access method would be most effective at this time?

HOW ARE SYMBOL SYSTEMS SELECTED?   A symbol is "something that stands for or represents something else" (Vanderheiden & Yoder, 1986, p. 15). More specifically, it is an arbitrary representation of a concept that speakers of a language agree has a specific meaning. Symbols can be spoken as in speech; graphically represented as in written language; presented in a tactile form such as Braille; or formed through hand shapes, as in sign language. Symbols are arbitrary because there does not need to be any clear relationship between the symbol and the concept. For example, all English-speaking people recognize that the graphic symbols "D," "O," and "G" represent specific sounds that when put together refer to a class of animals that have four legs and fur, bark, and are kept as pets. The symbol "dog" and the spoken word *dog* do not look or sound anything like the object to which they refer.

Selecting a symbol system is a critical component of an augmentative communication assessment. A symbol system can range from abstract symbols, such as the alphabet and words, to concrete systems such as real objects or tangible/tactile symbols. In between these two points on the continuum are symbol systems composed of line drawings, icons (stylized graphical representations), pictures, and photographs.

Symbol systems are classified according to their degree of **iconicity,** that is, the clarity of their meanings in isolation (Beukelman & Mirenda, 2005). Photographs and real objects are said to be **transparent** because their meaning is clear without any additional information. Written words and Braille labels are considered **opaque** because they can be understood only by people who can read. Symbol sets are said to be **translucent** when the meanings of some of the symbols are obvious, but other symbols are more abstract; translucent symbol sets are usually composed of line drawings: "Much of the magic of augmentative communication lies in the vast array of symbols, … other than those used in speech, that people can employ to send messages. Especially for individuals who cannot read or write, the ability to represent messages and concepts in alternative ways is central to communication" (Beukelman & Mirenda, 2005, p. 40).

Boardmaker (Mayer-Johnson) is a widely used application that is based on a system of line drawings called the Picture Communication Symbols. Many of the symbols for common nouns and verbs are easily understood and are considered transparent. Other symbols require some shared knowledge to understand; these are not as obvious and are considered translucent (see Figure 10.1 for examples of Boardmaker symbols). In designing an augmentative communication system, the team could choose to use either or both of these kinds of symbols. Pogo Boards, a Web-based picture system from Talk to Me Technologies, is another option for symbol systems.

Some augmentative communication users are able to use the alphabet and the written word, and prefer a text-based system as their symbol system. The advantage to a spelling system is that *any* idea or thought can be expressed. However, spelling out entire sentences is extremely time consuming and does not lend itself to spontaneous conversation. In addition, it requires high levels of literacy. Children and young adults who read below grade level do not have the necessary reading and spelling skills to use text-based symbol systems effectively. The slow rate

FIGURE 10.1 Sample Boardmaker symbols.

Boardmaker Symbol	Typical Meaning	Degree of Iconicity
	"ice cream"	Transparent
	"football"	Transparent
	"run"	Transparent
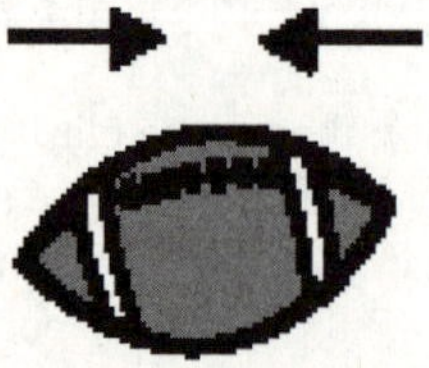	"football game"	Translucent
	"I don't like that show."	Translucent
	"I am so angry!"	Translucent

Boardmaker Symbol	Typical Meaning	Degree of Iconicity
	"That's so funny!"	Translucent
	"How do you play?" or "I don't know how to play this game."	Translucent
	"Can I play?"	Translucent
	"I have no one to play with."	Translucent
	"Please repeat that."	Opaque
	"I would like some more."	Opaque

(continued)

Boardmaker Symbol	Typical Meaning	Degree of Iconicity
	"I want…"	Opaque
	"Have you heard…?"	Opaque
	"Let's go home."	Opaque
	"Let's talk later."	Opaque

Source: The Picture Communication Symbols © 1981–2006 by Mayer-Johnson LLC. All rights reserved worldwide. Used with permission.

at which complex messages can be constructed using alphabet and word boards has led many augmentative users to prefer alternatives to text-based systems.

The challenge to any symbol system is the ability to generate a message as quickly and with as little effort as possible. Therefore, the way in which symbols are arranged and accessed must be as efficient as possible while matching the communicator's needs and abilities. There are many augmentative communication devices available commercially that use picture-based symbols that are designed to enhance symbol functionality. One such system is the pictorial language system called Minspeak (Semantic Compaction Systems), which forms the basis for the Unity system used in augmentative communication devices produced by the Prentke Romich Company. Minspeak and Unity are based on a visual language method called **semantic compaction** that uses a bank of carefully selected icons that can be easily combined to mean different things. The icons were selected deliberately to have multiple meanings and to be easily remembered. For example, to say the name of an animal, a user presses the "zebra" icon first. To say colors, a user presses the "rainbow" key first. Figure 10.2 contains examples of icon sequences. Learning the meanings of these icons and remembering how they are sequenced to convey different messages is known as **encoding**. Encoding enables an augmentative user to construct messages with less effort and time by striking fewer keys.

FIGURE 10.2 Sample Unity symbols. Courtesy of Prentke-Romich.

Building Basic Phrases and Sentences

With Unity, a client can select an icon to express single words and easily progress to building short phrases and complete sentences by using the same icons. The examples demonstrate how the natural language structure of Unity is used to build vocabulary.

The **action man** icon (or **verb** as it is labeled) is associated with verbs or things you do, such as "**drink**."

$+$ = *drink*

The **juice** icon plus the **adjective** icon communicates "**thirsty**."

$+$ = *thirsty*

The **he** icon represents the subject. The universally popular **sun** with a pleasant smiley face icon represents "**like**."

$+$ = *he likes...*

The **apple** icon followed by **action man** products the verb "**eat**."

$+$ = *eat*

Apple plus **adjective** produces the adjective "**hungry**."

$+$ = *hungry*

(continued)

Statements or questions can be easily created by simply reversing certain icon sequences.

How It Works

In Unity, the core vocabulary icons are simply used to teach an association. For example, the apple is associated with the concept of eating and the rainbow is associated with colors. Eventually, the communicator doesn't think "apple"; rather, he or she automatically touches the apple icon as part of saying the word "eat."

Source: Prentke Romich Company, http://www.prentrom.com/language/unity/index.php?page=5. Reprinted with permission.

The Vantage Lite (Prentke Romich) is a high-tech augmentative communication device that uses the Unity language system. It offer options for 4-, 8-, 15-, 45-, 60-, and 84-location displays so it can grow along with a child's language development. It is durable but lightweight and has a built-in handle for carrying.

Courtesy of Prentke-Romich.

The Unity series has a consistent set of icons for several levels, with consistent patterns for forming words and phrases. Each stage of Unity builds on the skills a student has already learned. The most advanced Unity system has a core vocabulary that represents the few hundred words that make up 85% of common conversation. High-end devices using Unity also include text-based features such as a QWERTY spelling keyboard and word prediction to facilitate the addition of custom vocabulary.

Some students with more complex disabilities and especially those who are blind or visually impaired often respond favorably to the use of real objects and/or tactile symbols for communication. The use of real objects is often the first example of emerging symbolic behavior in children. For example, infants are often observed getting excited when their parent reaches for

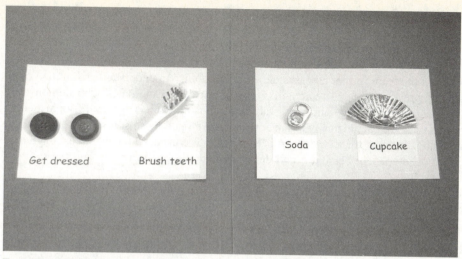

Two examples of tactile symbols that can be used for choice making. The tactile symbols on the left are used to answer the question, What do you want to do first—get dressed or brush your teeth? Those on the right are used to make a choice at snack time—Do you want soda or a cupcake?

Photo by Amy G. Dell

the car keys because they recognize a relationship between the keys and a car ride. An example of using real objects as a symbol system would be placing samples of favorite snack foods, such as Cheerios or chocolate candies, in small, clear plastic holders (available in the beads section of craft stores) that can then be presented to a student for him or her to communicate a choice. A bicycle handle used to represent the activity of exercising on a stationary bicycle is an example of a tactile symbol. During free play in a preschool when children are given the opportunity to choose the center in which they want to play, a student with deafblindness communicates her choice by selecting one of four tactile symbols: a small book for the reading center, a paintbrush to signify the art center, a small funnel to symbolize the water table, and a piece of cloth to represent the dress-up (make-believe) area.

Online Resource: Design to Learn

Design to Learn (http://www.designtolearn.com) is a group of researchers and special educators from the Oregon Institute on Disability and Development, a program of the Oregon Health & Science University (OHSU) in Portland, who specialize in developing effective assessment and teaching strategies that address the needs of children who are deaf-blind and children with autism spectrum disorders. Their Web site offers extensive resources in the development and implementation of tactile and tangible symbol systems and offers a free assessment protocol for early communication entitled The Communication Matrix. This assessment tool is designed to identify how a child is currently communicating and provides a framework for determining early communication goals.

From this brief discussion, it is clear that symbols vary in complexity from higher order symbol sets such as Unity and text to less complex symbols such as object cues that represent single activities. Determining which symbol set best matches a student's needs is, therefore, an important part of the augmentative communication assessment process.

The symbol assessment process begins with evaluating whether the student has a basic ability to determine the function of objects. At this stage, the team observes the student for evidence that he or she understands the fundamental link between an item and its use. For example, a cup is used for drinking or keys are used to start a car and go on a trip. From this point, the team progresses to transferring object symbols to less iconic representations such as photographs or line drawings. If the student successfully masters the match between objects and pictures, then the team further assesses the student's ability to understand and utilize more iconic symbol representations. Augmentative communication candidates who demonstrate an ability to understand language and words are better positioned to learn more sophisticated symbol systems than are candidates who have not yet developed these skills. Therefore, when identifying symbol systems for a student, it is important to consider literacy status, degree of communicative or interactive behavior, and demonstrated abilities to understand the symbol/concept relationship.

In addition to the team's assessment of the type of symbol system to use, team members must consider other variables that will influence the symbol system's effectiveness, including the following:

- Will the initial symbol system change as the student demonstrates more complex symbolic abilities? For example, will the symbol system change from simple objects to pictures or from pictures to line drawings?
- Will the symbol system effectively promote the student's skills and abilities to combine symbols to create unique messages?
- What is the most appropriate size for the symbols?
- How many symbols can be displayed at one time?
- How many symbols will be introduced at first?
- Can the student access multiple categories of symbols?

HOW IS VOCABULARY SELECTED?   Once the appropriate symbol system is identified, an initial vocabulary must be selected. It is especially important that the student continues or heightens his or her active role in the decision-making process. Vocabulary selection is a large factor in the successful use of any augmentative communication system (Balandin & Iacono, 1998). Many teams make the mistake of identifying vocabulary that is important to caregivers or teachers rather than to the student who will be using the system. Instead, the team must work to select vocabulary that is empowering to the student. This means communication must begin with messages that are highly motivating, such as requests for preferred objects or activities, questions that will enable the student to initiate conversation with another student, and comments that will get a reaction from other people. The selection of specific words and phrases should fit with the student's culture and age group. Teenagers, for example, do not want to sound like their (older) speech therapists or teachers; they want to use the same slang expressions that their peers are using.

For example, most teenagers do not say "How are you today?" or "I am fine, thank you." Instead, they have their own way of greeting each other and answering these kinds of questions, and the augmentative communication system's vocabulary should reflect this "kid-talk." Teachers need to become familiar with the slang their students use and incorporate these phrases in the device's vocabulary. Humor is often very motivating for students, so including jokes and sarcastic comments is often effective.

The following are guidelines to identify meaningful vocabulary:

- Provide messages that enable the student to **greet** other students and begin a conversation.
- Include vocabulary that enables the student to **comment** on events and activities, both as a way to express his or her opinion and as a way to continue a conversation.

- Provide vocabulary that includes specific people who are important in the student's life and enables the student to **call** them.
- Include favorite activities or objects and the vocabulary that enables the student to **request** them.
- Make sure the student has a way of **conveying his or her feelings**, such as "That makes me really angry."
- Include a method for **protest**. Provide a way of refusing or saying no. For example, "I don't want to do that," "I need a break," or "I want to be alone."
- Use **age-appropriate** and **culturally sensitive** words and phrases, including slang.
- Incorporate **humor** and sarcasm if age appropriate.

Identifying preferred vocabulary and words that have significance for the student is not a simple task. Many individuals do not have the ability to express the circumstances in which they would find communication the most powerful. Therefore, it is necessary for the team to look outward to other people in the student's life and to other assessment initiatives (Yorkston, Honsinger, Dowden, & Marriner, 1988). The team must employ multiple assessment strategies that may include the following:

- Interviews with family members, including siblings and grandparents
- Interviews with friends and same-age peers
- Preference inventories that detail an individual's likes and dislikes
- Direct observation across environments, activities, and people
- Analysis of challenging behavior

HOW ARE SYMBOLS GROUPED OR ARRANGED?   In addition to selecting the symbol system and the vocabulary, the collaborative team must decide how to arrange the symbols on the device. Symbol location can directly affect how well that symbol is perceived or recalled (Wilkinson & Jagaroo, 2004). Because efficiency in communicating is the greatest challenge to an augmentative communication user, the arrangement of symbols should maximize the student's rate of communication. Preferred layouts include those that allow the user easy access to words, phrases, and full sentences that are likely to be used often, as well as ease in constructing novel messages. A student who has control over only one hand, for example, needs frequently used words and phrases placed on the side of the device closest to the functioning hand. Decisions about symbol arrangement should consider the student's current developmental stage. For children whose language is still developing, a symbol array that provides practice in typical language skills may be helpful. For example, a child who is learning the rules of word order in sentences may benefit from a symbol array that groups parts of speech together—nouns on the left, verbs in the middle, adjectives on the right. As the child constructs a sentence, he or she moves from left to right, an essential skill in literacy development. Children who are learning about classifying items by attributes may need an array that groups categories of items together, such as foods, toys, and family members (Beukelmen & Mirenda, 2005).

Low-tech augmentative communication devices often rely on symbol sets that have been created on a computer and printed on paper using a graphics program such as Boardmaker (Mayer-Johnson) (See Figure 10.1). These paper overlays are easy to construct and can also be used as no-tech back-up systems. However, their static nature presents some limitations. When students have several overlays to be used on a single device, the overlay must physically be changed according to the appropriate communication context. Students with physical disabilities are often unable to manipulate the overlays and therefore must be dependent on an adult to

Student using an augmentative communication device to participate in a classroom activity.

Kevin J. Cohen. Used with permission.

make the change. An alternative system is one in which the symbol array is electronic and can be changed by a simple touch on a screen. This is called **dynamic display.** On a dynamic display device, vocabulary is shown as text and/or graphics on a touch screen; as one symbol is selected, the screen can change to another set of text and/or graphics.

Dynamic display systems are organized in a hierarchy in which each level of pictures increases in specificity. For example, the first display may offer an array of categories (e.g., food, activities, school). When a user selects the food category, an associated screen appears with specific items of food. The user navigates through these levels to get to his or her desired word or phrase. Dynamic display devices from Dynavox organize symbols in a file folder system that shows the major categories as tabs on the top of the files. Dynamic display devices are also available from Prentke-Romich.

Another type of symbol arrangement used on dynamic display devices for beginning communicators and those with more complex challenges is a **visual scene display.** This is a good choice for students who need contextual cues. Instead of simply arranging symbols in rows and columns, a visual scene display begins with a large picture or photograph that provides a context for more detailed information (Blackstone, 2004). As the student clicks on a part of the large picture, vocabulary related to that selection appears. For example, a picture of a classroom is shown and when the child points to a student's desk, vocabulary is shown related to the contents of the desk such as books, pencils, crayons, and paper. The items that are displayed within the desk may also lead the student to other scenes; for example, the student's science book may lead to vocabulary regarding a recent unit of study. The use of visual scene displays in augmentative communication devices creates a shared context for vocabulary. Research suggests it reduces the learning demands on young users and shifts the focus away from simple requests for desired objects to social interaction (Blackstone, 2004).

DynaVox m3 augmentative communication device showing a visual scene display.Courtesy of DynaVox Technology

USER PROFILE

Functional Communication for Students with Multiple Disabilities

The day begins in this self-contained classroom for students with multiple disabilities much like in other classrooms at the elementary school in this town. The students arrive, hang up their coats and bags, and greet the teacher and the assistant. However, here is where a difference arises. Of the 12 students in the class, ages 8–12, four of the students proceed to take their augmentative communication devices out of their backpacks and put on their speech wallets. The whole class puts on name tags imprinted with their name and favorite symbol. The name tags help develop sight words, and the symbols are cues for the students who use the augmentative devices to know which key to press to address that child.

VOCABULARY SELECTION

Ms. G., the special education teacher, has learned that to motivate her students to communicate, she must provide vocabulary that interests them. Before selecting vocabulary for a device, she works with the parents and the student to determine appropriate vocabulary. She makes a point of including favorite activities; expressions of emotions; humorous messages; and, if appropriate, sarcastic comments. Ms. G. recommends listening to other students in the school to find out what expressions are current and popular. Some of her favorites include "Yea, no school!" "See you later, alligator," and "Stop being a crybaby." Other high-interest messages that are stored on the students' devices are listed next.

SAMPLE AGE-APPROPRIATE MESSAGES STORED ON STUDENTS' AUGMENTATIVE COMMUNICATION DEVICES

- Wow, that was so cool!
- I don't want to play.
- We did something fun at school.
- School was yucky today.
- Don't tell me what to do.
- Will you help me call someone?
- That's great news.
- Can I go with my friends?
- I'm going to tell on you.
- I can do it myself.
- What's your problem?
- No way, man!
- Oh no. I have homework.
- She really makes me mad.
- He's so funny.

A COLLABORATIVE EFFORT

Ms. G. notes that it takes time and commitment on the part of the teacher, the speech-language specialist, the parents, and the students to integrate augmentative communication devices into the classroom. She attends training workshops with the parents, and she spends a good deal

(continued)

of prep time each week programming the devices with appropriate vocabulary for classroom activities. For each student, she makes a corresponding speech wallet that hooks to a belt loop to serve as a non-electronic backup to their high-tech devices. These manual backups are essential for those times when devices break or batteries run down.

Her efforts, however, have reaped many benefits in her classroom. She has seen communication initiation increase as her students now have a way to express emotions and ask for help. "I need to see the nurse," "I need help," and "Please leave me alone" are some of the initiations she has observed. The students also communi-cate with each other now. Christopher likes to stop students in the hallway to say, "Hi! How are you today?" When Seth killed a spider that the class had been watching, Christopher said, "Seth, I'm mad at you. That was not very nice. It is dead. Spider."

The class recently began a campaign to educate the regular education staff and students in their school about augmentative communication. Classes visit Ms. G.'s room to hear her students explain their devices and read the story *Brown Bear, Brown Bear, What Do You See?* to younger students. Christopher describes his device as follows:

This machine is called a Liberator. I use it to help me talk. Sometimes the battery gets low, and I have to plug it in. I can do it on my own. I wear a WalkerTalker [a simpler, low-tech device] around my waist. I wear it all the time.

Christopher, Eli, and Bobby then take turns reading pages of *Brown Bear, Brown Bear.* This experience gives the other classes an opportunity to learn about augmentative communication, see the devices in action, ask questions about them, and make some new friends. ■

Source: From "Functional Communication in a Life Skills Class," by Regina Quinn, 1996. *TECH-NJ, 7*(2), 6, 15. Reprinted with permission.

HOW IS THE ACCESS METHOD DETERMINED?   During the assessment process, the team is involved in discussions regarding appropriate features of the augmentative communication system. In addition to the symbol system, symbol arrangement and vocabulary selection, the team must consider the manner in which the student will access the vocabulary (i.e., the selection method) and the way in which the messages will be displayed (i.e., the system's output). Access to computers and selecting the most appropriate access methods were discussed in detail in Chapters 8 and 9. Many computer access methods discussed in these chapters are also available on augmentative communication systems. Therefore, this section focuses on access issues that are unique to augmentative communication.

Students who have a reliable point (the index finger extended at something) can use **direct selection** to construct messages on either low-tech language boards or high-tech computer-based systems. Direct selection may be accomplished in a variety of ways, including using direct finger pressure on specific keys, using a pointing device such as a headstick or chinstick, using an infrared beam that is mounted on the head, or pointing with the eyes (eye control, or eye gaze). Eye-gaze technology has become much more affordable, accurate, and easier to use in recent years and is now a realistic option for students who have extremely limited motor control but good vision and the ability to hold their heads still. However, many students do not have reliable motor abilities to use direct selection, and the team must collaborate to select and design a system that can be accessed through scanning.

Lori's user profile illustrates **single-switch scanning** as one alternative to direct selection for students to access their augmentative communication devices. Other methods include **encoding systems** such as Morse code that can be activated with two switches (one for dots and one for dashes) or the use of scanning with multiple switches or a joystick. It is critical that as the team considers the most efficient and effective access method for the student, it focuses on enhancing the rate of message selection through techniques such as word prediction and icon prediction.

USER PROFILE

Lori

Lori is a first-year high school student who uses a computerized voice output device that she accesses via single-switch scanning. She operates the device with a foot switch that when activated stops the scanning on her device at the desired selection. When she has completed composing a message, Lori scans to the Speak key and her device speaks the message using synthesized speech. Although this system is slower than direct selection, it is the most efficient system for Lori. This selection system enables Lori to construct any message she wants and gives her the freedom to communicate independently. ■

Student using direct selection to access her augmentative communication device.
Photo by Vicki Spence

WHAT OTHER FEATURES NEED TO BE CONSIDERED?   Other important features for the team to consider are the physical nature of the system and its compatibility with the natural environments in which the student will use it. The size, weight, mountability, degree of water resistance, and other characteristics must be considered during the selection process. A student who uses a wheelchair does not need a lightweight system but does need a system that can easily mount on his or her wheelchair. A student who is ambulatory (i.e., walks for mobility) needs a system that is portable and lightweight. A student who walks and has behavior problems may need a system that is not only portable, but durable as well.

Another decision to make when selecting an augmentative communication device involves the consideration of a dedicated versus a non-dedicated system. A **dedicated system** is a stand-alone device designed specifically for augmentative communication. Although these devices may include generic capabilities, they have been designed specifically for the purpose of expressive communication by individuals who are nonspeaking. A **non-dedicated system** refers to the use of a generic electronic device that has been designed for the general public, such as a laptop computer, tablet PC, or smart phone, that has been equipped with text-to-speech and augmentative communication software. There is a growing market of "apps" for smart phones (e.g., iPhone or Android), iPod Touches, and iPads that provide relatively inexpensive alternatives to dedicated augmentative communication devices. These new products may or may not meet the needs of the augmentative communicator. A student who has an accurate point, adequate vision, and good technical skills *may* be a candidate for an iPad or iPod Touch that has been equipped with communication software such as Proloquo2Go (see sidebar). On the other hand, a small, fragile iPod Touch may be a terrible choice for a student who has motor control issues, low vision, attention deficits, behavior problems, and/or cognitive disabilities. It is essential that the process to determine an appropriate augmentative system remain the same whether the outcome is a dedicated or non-dedicated device.

Many of today's high-tech dedicated devices offer Internet access as well as other standard computer applications. Others can easily be connected to a computer, and students can use the device in place of the standard keyboard for access. This gives them access to the Internet, e-mail, and other applications in which they are interested. Dedicated devices are more durable and offer greater volume control than do laptop computers or handheld devices. The main advantage to laptop computers and handheld devices is that they are less expensive than dedicated devices. However, third-party payers such as Medicaid and private health insurance companies do not consider a laptop computer or cell phone to be "durable medical equipment" and do not provide funding for them, even if their primary purpose is augmentative communication. This complicates the decision-making process.

As the team identifies the current skills of the student, the most appropriate symbol system, and the most efficient access method, consideration of specific devices—low, mid, and high tech—begins. It is at this point that the team begins to try out specific augmentative communication solutions that match the student's skills and needs. As the most appropriate and effective system becomes clear, the team then works to customize the system for the student's particular needs and interests.

Augmentative Communication Apps for iPod Touches, iPads, and Smart Phones

A growing number of applications have recently become available that can turn iPod Touches, iPads, and smart phones such as the iPhone or Android into augmentative communication devices. These apps take advantage of the devices' touch screen technology and are easy to use and customize. Proloquo2Go™ (AssistiveWare) provides natural-sounding text-to-speech voices, a library of picture symbols, a default vocabulary of 7,000 items, and the ability to expand both the picture library and the vocabulary. To provide some protection and louder speech output, the company also sells a protective case with built-in external speakers. SmallTalk (Lingraphica) is designed for people who have had strokes but with some tweaking could be useful for students with autism or cognitive disabilities. A starter set of icons is available free in the iTunes App Store, but the full version must be purchased to modify or expand the communication options. Voice4u and iComm are two apps that use icons and speech output to support young children and beginning communicators. These apps accept photographs and allow for recording human speech. TapToTalk, which is available for Nintendo handheld devices and Android phones as well as iPod Touches, iPhones, and iPads, does not offer text-to-speech—teachers or parents need to record messages—but it provides a Web-based program called TapToSpeak Designer for easy customizing. My

Talk Tools Mobile (2nd Half Enterprises) and SoundingBoard (AbleNet) are two other apps designed to provide opportunities for augmentative communication on various mobile devices. The Web addresses for these apps are found at the end of the chapter under Web Resources.

The Proloquo2Go app turns the Apple iPad (or iPod Touch) into an augmentative communication device
Courtesy of AssistiveWare.

USER PROFILE

Tim

Tim is a 12th-grade student who attends a program at his local high school that provides community-based vocational instruction. He has been sampling jobs in the community for the past 3 years and currently is working part time with supervision at the local video rental store. Tim has Down syndrome and has significant speech difficulties. In addition, Tim has a moderate bilateral mixed hearing loss that compounds his verbal intelligibility and receptive language skills. To help him communicate on the job, Tim's augmentative communication system consists of facial expressions and simple gestures and two aided components: (1) an iPod Touch with the Proloquo2Go app (see sidebar) and (2) an FM system to enhance listening circumstances (see Chapter 6). ∎

interAACT

Several assessment protocols for identifying and supporting augmentative communication systems have been developed. The DynaVox Mayer-Johnson Company provides a decision-making framework entitled InterAACT that is designed to guide practitioners in their considerations of the critical components of developing an individualized communication system. Although this framework is designed to be used with DynaVox applications and hardware, it offers more generic applications and is a useful resource for augmentative communication teams. The InterAACT framework considers the age and abilities of the student and the context of communicative interactions when deciding on structure, vocabulary, and an appropriate symbol set. It provides guidance on the arrangement of symbols sets to accommodate a student's current level of communication. Students are identified as one of the following: emergent communicators (functional), contextual communicators (situational), or independent (creative) communicators. The InterACCT system offers premade templates and has the flexibility to customize symbols and how they are displayed. Within the emergent or functional ranges, symbol sets are organized to reduce the cognitive demands of the communication system, for example, by providing symbols within a visual scene display that presents fewer options.

EVALUATING THE EFFICIENCY AND EFFECTIVENESS OF A STUDENT'S AUGMENTATIVE COMMUNICATION SYSTEM

After an augmentative communication system is selected and designed for a student, the team's work is not over yet. Communication ability is a work in progress. Most beginner augmentative communication users need years to develop their communication skills and to progress through a hierarchy of skill levels until true independent communication is realized. Therefore, ongoing evaluation of the effectiveness and efficiency of a system must be conducted. As students' skills improve or become more challenging, devices become outdated, students' environments change, and students' needs change. For these reasons, there has to be an ongoing assessment effort that continues to engage the student and his or her family and teachers. The conventional methods of monitoring a student's use of an augmentative communication system are primarily guided observations (including video recording) and data collection from trained observers. Students need to be monitored and evaluated on their gains in language development and competence, as well as on their efficiency in using the augmentative communication device (Hill, 2009).

Summary

- There are no prerequisites to augmentative communication. All people with communication difficulties can achieve enhanced communication abilities through the use of augmentative communication.
- Teachers need to be aware of the myths and realities surrounding augmentative communication so that they can provide appropriate supports for students who are—or soon will be—augmentative communication users in their classes.

- The process for selecting and designing an augmentative communication system must involve a collaborative team that includes a professional, such as a speech-language therapist, who is trained and experienced in augmentative communication assessment and applications; the student; his or her parent(s) or family members; and his or her teacher(s). Additional team members may include a physical therapist, occupational therapist, tech support person, a peer, or anyone else who works closely with the student.

- The selection process begins with the SETT Framework with the Task(s) item focusing on the parameters of communication and language development.
- Factors to consider during an augmentative communication assessment include the student's developmental status, current communication skills, attributes of the environment, and the student's current and future communication needs.

- The three major components of an augmentative communication system that must be determined are the symbol system, the vocabulary, and the student's access method. Other features to consider are portability, ruggedness, and the question of a dedicated device or a generic laptop computer.
- Ongoing evaluation of the effectiveness of the augmentative communication system is essential.

Web Resources

For additional information on the topics listed, visit the following Web sites:

More from Michael Williams, Writer and AAC User
AAC 101: A crash course for beginners
http://www.augcominc.com/newsletters/?fuseaction=newsletters&C=AS

AT/AAC Enables: How Assistive Technology (AT) and Augmentative and Alternative Communication (AAC) Enable Individuals with Disabilities to Participate in All Aspects of Life
Dispelling myths
http://depts.washington.edu/enables/myths/myths_intro.htm

Profiles of Augmentative Communication Users
http://depts.washington.edu/enables/profiles/profiles_at_aac.htm

Augmentative Communication Users Join the Working World
http://depts.washington.edu/enables/myths/myths_aac_people_working.htm

Augmentative Communication Devices
Prentke Romich Company
http://www.prentrom.com/

Assistive Technology, Inc.
http://www.assistivetech.com

Attainment Company
http://www.attainmentcompany.com

DynaVox Technologies
http://www.dynavoxtech.com/

Words+, Inc.
http://www.words-plus.com/index.htm

Collaborative Teaming for Assessment
QIAT Consortium: Quality Indicator #2
http://natri.uky.edu/assoc_projects/qiat

Cerebral Palsy
National Institute of Neurological Disorders and Stroke
http://www.ninds.nih.gov/disorders/cerebral_palsy/cerebral_palsy.htm

Symbol Systems
BoardMaker
http://www.mayer-johnson.com/

Pogo Boards
http://www.pogoboards.com

Minspeak
http://www.minspeak.com

Unity
http://www.prentrom.com/language/unity/index.php?page5

Visual Scene Display
http://www.imakenews.com/aac-rerc/e_article000344804.cfm?x=b11,0,w

Create your own Visual Scene Display
http://www.augcominc.com/newsletters/?fuseaction=newsletters&V=16&C=can

Tactile Symbols
The National Consortium on Deafblindness
http://nationaldb.org/ISSelectedTopics.php?topicCatID=14

Design to Learn
http://www.designtolearn.com

Apps for iPod Touches, iPads, and Smart Phones
Proloquo2Go™
http://www.AssistiveWare.com

SoundingBoard
http://www.ablenetinc.com/AssistiveTechnology/Communication/SoundingBoard/tabid/632/Default.aspx

SmallTalk
http://www.Lingraphica.com

Voice4u
http://voice4uaac.com/

iComm
http://www.miasapps.com/

TapToTalk and TaptoSpeak Designer
http://www.taptotalk.com/

MyTalkTools Mobile
http://www.mytalktools.com/dnn/

Research & Resources
AAC Institute
http://www.aacinstitute.org/index.html

AAC Rehabilitation Engineering Research Centers (RERC)
http://www.aac-rerc.com/

Suggested Activities

1. *Read profiles of augmentative communication users.* Visit the Web site of the Prentke Romich Company: www.prentrom.com/index. html and click on Success Stories. Read the archived profiles of four augmentative communication users and write a three- to five-page paper

on the themes that run through these personal stories. For example, consider the users' lives before they had access to augmentative communication and the power and control they gained after they became skilled augmentative communication users.

2. *Interview an augmentative communication user.* Find an adult augmentative communication user in your community and interview him or her regarding his or her life story.

   a. What have been the highlights of the individual's life? When did augmentative communication become a part of his or her life, and how has it contributed to the individual's accomplishments?

   b. Describe the augmentative system used by the person. For aided systems, indicate the brand name of the equipment and the means of indication used. What symbol system is used? Describe the layout of the overlay(s). Describe how the person is positioned to use the system.

   c. Describe the person's vocabulary on the augmentative communication device. Include specific examples of vocabulary use that you observed and other vocabulary the person is reported to use.

   d. How effective were the user's attempts at communicating with the system? What problem areas can you identify? What factors, such as the vocabulary available or the behavior of the communication partner, influenced the success of the communicative exchanges?

3. *Participate in a discussion board on augmentative communication.* Participate in an online discussion board that focuses on augmentative communication. Each week a new question or topic should be posted by either the instructor or students. Topics should reflect issues or practices that relate to the selection and design of augmentative communication systems, such as the teacher's role in the decision-making process, data collection procedures for monitoring a student's use of an augmentative communication system, the use of an augmentative communication system at home, the role of related services staff (e.g., speech therapist, occupational therapist) in selecting an augmentative communication system, and issues in identifying an appropriate symbol system.

4. *Attend a vendor exhibit.* Attend a vendor exhibit that features augmentative communication devices from several manufacturers, and spend time exploring a variety of mid-tech to high-tech systems. Vendor displays are found at consumer shows such as the Abilities Expo, and at state, regional, and national conferences of professional organizations such as the American Speech-Language-Hearing Association (ASHA). They are also featured at the three national conferences on assistive technology: Closing the Gap in Minneapolis in October, the Assistive Technology Industry Association (ATIA) in Orlando in January and in Chicago in October, and California State University–Northridge (CSUN) in Los Angeles in March. Gather literature on current augmentative communication systems, and inquire about devices under development. Add this literature to your assistive technology portfolio.

5. *Simulate and reflect.* Using a low-tech augmentative communication device such as an alphabet board, complete a routine activity within the community. You are to act as a nonspeaking person and utilize only the system that you have created for yourself. For example, you can order a meal at a restaurant using the device. Write a three- to five-page reaction paper that describes your experiences and outlines your further insights into the lives of augmentative communication users.

References

Balandin, S., & Iacono, T. (1998). A few well-chosen words. *Augmentative and Alternative Communication, 14,* 147–161.

Beukelman, D. R., & Mirenda, P. (2005). *Augmentative and alternative communication* (3rd ed.). Baltimore, MD: Brookes.

Beukelman, D. R., Yorkston, K., & Dowden, P. (1985). *Communication augmentation: A casebook of clinical management.* Austin, TX: Pro-Ed.

Blackstone, S. W. (2004). Visual scene displays. *Augmentative Communication News, 16*(2).

Bruder, M. B. (1994). Working with members of other disciplines: Collaboration for success. In M. Wolery & J. S. Wilbers (Eds.), *Including children with special needs in early childhood programs* (pp. 45–70). Washington, DC: National Association for the Education of Young Children.

Daniels, M. (1994). The effect of sign on hearing children's language. *Communication Education, 43*, 291–298.

Dowden, P., & Cook, A. (2002). Choosing effective selection techniques for beginning communicators. In J. Reichle, D. Beukelman, & J. Light (Eds.), *Implementing an augmentative communication system: Exemplary strategies for beginning communicators*. Baltimore, MD: Brookes.

Downey, D., & Hurtig, R. (2003). Augmentative and alternative communication. *Pediatric Annals, 32*(7), 467–474.

Erickson, K. A. (2000). All children are ready to learn: An emergent versus readiness perspective in early literacy assessment. *Seminars in Speech and Language, 213*, 193–203.

Finch, A., & Romski, M. (2004, January). *The myths of AAC*. Presentation at the American Speech-Language-Hearing Association 2004 Augmentative Communication Leadership Conference, Sea Island, GA.

Grady, A. P., Kovach, T., Lange, M., & Shannon, L. (1993). "Consumer knows best": Promoting choice in assistive technology. *PT: Magazine of Physical Therapy, 1*(2), 50–56.

Hetzroni, O. E. (2004). AAC and literacy. *Disability and Rehabilitation, 26*(21/22), 1305–1312.

Hill, K. (2009). Data collection and monitoring AAC intervention in the schools. *Perspectives on Augmentative and Alternative Communication, 18*, 58–64.

Hourcade, J., Everhart-Pilotte, T., West, E., & Parette, P. (2004). A history of augmentative and alternative communication for individuals with severe and profound disabilities. *Focus on Autism and Other Developmental Disabilities, 19*(4), 235–244.

Kangas, K., & Lloyd, L. (1988). Early cognitive skills as prerequisites to augmentative and alternative communication use: What are we waiting for? *Augmentative and Alternative Communication, 4*, 211–221.

Kroth, R., & Bolson, M. D. (1996). Family involvement with assistive technology. *Contemporary Education, 68*, 17–20.

Musselwhite, C., & King-DeBaun, P. (1997). *Emerging literacy success: Merging whole language and technology for students with disabilities*. Park City, UT: Creative Communicating.

Quinn, R. (1996). Functional communication in a life skills class. *TECH-NJ, 7*(2), pp. 6, 15.

Schlosser, R. (2003). Effects of augmentative communication on natural speech development. In R. Schlosser (Ed.), *The efficacy of augmentative and alternative communication: Toward evidence-based practice* (pp. 404–426). San Diego, CA: Academic Press.

Snell, M. E., & Janney, R. (2000). *Teacher's guide to inclusive practices: Collaborative teaming*. Baltimore, MD: Brookes.

Vanderheiden, G. C., & Yoder, D. E. (1986). Overview. In S. W. Blackstone (Ed.), *Augmentative communication: An introduction* (pp. 1–28). Rockville, MD: American Speech-Language-Hearing Association.

Van Tatenhove, G. M. (1987). Teaching power through augmentative communication: Guidelines for early intervention. *Journal of Childhood Communication Disorders, 10*, 185–199.

Wilkinson, K. M., & Jagaroo, V. (2004). Contributions of principles of visual cognitive science to AAC system display design. *Augmentative and Alternative Communication, 20*(3), 123–136.

Williams, M. B. (2005, March). *Why I use more than one communication device*. Presentation at California State University–Northridge's 20th annual international conference, Technology and Persons with Disabilities, Los Angeles, CA.

Yorkston, K. M., Honsinger, M. J., Dowden, P. A., & Marriner, N. (1988). Vocabulary selection: A case report. *Augmentative and Alternative Communication, 5*(2), 101–108.

Zabala, J. S. (2005). Ready, SETT, go! Getting started with the SETT Framework. *Closing the Gap, 23*(6), 1–3.

11

ASSISTIVE TECHNOLOGY APPROACHES TO TEACHING EARLY COMMUNICATION AND EMERGENT LITERACY

Focus Questions

1. What is the difference between communication and language?
2. What are the factors that promote communication and language development?
3. What are low-tech solutions to enhancing early communication in children with disabilities?
4. What is emergent literacy?
5. How can assistive technology be used to facilitate emergent literacy?

INTRODUCTION

In the previous chapter, we discussed how assistive technology can be used to provide a voice for students with disabilities who cannot speak. Some children who cannot speak have multiple and severe intellectual disabilities that interfere with the overall development of communication. These children have not yet learned the very early skills necessary to support the development of speech or language. Therefore, they do not possess the necessary abilities to use the sophisticated augmentative communication systems discussed in Chapter 10. For these children, other appropriate and effective applications of simple technology can contribute to further development of their communication skills. However, it should be noted that professionals within the field of augmentative communication are debating the value of introducing more complex devices to individuals who do not appear to have prerequisite skills and developmental correlates. This position supports the notion that augmentative communication users do not require a certain set of skills or perceived intact cognitive skills as a prerequisite for high-tech devices and symbol systems. In addition, the use of a hierarchy for symbol use is discouraged from the practice of eliminating augmentative communication candidates from access to conventional symbol systems (Barton, Sevcik, & Romski 2006). This is congruent with the "least dangerous assumption" (Donnellan, 1984) that states that without data to the contrary, educational decisions should be based on the assumption of competence.

The example of Clara (see sidebar) demonstrates several ways in which a teacher can use assistive technology to influence the early communication development of children with severe disabilities. However, although the technology itself may be simple, the appropriate application involves careful consideration and

Clara

Clara is a 6-year-old girl with significant developmental disabilities. She is a social and pleasant youngster who uses smiles, gestures, and vocalizations to indicate when she is happy, sad, or displeased with something. Because Clara has not developed speech, cannot walk, and has cognitive impairments, the experiences she needs in order to develop more effective communication skills are provided through the use of assistive technology. For example, Clara is presented with a variety of favorite toys that are activated by large single switches. She is given opportunities to choose from among these toys, allowing Clara to demonstrate her understanding that her deliberate actions (hitting the switch) can cause specific results or effects (activating a toy). There are other ways in which simple technology is infused into Clara's educational program to support her growing abilities to interact with others. A one-step digitized voice output device is programmed with a little girl's voice saying "Excuse me, but can someone come here for a minute?" Clara activates this simple augmentative communication device to get attention. It is available to her at all times so that she can use it as an alternative to gaining attention in negative ways such as by screeching. ∎

understanding of communication and language development. The professional literature clearly substantiates the importance of early communication to the development of more complex forms of communication such as language (Beukelman & Mirenda, 1998; Calandrella & Wilcox 2000; Warren & Yoder, 1998). Although a review of this literature is beyond the scope of this text, it is important to understand some basic concepts and parameters in order to use assistive technology as an instructional strategy for early communication.

WHAT IS COMMUNICATION?

Communication may be broadly defined as the exchange of information between people (Siegel-Causey & Guess, 1989). More specifically, it is

- the process of transmitting and receiving messages between two people; and
- occurs within the context of a socially supportive environment.

Communication occurs when one individual sends a message to another individual, who then acknowledges receipt and understanding. When this communication interaction is continued or sustained, it is called a **conversation**.

Although this description of the communication process is simple and most children develop communication with ease, a more detailed examination reveals a complex interdependent set of variables. These variables include the following:

1. The presence and participation of one or more partners
2. A socially and physically supportive environment
3. The ability and desire to send an intentional message and receive a message (Stremel-Campbell & Matthews, 1988)

Messages are created for a reason, have specific content, are communicated through some set of rules, and take some structure that can be expressed. The structure or mode of communication can be either symbolic (e.g., speech) or nonsymbolic (e.g., a gesture). This distinction represents

Child pointing to indicate his choice.

Photo by Tammy Cordwell

the difference between communication and language. **Language** is a form of communication that uses a set of symbols with rules for ordering that we all agree have a specific meaning. (See Chapter 10 for an explanation of symbols.)

It is important to understand that communication is not limited to language (Downing & Siegel-Causey, 1988). People communicate in a variety of nonsymbolic ways—through eye contact, body movements, facial expressions, gestures, and nonverbal vocalizations. Consider two friends unexpectedly running into each other at the mall. As they recognize each other from a distance, they wave enthusiastically and smile broadly, while their eyes widen and light up with excitement. Not a single word is exchanged, yet the meaning of their messages is clear without the use of language. This is **nonsymbolic communication**.

Nonsymbolic communication regularly occurs between babies and their parents. A baby's cry conveys hunger or tiredness or some kind of discomfort. Cooing communicates contentment. As the baby becomes a toddler, the point becomes a very effective gesture. The simplicity of the toddler's point does not compare to its power. With a single point, everyone in that toddler's environment understands that he or she wants *this*, not that, or wants to go *there*, not stay here.

HOW DO COMMUNICATION AND LANGUAGE DEVELOP?

Infants and early communicators (children with delayed speech and language) progress through a series of stages from unintentional to intentional forms of nonsymbolic communication. This comes about as a result of interactions and relationships with caregivers (Siegel-Causey, Ernst, & Guess, 1988). An **unintentional** form of communication is defined as a behavior that is merely *suggested* to have meaning or intent, such as a baby's first smile. These forms are then shaped into intentional communicative behaviors by the adults in the child's environment. (Consider the adults' reactions to the baby's first smile.) These early communication forms, or prelinguistic communicative behaviors, are important precursors to later language development (Warren & Yoder, 1998).

Infants then develop deliberate behaviors to influence others in their environments through a developmental process involving reciprocity between babies and their caregivers. For example, a baby responds to a familiar vocal cue and facial expression of his or her mother by gazing back into her eyes and smiling, cooing, or mimicking her facial expression. This is called a **reciprocal interaction** because it involves the basic back-and-forth elements of a conversation.

FIGURE 11.1 Communication model.

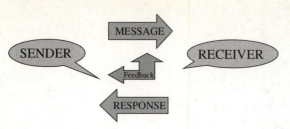

These elements include someone sending a message, another person receiving and responding to the message, and then continuing the exchange until someone stops the exchange or ends the conversation. This game is played over and over and, in effect, establishes the back-and-forth (reciprocal) nature of communication.

Children need practice to learn to communicate and interact. Infants enjoy and benefit from repeating routines involving familiar objects or toys and adults. For example, babies never seem to be tired of playing a game of peek-a-boo while getting dressed in the morning or getting dried off after a bath. Peek-a-boo games are good illustrations of the fact that communication and language development are rooted in social behavior and are dependent on the social environment (Bates, 1976; Bloom, 1993; Moore & Corkum, 1994; Wetherby & Prizant, 1992). Children interact with people and objects within their environments to learn the rules and patterns of effective communication (see Figure 11.1). Eventually, language is generated, and in place of the prelinguistic forms of communication are words, sentences, and language-based conversations.

What Factors Promote Communication and Language Development?

The factors that promote communication and language are both within and outside children. A child's capacity to interact with people and objects in the environment is influenced by his or her ability to see, hear, touch, smell, move, and solve problem. When these abilities are severely compromised, the development of communication and language is interrupted.

However, it is the factors *outside* the child that may have the greatest effect on communication development. Communication is developed by parents, siblings, and other more competent communicators being responsive and interactive with the child. It is the child's environment and the behavior of those people within it that can be influenced or changed to promote the communication development of the child.

Communication is stimulated within the context of routines, people, and objects that are present in the child's environment. An environment that is rich in activities and interesting objects gives children and their partners more opportunities to communicate or interact. It also supports the development of critical cognitive concepts such as cause and effect. Cause and effect is the understanding that your behavior can deliberately cause something to occur. ("If I do X, then Y will happen.") For example, "If I shake this rattle, it will make a funny noise," or "If I point at the cookie jar, Grandma will give me a cookie." This is increasingly important for children who are nonspeaking and in the early stages of developing communication skills. Children need to be *provided with opportunities* for frequent communicative interactions *with competent partners for a variety of reasons* so they, in turn, will learn to communicate for a variety of purposes.

Choice making is a powerful skill that presents a context for early communication development. Children are motivated to communicate their wants and needs when presented with a choice. For example, a toddler is more ready to get dressed in the morning when given an

USER PROFILE

Justin

Justin is a nonambulatory 3-year-old who does not speak and has limited use of his hands. At home, his parents appear to know when he needs comfort, is hungry, or wants attention. However, in preschool Justin's intentions are not as well understood. Therefore, he uses a colorful BIGmack (AbleNet, Inc.), a single-message communication device that will ask for someone to attend to him when he presses it with his fist. Justin presses the switch, a recorded voice says "I need someone to come over here," and a teacher approaches, inferring that he either wants attention or needs something. This is teaching Justin the beginning skills of initiating communication. ■

opportunity to choose between a selection of two outfits. This reinforces individual control and power, as well as providing a meaningful opportunity to interact with another person.

Another example of communication as power occurs when a child initiates a communicative exchange. Typical children learn to initiate and express intentions; they do not wait to be asked by an adult. This is usually done in an environment that contains interesting and novel objects and activities, as well as people who are able to interact with the child. For students who have severe disabilities, simple technology can be harnessed to provide opportunities to initiate communication, as illustrated in the following user profile.

Attention to both initiated communication and the response from a caregiver are equally critical in creating optimal environments for the development of early communication (Noonan & Siegel-Causey, 1997). Caregivers such as parents and teachers must be deliberate and consistent in their initiating and sustaining conversations with young children. Typically developing children require thousands of exchanges to gain the skills of having a conversation, and children with disabilities will need as many or more.

PROBLEMS STUDENTS WITH DISABILITIES HAVE WITH EARLY COMMUNICATION DEVELOPMENT

Children with severe social, cognitive, motor, and sensory disabilities are at risk for delays in developing effective communication and language skills (Stremel-Campbell & Matthews, 1988). As stated, early communication development requires that children participate actively in their environment. Children participate actively through play, interactions with other children, interactions with adults during daily routines (e.g., dressing, eating, bathing), and other activities that are repeated over and over. This becomes extremely challenging for children who have significant social, cognitive, motor, and sensory disabilities. They often (1) cannot independently interact with people and objects in the environment due to hearing, vision, or motor difficulties; (2) do not present the cognitive abilities to become fully symbolic communicators independently; and (3) are not provided with multiple opportunities to engage in communicative-rich environments with a variety of competent partners.

As a result of these delays in developing language, children with severe disabilities may remain dependent on nonsymbolic behaviors as their primary system of communication (Ogletree, 1996). For example, they use facial grimaces to express dislike, protest through the use of crying, or exhibit problematic behavior as a means to communicate their needs.

TABLE 11.1	Supports and Barriers to Early Communication		
Factors Supporting Communication Development	**Barrier**	**Effect**	
Intentionality and causality	Motor, sensory, and cognitive disabilities limit the number of opportunities to engage in routines that support intentionality and causality.	Child does not develop skills that promote early nonsymbolic communication.	
Choice making	Direct instruction in choice making and/or multiple opportunities for choice making are not provided to the child.	Child either does not develop the skills for choice making or does not make choices.	
Frequent and rich interaction with objects and people	Motor, sensory, and cognitive disabilities limit the availability of objects and people.	In cooperation with a communication partner, the child does not gain joint attention to objects or other people in the environment.	
Frequent and consistent practice of having conversations with others	Limited and inconsistent opportunities to practice the give and take of a conversation.	Child does not initiate or sustain a communication exchange.	
The overall presence of early communication forms	No way to communicate basic needs effectively.	Child exhibits inappropriate and problematic behavior.	

Table 11.1 offers a view of these limitations as they relate to the critical elements of communication and language development already discussed. The barriers represent attributes often recognized in children with severe or profound disabilities.

TECHNOLOGY TOOLS THAT SUPPORT EARLY COMMUNICATION DEVELOPMENT

Whereas most children learn communication skills through typical daily interactions, children with significant disabilities require direct, systematic instruction (Noonan & Siegel-Causey, 1997). They must be taught the fundamental concept that their actions can influence the environment and that their deliberate interactions can achieve desired ends (i.e., cause and effect). The use of assistive technology can bridge this gap for many children with cognitive, motor, and sensory impairments. It offers solutions to the problem of providing these children with the same opportunities as typically developing children to communicate and make choices. Through the use of devices to request attention, develop understandings of consequences, and stimulate the sensory system, children with disabilities can be provided with opportunities to access environments rich in interesting objects and people.

Direct instruction in **cause and effect** can be provided through the use of simple technology. **Switches** enable students who have limited motor control to activate battery-operated toys and other electronic equipment with a single movement. They enable students with disabilities to achieve positive interactions with their immediate surroundings and exert control over relevant stimuli (Lancioni et al., 2002; Langley, 1990). For example, a simple switch can be used to turn on a model race car that moves, makes sounds, and displays lights; a vibrating pillow that tickles; or a

Two types of switches from AbleNet,
Inc.—Microswitch & Big Red switch.

Courtesy of AbleNet, Inc.

CD player that plays a child's favorite songs. Each time the child presses the switch, the enjoyable consequence results. To be effective in teaching cause and effect, it is essential that switches are connected to toys, CDs, or objects that the child finds entertaining and are age appropriate.

In addition to teaching cause and effect, switches can be used to teach **choice making** to children with disabilities (Lancioni et al., 2002). Typically developing children learn to make choices over time through multiple opportunities provided within natural settings, but many children with disabilities are limited in their ability to express a choice and do not have the equivalent opportunities. Choice making is an important developmental skill that must be exercised often, especially for the student who is still developing intentional communication. The use of switches can be an excellent strategy to assist in the development of choice-making behavior and in providing opportunities to practice making choices. Choice making provides students with a sense of power. For example, during free play or break time, students can choose what they would like to listen to on their MP3 Player: a rap song or a country music song, or perhaps a book-on-CD or a podcast of their favorite radio show. Other students will use multiple switches to choose one battery-operated toy (a dancing pig, perhaps) over another (a noisy truck).

Switch-operated toy with
a Jelly Bean switch.

Photo by Amy B. Dell

Daniel

Daniel is a 3-year-old who has motor and cognitive disabilities. He is nonverbal and cannot ambulate independently, but he can reach and grasp with one hand. He attends a preschool program with typically developing children and is provided special education support services. His special education teacher has developed a variety of activities using assistive technology to provide Daniel with opportunities to understand that his deliberate actions can influence a desired effect. Daniel operates a remote control train set by activating a switch connected to the train and turns the pages of a talking computer-based storybook by pressing a Jelly Bean switch. Using switch technology, the special education teacher has provided multiple opportunities for Daniel to participate in his preschool routines and learn the power of his direct influence. ■

In addition to promoting students' prelinguistic skills of cause and effect and choice making, switches can be used as simple augmentative communication devices. Building on the switch activation skills a student has been taught, a single-message communication device (e.g., BIGmack, LITTLEmack [both by AbleNet, Inc.]) can be used to deliver a recorded message. Single-message communication devices look very similar to switches but contain sound chips that can be recorded with spoken messages. Students with disabilities can activate these prerecorded devices to initiate communication or respond to another person. For example, a child can use a single-step communication device to invite another person to play a game or read a story by pressing a single-message communication device that asks, "Does anyone want to play a game?" or "Will someone read me a story?" Single-message communicators are often used as calling or alerting devices that enable a student to request attention in an appropriate manner.

As students with severe disabilities are being educated within general education settings, single-switch communication devices can be extremely useful. Such devices can be programmed so that students with disabilities can actively participate in groups of typical peers. For example, a single-switch communication device can be programmed for participation in a morning exercise such as asking the other children what they did over the weekend. Single-switch communication devices can be programmed to provide anticipated answers to questions within an activity, such as "It's snowing today" during morning circle time. A student can use a single switch to answer questions during a social studies lesson, for example, "What is the capital of our state?" or "Who was the first president of our country?" These devices are easy to program, enabling teachers to be creative in finding ways for students to participate within their classrooms.

Multiple-step communication devices are also available for use by children who are early communicators and present complex disabilities. These devices look just like a single-step communicator or switch but can be programmed with a sequence of messages. For example, the first activation says, "I have a secret!" The second hit of the switch says, "Come closer and I will tell you." And the third activation says, "It is Mrs. Jones's birthday." The use of multiple-step communication devices enables nonverbal children to experience a conversation rather than a simple one-turn communication episode.

Types of Switches to Promote Early Communication

An array of options is available to meet the unique needs of every student. Some switches are large and can be pressed with a fist or foot. Others are tiny, require only a light touch, and can be activated with a single finger movement. Commercially available switches are usually categorized

USER PROFILE

Jane

Jane is another child in Daniel's preschool class. She receives similar special education services within the context of the general preschool program. Jane has been identified with a developmental disability that manifests limited speech, global difficulties in problem solving, and fine motor delays. Each activity in Jane's preschool program includes the use of some assistive technology that reinforces the fundamental understanding of cause and effect and choice making. For example, Jane is offered two switches that advance or reverse a page in a computerized storybook. In addition, she is provided with a choice of two switches to answer simple yes and no questions. The teacher asks, "Do you want to play a game with Daniel?" and Jane can make a choice. At first, it was not clear if Jane's selections were random or deliberate, but as time went on and she had more exposure to choice-making opportunities using switches, it became clear that her choices truly reflected her preferences. ■

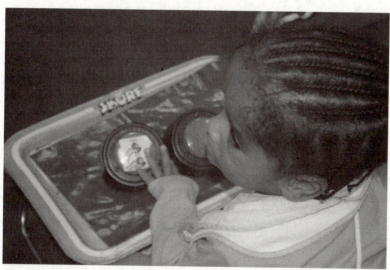

Student using a single-message communication device.
Photo by Vicki Spence.

by their activation features (see Table 11.2). Students must have a reliable movement to activate the switch independently, such as flexing a fist, extending a hand, or turning the head to the side. Physical or occupational therapists should be consulted to determine a student's most functional movement. (See Chapter 10 for a detailed discussion of how to select appropriate technology.) Switches may be mounted or positioned in a variety of ways to facilitate activation. Many of the switches and multiple-step communication devices mentioned in this chapter can be mounted for activation by a hand, head, foot, elbow, or any other available body part.

Commercially available battery-operated toys can be easily adapted for use with switches. Companies that produce switches, such as AbleNet, Inc., market a "battery device adapter" that is inserted in the battery compartment between the battery and the leads; it connects to the switch by a simple jack. In addition, there are switch interfaces that allow the use of multiple switches for choice making.

TABLE 11.2 Types of Commercially Available Switches	
Switch	**Activation Features**
Generic push	This switch comes in all sizes, shapes, and colors.
	The student pushes down on the switch and it activates the toy it is connected to. Some of these switches are designed for use as head switches or foot switches or are positioned near unique access points such as a student's knee or thigh.
Leaf	A plastic flap that is activated by swiping lightly against the leaf in one direction.
Squeeze/Pinch	A soft rubber ball-like or thin plastic switch that is activated by squeezing or pinching.
Mercury	A switch that is activated by tilting; usually mounted on a headband or hat and activated by head movement.
Pneumatic	This switch operates by changing air pressure. The student puffs air into a tube, or in the case of the sip and puff switch, blows into a tube for one activation and sucks air out of tube for a second activation.
Muscle/Twitch	The muscle/twitch switch is activated by small muscle movement, such as wrinkling the forehead, and can be adjusted to increase or decrease the amount of muscle movement needed to easily activate it.
Light Sensitive	The light switch activates by a change in lighting. Students can place a finger or hand over a sensor with no pressure and activate the switch.
Vibration	This switch activates by movement or vibration and can be calibrated for sensitivity.

The use of switches for students with complex disabilities is also used to promote inclusion with typical peers. As inclusion within general education classrooms has increased for these students, switch skills applications for two or more students have been developed. These programs allow students with severe disabilities to play games with typical peers, become actively engaged in computer use, and provide a context for peer-supported activities.

Determining the Use of Switches for Early Communication

The decision to use switch technology must be made by a team of professionals such as the collaborative team discussed in Chapter 10. The teacher need to collaborate with colleagues such as a speech-language specialist, whose expertise includes early communication; an occupational therapist, whose expertise is in fine motor development; a physical therapist, whose expertise involves seating and other gross motor skills; and with the student's parents, whose expertise includes knowledge of their child's likes and dislikes. Because switches are not an end result in themselves—they are employed within the broader context of an activity—they must have a specific function within a child's educational program (see Figure 11.2).

Once it is determined that a switch will be used for a specific activity, the time and place the child will engage in the activity need to be decided. As York, Nietupski, and Hamre-Nietupski (1985) suggest, the decision-making process then needs to address the following:

1. The optimal position the child will be placed in for the activity
2. The specific motor behavior that the child will use for activation
3. The best type of switch to use
4. The instructional procedures that will be used to teach the student to use the switch set-up, such as a prompting hierarchy or modeling

Each of these decision-making steps must involve the team, and consideration should begin with the least complex solutions. In addition, a record-keeping system should be designed and implemented to determine if expected progress is being made. In the absence of this kind of systematic approach, students are often saturated by the endless presentation of the same switch and switch-activated device, and learning fails to take place. Lastly, it is critical to engage the student in the decision to use a specific switch, making sure he or she is able to activate it comfortably.

FIGURE 11.2 Suggested inquiry for determining the use of switches for early communication development.

- At what stage of communication development is the child?
  - Understanding cause and effect
  - Making choices
  - Interacting with his or her environment
  - Initiating communication
  - Beginning conversations
- How can this child's communication development be enhanced through the use of switches?
- In which activities within the child's educational program can you embed communication through the use of switches?
- How can the use of switch technology support the child's participation in the classroom, school, community, and home?

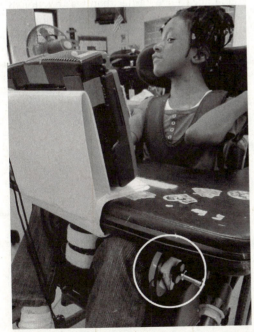

Student activating a switch with her knee to access her augmentative communication device with single switch scanning.

Photos by Vicki Spence

Examples of Switch Technology for Early Communication in the Classroom

There are hundreds of ways in which switch technology can be used within the classroom to promote the early communication development of children with disabilities. Although most of the examples within this chapter have focused on early childhood, many older children and adults remain rooted in the use of simple communication systems. There is debate within the professional community on whether or not there should be prerequisites for using more sophisticated augmentative communication systems. However, the fact remains that for many older children the use of switches continues to be a viable assistive technology solution to participation in classroom activities and expressive communication. The following user profile highlights the use of switch technology for a high school student's communication in the classroom.

Students with disabilities who are early communicators can be provided with an array of simple technology solutions to enhance their expressive communication. They need to be provided with multiple opportunities to use these solutions as they develop the skills to use additional options in augmentative communication. The next chapter presents strategies for integrating augmentative communication into the classroom and discusses the roles of the classroom teacher in supporting students who use technology to communicate.

EMERGENT LITERACY

Closely related to the development of language and communication is the development of literacy. In the past, literacy was defined only as the ability to read and write. However, the definition has been expanded to include skills regarding the ability to locate, evaluate, use, and communicate using a wide range of resources, including text, visual, audio, and video sources (Erickson & Koppenhaver, 1995). Current theory and practice demonstrate that the behaviors of reading and writing begin to develop at a very young age, much earlier than was previously realized. In the past, students with disabilities who experienced difficulties in the development of communication were not considered candidates for learning to read or write. Consequently, no effort was made to teach them early literacy skills (Koppenhaver & Yoder, 1993). However,

---

USER PROFILE

Joel

Joel is a 16-year-old, nonverbal student who attends a special education program within his local high school. He uses a power wheelchair with supervision and participates in school activities with his typical peers. Joel has been using switch technology for communication since he was in elementary school. Within his secondary education program, he continues to show effective use of communication through the use of switch technology.

- To greet his peers in the morning, Joel activates a one-step communication device with his foot. Using his foot leaves his left hand free to independently navigate his power wheelchair.
- Joel opens his locker with a remote control switch that is positioned on his wheelchair tray.
- During physical education, Joel activates a spin dial device with a single switch that randomly chooses teams for the other students.
- Joel calls for his personal care attendant by hitting a big button switch that activates the attendant's vibrating beeper. ■

Peter

Peter is a friendly, curious, and attentive 7-year-old who attends his local elementary school. For the majority of the day, he is included in a first-grade classroom and has been assigned a one-to-one aide who provides instructional support and personal care services. Peter has significant challenges due to global developmental disabilities of prematurity, cerebral palsy, and birth trauma. He is nonspeaking, uses a wheelchair with assistance, and has limited use of his hands. Peter has peers who interact with him; however, he rarely initiates an interaction. Because Peter does not have conventional symbolic communication strategies, his interactions are often not sustained. However, his peers indicate that Peter uses a reliable yes and no response by shaking his head. A combination of several switches has been incorporated into Peter's educational program to foster his communication and provide opportunities for him to initiate communication with his peers:

- Peter activates a single-message communication device, which is recorded by his brother, to greet his peers and ask questions. For example, in the morning when he presses the device, it says, "Hey! Ask me what I did last night!" and he is prepared with an object or picture that represents the answer (e.g., an advertisement for the movie he saw). Thus, a simple conversation takes place between Peter and his classmates.
- When Peter needs help, he calls his aide with another single-step communication device that is programmed with the aide's name.
- Peter uses a talking photo album to share a weekend experience. He chooses among a sequence of four pictures, each of which has a message recorded on its sound chip. When he activates each message, it retells his experience.
- Peter and a peer engage in a computer activity that uses a two-switch setup to build a picture, thereby using joint decision-making skills and cooperation. ■

reading, writing, speaking, and listening develop concurrently within children (Sulzby & Teale, 1991), and these early forms are identified as **emergent literacy.**

The term *emergent literacy* refers to a range of behaviors related to reading and writing that occur prior to conventional literacy (Sulzby & Teale, 1991). According to Kopppenhaver and Erickson (2003), "Emergent literacy includes all of the actions, perceptions and mistakes that early learners are engaged in regarding their attempts to create or use written language." For example, many infants enjoy looking at and turning the pages of a book, following along with their eyes as an adult reads a book aloud. In the popular book *Pat the Bunny* (Kunhardt, 1940), very young children follow directions such as, "Judy can pat the bunny. Can you pat the bunny?" Toddlers often page through books and bring familiar books to an adult to be read over and over again. Toddlers and preschoolers often use crayons and markers to imitate writing. In many homes and preschools young children are exposed repeatedly to print and the behaviors involved in reading and writing.

Eventually, children progress through the emergent to conventional literacy continuum and for most this transition is seamless (Erickson & Koppenhaver, 1995). Conventional literacy is defined as the outgrowth of early literacy behavior and it is characterized by reading, writing, and spelling of text in the form of symbols such as words. It is the ability to gain and provide meaning through print. With formal reading instruction, most children become literate adults with multiple abilities to express themselves.

For children with severe disabilities, however, the motor, cognitive, and sensory impairments that interfere with their communication development also interfere with their access to early reading and writing activities. Often, nonverbal children are not viewed as having the potential for the development of conventional literacy and are therefore not provided the opportunities to exercise communication through reading and writing. This in turn eliminates the breadth and scope of planned emergent literacy activities that parents and teachers typically employ with children. Therefore, it is essential that along with learning to use technology to communicate, children with severe disabilities are actively engaged in activities that promote emergent literacy with the expectation that they will gain conventional literacy skills (Erickson & Koppenhaver, 1995; Koppenhaver, Pierce, Steelman, & Yoder, 1994; Light & McNaughton, 1993). These children need direct and deliberate instruction and exposure to early literacy activities regardless of the severity of their disabilities (Musselwhite & King-DeBaun, 1997). It seems that many adults conclude without any substantial proof that children with complex communication needs and multiple disabilities cannot develop literacy. Under Donellan's least dangerous assumption paradigm (1984), parents and educators are directed to assume that *all* children present the capacity to develop literacy, and every effort should be made to enhance reading, writing, listening, and speaking skills.

With the use of assistive technology, students who have significant disabilities can engage in literacy-focused activities. Switches and one-step communicators can be used to enhance early literacy activities such as participating in story reading and storytelling. For example, preschool stories often include repetitive refrains that children remember and enjoy reciting as the story is retold. This repeat or choral verse, such as "He huffed and he puffed and he blew the house in" from the *Three Little Pigs* can be stored in a one-step communication device and activated by a child at the appropriate time. Tufte and Maro (1999) present several suggestions for facilitating communication development through literature-based activities and the use of simple switches. These include using several one-step communication switches that have been programmed with generic story-reacting vocabulary such as "Turn the page," "I can't see," and "I know what happens next!"

Both switch and augmentative communication technology can be harnessed to provide opportunities for children with disabilities to engage in instructional activities that support literacy development. Teachers can make simple books for children who require tangible symbols, such as those who are blind or visually impaired, by gluing or using Velcro to attach to real objects representing elements of the story to a book or collecting these items in a ziplock bag and attaching them to the book (Lewis & Tolla, 2003). A piece of blanket-like fabric, for example, can be glued to the page in which Goldilocks tries out the bears' beds and a piece of dry cereal where she tastes the oatmeal. Single-message communicators can be set up to recite the refrain of a story so a child can participate in the choral part of storytelling (e.g., *Goodnight Moon*). Step-by-step communicators can be recorded with sequential refrains.

Board books that talk are now widely available commercially. When a child presses a designated button, a sentence corresponding to the picture on the page is read aloud. Teachers can easily make similar books by buying inexpensive sound chips in a craft store, attaching them to each page of a child's favorite book, and recording the story, page-by-page. The child can then listen to the story by pressing on the button on each page. These low-tech adaptations enable children with disabilities to begin to handle books, interact with print, and listen to the rhythms of spoken stories.

Young children can listen to stories and children's books on CD or MP3 players (e.g., an iPod or iPad) while they follow along in the actual book. A CD player can be adapted so that a child can start and stop it with a single switch. Many children's books are available for download as digital audio files on Internet sites such as Project Gutenberg and Bookshare (as discussed in Chapter 3). These files can be transferred to a portable MP3 player so children can listen to them without being tethered to a computer. Other Web sites, such as Starfall, offer numerous simple books that are read aloud on a computer. The Tar Heel Reader, a free Web site sponsored

USER PROFILE

Angela

Angela is a 7-year-old first grader who attends her neighborhood elementary school. As a result of a rare genetic syndrome, she has a variety of challenges that affect her development and learning. She began to walk when she was 3 years old but remained nonspeaking due to a combination of factors related to cognition and oral motor functioning. Angela has developed an understanding of cause and effect and accurately uses a variety of switches and a four-panel voice output device. She participates in the following literacy-based activities:

- A story bag filled with objects is collected for the weekly storybook that the teacher reads to the class. These objects are representations for events that occur in the story. They reinforce the story line and can be used to indicate order of events or to reinforce a component of the story. By selecting or arranging the objects, Angela can comment or provide information to others.
- An overlay for her four-panel communication device is created for each story. Angela presses a button to answer the teacher's story comprehension questions such as "What do you think will happen next?"
- Angela's speech therapist comes in the classroom during the students' free time and reads familiar stories to a small group of children who require articulation therapy. These stories are engineered for the children to practice specific sounds; for Angela, they provide instruction in early phonics. She uses a one-step communicator to answer questions about initial consonant sounds. For example, Angela presses the communicator when the therapist asks, "What sound does 'Silly Sam the Snake' make?"
- On all of her switches, one-step communicators, and the four-panel communication device, the written word appears along with the picture symbols. This creates a text-rich environment and contributes to Angela's beginning understanding of the use of words as symbols. ■

by the Center for Literacy and Disability Studies at the University of North Carolina, provides a depository of more than 8,000 simple early language books that can be downloaded as slide shows in PowerPoint, Impress, or Flash format. Each book can be speech enabled and accessed using multiple interfaces, including touch screens, IntelliKeys, and switches. Video streaming is another technology that offers read-aloud stories. Storyline Online, for example, a Web site run by the Screen Actors Guild Foundation, presents videos of actors and actresses reading favorite children's books aloud while showing the words and illustrations.

Apps that run on smart phones, the iPod Touch, and iPad offer high-tech solutions to engaging young children in early literacy activities. Hutinger, Bell, Daytner, and Johanson (2006) categorized early literacy software into three types: (1) interactive literacy-based programs; (2) graphics and story-making applications; and (3) authoring applications such as Crick Software's *Clicker 5*, which can be used by teachers and parents to create their own stories based on children's individual experiences. Interactive literacy-based e-books and apps convert popular children's books from the standard presentation of text with pictures in a bound book to a multimedia display that may read the text aloud, provide music or sound effects, and/or offer young readers opportunities to make things happen on the screen. They also allow children to control the timing and repetition of words and sentences (Hutinger et al., 2006). Smart phones, iPod Touches, and iPads offer an ideal platform for this early literacy experience because of their use of touch screen technology; with simple points, pinches, and "swipes," children can "play" with the pictures, text, and characters. The adaptive inputs discussed in Chapter 8 can make these kinds of software programs accessible on computers to children who use single switches. (At the time of this writing, switch interfaces for the iPad were beginning to become available.)

Graphics and story-making applications enable children to create pictures and stories of their own design. Using whatever access method they need, children can choose pictures, colors, letters, sounds, clips of music, even video clips; arrange them on the screen; and manipulate them. This type of application empowers children to create pictures and storybooks that far exceed their abilities to draw and write. For children who cannot hold a crayon or paintbrush due to physical disabilities, this type of program enables them to produce a creative work that would be impossible without technology.

Simple authoring applications such as *My Own Bookshelf* (SoftTouch) enable teachers and parents to create interactive stories that children can access on computers. The computer reads aloud the text while displaying whatever pictures the teacher or parent has selected for the book. In addition to offering the opportunity to create stories that relate to a child's specific experiences, this technology enables parents and teachers to import photos from a digital camera and write stories that *include* the child in them. For students progressing from emergent to conventional reading, picture-assisted literacy programs such as Pixwriter or PictureIt (Slater Software) that automatically match pictures to words can assist in the literacy development process. Educators can use these programs to create age-appropriate stories that use simple language and provide pictures associated with each word to enable students to read text more easily.

Teachers and parents can also create simple switch-accessible talking books using Microsoft *PowerPoint*, a software program with which many people are already familiar (Spring, 2004). Step-by-step instructions are available on the following Web site: Assistive Technology Training Online Project at the University of Buffalo, http://atto.buffalo.edu/registered/Tutorials/talkingBooks/powerpoint.php. Anybody with basic computer skills should be able to create a talking book following these instructions. It is recommended that professionals and parents spend a little time creating a template so that they can produce several books more quickly, that is, by just changing the text and pictures.

The journey from emergent to conventional literacy requires attention to a range of developmental skill sets that include writing. For students who do not have the motor or sensory skills to handle conventional writing with a pencil, the Center for Literacy and Disability Studies has

USER PROFILE

Perry

Perry is a 10-year-old student who is in a self-contained classroom in his home district. He has global developmental disabilities that include being unable to speak or move on his own. He does not have the ability to point or direct select in any way. For the past several years, Perry has been learning to communicate using a low-tech eye-gaze board. His accuracy has been improving noticeably since his teacher began using the alternate pencil illustrated in Figure 11.3 After approximately 2 months of training in the use of the eye-gaze alphabet, Perry has been able to spell his name and select at least five sight words.

Perry's overall profile as a student with extensive disabilities had previously prevented his IEP team and his parents from expecting him to develop the skills of reading and writing. They had always assumed that Perry would have to demonstrate proficiency in expressive communication before he would be able to read or write. However, as a result of hard work and continued emphasis on literacy, Perry is developing skills of literacy and communication. He is learning to choose pictures that represent answers to test questions to demonstrate his understanding of basic math, science, and social studies content, and his teacher is now working to transfer his eye-gazing skills to an eye-gaze system for accessing a computer. ■

introduced a variety of "alternative pencils." These are low-tech solutions for students who do not present the ability to use a pencil or a computer keyboard. These alternative writing systems use partner-assisted scanning in which an adult or peer interprets from a child's gaze what letter or picture he or she is choosing (Hanser, 2006). Figures 11.3 and 11.4 show two types of alternate pencils that were developed by the Center for Literacy and Disability Studies.

Another helpful resource for developing literacy in children with severe disabilities is the comprehensive literacy curriculum MEville to WEville (AbleNet). Results from an evaluation

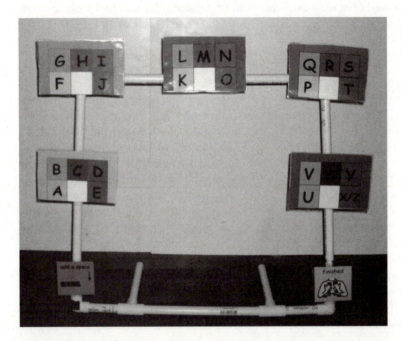

FIGURE 11.3 Alphabet eye-gaze frame.

Photos by Gretchen Hanser.

FIGURE 11.4 The print alphabet flip chart. The alphabet is presented in groups of large font letters, one page at a time, with symbols that indicate "turn the page," "add a space," "not what I meant," and "finished." Through "partner-assisted scanning," with the partner slowly flipping from page to page, the child signals when to stop on a desired page. The partner then slowly points to each letter and symbol on the page, and the child again signals when partner reaches the desired item.

Photos by Gretchen Hanser.

of this program conducted by the Center for Literacy and Disability Studies demonstrated that children initiated more communication and interaction during the use of the curriculum; they developed stronger social relationships with their peers in special and general education; they became more socially responsive; and teachers were able to spend more time addressing communication and literacy in their classrooms (AbleNet, n.d.).

Perry's and Angela's user profiles illustrate the link between early communication and the development of emergent literacy skills. With literacy-rich environments and assistive technology that may include switch technology, augmentative communication devices, and/or computer access, children who previously were not provided with opportunities to read and write are now accessing print and developing early literacy skills (Musselwhite & King-DeBaun, 1997).

Summary

- All children, regardless of the severity of their disabilities, can communicate. However, opportunities and supportive environments must be established and provided.
- Children can communicate in the absence of language. The goal of intervention and education is to encourage the further development of communication through symbolism or language.
- Children with motor, cognitive, and sensory disabilities require deliberate and systematic intervention to develop a functional system of communication.
- Assistive technology can be used to enhance the early communication efforts of children with significant disabilities.
- The use of switch technology for communication must be infused within the context of daily routines and classroom activities throughout the day.
- Communication is further developed by teaching the emergent literacy skills of early reading and writing.
- Children with significant disabilities should be exposed to print and writing to enhance their communication development and abilities.

Web Resources

For additional information on the topics listed, visit the following Web sites:

Low-Tech Communication Devices
Go Talk and other communication aids from Attainment Company
http://www.attainmentcompany.com
Hawk, Blackhawk, Lighthawk, Superhawk
http://www.adamlab.com/
Step-by-Step Communicator (AbleNet, Inc.)
http://www.ablenetinc.com/AssistiveTechnology/CommunicationProducts/tabid/56/Default.aspx
Communication Builder
http://enablingdevices.com/catalog/assistive_technology_devices_used_in_education/
communication-builders Early Language Development

Tangible and Tactile Symbols
Design to Learn
http://www.designtolearn.com/

Tactile Systems from the Texas School for the Blind
http://www.tsbvi.edu/Education/vmi/tactile_symbols.htm

Strategies to Teach Early Communication
Learning to Communicate: Strategies for Developing Communication with Infants Whose Multiple Disabilities Include Visual Impairment and Hearing Loss (PDF)
http://www.osepideasthatwork.org/parentkit/Learning_EngVer.asp

Emergent Literacy
Center for Literacy and Disability Studies at University of North Carolina
http://www.med.unc.edu/ahs/clds/

Literacy for All! By Gretchen Hanser
http://www.cs.unc.edu/Research/assist/et/2006/attach/HanserNotes/EnginTalkHO.pdf

Caroline Musselwhite's Web site: Activities & Materials
http://www.aacintervention.com/

Do2 Learn
http://www.dotolearn.com

News-2-You: Subscription service to newspapers written at beginning literacy levels, including with communication symbols
http://www.news-2-you.com/index.aspx

Digital Books for Emergent Literacy
Starfall
http://www.starfall.com

Tar Heel Reader
http://tarheelreader.org/

Storyline Online (a project of the Screen Actors Guild Foundation)
http://www.storylineonline.net

My Own Bookshelf (SoftTouch)
http://softtouch.com

PixWriter and PictureIt (Slater Software)
http://www.slatersoftware.com

Instructions for creating switch-accessible talking books using PowerPoint
http://atto.buffalo.edu/registered/Tutorials/talkingBooks/powerpoint.php

Literacy Curriculum for Students with Severe Disabilities
MEville to WEville (AbleNet)
http://ablenetinc.com/CurriculumSoftware/MEvilletoWEvilleLiteracy/tabid/132/Default.aspx

Suggested Activities

1. *Observe a classroom.* In small groups of two or three students, conduct a 2- to 3-hour observation of a child who has significant disabilities and is nonspeaking. During this observation, collect data regarding the following: (a) the frequency and types of expressive communication by the child, (b) the frequency with which the child has an opportunity to communicate with others, (c) the content of the communication that is presented (e.g., how often is the child given the opportunity to comment or protest?), and (d) the number and types of people who are available and who interact with the child. Based on these data, develop recommendations for the classroom teacher to enhance communication for this student.

2. *Develop an early communication parental workbook.* Develop a workbook that guides parents in understanding their child's early communication development. The workbook should provide a framework to promote communication within the home and community. In addition, include a list of references and resources in the workbook.

3. *Explore a toy store.* Take a trip to a local toy store and inventory the various battery-operated toys and games that could be adapted with switches to be used to promote interactive play with typical peers. Develop an annotated list including the name of the toy or game, the company that produces it; the suggested manner in which it can be adapted, and your suggested uses for independent activities or activities with typical peers.

4. *Create an object story bag.* Select two children's books appropriate for early elementary school students. Create a story bag of objects that can be used as the books are being read out loud.

5. *Build and use an alternative pencil.* Using a specific student who may be described as an emergent reader and does not have the ability to access a writing tool, design and implement an instructional program to support the use of an alternative pencil as described by the Center for Literacy and Disability Studies at the University of North Carolina: http://www.med.unc.edu/ahs/clds.

6. *Create PowerPoint books with related objects.* Develop a series of PowerPoint books using a central theme such as fairy tales or the Wild West. Choose objects to go along with the story so that students can become more engaged and relate to the sequence of story events. An alternative would be to print out the PowerPoint book and attach objects or two-dimensional cues with Velcro so that students can take them off as the story progresses.

References

AbleNet. (n.d.). *MEville to WEville Early Literacy Program.* Retrieved July 28, 2010, from http://www.ablenetinc.com/CurriculumSoftware/MEvilletoWEvilleLiteracy/tabid/132/Default.aspx

Barton, A. E., Sevcik, R. A., & Romski, M. A. (2006). Visual-graphic symbol acquisition by pre-school age children with developmental and language delays. *Augmentative and Alternative Communication, 22,* 10–20.

Bates, E. (1976). *Language and context: The acquisition of pragmatics.* New York: Academic Press.

Beukelman, D., & Mirenda, P. (1998). *Augmentative and alternative communication: Management of severe communication disorders in children and adults* (2nd ed.). Baltimore, MD: Brookes.

Bloom, L. (1993). *The transition from infancy to language.* Cambridge, Eng.: Cambridge University Press.

Calandrella, A. M., & Wilcox, M. J. (2000). Predicting language outcomes for young prelinguistic children with developmental delay. *Journal of Speech, Language, and Hearing Research, 43,* 1061–1071.

Donnellan, A. M. (1984). The criterion of the least dangerous assumption. *Behavioral Disorders, 9*(2), 141–150.

Downing, J. E., & Siegel-Causey, E. (1988). Enhancing the nonsymbolic communicative behavior of children with multiple impairments. *Language, Speech, and Hearing Services in Schools, 19,* 338–348.

Erickson, A., & Koppenhaver, D. (1995). Developing a literacy program for children with severe disabilities. *The Reading Teacher, 48*(8) 676–684.

Hanser, G. (2006). Fostering emergent writing for children with significant disabilities: Writing with alternative pencils. *Technology: Special Interest Section Quarterly, 16*(1), 1–4.

Hutinger, P., Bell, C., Daytner, G., & Johanson, J. (2006). Establishing and maintaining an early childhood emergent literacy technology curriculum. *Journal of Special Education Technology, 21*(4), 39–54.

Koppenhaver, D. A., & Erickson, K. A. (2003). Natural emergent literacy supports for preschoolers with autism and severe communication impairments. *Topics in Language Disorders.* 23(4), 283-292.

Koppenhaver, D., & Yoder, D. (1993). Classroom literacy instruction for children with severe speech and physical impairments (SSPI): What is and what might be? *Topics in Language Disorders, 13,* 1–15.

Koppenhaver, D. A., Pierce, P. L., Steelman, J. D., & Yoder, D. E. (1994). Contexts of early literacy intervention for children with developmental disabilities. In M. E. Fey, J. Windsor, & S. F. Warren (Eds.), *Language intervention in the early school years* (pp. 241–274). Baltimore, MD: Brookes.

Kunhardt, D. (1940). *Pat the bunny.* New York: Golden Books.

Lancioni, G. E., O'Reilly, M. F., Singh, N. N., Oliva, D., Piazzolla, G., Pirani, P., et al. (2002). Evaluating the use of multiple microswitches and responses for children with multiple disabilities. *Journal of Intellectual Disability Research, 46*(4), 346–351.

Langley, M. B. (1990). A developmental approach to the use of toys for facilitation of environmental control. *Physical and Occupational Therapy in Pediatrics, 10,* 69–91.

Lewis, S., & Tolla, J. (2003). Creating and using tactile experience books for young children with visual impairments. *Teaching Exceptional Children, 35*(3), 22–28.

Light, J., & McNaughton, D. (1993). Literacy and augmentative and alternative communication (AAC): The expectations and priorities of parents and teachers. *Topics in Language Disorders, 13*(2), 33–46.

Moore, C., & Corkum, V. L. (1994). Social understanding at the end of the first year of life. *Developmental Review, 14,* 349–372.

Musselwhite, C., & King-DeBaun, P. (1997). *Emergent literacy success: Merging technology and whole language for students with disabilities.* Park City, UT: Creative Communicating.

Noonan, M. J., & Siegel-Causey, E. (1997). Special needs of young children with severe handicaps. In L. McCormick, D. Loeb, & R. Schiefelbusch (Eds.), *Supporting children with communication difficulties in inclusive settings: School-based language intervention* (pp. 405–432). Boston, MA: Allyn & Bacon.

Ogletree, B. T. (1996). Assessment targets and protocols for nonsymbolic communicators with profound disabilities. *Focus on Autism and Other Developmental Disabilities, 11*(1).

Rowland, C., & Schweigert, P. (1993). *The early communication process using microswitch technology.* Tucson, AZ: Communication Skills Builders.

Siegel-Causey, E., Ernst, B., & Guess, D. (1988). Nonsymbolic communication in early interactional processes and implications for interventions. In M. Bullis (Ed.), *Communication in young children with deaf-blindness: Literature review III.* Monmouth, OR: Teaching Research.

Siegel-Causey, E., & Guess, D. (1989). *Enhancing nonsymbolic communication interactions among learners with severe disabilities.* Baltimore, MD: Brookes.

Spring, D. (2004). *Assistive technology supports for early childhood literacy.* Retrieved June 17, 2011 from *www.ecac-parentcenter.org/childhood/documents/AssistiveTech.pdf*

Stremel-Campbell, K., & Matthews, J. (1988). Development of emergent language. In M. Bullis (Ed.), *Communication in young children with deaf-blindness: Literature review III.* Monmouth, OR: Teaching Research.

Sulzby, E., & Teale, W. (1991). Emergent literacy. In R. Barr, M. L. Kamil, P. B. Mosenthal, & P. D. Pearson (Eds.), *Handbook of reading research* (Vol. 2, pp. 727–757). New York: Longman.

Tufte, L., & Maro, J. (1999). *Creating literature-based communication boards.* Retrieved July 22. 2010, from http://www.aacintervention.com/litboards.htm

Warren, S. F., & Yoder, P. J. (1998). Facilitating the transition from preintentional to intentional communication. In A. Wetherby, S. Warren, & J. Reichle (Eds.), *Transition in prelinguistic communication* (Vol. 7, pp. 365–385). Baltimore, MD: Brookes.

Wetherby, A. M., & Prizant, B. M. (1992). Profiling young children's communicative competence. In S. F. Warren & J. Reichle (Eds.), *Communication and language intervention:* Vol. 1. *Causes and effects in communication and language intervention* (pp. 217–251). Baltimore, MD: Brookes.

York, J., Nietupski, J., & Hamre-Nietupski, S. (1985). A decision-making process for using microswitches. *Journal of the Association for Persons with Severe Handicaps, 10*(4), 214–223.

12 | INTEGRATING AUGMENTATIVE COMMUNICATION IN THE CLASSROOM, HOME, AND COMMUNITY

Focus Questions

1. How can teachers effectively integrate a student's use of his or her augmentative communication system within the classroom and school?
2. How can peers provide support for students who use augmentative communication?
3. What strategies can teachers use to overcome "learned helplessness?"
4. How can augmentative communication be integrated into the IEP?
5. Why is it important to support the use of augmentative communication systems at home and in the community?
6. How can a student's augmentative communication system be designed to meet the communication demands of home and the community?
7. How can the progress of a student using augmentative communication be monitored for rate and quantity of progress in the development of language and communication?

INTRODUCTION

Chapter 6 introduced the benefits of augmentative communication for students with disabilities who cannot speak. Chapter 10 described the primary components of augmentative communication systems and outlined the collaborative process for selecting and designing a system for a specific student. Chapter 11 discussed specialized issues related to low-tech approaches to augmentative communication for early communicators. This chapter focuses on the *teacher's critical role* in teaching effective communication skills by integrating augmentative communication into the curriculum and daily classroom routines.

Too often, students who have been equipped with augmentative communication systems attend school in environments that do not provide adequate opportunities for communication. As a result, the systems are used only minimally or may be abandoned completely. As students with disabilities are being educated within general education settings, there are many opportunities to weave augmentative communication users within the fabric of their schools and communities. In these settings, students are surrounded by a milieu of functional and social communication, and they have access to competent communication partners. This presents both opportunities and challenges to the ongoing development of their augmentative communication skills.

SUPPORTIVE ENVIRONMENTS FOR AUGMENTATIVE COMMUNICATION USERS: THE TEACHER'S ROLE

Neighborhood schools and general education classrooms represent the context in which all students achieve and progress in academic and social learning. Central to this context for any beginner or seasoned augmentative communication student user is the classroom teacher. The teacher may be the single most influential variable in ensuring that students who use augmentative communication are successful. Once a system is designed by the collaborative team, it is the teacher who guides the implementation. It is the teacher (and other teaching staff) who creates classroom environments that facilitate social interaction and communication.

What specifically can teachers do to support augmentative communication users? Locke and Mirenda (1992) studied the responsibilities of special education teachers who serve on collaborative teams for augmentative communication. They found that teachers have many key roles to play, as summarized in Table 12.1.

Curriculum Issues

Many units of study taught in school use specialized terms and proper nouns. If students who are augmentative communication users are to be able to answer their teachers' questions and participate in classroom activities in these subjects, they need this specialized vocabulary added to their augmentative communication systems. For example, students studying the American Revolution in social studies class will need to be able to communicate names such as George Washington, Thomas Jefferson, Paul Revere, as well as the battles of Lexington and Concord. In English class, students need access to the names of literary characters and literary terms. The teacher is the one person who knows what new vocabulary will be covered. Therefore, it is the teacher's role to add curriculum-related vocabulary to students' augmentative communication systems or to provide this vocabulary ahead of time to a staff person who has been designated to do this task. Depending on the school staffing, this person could be a speech-language therapist or a teacher's aide (paraeducator).

Ongoing Skill Development in Communication

Teachers must seek every opportunity for students to practice their communication skills and conduct conversations throughout the school day. They need to provide deliberate interventions that support the use of augmentative communication systems. Using the context of daily routines and naturally occurring events in the classroom and other school environments is recognized as a powerful approach to communication skill development. A specific protocol for this practice,

---

TABLE 12.1   Teachers' Roles in Augmentative Communication

- Adapting the curriculum
- Writing goals and objectives for augmentative communication users
- Acting as a liaison between the team and the student's parents
- Providing for ongoing skill development in communication
- Identifying appropriate vocabulary
- Determining students' communication needs
- Training others in using the augmentative communication system

Source: Information from "Roles and Responsibilities of Special Education Teachers Serving on Teams Delivering AAC Services," by P. A. Locke and P. Mirenda, 1992, *Augmentative and Alternative Communication, 8*, pp. 200–214.

Child using a Springboard augmentative communication device (Prentke Romich Company) in the classroom to play a board game.

Photo by Vicki Spence

environmental communication teaching (ECT), was developed by Karlan (1991). This method focuses on identifying the communication demands of natural environments, providing partners to prompt communication messages, and systematically arranging to expand communication exchanges. The user profile provides a clear illustration of ECT in use.

There are a variety of strategies for the promotion of communication using augmentative and alternative communication that have their roots in effective instruction. The use of positive social reinforcement through a hierarchy of prompting or modeling is an approach to instruction in any skill. Therefore, often skill development training in the use of a communication device and system will require the teacher to provide direct instruction by fading from physical coactive prompting to complete independent use of the device. This systematic use of instruction shares its efficacy with a host of other behaviorally oriented approaches to instruction. Students with autism have responded positively to the use of such techniques as pivotal response training.

Pivotal response training (PRT) is a behavioral strategy based on the principles of applied behavior analysis (Koegel & Koegel, 2006; Koegel, O'Dell, & Dunlap, 1988; Koegel, O'Dell, & Koegel, 1987). The assumption is that motivation and responsiveness to a variety of cues affect behaviors that are central to a wide area of functioning. PRT promotes motivation by combining skill development (including skills in communication) with highly motivating variables such as child choice, taking turns, and other reinforcing events.

Another behavioral approach to promoting the use of augmentative communication systems for students with autism who are nonspeaking is the use of the Picture Exchange Communication System (PECS) and other similar visual communication strategies. The Picture Exchange Communication System is a method for teaching children with autism and related developmental disabilities a functional communication system. Its theoretical roots combine principles from applied behavior analysis and guidelines established within the field of augmentative communication. It uses direct instruction and modeling of an exchange of simple to more complex symbol/picture exchanges (Bondy, 2001; Bondy & Frost, 2001; Frost & Bondy, 2006).

Although direct behavioral intervention is an important vehicle in the development of language and effective communication, it must accompany an understanding that this occurs within a social context. Therefore, consistent and frequent social exchanges that represent an appropriate balance of pragmatic structure and turn taking are critical to the success of using any communication system. Teachers can employ various strategies to ensure that communication is taking place by creating a need. One such strategy is the use of *sabotage* to stimulate a need

Teaching Communication in Natural Environments

"Bernie, stand up. Are you buying lunch? Did you bring a lunch?"

"I am buying lunch."

"Ashley, stand up. Are you buying lunch? Did you bring a lunch?"

"I brought my lunch."

Taking the lunch count is a daily ritual performed by most elementary teachers, so at first glance this communication exchange seems quite ordinary. However, lunch count in this Life Skills class is not just another teacher-directed routine that has to be completed before learning can occur. In this class, lunch count *is* learning.

IMPLEMENTING ENVIRONMENTAL COMMUNICATION TEACHING

The classroom teacher, assistant teacher, and speech-language consultant have been implementing environmental communication teaching (ECT). ECT is designed to assist classroom teams in delivering communication intervention within the context of existing natural environments. The teams learn to develop activity-based objectives; sequences of cues, prompts, and feedback; and techniques to integrate augmentative communication in their classrooms. Teachers and parents who attend ECT training learn to change communication interactions from being teacher directed to being student directed, and to target communication skills in every classroom activity. Team members also learn to reduce the number of verbal and nonverbal prompts they give to students, and to change prompts when needed from yes/no questions and directives to open-ended questions and indirect prompts.

One of the hardest lessons of ECT is learning to pause to allow students the opportunity to process and initiate or respond. "We thought we were pausing to give the kids a chance to answer," reported the classroom teacher. "But we were amazed to see [on a videotape recorded in the classroom] just how quickly we jumped in to help the kids. Before ECT, we never would have waited as long as we do now, but the wait is worth it when a student finally answers a question on his own."

INTEGRATING AUGMENTATIVE COMMUNICATION INTO THE CLASSROOM

Of the 10 students in this class, only 4 have speech that is somewhat intelligible. Therefore, several students are learning to use augmentative communication devices. The devices in the room are on the low-tech end of the spectrum—devices such as the Hawk (Adamlab, LLC) that offers about 32 messages. One of the opportunities created for the students to learn and practice communication skills is the daily lunch count.

On the blackboard are photos of each student and a poster with a symbol for "lunchbox" on the left, "cafeteria tray" on the right; Velcro strips run vertically beneath the symbols for "They're not here" and "I'm finished." Next to the augmentative communication devices are laminated strips with the children's names. Jamillah, the lunch count taker of the day, removes Ashley's photo from the board and presses Ashley's picture on her device. As the device says "Ashley, stand up," Jamillah deposits Ashley's photo in the "All Done" box, then presses the question marks to ask "Are you buying lunch? Did you bring lunch?" Ashley presses the symbol of the cafeteria tray to answer, "I am buying lunch." She then finds her name and places it on the poster under the tray symbol.

Jamillah continues this routine until all students have been called. If a child is absent, Jamillah puts his or her photo in the "All Done" box and presses "They're not here." When the job is done, she tells the teacher "I'm finished" and sits down. The entire student-directed routine has once again been initiated, maintained, and completed by a 6-year-old student who has Down syndrome, visual and hearing impairments, and unintelligible speech.

INCREASING INDEPENDENCE AND COMPETENCE

Julie, another 6-year-old student, has also achieved a new level of independence. Julie's job is to go to the office to get the mail from the teacher's mailbox. Analyzing the task and Julie's educational objectives, the team determined that Julie had to (1) identify the teacher's mailbox, (2) handle both the mail and her augmentative communication device, and (3) communicate socially and request help if needed. Solution #1: The teacher's mailbox is now labeled with her picture instead of her name. Solution #2: Julie's augmentative communication device sits in the top basket of a three-tiered rolling cart so her communication system is readily available and the mail can be carried in the second basket to be wheeled

(continued)

back to the classroom. Solution #3: Julie uses the device to communicate to the office staff: "Hello," "It's time to get the mail," "I need help," and "Thank you." Upon returning to the classroom, she reports, "The mail is here" or "There wasn't any mail today." Julie completes this job entirely on her own; she no longer requires adult assistance.

The augmentative communication devices and manual communication boards are now an important component of a classroom that was already filled with line-drawn symbols, photographs, and words attached to the objects they represent. The team believes in using pictures with students in the Life Skills program to augment verbal messages from both the teachers and the students. "Symbols or pictures provide another avenue for the children to communicate, and also for understanding what we say to them," explains the teacher. As a result, all storage bins and cabinets are labeled with symbols

for the objects they contain. The daily schedule is displayed in symbols on Velcro; changing the schedule is part of the morning routine, and following the schedule throughout the day is a lesson in sequencing.

CREATING AND ORGANIZING ALL THE OVERLAYS AND SYMBOLS

Using Boardmaker (Mayer-Johnson), the team creates a plethora of communication materials for every activity and lesson, including overlays for the students' communication devices, manual picture boards for students who are moderately intelligible but have limited expressive vocabularies, and enlarged individual symbols for object-symbol matching activities as new vocabulary is introduced. Because they use these materials during snack, crafts, story time, music, morning circle, cooking, grooming, and free play, a clear system for organization is a must. All

device overlays and manual boards, along with manila envelops of the related individual symbols, are kept in a three-ring binder, one for each month of the school year.

POSITIVE RESULTS

With ECT, the team has learned new instructional and implementation strategies, as well as the value of the team approach. "We've proved the old saying, 'Three heads are better than one.' Each one of us has contributed insights and ideas that have benefited the kids." The acquisition of Boardmaker has opened up a world of creative possibilities for symbol use in the classroom, and the use of augmentative communication systems has given children who would have little chance of effective communication independence a means to both. ■

Source: From "Teaching Communication in Natural Environments," by P. L. Mervine, 1995, *TECH-NJ, 6*(1), pp. 3, 16. Reprinted with permission.

---

for communication. For example, a teacher may pretend not to see the attendance sheet that is behind him or her. "Where did I put that attendance sheet? I wonder where it could be." This creates an opportunity for students to respond using their devices, "I see it!" and then pointing. Other examples of the sabotage strategy are to "forget" an item that is needed for a class activity, such as the crayons for an art project or an ingredient for a cooking project (Mervine, Mark, & Burton, 1995). This provides the occasion for students to communicate, "I need a [item]."

Importance of Monitoring Communication Development

Once a student is provided with an augmentative communication system following a well-implemented assessment process, it is critical to monitor the quality and quantity of the student's use of the system (Kohn, LeBlanc, & Mortola, 1995). This monitoring process must be ongoing from the outset to ensure that progress in communication and language development is made. Traditional methods of data collection such as collecting frequency of use data or content and length of communication exchanges are effective if analyzed and used to provide continued and individualized support. An increasing number of augmentative communication devices have features that automatically monitor use and can provide valuable information (Hill & Romich, 2000). Although these features are convenient, they do not preclude the need for observer-driven data collection and analysis especially regarding the ease in which a student engages in a conversation.

In addition to the monitoring a student's augmentative communication use, it is critical to collect information on the responses of teachers and other school personnel to the student's use of the augmentative system across classroom activities (Soto, Muller, Hunt, & Goetz, 2001). The role of the teacher and other instructional staff in promoting the use of a student's augmentative communication system is paramount to realizing success. In the absence of quality monitoring and associated adjustments to communicative supports, students will not make the transition from old patterns of inefficient communication (e.g., screaming for attention), especially if they perceive the use of their device as more of a struggle than a benefit (Johnson, Reichle, & Evans, 2004).

Importance of Selecting Appropriate Vocabulary

As illustrated in the user profile, Teaching Communication in Natural Environments, routine daily activities that occur in schools present excellent opportunities for communication. Other infrequent but planned activities such as pep rallies present additional opportunities. To ensure full participation in these activities, appropriate vocabulary needs to be added to the augmentative communication system. For example, a teacher or aide can work with the student user to construct a stored daily announcement that can be transmitted via the school's public address system. Low-tech language boards can be constructed for field trips so that the student has access to vocabulary related to that specific destination. For example, on a field trip to the zoo, a student will probably want to communicate his or her reactions to the strange sights and smells (e.g., "Oh boy, that stinks!" "That is so ugly!" "Gross!"). The vocabulary for a visit to an art museum, however, will likely be different. The student will probably want to express opinions about the paintings and sculpture ("That's beautiful." "I really like/don't like that.") and possibly ask questions about the artists.

The school environment offers hundreds of opportunities to communicate and interact with peers. In addition to their regular classroom setting, students need to respond to the demands of the playground, hallways, and lunchrooms. Therefore, vocabulary made available to students in their augmentative communication systems needs to be ecologically sound; that

FIGURE 12.1 This communication board (which was made using BoardMaker) enables a child to participate in music class.

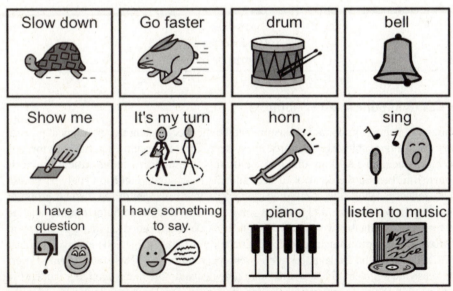

is, it must reflect the needs of the environment. Because it is difficult to predict the needed vocabulary for every school-related event or activity, teachers and classroom staff need to observe other children talking. Peer-referenced vocabulary is easily obtained by documenting frequently used phrases (e.g., "awesome," "cool," "no way") and by directly involving peers in vocabulary selection. Table 12.2 includes examples of age-appropriate vocabulary. Table 12.3 provides a checklist regarding the effectiveness of an augmentative communication system for supporting students' participation in general education classrooms.

TABLE 12.2 Examples of Vocabulary and Communicative Functions	
Function of the Communication Message	**Sample Vocabulary**
Commenting	"That's cool!"
	"I am not a fan."
	"No fair!"
Questioning	"What did you watch last night?"
	"What is your favorite TV show?"
	"What do you mean?"
Protesting or rejecting	"No, I don't wanna."
	"Leave me alone. "
	"I hate this!"
Requesting	"Ms. C., I need help."
	"Can I play?"
	"Can I have a snack?"
	"Could you explain that again?"
Commanding	"Cut it out!"
	"Stop bothering me!"
	"Get out of the way!"
	"Change the channel."

Use of Peers as Communication Facilitators

Deliberate training of peers is important to ensure that they feel competent in communicating with someone who uses an augmentative communication system. This can occur in natural ways through teacher or peer guidance. One strategy that may be used is to establish a **communication circle of peer support**. Building on the concept of peer support to facilitate inclusion (Falvey, Forest, Pearpoint, & Rosenberg, 1994), the communication circle involves identifying a small group of peers who meet regularly to discuss and problem solve issues related to providing communication opportunities for the augmentative communication user. A communication circle of peer support can be an effective tool for refreshing available vocabulary and identifying needed new vocabulary (see Figure 12.2). To set up the circle, a teacher requests peer volunteers. This small group of peers is taught how to use the augmentative communication device and how to engage other students in social interactions with the augmentative communication user. The group meets weekly with the teacher and the student to review communication progress and brainstorm solutions to problems.

FIGURE 12.2 Communication Circle of Peer Support summary protocol.

Chris's Communication Support Circle

Today's Date:

Circle Members: _____

_____

_____

_____

| **Description and Feeling Words** |
| **About This Week** |
| |

Were there any communication challenges?

Challenges	What Did You Do About It?

How can Chris and his circle members make it a better week?

❏ No way! It was a perfect week.

❏ Keep trying what we have been doing.

❏ There are some ways to make things better.

Circle Members Can ...	Chris Can ...

It's a wrap. Any final thoughts?

Examples of Partial Participation

- During roll call, the augmentative communication user announces the names of each student while another student records the attendance records.
- During read-aloud time, the augmentative communication user repeats the refrain of a book or poem while other students read the entire book out loud. For example, when reading from *The Very Hungry Caterpillar,* the refrain might be "But he was still hungry!" (Carle, 1969).
- During break time, the augmentative communication user participates in a game of Simon Says by "being Simon," that is, by calling out the commands.

Example of partial participation: Although the child cannot physically "pick a card," he takes his turn by using a switch to spin a dial.

Photo by Vicki Spence

TABLE 12.3   Augmentative Communication Checklist for Participation in General Education Classrooms

Yes	A Little	No	
❐	❐	❐	Does the student's system enables him or her to participate in classroom discussions?
❐	❐	❐	Does the student's system enables him or her to answer questions?
❐	❐	❐	Does the student's system enables him or her to ask questions?
❐	❐	❐	Can the student use his or her system for quick responses or messages?
❐	❐	❐	Is there a way for the student to gain attention from a distance?
❐	❐	❐	Does the student's system enables him or her to initiate a conversation?
❐	❐	❐	Does the student's system enables him or her to protest or reject something he or she does not want to do, to say "no"?

Yes	A Little	No	
❏	❏	❏	Does the student have a way to use unique and personalized vocabulary?
❏	❏	❏	Does the student have ways to express feelings and opinions?
❏	❏	❏	Is the student communicating efficiently with his or her peers?
❏	❏	❏	Is the student successfully communicating in other areas of the school, such as the playground, at lunch, or in the gym?
❏	❏	❏	Is the student increasing his or her overall skills in functional communication?
❏	❏	❏	Are there communication demands of specific activities that are not being met?
❏	❏	❏	Does there seem to be a need to expand the system to include additional solutions?

Other Strategies

Students who use augmentative communication must be *active* participants—not passive non-participants—within the classroom (Beukelman & Mirenda, 2005). If the user is not actively involved in an activity, lesson, or social event, his or her presence alone is not participation. Beginning users are often unskilled in initiating active participation, so teachers need to model effective ways to invite them into the process. Also, some nonspeaking students may be unable to participate fully in an activity because of the nature and scope of their disabilities. In these cases, partial participation is better than no participation. The sidebar provides specific examples of using partial participation to develop communication skills.

In addition to understanding the value of partial participation, teachers need to recognize that some students may have developed a pattern of learned helplessness through years of disempowerment (Reichle, York, & Sigafoos, 1991; Scherer, 2000). Providing students with a voice can be very powerful; however, many initial augmentative communication users do not know what to do with their newfound power. Therefore, teachers must be able to identify learned helplessness (Petersen, Maier, & Seligman, 1995) and provide support to overcome the passive responses of students who have yet to learn that they can exert control over their environments. See the sidebar, Tips for Overcoming Learned Helplessness.

Need for Teacher Training

Another reason students experience missed opportunities or limited practice for communication is that the teacher is often unfamiliar with the augmentative communication system or has little technical support for troubleshooting. If a system is a mystery to teachers and other educational staff, the likelihood of the student being able to use it effectively is diminished. Therefore, it is important that the student's primary teacher and aide or paraeducator are involved in initial and ongoing training in the use of the augmentative communication system. In addition, a tech support

Tips for Overcoming Learned Helplessness

- Build a daily expectation of communication through specific activities such as choosing the activity during recess, picking a book to read, or identifying where to eat lunch.
- Construct a brief daily report to parents that is communicated by the student.
- Allow natural consequences to occur and provide avenues for repair. This includes setups that alter the environment to provide less support or sabotage.
- Provide for choice making whenever possible that requires the student to use his or her augmentative communication system.
- Provide powerful phrases on the device for students to reject or protest something.

Child making a request using her Dynavox V augmentative communication device.

Photo by Vicki Spence.

staff member in the district should be designated as a technical assistance provider for the system to provide first-level troubleshooting and to address issues related to connecting to the school network.

Comprehensive (and free) resources for professional development are available from professional organizations such as the American Speech, Language, Hearing Association (ASHA) and the International Society for Augmentative and Alternative Communication

(ISAAC) and from several companies that develop and sell augmentative communication devices. The Implementation Toolkit from DynaVox Mayer-Johnson and the e-Training Program from Prentke-Romich are two highly informative training resources.

Not Everything Is High Tech

Making simple communication more complex than necessary can be a mistake that teachers make in their attempts to be communication facilitators. Students need to be provided with an array of strategies to respond as efficiently as possible to simple communication demands. Students are often required to answer simple questions or make quick decisions regarding anything from lunch preferences to recess options. In these frequent and quick-moving situations, it is critical that the augmentative communication user have access to a simple no-tech or low-tech response such as using an unaided conventional gesture (e.g., shaking the head no) or a low-tech single-switch device that is easily accessible to the student at all times (Downey, Daugherty, Helt, & Daugherty, 2004).

INFUSING COMMUNICATION DEVELOPMENT WITHIN THE IEP

The teaching of communication skills is guided by the individualized education program (IEP). Augmentative communication evaluations should be a component of the program development process and must be carefully considered for all nonspeaking students. Once determined to be necessary for a student, the components of the system should be outlined within the IEP. In addition to specifying the system components, the IEP should also include the *use* of the augmentative communication system within the student's educational program. This will ensure that fundamental opportunities are provided for the student to practice communication skills within the context of his or her overall program. A student's academic goals and objectives should assume that his or her participation and evaluation will be achieved through the use of the augmentative communication system. However, every student user must have goals and objectives that reflect the use and continued development of the system. Table 12.4 presents sample IEP goals related to augmentative communication.

When constructing an IEP for a student who uses augmentative communication, it is important that the student's use of the system is integrated within and across the school day, including both instructional and noninstructional periods. To realize a plan that is aligned to all of a student's instructional program components and expected outcomes requires a heightened level

---

TABLE 12.4   Sample IEP Goals of Communication

- The student will increase his or her spontaneous use of appropriate communication with familiar partners for at least three communicative purposes (e.g., initiating, rejecting, and commenting).
- The student will increase his or her use of appropriate communication with unfamiliar partners within the community.
- The student will independently navigate the augmentative communication device without assistance or prompts.
- The student will independently change his or her augmentative communication device overlay to increase available vocabulary and complexity of expression.
- The student will communicate more complex messages by selecting a three-icon sequence.

TABLE 12.5   Sample IEP Goals to Support Instruction and Academics

- Parker will use his augmentative communication device to make a brief presentation to the class about the history of the global race to space.
- Barbara will participate in social studies class through a specifically designed overlay that is developed for her augmentative communication device for each unit. She is expected to volunteer answers to at least two questions per lesson.
- Jackie will participate in a cross-content unit of study such as a class play about the state of New Jersey by using preconstructed messages on her augmentative communication device.

of collaboration among IEP team members (Hunt, Soto, Maier, Muller, & Goetz, 2002). The IEP must include clear statements reflecting the student's communication needs across environments and descriptions of how the specific features of the system will be used by the student. For example, Borey will be provided with a dedicated voice-output device that uses synthesized speech to communicate in school. He will be given up to 1 minute to respond to unexpected interactions and 20 seconds for routine responses. He may require some prompting to facilitate his communication.

When the team develops IEP goals, it is important to remember that the augmentative communication device is not an IEP goal in itself but rather a means to accomplishing a goal. There are three goal areas to consider for augmentative communication users: communication (see Table 12.4), instruction/academic (Table 12.5), and social interactions (Table 12.6). The IEP team must determine goals for developing more effective and efficient communication using the augmentative communication device, and also how the use of augmentative communication will enhance the student's participation in the instructional process and in social interactions.

Two additional components that must be included in an IEP for a student using augmentative communication are a list of the augmentative communication services to be provided by related service personnel (such as the speech/language pathologist and occupational therapist) and identification of the party responsible for device maintenance and operations. Like most technology, augmentative communication devices are subject to technical glitches and breakdowns. A plan for who will troubleshoot, who will be responsible for its repair, and what the student will use while his or her device is being serviced must be delineated within the IEP. This will prevent long periods of time when the student has no voice and no way to interact with others or participate in classroom instruction.

TABLE 12.6   Sample IEP Goals to Support Social Interaction

- David will use his augmentative communication device to engage in three to four conversational turn takings with other students in four out of five opportunities to do so.
- Michelle will use her augmentative communication device to sustain conversation by asking appropriate questions of others regarding topics initiated by herself or others.
- Lori will use her augmentative communication device to comment appropriately or ask for assistance from a peer when engaged in play activities during free time within the classroom or playground.
- Jake will greet three people using a low-tech Talking Brix while engaged in a vocational activity in the community.
- Roberta will use her augmentative communication device to spontaneously indicate to a peer or teacher that she needs additional "wait" time to process information before responding.

TRANSITION FROM SCHOOL TO SCHOOL AND TEACHER TO TEACHER

When a student is transitioning from one school to another or from one teacher to another, it is critical to apply the protocols of comprehensive transition planning to ensure continued progress in the student's communication skills. These protocols include specific steps to take to assure that (1) teachers and other school staff are properly trained in supporting the communication of the student and (2) a specific person is identified to maintain and troubleshoot the device in the case of system failure. This written plan should be included as a component of the student's IEP. Every effort should be made to ensure that the student does not experience regression or diminished opportunities for communication and participation. Training and technical assistance to the new teaching staff should be provided. Other effective practices include teacher observations in the current environment; written protocols for the support that new teachers can expect; training of new peers; and, as stated earlier, the designation of a central point person for troubleshooting.

A consideration when a student is moving out of district is the likelihood that components of the augmentative communication system may remain with the old district. Without advanced transition planning, the student will be without his or her device for an extended period of time (Behnke & Bowser, 2010). Therefore, it is essential that transition planning be expected and well coordinated in advance in order for a student to continue to have access to his or her voice.

HOME AND COMMUNITY USE

Although students receive direct instruction and guidance in developing augmentative communication skills in school, they must practice and use their system at home and within their communities. Using their systems in these other places reinforces the communication skills learned in school and helps generalize them to other settings. This requires expanded consideration of family involvement, issues related to culture, and the identification of places or activities in which the student is active. Teachers must be actively involved in ensuring that there is appropriate carryover and use within the home, among the family members, and across community sites.

The development of a working relationship between school and home is critical to the success of augmentative communication. Both environments reflect different and varied communication demands, and coordinated efforts can significantly increase the likelihood of effective communication. Training in the use of augmentative communication systems should be provided to families. This may include strategies for expanded use of the system and providing new vocabulary for the unique communication demands of home and community. For example, family members may want their nonspeaking child to participate in family birthday celebrations, religious activities, or a community group such as scouting.

It is strongly recommended that patterns of family functioning and cultural diversity be actively considered at the initial stages of development and throughout the implementation process (VanBiervliet & Parette, 2002). Family members, including siblings, grandparents, and extended family, must be included in the evaluation and implementation processes. Parents are familiar with the need to have conversations with their children and to facilitate their appropriate interaction with others. They do this with ease and consistency when at home or in other settings. However, this parenting skill is more challenging when a system of augmentative communication is introduced into the process. School personnel must provide direct instruction to the

Tips for Guiding Parents to Promote the Use of Augmentative Communication

- **Provide Direct Instruction on the Use of the *System*:** A selected group of family members should be assigned as primary at-home support for the student. This enables the school to provide intense and comprehensive training to a few people who will provide support at home. The more that family members can appropriately troubleshoot technical and pragmatic problems, the less likely they will need to depend on school staff.
- **Identify Vocabulary That Is Relevant to the Home:** Phrases such as "What's for dinner?" or "Change the channel" should be available for home use. A guided interview with the family can identify the specific communication demands of the home and most frequented community environments.
- **Teach Family Members to Provide Opportunities for Communication and to Wait:** Parents tend to anticipate the needs of their children and thereby create no real need to communicate. This tendency to speak for their child or assume that they know what the child wants must be replaced with strategies that encourage communication.
- **Provide Simple Data and Evaluation Sheets for Home and Community Use:** School staff should request families to report on their child's augmentative communication system use. Providing simple report protocols will enable the team to monitor the system's use outside the school and determine if and where assistance is needed.
- **Give Parents Permission to Expand the Child's Communication:** Parents should be reinforced for reported occurrences of communication practice and moving their child to expand his or her communication partners and experiences. The more novel people and places the student can communicate about and among, the better.
- **Keep It Simple:** If parents are expected to promote the use of augmentative communication to others, then the explanation of the system's use must be simple. Provide parents with clear, simple descriptions of their child's device—what it does and how the student uses it.

parents, who in turn can teach other family and community members to interact with their child. Because some augmentative communication systems can be quite complicated to operate, consideration should be given to the current level of the family members' familiarity with computers and technology and their willingness to learn, prior to deciding on the most appropriate system. This will enable the school staff to plan the most appropriate home supports and expectations. It is important for the family to feel comfortable with the system and to understand the impact that communication practice will have on future success. See the sidebar, Tips for Guiding Parents to Promote the Use of Augmentative Communication.

Using Augmentative Communication in the Community

Using augmentative communication systems in school and at home has the advantage of involving people who are interested in making sure it is successful. In contrast, the community at-large is less familiar with the augmentative communication user and may be less willing to accept the unfamiliar approach to communication. Communicating with unfamiliar partners is extremely challenging for most users. Unfamiliar partners are people who have no shared knowledge with the user, no understanding of the system, and no understanding of the rules of communicating with an augmentative communication user (Wagner, Musselwhite, & Odom, 2005). Teachers can facilitate positive experiences with novel communication partners through schoolwide special activities or assemblies and through planned field trips in the community. In this case, the devices can be programmed to ask specific questions and guests can be directed toward the augmentative communication user to answer a question. This will enable the student to practice interacting with unfamiliar partners.

How to Talk to an Augmented Communicator

As an AAC user, I often find people don't know how to treat me or how to talk to someone with a device. It often leaves them feeling uncomfortable and me feeling frustrated. I have put together some guidelines to help people communicate effectively with augmented communicators. Hopefully these guidelines will help them feel more comfortable.

- Just be yourself. A lot of times people will get nervous when they are talking to me the first time. I'm just like the average person when you are having a conversation with me– I just speak differently than you do. Don't be nervous. I don't bite.
- Talk to the user at an age-appropriate level. I'm a 24-year-old college student. Some people are fully aware of this fact, yet they still talk to me as if I have no idea what is going on. Try to find out more about me through conversation. Although some people who use AAC devices have cognitive disabilities, I do not and if you speak to me, you'll find that out.
- Talk to the **user**, not to the person who is with them. This happens to me a lot. People will ask my mom what I want to eat, or doctors will ask my attendants why I came to see them when I am right there. It's like I'm invisible. I have a button programmed on my Vmax that says, "not to be rude. But you can talk to me and not to…"
- Always ask if you can read their screen or if you can guess what the user is saying. Everyone is different with this. Personally, I like it when somebody I know does this so that we can have a faster conversation, but whenever I'm in a group or telling a story I like to type everything out myself. However, I know people who do not like it when someone tries to guess what they are about to say.
- If you are having a regular conversation, try not to praise the user. Sometimes when I ask people who I don't know how they are doing, they will completely ignore the question and tell me I'm amazing. I totally understand that people who have never seen a DynaVox before think it is amazing, and it is. However, it's still just my voice.

Source: How to Talk to an Augmented Communicator by Sara Pyszka, Retrieved July 22, 2010, from http://www.voiceforliving.com

AUGMENTATIVE COMMUNICATION RESOURCES FOR TEACHERS

Providing new opportunities for communication for students who use low-tech communication devices does not need to entail time-consuming construction of communication boards. A wealth of resources have been developed to infuse the practice of augmentative communication within activities in school, home, and the community. *I Can Cook, Too!* (Mervine, Mark, & Burton, 1995) and *Art for Me, Too!* (Mervine, Burton, & Wood, 1996) are two collections of classroom activities that are designed to encourage communication. In addition to providing detailed instructions for implementing the cooking and art activities, these volumes provide communication boards that were designed using Boardmaker (Mayer Johnson) for augmentative communication users. The vocabulary on each of these communication boards matches the communication demands of each activity. Teachers are encouraged to copy the boards, laminate them, and use them in the context of the cooking and art activities to provide multiple opportunities for students to practice their communication skills. Figure 12.3, 12.4, and 12.5 illustrate the communications materials that are provided for one cooking activity in *I Can Cook, Too!*

FIGURE 12.3 Sample picture recipe for "Dirt Cups."

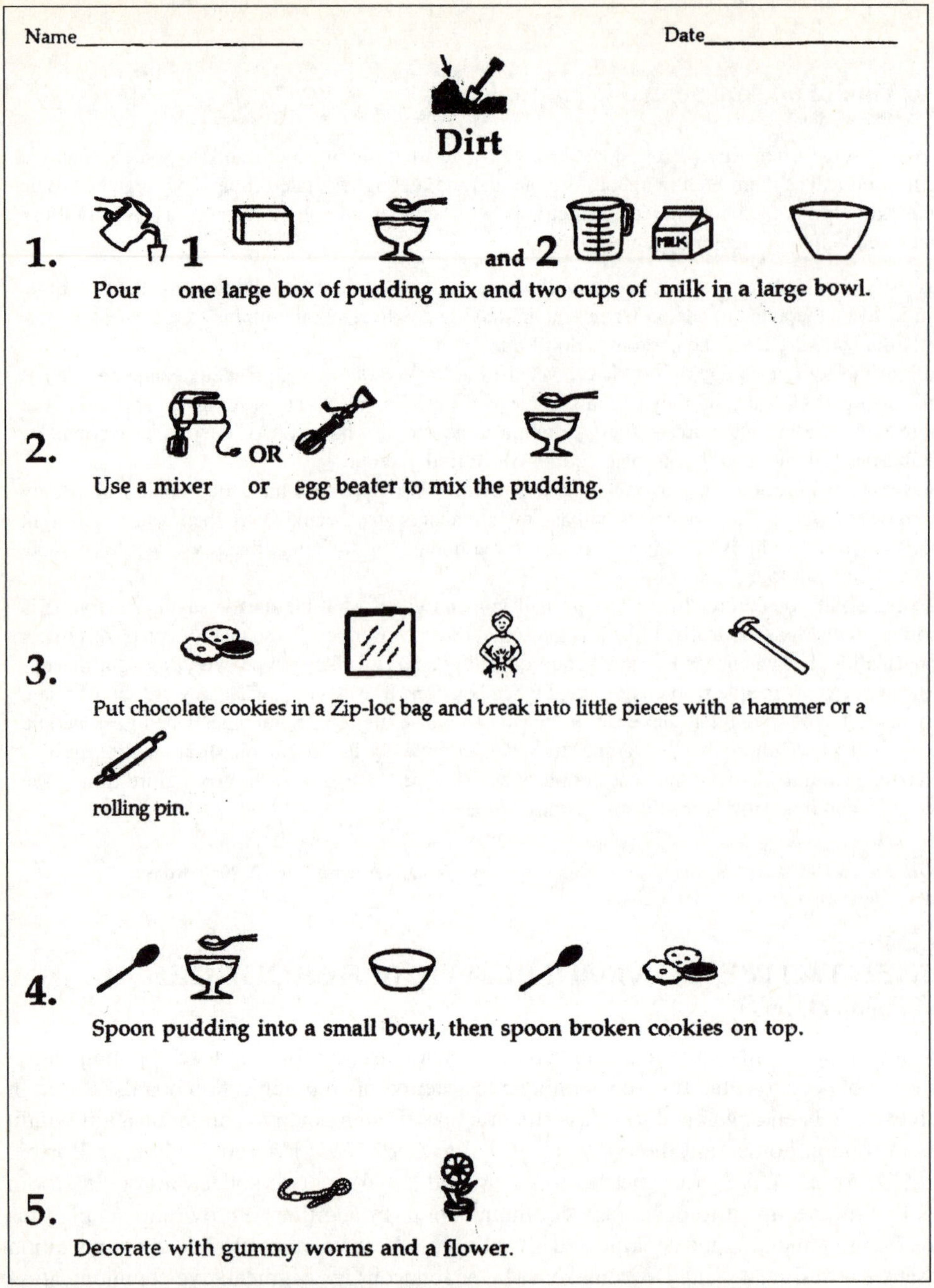

Name_____   Date_____

Dirt

1. Pour   one large box of pudding mix and two cups of milk in a large bowl.

2. Use a mixer   or   egg beater to mix the pudding.

3. Put chocolate cookies in a Zip-loc bag and break into little pieces with a hammer or a

   rolling pin.

4. Spoon pudding into a small bowl, then spoon broken cookies on top.

5. Decorate with gummy worms and a flower.

Source: From *I Can Cook, Too!* by P. L. Mervine, M. Mark, & M. Burton, 1995, Solana Beach, CA: Mayer-Johnson. Reprinted with permission.

FIGURE 12.4 Communication boards to use with the recipe for Dirt Cups.

Source: From *I Can Cook, Too!* by P. L. Mervine, M. Mark, & M. Burton, 1995, Solana Beach, CA: Mayer-Johnson. Reprinted with permission.

FIGURE 12.5 Standard vocabulary strips (mini-communicator boards) for cooking activities.

Standard Vocabulary Strip: Copy, color, and glue to placemat.

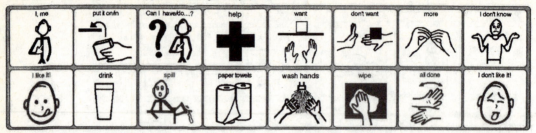

Number and Color Strip: Copy, color, and glue to placemats, or use separately by attaching to an oaktag strip & laminate.

If the child has a reliable yes/no, or is working toward one, please use it! These symbols are provided only for those children who do not have a yes/no response yet.

Source: From *I Can Cook, Too!* by P. L. Mervine, M. Mark, & M. Burton, 1995, Solana Beach, CA: Mayer-Johnson. Reprinted with permission.

Summary

- The teacher has a critical role to play in teaching effective communication skills by integrating augmentative communication into the curriculum and daily classroom routines.
- Of the many roles teachers fill, providing opportunities for communication and teaching communication skills are among the most important.
- Peers also have an important role to play in teaching communication skills. Organizing a communication circle of peer support is one way to involve peers in communicative interactions and problem-solving issues related to providing communication opportunities for the augmentative communication user.
- Teachers need to recognize learned helplessness and use strategies to overcome it.
- In addition to specifying system components, IEPs of augmentative users should also include the use of the augmentative communication system within the student's educational program. This is to ensure that fundamental opportunities

are provided for the student to practice communication skills.

- Communication demands of home and community can differ considerably from those at school. Parents and other family members need to be included in augmentative communication planning and implementation so that they can support their child's communication attempts in these other environments.

- Each student who uses an augmentative communication system must be monitored for his or her progress in increasing and developing communication skills. Their instructors' behavior related to their augmentative communication must also be monitored to document and/or adjust the supports they provide.

Web Resources

For additional information on the topics listed, visit the following Web sites:

Benefits of Inclusion
Article by J. Katz and P. Mirenda in *International Journal of Special Education*
http://www.internationalsped.com/documents/Educ._Benefits(2).doc

Teacher's Role in Augmentative Communication
http://www.speakingofspeech.com

Pivotal Response Training
R. Koegel, et al., *How to Teach Pivotal Behaviors to Children with Autism: A Training Manual*
http://www.users.qwest.net/~tbharris/prt.htm

Picture Exchange Communication System (PECS)
Pyramid Educational Consultants, Inc
http://www.pecs.com/

Joke Telling to Encourage Social Interaction
Linda Burkhart's recommendations: Web sites for jokes and riddles
http://www.lburkhart.com/jokes.htm

Augmentative Communication Online Communities
Voice for Living
http://www.www.voiceforliving.com
ACOLUG (Augmentative Communication OnLine Users Group): Hosted by Temple University's Institute on Disabilities
http://listserv.temple.edu/archives/ACOLUG.html

General Information Regarding Advancements in Augmentative Communication
Rehabilitation Engineering Research Center (RERC)
http://www.aac-rerc.com

Parent Advocacy and Home-School Collaboration
PACER Center (Parent Advocacy Coalition for Educational Rights) and Simon Technology Center at PACER
http://www.pacer.org/stc/index.htm

Infusing Augmentative Communication in the IEP
Guiding Document: Including Assistive Technology in the IEP
*http://natri.uky.edu/assoc_projects/qiat/documents/GuideDocATinIEPintent%2010-09%20
FINAL.pdf*

Suggested Activities

1. *Conduct an ecological inventory.* Conduct an ecological inventory or assessment of a classroom, identifying the communication demands and opportunities presented to the students. Using the questions *Who, What, Where, Why,* and *How,* analyze the opportunities for communication available. Discuss additional strategies that the teacher can use to promote communication.

2. *Develop a peer support training manual.* Develop a peer support training manual that focuses on creating understanding of and skills in supporting the communication efforts of augmentative communication users. What do peers need to know about communicating with a fellow student who uses augmentative communication? Write the manual for a specific age group and be sure it reflects age-appropriate and practical advice. The manual should be written without jargon and in easy-to-understand language.

3. *Infuse augmentative communication in the IEP.* Review three sample IEPs that are available on the Family Village Web site: http://www. familyvillage.wisc.edu/education/iepsamples. html. Modify the goals and objectives to infuse and operationalize the use of an augmentative communication system.

4. *Brainstorm for vocabulary selection.* The class will be divided into three groups, with each group assigned a grade level and an activity:

   a. Group A: Kindergarten, story time
   b. Group B: Fourth and fifth grade, nature hike
   c. Group C: High school, at the mall

   Brainstorm with the members of your group and develop a list of vocabulary that would be needed for an augmentative communication user to participate actively in the activity. Remember to include vocabulary that is age appropriate and that provides a variety of communicative functions.

References

Behnke, K. D., & Bowser, G. (2010). Supporting transition of assistive technology users. *Journal of Special Education Technology, 21*(1), 57–62.

Beukelman, D. R., & Mirenda, P. (2005). *Augmentative and alternative communication* (3rd ed.). Baltimore, MD: Brookes.

Bondy, A. (2001). PECS: Potential benefits and risks. *The Behavior Analyst Today, 2,* 127–132.

Bondy, A., & Frost, L. (2001). The picture exchange communication system. *Behavior Modification, 25,* 725–744.

Carle, E. (1969). *The very hungry caterpillar.* New York: Philomel.

Downey, D., Daugherty, P., Helt, S., & Daugherty, D. (2004). Integrating AAC into the classroom: Low-tech strategies. *The ASHA Leader,* 6–7, 36.

Falvey, M. A., Forest, M., Pearpoint, J., & Rosenberg, R. (1994). *All my life's a circle. Using the tools: Circles, MAP's and PATH.* Toronto, Ontario, Canada: Inclusion Press.

Frost, L., & Bondy, A. (2006). A common language: Using B. F. Skinner's verbal behavior for assessment and treatment of communication disabilities in SLP-ABA. *The Journal of Speech-Language Pathology and Applied Behavior Analysis, 1,* 103–110.

Hill, K., & Romich, B. (2000, August). *AAC best practice using automated language activity monitoring*. Paper presented at the Biennial Conference of the International Society of Augmentative and Alternative Communication, Washington, DC.

Johnson, S. S., Reichle, J., & Evans, J. (2004). Supporting augmentative and alternative communication use by beginning communicators with severe disabilities. *American Journal of Speech-Language Pathology, 13*, 20–30.

Hunt, P., Soto, G., Maier, J., Muller, E., & Goetz, L. (2002). Collaborative teaming to support students with augmentative and alternative communication needs in general education classrooms. *AAC Augmentative and Alternative Communication, 18*, 20–35.

Karlan, G. (1991). *Environmental communication teaching training*. Field-Initiated Research Grant Award No. H023C9005, Office of Special Education Programs, U.S. Department of Education. Lafayette, IN: Purdue University.

Koegel, R. L., & Koegel, L. K. (2006). *Pivotal response treatments for autism*. Baltimore, MD: Brookes.

Koegel, R. L., O'Dell, M. C., & Dunlap, G. (1988). Motivating speech use in nonverbal autistic children by reinforcing attempts. *Journal of Autism and Other Developmental Disorders, 18*, 525–537.

Koegel, R. L., O'Dell, M. C., & Koegel, L. K. (1987). A natural language teaching paradigm for nonverbal autistic children. *Journal of Autism and Developmental Disorders, 17*, 187–200.

Kohn, J. G., LeBlanc, M., & Mortola, P. (1995). Measuring quality and performance of technology: Results of a prospective monitoring program. *Assistive Technology, 6*, 120–125.

Locke, P. A., & Mirenda, P. (1992). Roles and responsibilities of special education teachers serving on teams delivering AAC services. *Augmentative and Alternative Communication, 8*, 200–214.

Mervine, P. L. (1995). Teaching communication in natural environments. *TECH-NJ, 6*(1), 3, 16.

Mervine, P. L., Burton, M., & Wood, L. (1996). *Art for me, too!* Solana Beach, CA: Mayer-Johnson.

Mervine, P. L., Mark, M., & Burton, M. (1995). *I can cook, too!* Solana Beach, CA: Mayer-Johnson.

Petersen, C., Maier, S. F., & Seligman, M. E. P. (1995). *Learned helplessness: A theory for the age of personal control*. New York: Oxford University Press.

Reichle, J., York, J., & Sigafoos, J. (1991). *Implementing augmentative and alternative communication: Strategies for learners with severe disabilities*. Baltimore, MD: Brookes.

Scherer, M. J. (2000). *Living in the state of stuck: How assistive technology impacts the lives of people with disabilities*. Newton, MA: Brookline Books.

VanBiervliet, A., & Parette, H. P. (2002). Development and evaluation of the families, cultures and augmentative and alternative communication (AAC) multimedia program. *Disability and Rehabilitation, 24*(1/2/3), 131–143.

Wagner, D., Musselwhite, C., & Odom, J. (2005). *Out and about: AAC in the community*. Litchfield Park, AZ: C. Musselwhite.

PART 4

MAKING IT HAPPEN

CHAPTER 13

Implementation of Assistive Technology in Schools

CHAPTER 14

Implementation of Assistive Technology in Transition Planning

13 | IMPLEMENTATION OF ASSISTIVE TECHNOLOGY IN SCHOOLS

Focus Questions

1. What laws influence assistive technology provision in P–12 education?
2. How can assistive technology be integrated into the IEP?
3. What are some of the critical issues related to assistive technology implementation?
4. How does each issue affect assistive technology implementation?
5. What are the major funding sources of assistive technology for students?
6. What resources are available to support the implementation of assistive technology?

INTRODUCTION

Assistive technology offers numerous benefits for students with disabilities, as discussed in the preceding chapters. However, many students with disabilities are not being provided with the assistive technology tools and training that they need. Many students with learning disabilities continue to struggle with reading and writing, falling further and further behind in their work because their schools have not made talking word processing, word prediction, or scan/read software available to them. Many students with physical disabilities or autism continue to be frustrated by their inability to communicate and are unable to demonstrate their intelligence because their schools have not provided them with appropriate augmentative communication systems. The gap between the *possibilities* of assistive technology and the actual implementation of it in our schools is substantial. This chapter focuses on the key issues that need to be addressed to get assistive technology into the hands of the students who will benefit from it. The place to start is examining the legal basis for assistive technology.

LEGAL BASIS FOR ASSISTIVE TECHNOLOGY

The United States Congress has underscored the importance of assistive technology to the education of students with disabilities by stating the following:

> Almost 30 years of research and experience has demonstrated that the education of children with disabilities can be made more effective by …

(H) supporting the development and use of technology, including assistive technology devices and assistive technology services, to maximize accessibility for children with disabilities. (IDEA 2004)

We can say, therefore, that provision of assistive technology is not only a good idea, it is the law. Students with disabilities are entitled to assistive technology if it is essential for accessing education and education-related resources. The Individuals with Disabilities Education Improvement Act of 2004 (IDEA 2004), Section 504 of the Rehabilitation Act of 1973, and the Americans with Disabilities Act (ADA) ensure that students with disabilities have access to education and that they are protected from discrimination based on having a disability. Each of these laws is relevant to our discussion of assistive technology (see Chapter 1 for detailed information). However, IDEA 2004 is the law that has the greatest impact on Preschool through Grade 12 students with disabilities because it requires consideration of students' needs for assistive technology during the development of their individualized education programs (IEPs).

INTEGRATING ASSISTIVE TECHNOLOGY INTO THE IEP

Because the IEP drives the provision of special education services to students with disabilities, any discussion of assistive technology implementation must address the need to integrate assistive technology into the IEP. Assistive technology is one of the **special factors** that must be considered when developing each student's IEP. (See Chapter 9 for a discussion of assistive technology consideration.) The IEP must document that assistive technology has been considered. If the IEP team determines that assistive technology is not needed, this must be noted, along with the reason for this determination. If the IEP team determines that assistive technology is needed, this needs to be documented as well.

The documentation of the need for assistive technology may be incorporated throughout the IEP; however, there are three places in the IEP where specific assistive technology needs usually appear:

1. In the description of specially designed instruction
2. In the description of supplementary aids and services
3. In the description of related services (Bauder, Lewis, Bearden, & Gobert, 1997, p. 19)

It is also common to integrate assistive technology into the IEP in the section addressing present levels of academic achievement and functional performance. In IDEA 1997, this section was called the "present level of educational performance" (PLEP). The name change makes more explicit the intended purpose of this section, which is (and has been) to provide information about "the present level at which the student is functioning in physical, social, academic, emotional, and transitional areas" (Wallace, 1999, p. 10). *Assistive Technology in the IEP* (Pennsylvania Training and Technical Assistance Network [PaTTAN], n.d.) provides many examples of acceptable statements (see Figure 13.1), along with the following guidance: "If the student is currently using assistive technology in his/her educational program, summarize how it is being used and how it relates to the student's performance" (p. 10).

Specially Designed Instruction

Assistive technology is often included in the goals or objectives of students' IEPs. Goals are relatively broad statements related to achievement expectations for students: "Goals should relate to the general education curriculum with assistive technology used as a tool to reach the curriculum goals" (PaTTAN, n.d., p. 14). That is, "assistive technology may be a means to help the child reach a goal. It should not be the goal itself" (Connecticut State Department of Education and

FIGURE 13.1 Sample statements for IEPs: Present Level of Academic Achievement and Functional Performance.

- Uses adapted pencil grip for all written work.
- Uses slant board for all written work.
- Can complete written work using a computer adapted with a mini-keyboard.
- Completes written work using a word processing program with speech feedback and headphones.
- Completes % of written work compared to peers when using assistive technology and % if not using assistive technology.
- Uses adapted chair for toileting.
- Self-propels adapted wheelchair for mobility in school.
- Plays with other students in competitive games using assistive technology.
- Uses a voice output device to communicate within the classroom.
- Uses a communication board to interact with peers.
- Uses a personal FM amplification system to comprehend classroom instruction.
- Uses an FM sound field system to improve his or her attention to spoken messages.
- Completes written assignments using a computer with a voice recognition program.
- Uses a closed-circuit television (CCTV) to read printed material.
- Completes functional tasks using environmental controls.
- Participates in leisure activities using an environmental control unit.
- Accesses emergency evacuation information using visual, auditory, and tactile cues.

Source: From *Assistive Technology in the IEP*, by the Pennsylvania Training and Technical Assistance Network (n.d.), Harrisburg, PA: Pennsylvania Department of Education. Reprinted with permission.

Connecticut Birth to Three System, 1999, p. 32). For example, a student may have a goal targeting the improvement of skills in written expression. If assistive technology is needed to support the attainment of this goal, the goal might be stated as "Joseph will demonstrate improvement in written expression using a talking word processing program and word prediction." The focus should be on the skill acquisition, not the use of technology.

Objectives, or benchmarks, are the intermediary steps that must be reached in order to achieve the goals. Assistive technology is often included in objectives. This is good practice if using assistive technology is the means by which students will be able to demonstrate they have successfully accomplished their objectives. Another reason for including assistive technology is that "with objectives that include the specific technology, everyone involved in implementing the IEP knows and understands what is expected and what will be used" (Connecticut, 1999, p. 33). As an example, an appropriately worded objective for Joseph (mentioned earlier) might be "Joseph will compose a complete paragraph with appropriate punctuation using talking word processing and word prediction programs."

Assistive technology may also be included in the IEP section dealing with **accommodations** and **modifications**. Any modifications to instructional methods or materials that will be required to make the general education curriculum accessible to students with disabilities should be noted. It is often beneficial to list assistive technology in this section even if it was mentioned in other sections of the IEP. For example, a student with a learning disability who is a struggling reader might have a modification that states, "all worksheets and handouts will be provided in an electronic format that can be read aloud by a text-to-speech program."

Supplementary Aids and Services and Related Services

The sections of the IEP concerned with supplementary aids and services and related services are appropriate places to integrate assistive technology. IDEA 2004 defines **supplementary aids and services** as "aids, services, and other supports that are provided in regular education classes

Sample Assistive Technology Implementation Plans

Sample assistive technology implementation plans can be found at the following Web sites:

Oregon Technology Access Program

Assistive Technology Model Operating Guidelines for School Districts and IEP Teams
http://www.otap-oregon.org/Documents/AT%20Model%20Operating%20Guidelines.pdf

Minnesota Assistive Technology Manual

http://education.state.mn.us/mdeprod/groups/SpecialEd/documents/Manual/001089.pdf

---

or other education-related settings to enable children with disabilities to be educated with non-disabled children to the maximum extent appropriate."

Related services are defined as

> transportation, and such developmental, corrective, and other supportive services … as may be required to assist a child with a disability to benefit from special education.… The term does not include a medical device that is surgically implanted, or the replacement of such device. (IDEA, 2004)

Clearly, assistive technology can provide students with access to the curriculum, enable them to be educated in the regular education classroom, and help them benefit from special education. For these reasons, assistive technology can be considered supplementary aids and services or a related service and included as such in the IEP.

Including assistive technology in the IEP is the first step, but it is only the beginning. It does not guarantee that the potential benefits offered by technology will be realized by a student. Anecdotal evidence and a growing body of literature point to the need for systematic planning of assistive technology *implementation*. This critical topic is highlighted by the QIAT Consortium (see Chapter 9) who, in the Quality Indicators for Assistive Technology Implementation, identify best practices for AT implementation. Each of these quality indicators is supported by legal mandates in IDEA under the definition of assistive technology services, the research base on AT implementation, and the collective wisdom of the field. (See Figure 13.2.)

The National Assistive Technology Research Institute (NATRI) developed a form for use by teams called the Assistive Technology Implementation Plan whose purpose is to "guide teams through a planning process that will ensure proper implementation of a student's AT" (Bausch & Ault, 2008, p. 7). The form collects information and provides written documentation on the following details:

- Names and positions of each member of the implementation team.
- Specific hardware, software, and assistive devices to be used and the status of each (e.g., to be purchased, already in district, owned by family).
- Tasks related to hardware, software, and assistive devices that need to be completed by team members, the specific person responsible for each task, and a deadline.
- Training needs, including who needs the training, who will provide it, dates of trainings, and follow-up plans.

FIGURE 13.2 Quality Indicators for Assistive Technology Implementation.

Assistive technology implementation pertains to the ways that assistive technology devices and services, as included in the IEP (including goals/objectives, related services, supplementary aids and services, and accommodations or modifications), are delivered and integrated into the student's educational program. Assistive technology implementation involves people working together to support the student using assistive technology to accomplish expected tasks necessary for active participation and progress in customary educational environments.

1. Assistive technology implementation proceeds according to a collaboratively developed plan.
2. Assistive technology is integrated into the curriculum and daily activities of the student across environments.
3. Persons supporting the student across all environments in which the assistive technology is expected to be used share responsibility for implementation of the plan.
4. Persons supporting the student provide opportunities for the student to use a variety of strategies—including assistive technology—and to learn which strategies are most effective for particular circumstances and tasks.
5. Training for the student, family, and staff are an integral part of implementation.
6. Assistive technology implementation is initially based on assessment data and is adjusted based on performance data.
7. Assistive technology implementation includes management and maintenance of equipment and materials. This may include organization of equipment and materials; assigning responsibility for acquisition, set-up, repair, and replacement in a timely fashion; and assurance that equipment is operational.

Source: QIAT Consortium (2005). *Quality Indicators for assistive technology services.* Retrieved July 12, 2010, from http://natri.uky.edu/assoc_projects/qiat/qualityindicators.html

- Classroom implementation information: brief list of relevant IEP goals linked to the specific assistive technology tool that will be used to meet that goal, any customized settings that will be needed, and the person responsible.
- Home implementation information: the IEP goals and assistive technology tools and settings that will be used at home. Parents and/or students are usually the people identified as being responsible for carrying out this part of the plan.
- Monitoring and evaluation: strategies that will be used to teach the student to use the technology, methods of data collection, and person(s) responsible.

CRITICAL ISSUES IN ASSISTIVE TECHNOLOGY IMPLEMENTATION

What kinds of obstacles do teachers and teams face as they try to integrate assistive technology into the curriculum? Research and practice show that it is possible to avoid problems if they are identified and anticipated in advance so that collaborative teams can address them directly. The following sections focus on critical issues impacting assistive technology implementation and include suggestions and resources for avoiding or overcoming common barriers.

The Digital Divide

Educational and civil rights laws apply to all students with disabilities in P–12 settings. However, professionals and parents recognize the existence of a basic inequity with regard to application of these laws. In many respects this equity gap mirrors the **digital divide**, a phrase that is often used to identify the gap between people who have access to information technology and people who do not. There is also a digital divide in terms of access to assistive technology.

A clear understanding of the digital divide is essential for understanding its impact on assistive technology. Webopedia (n.d.), an online dictionary focusing on computer technology, provides the following definition of *digital divide*:

> A term used to describe the discrepancy between people who have access to and the resources to use new information and communication tools, such as the Internet, and people who do not have the resources and access to the technology. The term also describes the discrepancy between those who have the skills, knowledge and abilities to use the technologies and those who do not.

As you might surmise, many school districts serving upper- and middle-class students are among the "haves," and many districts serving predominantly low-income and minority students are among the "have-nots" (Lever-Duffy & McDonald, 2011). Brown, Higgins, and Hartley (2001) identify the have-nots as

> students from diverse ethnic backgrounds, students living in inner cities, female students, students with disabilities, rural children, English language learning (ELL) children and their families, and students unlikely to graduate or who leave school without an adequate level of basic skills. (p. 33)

Not surprisingly, many of those who are have-nots with respect to information technology are also have-nots with respect to assistive technology. The financial resources of school districts account in large part for both forms of the digital divide; districts that have extremely limited funds simply have less money to invest in information technology and assistive technology. However, other factors also contribute to the inequity. Culture, access to information, and advocacy skills are among the factors that strongly influence assistive technology implementation.

Culture

Culture can have a tremendous impact on one's view of disability as well as acceptance of interventions, including assistive technology. **Culture** can be broadly defined as a system of learned and shared standards for perceiving, interpreting, and behaving in interactions with others and the environment (Jezewski & Sotnik, 2001, p. 3). Jezewski and Sotnik identify dietary practices, religion and religious practices, language, child-rearing practices, and family and social relations among the elements of a culture system; some of these elements have a stronger influence than others on how disabilities are viewed and treated. In some cultures, disabilities are considered shameful because they are viewed as punishment for sins or actions of the parents or sins committed in past lives. Individuals subscribing to this cultural view may simply accept the disability as predetermined and not seek medical or rehabilitation services to address it. When disabilities are considered shameful, families may prefer to have their children with disabilities keep a low profile; they may not embrace the use of assistive technology because it would call attention to their child.

Some cultures are more collectively than individually oriented. The American culture values independence and self-reliance, whereas other cultures put the needs of the family above those of the individual. People from collectivist cultures may live with extended family and may have many family members to help an individual with a disability. They do not value independence and may not see a need to use assistive technology to increase independent functioning.

Cultural diversity can make it challenging to maintain effective communication and interactions among students with disabilities, their family members, and IEP team members. The rules governing communication style (e.g., formal or informal), acceptable forms of address, use of eye contact, attitudes toward punctuality, and other matters vary from culture to culture. Speaking or acting in ways that may unintentionally be taken to be offensive often causes communication breakdowns.

In our increasingly diverse communities, it is important to consider the cultural beliefs of students with disabilities and their families in order to provide culturally sensitive AT services. Teachers and IEP team members need to search out community and school resources to familiarize themselves with the cultures of their students. The monograph series, *The Rehabilitation Provider's Guide to Cultures of the Foreign-Born,* available from the Center for International Rehabilitation Research Information and Exchange (CIRRIE), is a useful resource to augment local resources (see sidebar). Although information provided in these monographs, as well as information garnered from other sources, applies to many people from a given culture, it is important to refrain from generalizing or stereotyping as there are always intra-cultural differences—that is, not everyone from a particular culture will ascribe to the exact same beliefs or communicative behaviors.

Cultural Monograph Series

The Center for International Rehabilitation Research Information and Exchange (CIRRIE) provides a 13-volume monograph series entitled *The Rehabilitation Provider's Guide to Cultures of the Foreign-Born.* The series includes an introductory monograph, *Culture Brokering: Providing Culturally Competent Rehabilitation Services to Foreign-Born Persons*, which provides practical information related to outreach strategies, becoming familiar with and trusted by other cultures, the importance of understanding one's own culture, and using translators effectively. Each of the other 12 monographs contains general information about a particular culture, its values, recommendations for interacting with people from that culture, and information on the culture's view of disability and rehabilitation. The following cultures are represented in the series: Mexico, China, Philippines, India, Vietnam, Dominican Republic, Korea, El Salvador, Jamaica, Cuba, Haiti, as well as Muslim perspectives.

Another relevant issue related to culture is that parents of students with disabilities from diverse cultures may have less access to information about assistive technology and their children's rights under IDEA, including an entitlement to assistive technology consideration. It may be difficult or impossible to access print and online resources because they may not be available in the parents' native language.

Well-informed parents are better able to advocate their children's rights and bring important assistive technology information to the attention of IEP teams. As mentioned in Chapter 9 and discussed later, IEP team members may have received little, if any, preservice or in-service training in assistive technology. This problem is compounded by rapidly changing technological advances, making it difficult to keep abreast the latest products and developments. Parents can be instrumental in bringing categories of assistive technology or specific products to the attention of IEP teams, thereby increasing the probability that their children will benefit from appropriately selected and implemented technology. Those families with greater access to information are better able to contribute to the assistive technology consideration process and advocate their children's technology needs during IEP meetings.

Assistive Technology Consideration Misunderstood

Despite the clear mandate to consider the assistive technology needs of all students receiving special education services, many obstacles prevent this ideal situation from becoming a reality. One problem stems directly from the language used in IDEA. Although assistive technology consideration is required, the term consideration is not clearly defined. State and local education agencies may have disparate interpretations and actualizations of consideration. Some educational agencies include a checklist of assistive technology solutions along the full assistive technology continuum as part of the IEP document and have policies and procedures in place to obtain an evaluation if team members believe they cannot adequately consider a student's needs. In other districts, consideration is reduced to a statement on the IEP that assistive technology has been considered and is accompanied by checkboxes to indicate that technology is or is not necessary. "Is not" may be checked routinely simply because those doing the considering lack the necessary knowledge and skills in assistive technology.

Resources for Teachers, IEP Teams, Administrators, and Parents

Good resources on considering assistive technology during the IEP process and implementing assistive technology in the classroom are available from the Technology and Media Division (TAM) of the Council for Exceptional Children (CEC). The monograph *Considering the Need for Assistive Technology Within the Individualized Education Program* (Center for Technology in Education at Johns Hopkins University and Technology and Media Division of CEC, 2005) provides essential information on the process for IEP teams. A second monograph *A School Administrator's Desktop Guide to Assistive Technology* (Bowser & Reed, 2004) is specifically geared to principals and other educational leaders so they will be prepared to support assistive technology use in their schools.

A kit called the *Assistive Technology Planner: From IEP Consideration to Classroom Implementation* (Bausch, Ault, & Hasselbring, 2006) consists of a form for assistive technology implementation planning and three informative manuals: one for teachers, one for administrators, and one for families. Each booklet is tailored to its audience with information on its particular roles in the process and specific strategies that are relevant to those roles. For example, the guide for teachers lists the following roles: (1) familiarizing oneself with assistive technology tools, (2) organizing the classroom environment and routines to support the use of assistive technology; (3) arranging for assistive technology to be used consistently, (4) monitoring student progress on assistive technology use, (5) maintaining communication with colleagues and parents about students' use of assistive technology, and (6) committing to further professional development on assistive technology. These resources are all available from http://www.tamcec.org/publications/

Educational Professionals' Lack of Knowledge and Skills

A major obstacle to assistive technology implementation arises from a lack of knowledge and skills in assistive technology among educational professionals. Although IDEA has mandated assistive technology consideration since the 1997 reauthorization, many educational personnel who are responsible for considering students' technology needs are unprepared to do so (Bausch & Hasselbring, 2005; Derer, Polsgrove, & Rieth, 1996). Additionally, simply identifying the assistive technology needed by a student does not equate to successful implementation. Levin (2005) cautions that "teachers may not have the training and support they need to help their students to make the most effective use of the technology tools and resources at their disposal" (p. 32). This barrier occurs because training for special education teachers is either missing entirely or is inadequate at both the preservice and in-service levels. Often when assistive technology training does occur, it focuses on learning to use *devices*, rather than on using the devices *to learn*: "Training does not typically include using assistive technology to access the general-education curriculum, which is a key component to the successful use of assistive technology" (Bausch & Hasselbring, 2005, p. 9). Consequently, a lack of training for professionals continues to hinder the successful implementation of assistive technology in our schools (Gruner et al., 2000). Special education teachers entering the field today may be no more informed about, able to use or skilled at identifying appropriate assistive technology than were teachers 10 years ago.

Opportunities for *quality* in-service assistive technology training are often not made available to increase the competency of teachers and other educational personnel. This may be the case despite the fact that technology training may be provided during school district professional development days. Newton and Shiller (2005) report that special education teachers and staff are often required to attend the same technology trainings as general education teachers, regardless of whether or not the training is appropriate for them.

It does not have to be this way. Extensive resources for building assistive technology knowledge and skills are readily available in the form of interactive Web sites, multimedia presentations, webinars, and manuals and documents that can be obtained in hard copy or downloaded from the Internet. A sampling of these resources is found in Table 13.1.

Information Technology Policies

Assistive technology practitioners and teachers lament the fact that policies established to protect information technology (IT) systems can become barriers to assistive technology implementation (Newton, 2002). Access to operating system resources such as control panels are often a "privilege" reserved for IT personnel. As a result, assistive technology practitioners and teachers are unable to implement simple modifications such as activating StickyKeys or MouseKeys (see Chapter 7), and they cannot install software programs or assistive devices that are mandated by students' IEPs. At times, these problems are transitory and easily resolved when IT personnel respond to requests to provide required services. However, at other times, the IT policies result in denying students the assistive technology to which they are legally entitled. Teachers and assistive technology practitioners report that requests for software or hardware installation are sometimes denied because IT policies dictate that every computer in a school or district be configured the same way; therefore, if a program is not on *every* computer, it cannot be on *any* computer (Newton, 2002).

Collaboration and cooperation between AT and IT professionals are essential to avoid conflict and contribute to successful assistive technology implementation. Newton and Dell (2009) offer insights into practices that foster collaborative relationships. In brief, they find that when AT and IT professionals make an effort to learn about each other's domains and develop respect for each other's concerns and priorities, collaboration and cooperation are more likely to occur. More detailed information is found in the sidebar.

TABLE 13.1   Resources for Developing Professionals' Assistive Technology Knowledge and Skills

Resource	Description	URL
Assistive Technology Training Online Project (ATTO)	This interactive Web site provides information on assistive technology for access to computers and for access to the curriculum	http://atto.buffalo.edu/
Valdosta State University in collaboration with the Georgia Project for Assistive Technology	A collection of video tips related to both assistive technology devices and assistive technology services	http://www.valdosta.edu/coe/ecre/ATRB/Video_Tips.htm
A Resource Guide for Teachers and Administrators About Assistive Technology	An overview of assistive technology, information about various types of assistive technology, and a listing of additional assistive technology resources	http://www.wati.org/content/supports/free/pdf/ATResourceGuideDec08.pdf http://www.wati.org/content/supports/free/pdf/ATResourceGuideDec08.pdf
Michigan's Integrated Technology Resource	Provides a series of tutorials, resources and training modules.	http://mits.cenmi.org/Resources/AssistiveTechnology/SharedTutorialsandResources.aspx
Texas Assistive Technology Network	A series of online training modules. One focuses on assistive technology for reading, and one on assistive technology for writing.	http://www.texasat.net/default.aspx?name=trainmod.home

Suggestions for Developing Collaborative Working Relationships with IT Staff

Learn about the other's working universe and respect each other's territory: Special education teachers and/or assistive technology staff need to make an effort to understand the priorities and concerns of their schools' IT staff. What problems do they deal with on a daily basis? What are they trying to accomplish with their restrictions on software installations, downloading files from the Internet, etc.? Understanding their perspective will help you propose solutions that are likely to be more acceptable to them….

Improve your computer technology skills so that you earn a reputation for competence: You will only be able to understand the priorities and concerns of your district's IT staff if your computer skills are strong. It is not enough to know which assistive technology tools meet the needs of specific students and how to use those tools. Special education teachers and/or assistive technology staff need to be competent and independent with utilizing the basic features of the computer operating systems and commonly used applications…. They need to use the correct terminology when referring to computer hardware and operating system components, which requires keeping current with the latest computer technology advances….

Show the power of assistive technology: Many IT staff members have no experience in special education or with students who have disabilities. Just as it is important for those who support the use of AT to know and understand the universe of IT personnel, it is equally important that IT personnel come to know and understand the AT world…. One simple way to introduce assistive technology into the IT universe is to make a point of including information about AT in discussions with IT staff; letting them know what a product does and why a student needs it helps to build their knowledge base over time…. Explaining the law and the legal implications surrounding students' rights to assistive technology can help IT staff understand concerns about providing the AT as quickly as possible…. Invite administrators and IT staff to see assistive technology in action and to observe its impact on students.

Raise AT awareness through hands-on training: Arrange for brief hands-on experiences where IT staff can try out various assistive technology tools themselves. This has a much greater impact than simply explaining what it is like to be a computer user with a disability. For example, give them each an unsharpened pencil to hold in their fists as a dowel, and have them type a short passage so they can experience the typing task as a one-finger typist might…. Take away the computer mouse and they will quickly see the need for MouseKeys as well as the need to adjust the mouse speed….

Problem-solve collaboratively: Once you have a better understanding of the concerns of your IT staff, and they have a better understanding of the needs of students who use assistive technology, it is more likely that you can work together to come up with mutually acceptable solutions. Special education staff involved in assistive technology need to communicate with IT staff during the entire process of assistive technology consideration, assessment, and implementation so that due consideration can be given to network issues….

Be proactive: Find out how decisions about technology purchases and policies are made in your school or district, and try to get involved…. There needs to be special education/assistive technology representation on these committees… to speak out about the needs of students who use assistive technology so that their technology needs will not be left out of district-wide decision-making.

Source: Newton, D. A., & Dell, A. G. (2009). Issues in assistive technology implementation: Resolving AT/IT conflicts. *Journal of Special Education Technology, 24*(1), 51–56. Used with permission from the copyright holder, the Technology and Media Division of the Council for Exceptional Children (TAM) (www.tamcec.org).

Funding

Funding for assistive technology is available from a number of sources, yet it continues to be among the predominant concerns for many schools, organizations, and individuals. This concern is certainly warranted; lack of funding is one of the major barriers to the successful implementation of assistive technology (National Task Force on Technology and Disability [NTFTD], 2004). Although IDEA mandates assistive technology consideration, it does not provide adequate funding for the technology that may be considered appropriate. Whereas the cost of low-tech assistive technology is usually minimal, further along the assistive technology continuum the cost increases. In school districts already facing financial challenges, funding may be viewed as an insurmountable barrier to assistive technology implementation.

Funding issues negatively affect assistive technology implementation in ways other than simply the expense involved in acquiring the assistive technology. Purchase price does not represent the total cost of most assistive technology devices; there are costs associated with insuring, maintaining, repairing, transporting, and updating the purchased items. Of particular concern is providing training for the students and adults who support the students' use of the technology, and training costs money. Unfortunately, when funds are short, adequate training is not provided; in this case, students end up with the assistive technology that they need, but they do not benefit from it because no one knows how to use it or integrate it correctly into students' educational programs.

School district budgets, public and private insurance, and other sources may be accessed to pay for assistive technology for P–12 students. The following text discusses these, as well as other, possible funding sources for assistive technology.

IDEA requires that **school districts** provide assistive technology devices and services at no charge to students' families if the assistive technology is necessary for students to benefit from a free appropriate public education (FAPE). School districts must provide any assistive technology that is identified in students' IEPs regardless of cost. However, simply providing devices does not meet the legal obligations mandated by IDEA. Assistive technology *services*, such as technology evaluations; training for students, school personnel, and others who will support students' use of assistive technology for academic purposes; and repair and maintenance of technology must be provided at no charge to students' families.

Often special education budgets are the source of funds for purchasing assistive technology; however, this need not, and in fact should not, be the sole source of funding for devices and services. The Connecticut State Assistive Technology Guidelines add emphasis to this by stating

> Assistive technology should be a part of every district's technology plans and purchases so that schools begin to deal with assistive technology needs pro-actively instead of reactively. In setting up technology plans, districts should incorporate basic assistive technology software, for example, when setting up computer labs. They should take into account student access to computers and carefully examine the environment so that at least some of the equipment is accessible to all students in terms of scheduling, workstation access, keyboard use, etc. Districts ought to include awareness level training in assistive technology use as part of their in-service technology training sessions, requiring that all teachers and support personnel become aware of the full range of assistive technology devices and services. (Connecticut, 1999, p. 41)

IDEA provides an option for acquiring medically necessary assistive technology through funding sources other than school districts. Use of Medicaid and parents' private health insurance to purchase assistive technology was authorized by IDEA 1997, and IDEA 2004 does not change this. However, because assistive technology must be provided at no cost, parental agreement to the use of these alternate funding sources is voluntary.

Medicaid is a joint federal-state program that provides funding for medical care, rehabilitation, and other services to individuals who meet eligibility requirements that include financial need. The Medicaid program varies from state to state: Each state's program must provide a certain set of mandatory services, and then the state can elect to provide a number of optional services for adult beneficiaries. Children with disabilities receive Medicaid benefits under Early Periodic Screening, Diagnosis, and Treatment (EPSDT) provisions and are eligible for the full range of Medicaid services, even those that may not be available to adult beneficiaries in their state (Sheldon & Hager, 1997). Regardless of a beneficiary's age, Medicaid provides assistive technology only if it is judged to be **"medically necessary."** At times, assistive technology deemed medically necessary, such as an augmentative communication device, also enables students to benefit from FAPE. In such cases, Medicaid funds, with parental approval, can be used to purchase the assistive technology.

For students who do not qualify for Medicaid, assistive technology that is medically necessary may be covered under the **family's private health insurance.** Parents may elect to use their private insurance rather than school funds to pay for assistive technology. If parents elect to do this, they own the assistive technology device, but that does not negate the school's obligation to provide associated assistive technology services. When private insurance is used, schools are still obligated to meet IDEA's mandate that assistive technology be provided at no cost to families; therefore, they may need to reimburse parents for copayments or deductibles (Hager & Smith, 2003).

Despite reimbursement for out-of-pocket expenses, there is often an unseen cost to parents when they agree to use private insurance to pay for assistive technology—a reduction in the annual or lifetime cap for medical benefits. Hager and Smith (2003) state, "For some students with significant needs, even a very substantial lifetime cap could be quickly used up, requiring the family to be very careful about when the insurance policy is used" (p. 38). School districts are required to inform parents that the use of private insurance is voluntary, and schools must provide the assistive technology if parents decline to use their private insurance.

Vocational rehabilitation (VR) agencies and the services they provide vary from state to state. In some states, VR may be a funding source for assistive technology for students with disabilities. An **individual transition plan (ITP)** must be established as part of the IEP process when students are 16 years old. As part of the ITP, agencies that will be needed to support

---

Sources for Grant Writing and Identifying Possible Funding Sources

Grant Writing Resources

SchoolGrants provides free grant information and grant writing resources targeting P–12 school grant opportunities. Grant writing tips and sample proposals are available to help novice grant writers. http://k12grants.org/

GRANTwriters Online provides easy-to-understand guidance and tips for writing successful grants. Sample grant proposals are available for review. http://www.grantwritersonline.com/index.html

Locating Grant Opportunities and Funding Sources

Grants.gov is the place to locate and apply for federal grants. Web site visitors can sign up for e-mail alerts about new grant opportunities. http://www.grants.gov/index.jsp

ED.gov, the Web site of the U.S. Department of Education, provides information about available federally funded technology grants, including grants related to assistive technology. http://www2.ed.gov/about/offices/list/os/technology/edgrants.html

Fundsnet Services Online provides free access to its fund-raising and grants directory. Education and Literacy, Technology, and Disability Grants are among the 28 categories that can be reviewed for grant offerings. http://www.fundsnetservices.com/

The Foundation Center, a nonprofit organization, helps grant seekers identify funding sources. Free access to resources is available at the five library/learning centers located in New York, Atlanta, Cleveland, San Francisco, and Washington, DC. Web site visitors must complete a free registration process to access limited free resources; a fee is required to access other resources. http://foundationcenter.org/

Grant Wrangler provides a free, searchable database of grants and awards to make it easier for teachers, librarians, and parents to locate funding opportunities. Visitors to the Web site can subscribe to the Grant Wrangler Bulletin to receive a biweekly e-mail update on K–12 school and teacher grants. http://www.grantwrangler.com/

Disability.Gov is a federal Web site providing access to information about disabilities and opportunities in a variety of areas, including technology. Selecting Technology from the menu on the home page will reveal a link to Funding Sources. The Funding Sources page provides links to other government Web site pages as well as to external Web sites. http://www.disability.gov/

students after high school graduation should be involved in the transition planning process. State VR agencies are often involved in the transition plans of students with disabilities, especially those with the most severe disabilities. VR agencies may provide assistive technology while students are still in high school if the assistive technology will increase the students' chances for successful employment or pursuit of postsecondary education. Because VR funds must be targeted to improved employment outcomes, Kemp, Hourcade, and Parette (2000) suggest that "requests made for assistive technology through a state's Department of Vocational Rehabilitation might especially highlight the contributions that the technology will make towards the student's potential for vocational independence and/or productivity" (p. 7).

School district budgets, Medicaid, private insurance, and VR agencies are the major funding options available to school districts for purchasing assistive technology, but some districts pursue additional resources in their local communities. **Local civic organizations** such as the chamber of commerce, Lions club, Kiwanis club, and Rotary clubs are often tapped for support of assistive technology purchases. School and community fund-raisers may be other sources of funding (Bauder et al., 1997; Connecticut, 1999; Montana Office of Public Instruction, 2004). Renting or borrowing assistive technology, rather than outright purchase, can be considered as well. Regardless of the source of funding, "it is important to note … that the implementation of the devices and services required in the IEP cannot be delayed while the school system tries to find alternative funding sources" (Connecticut, 1999, p. 55).

In addition to the previously mentioned sources of funding, grant funding may be available for assistive technology. To be eligible to receive grant funding, applicants must demonstrate that they meet eligibility criteria and must provide sufficient, detailed documentation to convince the grantor that their proposal is worth supporting. Information associated with grant writing and funding sources can be found in the sidebar.

Implementing Assistive Technology Recommendations

A common complaint is that recommendations for the use of assistive technology fail to get implemented despite the technology having been acquired and delivered to the student's classroom (Bell & Blackhurst, 1999). Even ensuring that professionals have the requisite technological knowledge and skills does not equate to successful implementation. A number of other details must be addressed, or effective assistive technology implementation within students' educational programs is unlikely to happen.

Consider, for example, that a scan/read system has been recommended for a high school student with a learning disability to compensate for an inability to decode printed text. The system is purchased and everyone maintains high expectations for the student's academic success because of this acquisition. However, as the school year starts, the student's textbooks and other required reading materials are not available in electronic format. No one had been assigned to investigate whether there is a source for obtaining the needed materials in electronic format, and if so, to acquire them. Indeed, aside from the textbooks, no one even knows what other materials will be needed (e.g., the novels that will be read in English classes or the genre of books required for book reports). The textbooks have not been scanned because no one was assigned responsibility for this task, and it becomes apparent that scanning will be a lengthy and time-consuming process because the school does not have a high-speed scanner. No provisions have been made for scanning day-to-day printed materials such as handouts, worksheets, and study guides.

Implementation planning is vital to successful use of assistive technology, to avoid assistive technology abandonment, and to avoid scenarios such as the one just presented. For successful assistive technology implementation, a collaboratively developed **assistive technology**

TABLE 13.2   Assistive Technology Implementation Resources

Resource	URL	Comments
Assistive Technology Implementation: Working Together to Make a Measurable Difference	http://www.texasat.net/default.aspx?name=trainmod.implem	This is a complete instructional module on AT implementation from the Texas Assistive Technology Network that includes an implementation form
Assistive Technology Model Operating Guidelines	http://www.otap-oregon.org/Pages/Default.aspx	Find the complete guidelines by clicking on OTAP Publications. Implementation plan available separately at www.otap-oregon.org/Documents/AT%20Implementation%20Plan.doc
University of Kentucky Assistive Technology (UKAT) Project	http://edsrc.coe.uky.edu/www/ukatii/toolkit/index.html	This implementation form is one of the tools in the UKAT Toolkit.
Making It Work: Effective Implementation of Assistive Technology Guide	http://www.setbc.org/setbc/topics/effective_implementation_of_assistive_technology.html	The Introduction and seven downloadable sections are devoted to specific steps in the AT implementation process.

implementation plan (Quality Indicator #1) must incorporate many of the other Quality Indicators for Assistive Technology Implementation. *At a minimum,* the plan must do the following:

- Identify the specific individuals responsible for particular elements of the plan (Quality Indicator #3).
- Specify any necessary training that must be provided and those who need to be trained (Quality Indicator #5).
- Provide for follow up to determine if the assistive technology is working so adjustments or modifications can be made if needed (Quality Indicator #6).

It is fortunate that a wide variety of resources are available to help with developing implementation plans. Resources developed by organizations and individual leaders in the field of assistive technology are freely shared. Table 13.2 directs readers to these assistive technology implementation resources.

Students will realize the full potential of assistive technology only if it is **integrated into the curriculum**. This integration allows students with disabilities to more fully participate in the typical activities that occur within the classroom. Such integration does not occur by happenstance; it requires making purposeful decisions to consider the learning needs of all students and creating technology-enhanced lessons. Collaboration among the special education teacher, the classroom teacher, special education assistants/aides, and other members of the IEP team, as appropriate, is essential. It takes additional planning time to ensure lessons will be accessible because customized computer-based activities may need to be created with authoring software, Web sites that provide alternatives to hands-on activities may need to be located, and assistive technology and computers need setup time. Table 13.3 directs readers to resources that can help with the integration of assistive technology.

TABLE 13.3   Resources for Assistive Technology Integration

Resource	Description	URL
Georgia Project for Assistive Technology	Provides downloads on supporting participation in typical classroom activities, Creating Technology Enhanced Lesson Plans, and AT Intervention Plan	http://www.gpat.org/resources.aspx?PageReq=GPATImp
Learning Grids World	Provides free, downloadable curricular activities for use with Clicker 5, ClozePro, and Write Online by Crick Software	http://www.learninggrids.com
Classroom Suite Activity Exchange	Provides free downloadable curricular activities for use with Classroom Suite	http://www.intellitools.com/
National Center on Accessible Instructional Materials	Offers presentations, webinars, teleconferences, conference presentations, and workshops. The AIM Navigator uses a question-and-answer format to guide teachers through the selection and use of accessible instructional materials by IEP teams.	http://aim.cast.org/
Special Education Technology—British Columbia (SET-BC)	Section Six: Adapt Lessons for Technology Integration	http://www.setbc.org/download/LearningCentre/Topics/MakingItWork_Section6.pdf

Summary

- The Individuals with Disabilities Education Improvement Act of 2004 (IDEA 2004), Section 504 of the Rehabilitation Act of 1973, and the American with Disabilities Act (ADA) are the laws that entitle students in P–12 education to assistive technology in order to access education and education-related resources.
- Assistive technology must be *considered* for each student receiving special education services.
- Because the IEP drives the provision of special education services to students with disabilities, any discussion of assistive technology implementation must address the need to integrate technology into the IEP.
- Despite the legal mandates, there are many critical issues to address for successful consideration and implementation of assistive technology. Critical issues include the digital divide, cultural issues, misunderstandings about what constitutes assistive technology consideration, a dearth of assistive technology skills among educational professionals, school districts' information technology policies, funding, and implementation of technology recommendations,

- Recognizing these issues is a necessary first step to keep them from becoming obstacles to successful assistive technology implementation.
- The QIAT Consortium sets standards for effective assistive technology implementation.

- School district budgets, Medicaid, private insurance, and vocational rehabilitation agencies are the major funding options available to school districts for purchasing assistive technology, but some districts pursue additional grant opportunities and/or resources in their local communities.

Web Resources

For additional information on the topics listed, visit the following Web sites:

Making It Work: Implementation Issues
National Center for Technology Innovation
http://www.nationaltechcenter.org/index.php/category/i-can-soar/

Ottawa Network for Education's Implementing Assisitve Technology in the Classroom videos
http://www.scriptreaction.com/clients/ocri/teachers/videos/

Assistive Technology and the Law
U.S. Department of Education: Building the Legacy: IDEA 2004
http://idea.ed.gov/

Texas Assistive Technology Network: Providing Assistive Technology: A Legal Perspective (PDF)
http://www.texasat.net/docs/Legal.Persp.Guides.pdf

Digital Divide
ISTE Educator Resources
http://www.iste.org → Educator Resources → Equity → Digital Divide

Alliance for Digital Equality
http://www.digital-equality.org/

The Rehabilitation Provider's Guide to Cultures of the Foreign-Born
http://cirrie.buffalo.edu/monographs/index.php

Family Information Guide to Assistive Technology
http://www.fctd.info/resources/fig/Building Assistive Technology Skills

Resources for Assistive Technology Implementation
Georgia Project for Assistive Technology: Implementation and Intervention
http://www.gpat.org/resources.aspx

Oregon Technology Access Program: Assistive Technology Model Operating Guidelines
http://www.otaporegon.org/documents/at%20model%20operating%20guidelines.pdf

Videos of assistive technology from Valdosta State University
http://www.valdosta.edu/coe/ecre/ATRB/Video_Tips.htm

National Assistive Technology in Education Network
http://www.natenetwork.org/professional-support

Suggested Activities

1. *Check out the QIAT listserv.* Monitor the messages posted to the QIAT listserv by reviewing the archived postings available at http://lsv.uky.edu/archives/QIAT.html. Be prepared to discuss or write about the postings during class sessions.

2. *Add to your portfolio.* Add a copy of the standards of practice for your professional organization to your portfolio. Identify and highlight the standards related to assistive technology.

3. *Complete a self-evaluation.* Print a copy of the section titled "Knowledge and Skill Base for Special Education Technology Specialists" from the CEC publication *What Every Special Educator Must Know: Ethics, Standards, and Guidelines for Special Educators.* Access the publication by clicking on the "Professional Standards" link at the CEC Web site (http://www.cec.sped.org). Complete a self-assessment by reading each indicator, considering your skill level, and indicating whether you are at a novice or proficient level for each indicator. When you have completed the self-evaluation, create a professional development plan to address your area of greatest need.

4. *Integrate a low-tech device in the IEP.* You have a student who requires the use of a slant board to complete handwriting tasks. In which sections of the IEP might you include reference to using a slant board? Write statements that would be appropriate for each section.

5. *Research assistive technology in the IEP.* Interview a member of a local IEP team. Ask the following questions as well as others that you think are relevant. Submit a written summary of the interview and be prepared to discuss the interview in class.

   • Does the district have a prescribed process for assistive technology consideration while developing an IEP? If yes: What is the process?

   • How does the district document that assistive technology has been considered?

   • If assistive technology is included in the IEP, is an implementation plan developed? If yes: What is included in an implementation plan? If no: How do you make sure the assistive technology gets purchased and implemented?

   • Has any assistive technology training been provided for IEP team members?

6. *Conduct a school profile survey.* The School Profile of Assistive Technology Services is a survey designed to help improve assistive technology service delivery. Have at least two special education teachers at a school of your choice complete the survey. The school profile can be purchased from WATI (http://www.wati.org/products/products.html) or you can download a copy of the completed Wisconsin profile and edit it for your use (http://www.wati.org/AT_Services/pdf/profile.pdf, permission granted by WATI). Summarize the data from the completed surveys, identifying areas of strengths and areas in greatest need of improvement.

References

Bauder, D. K., Lewis, P., Bearden, C., & Gobert, C. (1997). *Assistive technology guidelines for Kentucky schools.* Frankfort, KY: Kentucky Department of Education.

Bausch, M. E., & Ault, M. J. (2008). Assistive technology implementation plan: A tool for improving outcomes. *Teaching Exceptional Children, 41*(1), 6–14.

Bausch, M. E., Ault, M. J., & Hasselbring, T. S. (2006). *Assistive technology planner: From IEP consideration to classroom implementation.* Lexington, KY: National Assistive Technology Research Institute.

Bausch, M. E., & Hasselbring, T. S. (2005). Using assistive technology: Is it working? *Threshold, 2*(1), 7–9.

Bell, J. K., & Blackhurst, A. E. (1999). *How assistive technology services can go awry.* Report of the University of Kentucky Assistive Technology Project. Retrieved April 3, 2007, from http://natri.uky.edu/resources/reports/awry.html

Bowser, G., & Reed, P. (2004). *A school administrator's desktop guide to assistive technology.* Arlington, VA: Technology and Media Division of the Council for Exceptional Children.

Brown, M. R., Higgins, K., & Hartley, K. (2001). Teachers and technology equity. *Teaching Exceptional Children, 33*(4), 32–39.

Center for Technology in Education at Johns Hopkins University and Technology and Media Division of CEC. (2005). *Considering the need for assistive technology within the individualized education program.* Arlington, VA: Technology and Media Division of CEC.

Connecticut State Department of Education and Connecticut Birth to Three System. (1999). *Guidelines for assistive technology.* Hartford, CT: Author.

Derer, K., Polsgrove, L., & Rieth, H. (1996). A survey of assistive technology applications in schools and recommendations for practice. *Journal of Special Education Technology, 13*(2), 62–80.

Gruner, A., Fleming, E., Carl, B., Diamond, C. M., Ruedel, K. L. A., Saunders, J., et al. (2000). *Synthesis on the selection and use of assistive technology* (Final report). Washington, DC: U.S. Department of Education.

Hager, R. M., & Smith, D. (2003). *The public school's special education system as an assistive technology funding source: The cutting edge.* Buffalo, NY: Neighborhood Legal Services.

Individuals with Disabilities Education Act of 2004, 20 U.S.C. § 1401D.

Jezewski, M. A., & Sotnik, P. (2001). *The rehabilitation service provider as culture broker: Providing culturally competent services to foreign born persons.* Buffalo, NY: Center for International Rehabilitation Research Information and Exchange.

Kemp, C. E., Hourcade, J. J., & Parette, H. P. (2000). Building an initial information base: Assistive technology funding resources for school-aged students with disabilities. *Journal of Special Education Technology, 15*(4), 15–24.

Lever-Duffy, J. & McDonald, J. B. (2011). *Teaching and learning with technology—4th edition.* Boston: Pearson.

Levin, D. A. (2005). From promise to practice: Honoring leadership in using technology for improved learning. *Threshold, 2*(1), 32.

Montana Office of Public Instruction. (2004). *A special education guide to assistive technology.* Helena, MT: Division of Special Education.

National Task Force on Technology and Disability. (2004). *Within our reach: Findings and recommendations of the National Task Force on Technology and Disability.* Flint, MI: The Disability Network.

Newton, D. (2002). *The impact of a local assistive technology team on the implementation of assistive technology in the school setting.* Unpublished doctoral dissertation, University of Cincinnati.

Newton, D. A., & Dell, A.G. (2009). Issues in assistive technology implementation: Resolving AT/IT conflicts. *Journal of Special Education Technology, 24*(1), 51–56.

Newton, D., & Shiller, B. (2005, October). *When assistive technology meets IT: The good, the bad, and the ugly.* Paper presented at the 23rd annual Closing the Gap Conference, Minneapolis, MN.

Pennsylvania Training and Technical Assistance Network. (n.d.). *Assistive technology in the IEP.* Harrisburg, PA: Pennsylvania Department of Education, p. 10.

QIAT Consortium. (2005). *Quality Indicators for assistive technology services: Research-based update.* Retrieved July 12, 2010, from http://natri.uky.edu/assoc_projects/qiat/qualityindicators.html

Sheldon, J. R., Jr., & Hager, R. M. (1997, May–June). Funding of assistive technology for persons with disabilities: The availability of assistive technology through Medicaid, public school special education programs and state vocational rehabilitation agencies. *Clearinghouse Review.* Retrieved February 25, 2006, from http://www.nls.org/atart.htm

Wallace, J. (1999). *Assistive technology in the student's Individualized Education Program: A handbook for parents and school personnel.* Richmond, VA: Virginia Assistive Technology System. Retrieved from the Virginia Assistive Technology System Web site: http://www.vats.org/athandbook.htm

Webopedia. (n.d.). Digital divide [Definition]. Retrieved July 30, 2010, from http://www.webopedia.com/TERM/D/digital_divide.html

14 IMPLEMENTATION OF ASSISTIVE TECHNOLOGY IN TRANSITION PLANNING

Focus Questions

1. How can assistive technology serve as a reasonable accommodation for students with disabilities in college?

2. What are the differences between the rights and requirements of the Individuals with Disabilities Education Act (IDEA) in the P–12 world and the rights and responsibilities under the Americans with Disabilities Act (ADA) in higher education?

3. What are the implications of assistive technology needs in college for transition planning and implementation in high school?

4. How can assistive technology help students who have autism, cognitive disabilities, or multiple disabilities achieve independence in home, work, and community settings?

5. How can apps for the iPhone, iPod Touch, and other handheld devices be used to provide visual supports for students with severe disabilities?

PREPARATION FOR TRANSITION FROM HIGH SCHOOL TO COLLEGE

The 1990s saw the first group of children with disabilities who had received a free appropriate public education (FAPE) under the Individuals with Disabilities Education Act (IDEA) graduate from high school. For many of these adolescents, going on to college was a logical next step, and, in fact, research reveals that the employment rate is substantially higher for people with disabilities who complete four years of college (50.3%) compared to those who complete only high school (30.2%) (Yelin & Katz, 1994). The number of students with disabilities attending college has increased significantly in the past decade. In one study, 9.3% of all undergraduates self-identified as having a disability (U.S. Department of Education Office for Civil Rights, 2002). Fifty-nine percent of these students were attending two-year programs. In another study, a breakdown by disability category revealed the following: 16% of first-year students with disabilities identified themselves as being blind or partially sighted, 15.4% self-reported health-related impairments, 8.6% reported deafness or hearing impairment, and 7% reported having orthopedic disabilities. The largest percentage reported among first-year students was learning disabilities—40.4% in 2000, in contrast to 16% in 1988 (Henderson, 2001).

Problems Students with Disabilities Face in College

Consider the typical tasks college students must complete in order to be successful in their academic endeavors. College students do a lot of reading—textbooks, journal articles, literary works, Web sites, and exams, to name a few. Many course assignments involve writing papers that require students to organize their thoughts, express themselves clearly, and demonstrate their knowledge. Students need to be able to attend lectures and discussions and simultaneously take notes. And finally, college students need to keep themselves organized and manage their time responsibly (e.g., turn in their assignments on time). (See Brinckerhoff, McGuire, & Shaw, 2002, p. 285, for a comprehensive list of the common demands placed on college students.)

Now consider the typical characteristics of students with learning disabilities. The National Joint Committee on Learning Disabilities (NJCLD, 1994), which developed the definition of learning disabilities that is accepted in higher education, defines **learning disabilities** as

> a heterogeneous group of disorders manifested by significant difficulties in listening, speaking, reading, writing, reasoning, or mathematical abilities. Problems in self-regulatory behaviors, social perception, and social interaction may exist with learning disabilities but do not by themselves constitute a learning disability. (pp. 65–66)

In other words, these are the students who tend to read slowly at best and struggle with reading comprehension; they have significant difficulties organizing their thoughts and expressing themselves in writing; they dread writing because they are poor spellers and the writing process is so frustrating; many cannot listen and take notes at the same time; some find math to be incomprehensible; some cannot master the intricacies of social interactions; and many students with learning disabilities are especially weak in executive functions such as task organization and time management.

Students with other disabilities also face obstacles in completing college-level work. For students with visual impairments, the tasks of reading, taking notes, researching information, and using a computer may be barriers to success. For students who are deaf or hard of hearing, listening to lectures and taking notes in class may present problems; communicating with faculty and peers and participating in group discussions pose additional obstacles for students who are deaf or hard of hearing. Students with physical disabilities may be extremely slow typists or may not be able to type on a computer at all.

Assistive technology offers solutions to these obstacles. With the right hardware, software, and assistive device, computers can help college students complete academic tasks in a timely fashion; decrease the anxiety and frustration associated with reading, writing, and communicating; gain access to and participate in the full range of learning opportunities; and maximize their independence (Burgstahler, 2003).

Typical Accommodations at College That Meet These Needs

Assistive technology can be used to help college students during classes and testing situations and in completing assignments. Chapters 2 and 3 of this text described specific ways computer technology can assist with writing, organizing, and reading; Chapter 6 addressed assistive technology tools that can enhance communication; and Chapters 7, 8, and 9 described multiple ways of accessing computers for students who cannot type on a regular QWERTY keyboard. All of these assistive technology tools may be helpful to college students *if* the tools meet the following criteria:

1. The assistive technology tool must be **easy to use** and **easy to customize**. The technology must make the accomplishing task *easier* and not more difficult for the student with a disability. Software that takes hours to set up or days to learn how to use is not appropriate. The device or software must also be easily customized to the student's specific needs or styles. If choosing a word prediction program, for example, the user will want to make sure he or she can add specialized vocabulary to the dictionary quickly and efficiently.

2. The technology tool must be **age appropriate**. Although there are many assistive technology devices and software programs that are effective at the elementary school level, college students will refuse to use them if they appear childish. The assistive technology tool chosen should blend in with the college environment. For example, college students who need word prediction (see Chapter 2) may prefer using a word prediction program that works along with Microsoft Word (a standard word processor) rather than a stand-alone program that has a simplified, juvenile-looking interface.

3. Closely related to the previous point, the assistive technology selected must be the **student's own choice**. It is extremely important that personal preference be a major criterion in technology selection in higher education (Burgstahler, 2003). The student has an understanding of his or her strengths, needs, and goals and priorities, which can be very helpful in determining appropriate technology solutions. It is also likely that the student has particular likes and dislikes. If these personal preferences are not honored, the student is unlikely to use the technology.

4. The technology tool must carefully **match the specific task** that needs to be accomplished and the **environment** in which it will take place. Note taking, for example, is a specialized form of writing. It needs to be done quickly, while the instructor is speaking or showing a video. Note taking takes place in a lecture hall or classroom, where there are other students present. Often there is no power source available. How does this affect the selection of assistive technology? Voice recognition is not likely to be a good choice because dictation will bother other students. Typing notes on a laptop that requires charging every 3 hours may not be effective because the course is in the afternoon, the laptop's power will be used up, and there may be no power outlet accessible to the student. In this case, the technology solution may be a LiveScribe Pulse Smartpen that records the professor's lecture and syncs it to the student's handwritten notes for review later on.

5. The assistive technology tool must be installed in a place that the student can **access easily**, whenever he or she needs it for completing college work. College students without disabilities usually have access to their institution's computers at least 16 hours a day; many colleges offer computer access 24/7. Assistive technology solutions must be available during the same time period as other technology resources. Computers and devices such as video magnifiers may be set up in a centrally located place such as the college library or a computer lab, or in a student's dormitory room. Software may be installed in computer labs or on students' own computers—this will vary by college. What must be avoided is installing the assistive technology in an office that is open only limited hours or a room that is inaccessible to the student who needs it.

6. **Training** and ongoing **technical support** must be provided to students and staff. Even if students already are skilled in using a particular piece of software, it is not unusual for technical problems to arise, especially on college computers that are set up for many different uses. Software and network conflicts are commonplace; therefore, provisions for providing technical support must be in place.

USER PROFILE

Serena

ASSISTIVE TECHNOLOGY AS A REASONABLE ACCOMMODATION IN COLLEGE

A desktop computer, screen-reading software, a scanner with an automatic document feed, scan/read software, a talking Braille note taker, a Braille embosser (printer), digital books, books-on-tape, and a tape player: These are the technology tools that Serena uses to complete her academic requirements in college. Serena, who is blind, is a first-year student who plans to major in either psychology or sociology, and to pursue her interest in Spanish. She takes notes in class using her lightweight Braille note taker, which has both speech output and a refreshable Braille display. It is also equipped with a Spanish

module so she can write and print out in Spanish as well as English. She writes papers using the Braille note taker or the desktop computer (she learned to touch-type in second grade); she can print Braille copies on the Braille embosser for her own reading and standard text copies on an inkjet printer for her professors.

Reading textbooks and other assigned readings requires a more elaborate arrangement. Some textbooks are available as digital books or books-on-tape from Recording for the Blind and Dyslexic (RFB&D); others are borrowed as Braille books or books-on-tape from the state Library for the Blind and Handicapped. Books and other reading material that are in the public domain are downloaded as electronic

text from a variety of Web sites and then read aloud by Serena's screen-reading program. A few textbook publishers have provided electronic files of their texts so they can be read by the screen-reading software. Reading assignments that are not available in any of these formats are scanned into her computer and read aloud via the scan/read software. The scan/read program can also send documents to the Braille note taker, which gives Serena the option of reading the books herself using the note taker's refreshable Braille display. This array of technology tools provides Serena with complete access to her college coursework. ■

Source: Adapted from "Utilizing Blindness Skills in College," by S. Cucco, *TECH-NJ, 16*(1), p. 6.

There Are No IEPs in College

Although many of the technology tools used at the college level are the same as those used in the P–12 environment, the laws affecting students with disabilities and the process of obtaining assistive technology are completely different. IDEA is not in effect in higher education. Colleges have no legal responsibility to identify students with disabilities or involve parents in decision making. There are no IEPs in college (Varrassi, 2004). In fact, there is no *right* to college; no one in this country—with or without disabilities—is *entitled* to a higher education.

Rather, in higher education, the relevant law is a civil rights law that protects people with disabilities from discrimination in admission to college and participation in college activities. The two federal laws that provide this protection are

- Section 504 of the Rehabilitation Act (originally passed in 1973, with subsequent reauthorizations)
- The Americans with Disabilities Act (ADA, passed in 1990)

The ADA upholds and extends the compliance standards of Section 504, which had been passed years earlier (AHEAD, 2001). Section 504 pertains only to those colleges and universities that receive federal funds, whereas the ADA applies to all entities—public, under Title II, and private under Title III. The ADA states

> No otherwise qualified individual with a disability shall, by reason of such
> disability, be excluded from participation in or be denied the benefits of the services,
> programs, or activities of a public entity, or be subjected to discrimination by any
> such entity. (www.wrightslaw.com/info/sec504.summ.rights.htm)

In other words, a disability cannot be grounds for excluding a person from a college, an academic program, a class, a residence hall, or a college activity, if the person is qualified. The ADA guarantees access to equal opportunity; you could say that it entitles students with disabilities to "an opportunity to compete with their non-disabled peers" (Rothstein, 2002, p. 77).

Reasonable Accommodations

Under Section 504 and the ADA, colleges must provide—at no cost to the student—reasonable accommodations to make their programs accessible to students with disabilities. Examples are scheduling a class in a first-floor classroom to accommodate a student who uses a wheelchair, providing sign language interpreters for a student who is deaf, and arranging for extended time on tests for a student who has learning disabilities. The second column in Table 14.1 lists typical accommodations that colleges provide matched to the corresponding task needing to be completed.

In many cases, providing an effective assistive technology tool is considered a reasonable accommodation. As in Section 504, Title II of the ADA uses the phrase "auxiliary aids and services" to refer to devices and services that make programs and materials available to people with disabilities:

> A public entity shall furnish appropriate aids and services where necessary to
> afford an individual with a disability an equal opportunity to participate in a service,
> program, or activity. (U.S. Department of Education, 1998)

Section 504 regulations state that auxiliary aids and services "are not required to produce the identical result or level of achievement" for people with and without disabilities, but they must afford people with disabilities *equal opportunity* to obtain the same result, to gain the same benefit, or to reach the same level of achievement" (U.S. Department of Education, 1998, italics added). Similarly, the *effectiveness* of an auxiliary aid or service is determined by whether or not it succeeds in equalizing the opportunity for the student with a disability to participate in the educational program.

For example, auxiliary aids and services for a student who is hard of hearing may include the use of an assistive listening system (see Chapter 6) because this device offers the student an equal opportunity to learn from a lecture. Auxiliary aids for a student who is blind and a Braille reader may include a Braille printer and Braille translation applications so that the student has an equal opportunity to produce written assignments. For a student who has visual impairments, providing screen magnification applications provides access to the college library's services and to computers for reading, writing, and research (see Chapters 7 and 8). For students who struggle with reading and writing, providing text-to-speech programs (e.g., talking word processing applications, text readers, or scan/read systems) for class assignments and testing may be an effective auxiliary aid (see Chapters 2 and 3). The third column in Table 14.1 lists common technology-based accommodations in college.

Of particular relevance to the topic of assistive technology is that although colleges are required to provide auxiliary aids and services, they are not required to provide the most sophisticated technology available. A college "has flexibility in choosing the specific aid

TABLE 14.1	Accommodations for College Students with Disabilities Linked to Tasks Required in College Coursework	
Task	**Typical Nontechnology Accommodations**	**Technology-Based Accommodations**
Note taking	Student note takers using carbonless paper	Use of a portable note taker (e.g., Neo) Smart pen to record lectures and sync to notes Whiteboard capturing devices
Understanding lectures	Sign language interpreters	C-print captioning Assistive listening system
Taking tests	Extended time on tests Distraction-free environment for testing	Word processing application for essay exams Use of spell-check feature or handheld speller Use of a calculator Text-to-speech software for reading support
Accessing course materials	Sign-language-interpreted videos Arranging for materials to be translated into Braille	Captioned videos Providing handouts in electronic format Making course Web sites accessible
Reading	Providing readers	Books in alternate formats (e.g., e-text) Scan/read systems with highlighting and text-to-speech Text readers Audio books Video magnifiers
Completing papers and other assignments		Screen magnification applications Screen-reading applications Text-to-speech and word prediction applications Voice recognition applications Graphic organizer applications
Accessing the Internet		Providing screen magnification, screen reading, or text-to-speech applications Making college Web pages accessible
Registering for classes	Priority registration	Making college Web-based systems accessible
Telecommunicating		Providing a telecommunications device for the deaf (TTY) E-mail Text messaging Instant messaging Video relay system

or service it provides to the student, as long as the aid or service selected is effective" (U.S. Department of Education, 1998). This means that a student may be provided with a different technology product from that which he or she requested. For example, the college may provide a different brand of screen-reading application than requested or an older FM system instead of the latest digital assistive listening system.

TABLE 14.2 College and Student Obligations Under the Americans with Disabilities Act (ADA)	
College's Obligations Under the ADA	**Student's Obligations Under the ADA**
Ensure that qualified applicants and students have access to the college's programs.	Self-identify that he or she has a disability (following the specific college's stated policies and procedures). Provide appropriate documentation of the disability.
Provide reasonable accommodations for the student's documented disabilities.	Request specific accommodation(s).
Demonstrate a good-faith effort to provide the student with meaningful access.	Follow the agreed-upon procedures for using the accommodations.

The term *reasonable* in the phrase "reasonable accommodation" is not defined in the law and is still being debated in the courts. It is generally understood to mean that providing the accommodation will not cause "undue burden" to the institution. Colleges would be hard-pressed to claim that purchasing a piece of software or a $100 flatbed scanner represents undue burden, considering the millions of dollars most spend annually on technology. Therefore, under Section 504 and the ADA, many college students with disabilities are finding access to assistive technology tools to be an important accommodation (Bryant, Bryant, & Rieth, 2002).

Procedures for Obtaining Assistive Technology in College

How is assistive technology provided to students with disabilities in college? To answer this question, we must examine the procedural requirements of the ADA. In higher education, the responsibility for documenting a disability and requesting accommodations falls on the *student*, not on the educational institution. The college is not required to find or assess students who have disabilities. If a student chooses to keep his or her disability a secret, that is the student's prerogative and the college is not required to provide any kind of auxiliary aid. If a student does not follow through on his or her obligations under the law, the institution is also not required to provide accommodations. Table 14.2 summarizes the obligations of colleges and students with disabilities under the ADA.

What is particularly important to note is that the student must specifically *request* a piece of assistive technology as an accommodation if he or she believes it will provide access to the curriculum and an equal opportunity to demonstrate his or her knowledge. The accommodation must be clearly linked to the student's particular needs. Table 14.1 illustrates the link between specific tasks students must complete and technology-based accommodations that may assist students in successfully completing those tasks.

Legal and Procedural Differences Between ADA and IDEA

Learning that the IDEA does not apply to higher education and that college students have a much greater responsibility if they are to receive accommodations (and parents have a greatly reduced role) is often a shock for students and their parents. Unlike the IDEA, which, under its zero reject policy, guarantees an education to all school-aged children regardless of ability, the ADA protects only those individuals who meet the stated qualifications of a college or program. The phrase "otherwise qualified" in the ADA means that only those people who are able to meet the technical and academic qualifications for entry into a school, program, or activity are protected by the ADA. This means that although colleges are required to make what are called "minor academic adjustments," they are *not* required to make substantial modifications to their curricula or course requirements. A good example of how this differs from the P–12 world is that although

TABLE 14.3	Comparison of the Requirements and Procedures of the Individuals with Disabilities Education Act (IDEA) and the Americans with Disabilities Act (ADA)	
	IDEA (K–12)	**ADA (College)**
Rights guaranteed by the law	Free appropriate public education (FAPE)	Prohibits discrimination on the basis of disability.
Who is covered	Every child; concept of zero reject	Students who are "otherwise qualified."
Identification and evaluation of students with disabilities	District responsible for identifying students with disabilities, evaluating them, and covering the costs	College has no such responsibility. Students must self-identify and provide appropriate documentation. If an evaluation is needed, the expense is the student's responsibility.
Determining services	Individualized education plan (IEP) developed by team Curriculum modifications and special programs are common	Reasonable accommodations, including auxiliary aids and services, must be requested by student. Academic adjustments that equalize opportunity for participation are required; substantial modifications to curriculum and lowering standards are not required.
Personal devices and services such as wheelchairs, hearing aids, and personal care attendants	Provided by district if determined to be necessary (and included in IEP)	Colleges are not required to provide these.
Role of parents	Parents must be included in decision making	College students are older than 18 and are considered adults. No parent consultation is required.
Appeals process	Right to due process as spelled out in the law	College grievance procedure and then a complaint with U.S. Department of Education's Office of Civil Rights must be filed.

a reasonable accommodation may be extended time on tests or a distraction-free environment for testing, the law does *not* require colleges to modify the *contents* of an exam. Another example is that colleges are not obligated to provide students with disabilities more intensive tutoring services than they provide to students without disabilities. Table 14.3 summarizes the major differences between the requirements and procedures of the IDEA and the ADA.

IMPORTANCE OF TRANSITION PLANNING IN HIGH SCHOOL

Because many of you are primarily concerned with the P–12 world, you may be wondering why this chapter has focused on students with disabilities who have exited high school. The reason is that in order to access and use technology tools effectively in college, students with disabilities must be adequately prepared in *high school*. Technology access that leads to greater success in high school and postsecondary environments "has the potential to improve career outcomes for people with disabilities" (Burgstahler, 2003, p. 8). However, the differences between the protections and procedures of the IDEA and the ADA described previously have been identified as a serious barrier to technology access for people with disabilities (National Council on Disability, 2000). These differences make transition planning in high school especially important for students in special education who want to go on to college.

IDEA mandates that **transition planning** begin at age 16; starting at age 16 means that most students will have 2 to 3 years to learn the skills they will need to succeed in college. What skills do they need to learn? Transition plans for students with disabilities who want to attend college must include the development of two kinds of skills:

1. Assistive technology skills for independence (Behnke & Bowser, 2010)
2. Self-advocacy skills

Assistive Technology Skills

High schools must make it a high priority to identify assistive technology tools that will help students with disabilities work more independently and efficiently. As mentioned in Chapter 9, students must develop skills in four different but complementary areas: operational skills, functional skills, strategic skills, and social skills (Behnke & Bowser, 2010). **Operational skills** are the technical skills that are needed for operating the device. For example, a student must know how to turn a device on and off, select the appropriate icons or keys, and use basic commands. **Functional skills** involve knowing how to do the tasks for which the device is intended and how to use the assistive technology tool to help with that task, such as writing or expressive communication. Strategic skills involve the ability to decide which tool or strategy to use for a specific activity and knowing when to use and not use an AT device. **Social skills** in the context of assistive technology involve knowing how to use the technology appropriately around other people. For example, a student may need to learn how to explain the use of a LiveScribe Smart Pen for note taking to a skeptical college professor. Students must be skilled in these four skill areas if they are to successfully use the technology in college.

High school is the perfect time and place to *teach* students these assistive technology skills. Brinckerhoff, McGuire, and Shaw (2002) provide a detailed timetable for transition planning in high school that recommends that students "try out auxiliary accommodations and auxiliary aids" (pp. 38–39) and learn about technology tools in Grades 9 and 10. Once appropriate technology tools have been identified (see the chapters in Parts I and II of this text), students need to be given multiple opportunities to *practice* their new technology skills so that they become comfortable with the technology, they learn to customize it to their specific needs and preferences, and they are able to use it quickly and effortlessly. If this kind of training begins in high school, by the time students enter college, they will be prepared to use assistive technology to meet the academic demands they will face in college.

Serena: Implementation Details

Reread the paragraph in Serena's user profile that describes the ways she obtains accessible textbooks. No fewer than five methods are utilized, including scanning one page at a time. This is a much more involved and time-consuming process than the traditional method sighted students use to obtain their textbooks—a trip to the college bookstore or a few mouse clicks at a Web site. It takes Serena up to 3 months to locate and obtain accessible versions of all of her textbooks. This means she must get reading lists from her professors well in advance, and she must contact the various organizations and check out several Web sites to see if the books are already available as recordings or electronic text. These tasks require Serena to manage her time carefully, keep track of all the information, and advocate for herself. Without her attending to these implementation details, the technology tools themselves would be ineffective.

Self-Advocacy Skills

Being skilled in using specific assistive technology tools, however, is not enough. In order to receive accommodations in higher education, college students need to be able to advocate for themselves so that they will be prepared for their increased responsibilities in accessing accommodations in college. Self-advocacy refers to "the ability to act as a causal agent in one's life and to make independent choices and decisions" (Behnke & Bowser, 2010, p. 58). College students with disabilities need to be able to articulate which assistive technology tools are effective for them. This means that self-advocacy skills need to be taught in high school. Barr, Harttnan, and Spillane (1995) provide a good explanation of self-advocates:

> People who can speak up in logical, clear and positive language to communicate about their needs. Self-advocates take responsibility for themselves. To be a self-advocate, each student must learn to understand his or her particular type of disability, and the resultant academic strengths and weaknesses. Most importantly, high school students with disabilities need to become comfortable with describing to others both their disability and the academic related needs. (p. 3)

In order to advocate for themselves in college, students with disabilities need to be able to explain the nature of their disabilities and to articulate the strategies and adaptations that will support their learning. Empowering adaptations often include assistive technology tools, so students need to learn—in high school—the advocacy skills they will need to request specific assistive technology solutions as reasonable accommodations in college. Brinckerhoff and colleagues (2002, pp. 38–39) recommend that students learn about the nature of their disability, their preferred learning styles, and their rights and responsibilities under Section 504 and the ADA in Grades 9 and 10. Combining the teaching of strong self-advocacy skills with appropriate assistive technology skills will enable students with disabilities to transition to the college environment smoothly and successfully.

Recognizing the importance of this combination of skills, the QIAT Consortium has developed a model of quality indicators that supports success in postsecondary education for students who use assistive technology. The QIAT-PS (Quality Indicators in Assistive Technology—Post-Secondary), called Self-Advocacy and Self-Determination, include two sets of guidelines: Student Guidelines and College Guidelines. The QIAT-PS Student Guidelines are intended to serve as a tool for students and families as they consider the transition from high school to the college environment. The seven Student Guidelines are organized by (1) a quality indicator, (2) questions students should ask themselves to see if they meet the indicator, and (3) other tasks that relate to the specific indicator. The QIAT-PS College Guidelines are intended as a tool for college personnel as they develop, articulate, and implement policies and procedures that contribute to the successful transition and inclusion of students with disabilities in all areas of college life. Table 14.4 summarizes these two sets of guidelines and highlights the relationship between the Student Guidelines and the College Guidelines. The seven quality indicators are the same for both, but the questions that need to be asked by students and those that need to be addressed by college personnel differ.

When students master the skills discussed earlier and both high school and college professionals provide appropriate supports, students' use of assistive technology will continue to be successful in new settings. An excellent resource called the *Student Transition Planning Guide for Assistive Technology* is available from the Texas Assistive Technology Network (TATN): http://www.texasat.net/docs/TXTransStudentPlanningguideforAT.pdf

TABLE 14.4   Quality Indicators in Assistive Technology—Post Secondary (QIAT-PS) Self-Advocacy & Self-Determination Indicators

Indicator	STUDENT Questions	COLLEGE Questions
1. Self Awareness: The student is aware of the various factors of his or her disability and is knowledgeable about needed accommodations.	Can I accurately describe my disability and its impact on my educational process, including educational achievement and participation in academic and campus life activities?	Are our disability support staff and others trained to work with students with disabilities and assistive technology needs to assist in defining their disability and determining their accommodations?
2. Self-Advocacy: The student understands that under ADA and other federal and state laws, he or she is responsible for disclosure of a disability that requires accommodations in order to gain access to the curricula and materials.	What do I want to disclose about my disability, and to whom?	Does the college have a campus culture of inclusiveness that facilitates self-advocacy and provides professional development to staff to enable student-faculty collaboration regarding accommodations and assistive technologies?
3. Communication: The student has the communication and interpersonal skills to communicate with faculty concerning confidentiality, documentation, evaluation, and grievance procedures.	Can I communicate my needs to the appropriate people in a timely manner?	Are our marketing materials, course catalogs, procedures, and Web resources accessible and assessed frequently regarding their appropriateness? Does staff have open communication policies?
4. Self-Advocacy and Leadership: The student makes a self-advocacy plan to guide staff in the provision of AT and accommodations that allow access to the curriculum and aid independence.	Do I have a plan regarding the assistive technology I need both for daily living activities and educational success?	Do we promote an inclusive campus culture and encourage and actively seek input from students with disabilities in assistive technology planning and implementation on campus, in campus living environments, and in online/distance learning environments?
5. Self-Evaluation and Self-Determination: The student evaluates his or her use of AT and makes adjustments to goals when necessary, including justifying and acquiring any new technology needed.	Do I understand the difference between my use of AT for daily living and AT for academic use, and what the college will legally provide?	Do we work with students to make timely changes to assistive technology supports and accommodations that may be necessary for different academic tasks and environments?
6. Student Initiative and Decision Making: The student independently chooses the appropriate AT for each situation and makes long-term decisions about assistive technology device acquisition and supports.	Is the assistive technology I need, or have been using, different from what the college provides?	Do we support the integration of personal assistive technology into the classroom and labs when appropriate, including the provision of professional development when needed?
7. Assistive Technology Problem Solving: The student identifies problems with AT use, is able to identify the AT supports and services needed to solve AT problems, and communicates these solutions to instructors and disability services staff	Do I have a plan to deal with assistive technology problems that may arise?	Do we promote collaboration among the student, various support services, and faculty in solving AT challenges and problems?

Source: From Quality Indicators in Assistive Technology—Post Secondary (QIAT-PS) by R. Holland, B. Ayres, J. Peters, & D. Wilkinson, 2010, *TECH-NJ, 21*, pp. 8–9. Reprinted with permission.

ASSISTIVE TECHNOLOGY FOR TRANSITION FROM HIGH SCHOOL TO HOME, WORKPLACE, AND COMMUNITY

Students with disabilities who are not headed for college also need careful planning for their transition from high school to adult life, and they, too, can benefit from the use of assistive technology. Many of these students have cognitive disabilities, autism, or multiple disabilities, and their transition plans often focus on the enhancement of their communication, social, self-care, leisure, and work skills. Chapters 10, 11, and 12 addressed the use of augmentative communication technology to support students whose speech is not adequate to meet their communication needs. This section summarizes other kinds of assistive technology that can help students who have severe disabilities develop skills for living and working in the community.

TECHNOLOGY TO TEACH FUNCTIONAL SKILLS

In Chapters 4 and 5, applications to teach academic skills were presented. Students with severe disabilities, especially cognitive disabilities, however, have learning needs that extend beyond the standard academic curriculum. Often, the goals for these students focus on optimizing independence in areas such as communication, vocation, personal grooming, laundry, dining, meal preparation, housekeeping, leisure activities, and money management (Rocchio, 1995). Collectively, these are known as functional skills.

Instructional Applications to Teach Functional Skills

Technology-based activities can be a highly motivating way to teach functional skills. Well-designed applications, as discussed in Chapter 5, provide students who have severe disabilities with the consistent, repetitive practice needed to master functional skills in risk-free environments. Programs typically focus on low-level content and provide simple, uncluttered presentations. It is essential that applications for students with severe disabilities offer options to customize both presentation features and content. Since most of these students are nonreaders or beginning readers, the application must provide graphics and spoken instructions that can be repeated as often as needed. To accommodate students' motor disabilities and/or attention deficits, the application should allow for adjustments in response time, and it should be accessible by a variety of methods, such as single-switch scanning. Auditory feedback often helps keep students engaged, but teachers must have the option to turn it off in case it is distracting instead of helpful. Most importantly, high-quality applications that teach functional skills enable teachers to set the level of difficulty and select specific content.

Instructional applications that meet these criteria are available from Laureate Learning Systems (http://www.laureatelearning.com). Laureate's programs teach functional skills such as cause and effect, turn taking, early vocabulary, syntax, cognitive concepts, and early reading. The programs can be accessed using a mouse, touch screen, or switch to accommodate a wide range of physical and cognitive disabilities (see Chapter 8). For example, My House: Language Activities of Daily Living teaches students vocabulary for items in six rooms of a typical home: living room, dining room, kitchen, bedroom, bathroom, and utility room. The teacher can preselect the vocabulary to be presented to match students' ability levels. In the kitchen, for example, students may be learning to identify only basic items such as the stove, refrigerator, table, and chair, or they may be at a more advanced level and learning to identify items such as utensils, hot water tap, potholder, and paper towel dispenser (see Figure 14.1). My School and My Town are similar programs that focus on the vocabulary students are likely to encounter in their schools and their communities.

FIGURE 14.1 Kitchen screen in My House: The Language Activities of Daily Living (Reprinted with permission of Laureate Learning Systems).

Attainment Company also publishes a series of customizable applications that focus on teaching functional skills such as basic money skills and time telling. First Money teaches students to identify money names and values; in Spending Money, students go from store to store to buy items on a shopping list; and in Making Change, students act as a store clerk as they practice making change. TimeScales provides multiple-choice questions and a set-the-clock option in three modules of increasing difficulty: hours of the day, minutes of the hour, and from time to time. Teachers can choose from varying clock faces or can select audio cues only. The Functional Skills System from the Conover Company includes a collection of applications that teach the reading of signs. Each module shows an actual sign, a video of a person in the community referring to the sign, a multiple-choice "find the sign" activity, and a generalization activity. Included are signs and words from a clothing store, grocery store, pharmacy, restaurant, school, public transportation, entertainment in the community, and an emergency situation.

Several companies publish applications that teach cause and effect to students with severe disabilities. These programs are also used to teach students how to use a switch for computer access or augmentative communication access. SoftTouch and Inclusive TLC offer a series of programs that are designed to teach students to interact with the computer. The programs use music, colorful graphics, morphing, and/or humorous pictures to get a student's attention and engage them. Auditory and visual prompts are provided.

Authoring Applications to Teach Functional Skills

Simple authoring programs, which were introduced in Chapter 5, can be used by teachers to create curricular activities appropriate and accessible for students with severe and/or multiple disabilities. My Own BookShelf (SoftTouch, Inc.), for example, allows teachers to create customized, accessible electronic storybooks (see Figure 14.2). Teachers can import pictures of their students to create personalized social stories, create stories on topics that appeal to individual students, create stories with controlled vocabulary, or create any other type of story. Any story created with My Own BookShelf is accessible using the standard keyboard or mouse, an adapted keyboard or mouse, or with the built-in scanning feature that makes it switch-accessible.

FIGURE 14.2 My Own Bookshelf offers teachers the option of designing books to meet their students' specific interests and needs.

Source: Image courtesy of SoftTouch, Inc.

ClozePro v. 2 (Crick Software) is another example of an authoring application that can be used to construct activities to teach functional skills (Figure 14.3). It can also be used to create assessments. Using ClozePro, teachers can create fill-in-the-blank activities on any topic to match students' reading levels, curricular content, visual presentation requirements, need for picture cues, and/or need for auditory output. Text-to-speech enables students to listen to the sentence they are working on and the multiple choices. Words can be supported with pictures for students with weak reading skills. Teachers can decide if students will have access to the prompt tool and, if so, the nature of the prompt that will be given. They can also choose how many choices to include in the answer blank. ClozePro is switch-accessible so it is easily used by students with severe physical disabilities for whom scanning is their access method.

Clicker 5 (Crick Software) provides teachers with the ability to create what Crick Software calls "hit and happen" activities; these are also known as cause-and-effect activities in which users simply execute a mouse click using a standard mouse, mouse emulator, or switch (see Chapters 8 and 11) to cause "something" to happen on the computer. The something can be a visual display, auditory output, or a combination of the two and can be customized to be meaningful, interesting, and/or motivating according to students' individual needs. Clicker 5 also functions as a talking word processor that affords teachers the opportunity to create grids containing word banks, phrases, sentences, numbers, pictures, or any combination of these that students can insert into a document with the click of a mouse (see Chapter 2). These features allow teachers to create literacy, science, and social studies activities for students who are non-readers or at the emergent literacy level (see Figure 2.4).

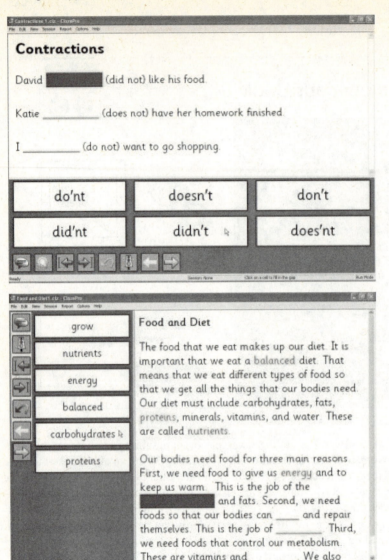

FIGURE 14.3 ClozePro's fill-in-the-blank activities can provide students with wordbars.

Source: Printed with permission of Crick Software, Inc.

Using computers to create learning activities takes time and practice, but teachers will find that the longer they work with a specific authoring program, the quicker they will become at creating activities. In addition, several companies now use their Web sites to provide a venue for teacher's to share teacher-created materials. Rather than always having to always design original activities, teachers can search their Web sites—such as Crick Software's Learning Grids Web site (http://www.learninggrids.com)—to see if someone else has already created an activity that can be used as is or modified to meet the needs of their own students.

Technology to Provide Visual Supports

Students who have cognitive disabilities, autism, and/or multiple disabilities often have difficulty with self-management and personal organization. Their lack of these skills has been successfully addressed through the use of visual supports such as picture schedules and activity sequences, which are sequential, pictorial representations of events or tasks that cue a student to complete them (McClannahan & Krantz, 1999). Similar to a "to-do" list, they provide a visual reminder of what happens next and what will occur later. Picture schedules (see Figure 14.4) help students see the day's structure at a glance and can reduce the anxiety that some students experience when it is time to transition from one activity to another. By helping students understand what is to come and what is expected of them, picture schedules can reduce confusion and acting-out behaviors (McClannahan & Krantz, 1999). Activity sequences (see Figure 14.5) are step-by-step pictorial representations of a particular task such as brushing one's teeth, cooking popcorn in the microwave, or taking out the trash. They are an effective strategy for shifting students from a reliance on verbal prompts (adult assistance) to more independent completion of self-care and vocational tasks (McClannahan & Krantz, 1999).

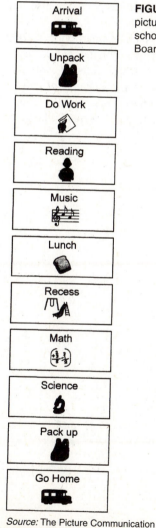

FIGURE 14.4 Sample picture schedule of a school day, made with Boardmaker.

FIGURE 14.5 Sample on-the-job activity sequence, made with Boardmaker.

Visual supports can make use of any of the symbol systems discussed in Chapter 10, such as line drawings or tactile symbols. For students who need concrete symbols, visual supports can be created by taking digital photos of the actual student in each environment or completing each step in an activity. The use of photos of people the student knows in environments with which the student is familiar is an effective strategy that reduces the need for generalization.

Computer technology offers several convenient ways to create and use visual supports. Boardmaker (Mayer-Johnson) or Pogo Boards (AbleNet), symbol-generating systems discussed in Chapter 10, offer templates for picture schedules and activity sequences. Using these templates, teachers and parents can create picture schedules and activity sequences quickly on a computer and then print them in color and laminate them for protection. Some teachers tape a student's daily schedule to a corner of his or her desk so that a visual reminder is always in the student's field of vision. For students who are learning or working in the community, a picture schedule or activity sequence can be folded up and put in a pocket. Visual supports can also be easily created in Microsoft Word or PowerPoint using clip art or digital photos.

With the advent of inexpensive, easy-to-use mobile technology such as smart phones, the iPod Touch, and the iPad, visual supports are increasingly being provided by handheld devices that utilize touch screen technology. iPrompts (HandHold Adaptive), which runs on Apple's iPhone, iPod Touch and iPad devices, presents picture-based prompts that have been configured by teachers and parents to help students stay on task and transition between activities. The app provides hundreds of stock photos and allows users to add digital pictures from their iPhone's built-in camera (see Figure 14.6).

FIGURE 14.6 Sample talking picture schedule created with the iPrompt app.
Source: Image courtesy of HandHold Adaptive, LLC.

iCommunicate (Grembe) and First-Then (Good Karma Applications) also use digital photos to create picture schedules and provide the option to record messages linked to each picture. The messages can be an audio version of the visual prompt or it can provide audio reinforcement. Picture Planner (Cognitopia) is designed so that students with cognitive disabilities can construct personalized picture schedules for themselves on a computer and then use the schedules either in a printed version or on mobile devices. The program provides line drawing symbols (students can also import photos of familiar people and objects) and text-to-speech feedback. Activity sequences can also be made using video clips on an iPod Touch.

Computer-Generated and Video-Based Social Stories

iCommunicate, Boardmaker, Pogo Boards, PowerPoint, and other programs can also be used to create social stories (see Figure 14.7). Social stories are teacher- (or parent-) authored short stories that are written to help a student who has autism learn "the social information he may be lacking" (Gray, 2000, p. 13-1). They take advantage of many children's strengths in the visual modality to

FIGURE 14.7 Sample pages from a social story.

This social story was written for a nine-year-old boy who had autism and a moderate hearing loss to address the disruptive vocalizations and hand flapping behaviors he displayed when entering the classroom and during reading instruction. The social story was developed to help him gain an understanding of social routines and expectations in the typical class. After two weeks of using the social story, the teacher reported a significant decrease in the target behaviors. The student continued to use the social story to remind him of the expectations.

When I enter reading class I should sit in my seat and keep my hands still and my voice quiet.

When I am quiet and still, it is easy for me to do what the teacher wants me to do.

I can help myself remember by reading my social story book.

When I follow the teacher's instructions, I am happy because I can do better work.

Source: Courtesy of Eva Scott, New Jersey Consortium of Deafblindness.

provide instruction without the complications of interpersonal interactions (Scattone et al., 2002). Social stories are often used as part of a social skills training curriculum to teach students how to interact with other people, and they address skills such as reading body language, looking at situations from another person's perspective, and responding in socially acceptable ways. Many teachers use them to help students cope with changes in classroom routines, such as the presence of a substitute teacher, an upcoming school assembly or field trip, or a planned fire drill (Gray, 2000).

Gray (2000) presents clear guidelines for the content and format of social stories, including the specific kinds of sentences that need to be included. Technology makes the creation and production of social stories easier, and it presents the added advantage of being able to personalize the story for each particular student. For example, if a student has problems waiting in line and acts out whenever the class is told to "line up," the teacher could write a simple social story and illustrate it with digital photos of the teacher standing at the door giving instructions; the other children lining up appropriately; this particular student getting in line appropriately; and the entire class, including this student, walking appropriately down the hall. This story could be created on a mobile device using iCommunicate, which could also read the story aloud, or it could be printed out and "bound" like a book for a low-tech version. Social stories created in PowerPoint can also be recorded and read aloud in the student's own voice.

Another technique that has been shown to be effective in teaching social skills to students on the autism spectrum is video modeling (Mc Coy & Hermansen, 2007). Kuder and Lord (2009) combined the idea of social stories with video modeling and presented modified video-based social stories on an Apple iPod to seven students with autism, ages 8 to 13. The iPod was chosen because of its age appropriateness, portability, and ease of use. The topics of the videos were crossing the street, shopping in a grocery store, and going to a restaurant. Findings from this study revealed that video-based social stories improved the students' ability to complete community-based social tasks, increased the frequency of appropriate communication, and led to improvements in their behavior in the three social situations.

Simple Technology for Self-Care and Leisure Activities

For many students who have severe physical disabilities that interfere with normal movement patterns, functional curriculum goals often involve increasing their participation in everyday

Example of using a switch for partial participation. Although the child does not have the motor skills needed to add ingredients to the mixer, he can participate in the cooking activity by turning the mixer on and off with his switch.

activities such as self-care, food preparation, leisure, and vocational tasks. Although these students may not be able to complete tasks completely independently, they can benefit from—and should be given opportunities to engage in—**partial participation**—completing a portion of the activity (Baumgart et al., 1982). Simple technology using adapted switches, which were discussed in Chapters 8 and 11, can be used to facilitate partial participation. Adapted switches can be connected to battery-operated devices such as audio players, funny toy animals that sing and dance, remote control cars, or other entertaining electronic gadgets. Through a special interface, they can also be connected to tabletop appliances such as hair dryers, fans, and kitchen mixers.

For example, a student who has spastic cerebral palsy that causes her hands to be fisted most of the time can participate in self-grooming by turning a hair dryer and a lighted makeup mirror on and off with an adapted switch that she activates with her fist (Levin & Scherfenberg, 1990). Although someone else needs to do the actual styling of her hair and putting on of makeup, the use of simple technology enables this student to be an active participant in these grooming tasks. This same student can help her mother bake cookies by turning the electric mixer on and off with the same adapted switch. Using simple technology for partial participation in vocational activities, this student could activate an electric stapler, electric three-whole punch, or a paper shredder if she works with a partner in an office environment (Levin & Scherfenberg, 1990).

For students who cannot use their hands at all, the switches can be mounted so that they are accessible to whatever body part the student can control. Some students have better head control than hand control, so a switch can be mounted next to their cheek or the side of their head for activation by a turn of their head. Switches also can be positioned so they can be activated by a foot, elbow, or knee. Smaller, more sensitive switches are also available for students who have only very limited, weak movements.

PLANNING FOR TRANSITION TO HOME, WORKPLACE, AND COMMUNITY

Just as students with learning disabilities need to be prepared for college by learning assistive technology tools in high schools, students with severe disabilities must learn to use the assistive technology tools that will help them function more independently in their homes and communities. In addition to the technology applications discussed in this chapter, students with severe disabilities can benefit from many of the tools discussed in Part I of this text (writing, reading, and instructional tools). They also need and benefit from many of the augmentative communication systems discussed in Chapters 6, 10, and 11. These students' transition plans need to address the same items discussed earlier in this chapter: identification of appropriate technology tools, training to help students become independent users of the technology, appropriate supports, and training in self-advocacy. The students need to be given multiple opportunities to *practice* their new technology skills and advocate for themselves while they are in high school so that when they exit high school at age 21, they will be better prepared for living as adults in their communities.

Summary

- The number of students with disabilities attending college has increased significantly in the past decade, and assistive technology offers solutions to the obstacles they face in meeting the academic demands of college.
- The assistive technology tools discussed in this text can help college students with

disabilities if they are easy to use, easy to customize, age appropriate, reflect the students' preferences, match the specific task that needs to be completed, are accessible to the students, and are supported with training and ongoing technical support.

- There are no IEPs in college. The laws and procedures governing services to college students with disabilities are very different from those in the P–12 world.
- Students need to learn about these differences and need to be taught self-advocacy skills so that they will be prepared to articulate their assistive technology needs and request tools as reasonable accommodations when they get to college.

- Assistive technology can also support students with disabilities who are not headed for college. Graphics applications and apps for mobile devices based on touch technology can be used to easily create visual supports such as picture schedules, activity schedules, and social stories. Simple technology using adapted switches can be used to facilitate partial participation in self-care, grooming, domestic, leisure, and vocational activities.
- Careful transition planning is essential so that students learn these assistive technology skills in high school before they make the transition to adult life.

Web Resources

For additional information on the topics listed, visit the following Web sites:

Students with Learning Disabilities in College
TECH-NJ at The College of New Jersey
http://www.tcnj.edu/~technj/2004/horne.htm
http://www.tcnj.edu/~technj/2004/farr.htm

Legal Issues in Higher Education
U.S. Department of Education Office for Civil Rights
Students with Disabilities Preparing for Postsecondary Education: Know Your Rights and Responsibilities
http://www.ed.gov/about/offices/list/ocr/transition.html
Heath Resource Center: Online Clearinghouse on Postsecondary Education for Individuals with Disabilities
http://www.heath.gwu.edu

Transition Planning in High School
TECH-NJ at The College of New Jersey
www.tcnj.edu/~technj/2007/plancollegesuccess.htm
www.tcnj.edu/~technj/2007/makingtransition.htm
Texas Assistive Technology Network (TATN)
http://www.texasat.net/default.aspx?name=trainmod.transition
Getting Ready for College Begins in Third Grade
C. Castellano, Charlotte, NC: Information Age Publishing, 2010
http://www.infoagepub.com/products/Getting-Ready-for-College-Third-Grade

Self-Advocacy
Advice for high school students
http://www.tcnj.edu/~technj/2007/advice.htm

Wrightslaw: Self-Advocacy: Know Yourself, Know What You Need, Know How to Get It
http://www.wrightslaw.com/info/sec504.selfadvo.ld.johnson.htm

QIAT-Post Secondary
http://www.qiat-ps.org

Student Transition Planning Guide for Assistive Technology
Texas Assistive Technology Network (TATN):
http://www.texasat.net/docs/TXTransStudentPlanningguideforAT.pdf

Technology to Teach Functional Skills

Laureate Learning
http://www.laureatelearning.com/

Crick Software
http://www.cricksoft.com/us/default.asp

SoftTouch
http://www.softtouch.com/

Attainment Company
http://www.attainmentcompany.com/home.php?cat=252

Conover Company
http://www.conovercompany.com/products/functionalskillssystem/

Technology-Based Visual Supports for Students With Severe Disabilities

Use Visual Strategies Web site
http://www.usevisualstrategies.com/index.html

Child Autism Parent Cafe
http://www.child-autism-parent-cafe.com/visual-pictureschedule-example.html

iPrompt (handHold Adaptive)
http://www.handholdadaptive.com

iCommunicate (Grembe)
http://www.grembe.com/home/communicate

First-Then (Good Karma Applications)
http://www.goodkarmaapplications.com

Picture Planner (Cognitopia)
http://www.cognitopia.com

Ablelink Technologies
http://www.ablelinktech.com

Social Stories

Carol Gray's Web site
www.thegraycenter.org/socialstorywhat.cfm

Simple technology at home: Linda Burkhart's Simplified Technology Web site
http://www.lburkhart.com/index.html

Self-Determination

ERIC Digest: Promoting the Self-Determination of Students with Severe Disabilities, by M. Wehmeyer
http://www.ericdigests.org/2003-4/severe-disabilities.html

Suggested Activities

1 *Research accommodations at your college.* Research the policies and procedures at your college regarding making its programs and services accessible to students who have disabilities. At which office does a student self-identify and provide documentation of a disability? How does your college publicize the procedure for requesting accommodations? What kinds of assistive technology does your college provide to make its programs and services accessible to students with disabilities?

2 *Investigate assistive technology and self-advocacy training in a high school.* Arrange to visit a high school in your area and interview a transition coordinator or a teacher who teaches transition skills. What kinds of assistive technology are students being taught to use? What is the curriculum for teaching self-advocacy skills? Based on what you have learned in this course, will these students have the assistive technology skills they will need to succeed academically in college?

3 *Create a picture schedule.* Locate a high school student who has autism, cognitive disabilities, or multiple disabilities. Work with his or her teacher to find out which tasks related to transitions are presenting challenges to this student that might be addressed with the aid of a visual support such as a picture schedule. Using Boardmaker or a digital camera, create a picture schedule that will support this student. Write a brief narrative explaining your decision making in designing and creating the picture schedule.

4 *Create a social story.* Go to Carol Gray's Web site at http://www.thegraycenter.org/socialstorywhat.cfm. After reading about social stories, go to the section titled "How Do I Write a Social Story?" Follow the instructions to create a social story in PowerPoint that specifically addresses a problem faced by one of your own students.

References

Association on Higher Education and Disability (AHEAD). (2001). *The Americans with Disabilities Act: The law and its impact on postsecondary education* (brochure). Boston, MA: Author.

Barr, V. M., Harttnan, R., & Spillane, S. (1995). *Getting ready for college: Advising high school students with learning disabilities.* Retrieved June 4, 2011 from the George Washington University HEATH Resource Center Web site: http://www.heath.gwu.edu

Baumgart, D., Brown, L., Pumpian, I., Nisbet, J., Ford, A., Sweet, M., et al. (1982). Principle of partial participation and individualized adaptations in educational programs for severely handicapped students. *Journal of the Association for the Severely Handicapped, 7,* 17–27.

Behnke, K., & Bowser, G. (2010). Supporting transition of assistive technology users. *Journal of Special Education Technology, 25*(1), 57–62.

Brinckerhoff, L. C., McGuire, J. M., & Shaw, S. F. (2002). *Postsecondary education and transition for students with learning disabilities* (2nd ed.). Austin, TX: Pro-Ed.

Bryant, B. R., Bryant, D. P., & Rieth, H. J. (2002). The use of assistive technology in postsecondary education. In L. C. Brinckerhoff, J. M. McGuire, & S. F. Shaw (Eds.), *Postsecondary education and transition for students with learning disabilities* (2nd ed., pp. 389–429). Austin, TX: Pro-Ed.

Burgstahler, S. (2003). The role of technology in preparing youth with disabilities for postsecondary education and employment. *Special Education Technology, 18*(4), 7–19.

Cucco, S. (2005). Utilizing blindness skills in college. *TECH-NJ, 16*(1), 6.

Gray, C. (2000). *The new social story book, illustrated.* Arlington, TX: Future Horizons.

Henderson, C. (2001). *College freshmen with disabilities: A biennial statistical profile.* Washington, DC: American Council on Education.

Holland, R., Ayres, B., Peters, J., & Wilkinson, D. (2010). Quality Indicators in Assistive Technology—Post Secondary (QIAT-PS). *TECH-NJ, 21,* 8–9.

Kuder, S. J., & Lord, D. (2009). Mi-Stories™: iPod Touch video social scenarios for students with autism. Paper presented at the American Speech

Language and Hearing Association Convention, New Orleans.

Levin, J., & Scherfenberg, L. (1990). *Selection and use of simple technology in home, school, work, and community settings.* Minneapolis, MN: AbleNet.

McClannahan, L. E., & Krantz, P. J. (1999). *Activity schedules for children with autism: Teaching independent behavior.* Bethesda, MD: Woodbine House.

Mc Coy, K., & Hermansen, E. (2007). Video modeling for individuals with autism: A review of model types and effects. *Education and Treatment of Children, 30,* 183–213.

National Council on Disability. (2000). *Federal policy barriers to assistive technology.* Washington, DC: Author.

National Joint Committee on Learning Disabilities. (1994). *Collective perspectives on issues affecting learning disabilities: Position papers and statements.* Austin, TX: Pro-Ed.

Rothstein, L. (2002). Judicial intent and legal precedents. In L. C. Brinckerhoff, C. Loring, J. M. McGuire, & S. F. Shaw (Eds.), *Postsecondary education and transition for students with learning disabilities* (2nd ed., pp. 71–106). Austin, TX: Pro-Ed.

Scattone, D., Wilczynski, S. M., Edwards, R. P. & Rabian, B. (2002). Decreasing disruptive behaviors of children with autism using social stories. *Journal of Autism and Developmental Disorders, 32,* 535–543.

U.S. Department of Education Office for Civil Rights. (1998). *Auxiliary aids and services for postsecondary students with disabilities: Higher education's obligations under Section 504 and Title II of the ADA.* Retrieved January 29, 2004, from http://www.ed.gov/about/offices/list/ocr/docs/auxaids.html

U.S. Department of Education Office for Civil Rights. (2002). *Students with disabilities preparing for postsecondary education: Know your rights and responsibilities.* Retrieved June 4, 2011 from http://www.ed.gov/about/offices/list/ocr/transition.html

Varrassi, V. (2004). *Personal communication.* Trenton, New Jersey.

Yelin, E., & Katz, P. (1994). Labor force trends of persons with and without disabilities. *Monthly Labor Review, 117*(10), 36–42.

INDEX